SOCIETY FOR NEW TESTAMENT STUDIES
MONOGRAPH SERIES
General Editor: R. McL. Wilson, F.B.A.
Associate Editor: M. E. Thrall

45

AUTHORITY IN PAUL AND PETER

Authority in Paul and Peter

The Identification of a Pastoral Stratum
in the Pauline Corpus
and 1 Peter

WINSOME MUNRO

Assistant Professor
University of Dubuque Theological Seminary

CAMBRIDGE UNIVERSITY PRESS

CAMBRIDGE
LONDON   NEW YORK   NEW ROCHELLE
MELBOURNE   SYDNEY

Published by the Press Syndicate of the University of Cambridge
The Pitt Building, Trumpington Street, Cambridge CB2 1RP
32 East 57th Street, New York, NY 10022, USA
296 Beaconsfield Parade, Middle Park, Melbourne 3206, Australia

First published 1983

Printed in Great Britain by
Redwood Burn Ltd
Trowbridge

Library of Congress catalogue card number:

ISBN 0 521 23694 0

CONTENTS

ACKNOWLEDGEMENTS

This study includes most of the textual analysis, plus historical explanations, included in my dissertation for the degree of Doctor of Education in the cooperative degree programme of Teachers College, Columbia University, and Union Theological Seminary, New York, conferred in May 1974.

I am indebted to faculty of both institutions for the genesis and progress of the enterprise; at Union Theological Seminary, initially, to Professor J. Louis Martin, who encouraged me to 'keep working on this', to Professor Raymond E. Brown for his searching criticism in his seminar on the Catholic Epistles, to Professor George M. Landes for clarifying some points relating to Hebrew and Aramaic, and particularly to Professor Reginald H. Fuller for his exacting guidance in the major New Testament area of investigation. To Professor Robert O. McClintock, my sponsor at Teachers College, I am grateful for the stimulation of ideas and insights.

I should like to mention yet earlier teachers who helped equip me for such study: Miss Florence Holden, my Latin teacher at the Girls High School, Potchefstroom, South Africa, who taught me Greek in her spare time and introduced me to the scholarly study of the New Testament; Miss E. M. Batten, O.B.E., formerly Principal of William Temple College, Rugby, England, who found means for me to fulfil a dream and hope; Miss O. Jessie Lace, formerly Senior Tutor at William Temple College, who taught me to read the Bible as if for the first time; the late Professor G. W. H. Lampe, my tutor for the B.D. degree of the University of Birmingham and subsequently Ely Professor and then Regius Professor of Divinity at the University of Cambridge.

I wish to thank Professor R. McL. Wilson and Dr M. E. Thrall for the close attention they have given to this manuscript, and for their editorial suggestions.

Most immediately, my thanks and appreciation go to Fr Michael D. Meilach, O.F.M., for his rapid and skilled typing of the manuscript and for his experienced editorial advice, and to Siena College for the generous grant facilitating preparation of the manuscript for publication.

A final credit: to my friends who went to prison in my home country with nothing to read but the Bible, one of whom wanted to know how Paul the prisoner could have written Rom 13:1-7.

Loudonville, N.Y., 1979   W.M.

The Greek text which forms the basis for the identification of the Pastoral stratum and the reconstruction of earlier material is *The Greek New Testament*, edited by K. Aland, M. Black, B. M. Metzger, A. Wikgren, published by the American Bible Society in 1966.

1 INTRODUCTION

Thesis

The problem addressed in the first instance is the presence in the Pauline corpus and 1 Peter of the teaching on subjection to authority, known as 'household tables' (*Haustafeln*) or codes of subordination. Investigation of its original setting and purpose led, however, to rejection of the prevailing view that the original writers had incorporated them from oral tradition in the churches. Instead, it will be argued, they are subsequent additions to the text, not as isolated interpolations accrued haphazardly, but as part of a later, redactional stratum extending across the ten-letter Pauline collection and 1 Peter, and emanating from the same or similar source as the Pastoral epistles.

That the Pastoral epistles are a post-Pauline development drawing on the earlier epistles in the Pauline corpus is a widely accepted notion on which there is near consensus. The converse possibility, that Pastoral influence has left its mark on the earlier epistles in the form of redactional shaping and interpolated additions amounting to an extensive later stratum, is a less familiar concept. It involves a paradigmatic shift which encounters considerable perceptual resistance among Pauline scholars.[1] There is now however a greater readiness than formerly to entertain the notion, for it is beginning to emerge as a logical next step without which little progress can be made in determining the redactional history of the Pauline writings.

Not only is it reasonable to reject the 'household tables' as elements of the Christianity contemporary with Peter and Paul; but, to carry the argument further, it can be maintained that the material in the ten letters is even later than the main body of Ephesians, which is taken to represent the Paulinism of the immediate sub-apostolic period. So extensive is the stratum of which it is part that it renders the earlier version a source incorporated in subsequent redaction.

The purpose here is not, in the first instance, to uncover the original, though that will be a partial outcome, but rather to identify the uppermost stratum in the writings in question to the extent that this is relevant to sustain the case for dissociating the subjection material from its literary surroundings. All the material of this nature seems to have been identified in 1 Peter, Ephesians, Colossians, and 1 and 2 Thessalonians, but not all in the remaining epistles. Thorough analysis of every part of the entire corpus is probably needed to locate all amendments, additions, and arrangements of a Pastoral character.

The association of the material with this literary strain means that it does not come from the original collector and redactor of a Pauline letter corpus, but from different circles at a more advanced stage of Christian history. The later stratum, together with the Pastoral epistles, will therefore be characterized as 'Pastoral' or trito-Pauline.

Regarding its relations with the rest of the New Testament, significant links will become evident with Luke–Acts. Close connections will also be found with such early patristic writings as 1 Clement, Polycarp's Epistle to the Philippians, the Epistles of Ignatius, and certain parts of the Didache and the Epistle of Barnabas, though these will not be examined exhaustively. The presence in 1 Clement and Polycarp's epistle of catalogues of duties resembling the 'household codes' of the New Testament gives these writings special relevance for the study. The Ignatian corpus also proves revealing for the context, purpose, and dating of the Pastoral material.

It will emerge that its milieu is the Roman hellenism of the first half of the second century, when the Christian movement was prey to sporadic persecution, but was nevertheless hopeful that it might gain recognition and tolerance from the Roman authorities under the Antonine emperors.

At this stage an attempt was made to present Christianity as the *paideia* of a philosophic school: in other words, a higher, divine, and essentially moralistic type of learning akin to the Stoicism of the period. In shaping Christian tradition according to this model the 'codes of subordination' were evidently intended to parallel Stoic categories of duties, just as was the somewhat similar teaching in the writings of hellenistic Judaism. Just how 'Pastoral' *paideia* compares with its Roman hellenistic and Jewish precedents, and how each *paideia* relates to the social patterns of authority and subjection of the patriarchal household cannot be shown here, but is set out in the longer, original version of this study.[2]

Though hellenistic Judaism is evidently taken as an example to be followed, the Pastoral material is concerned to achieve dissociation from Judaism, and to give assurances of support for the major institutions of Graeco-Roman society: the patriarchal household, slavery, the imperial state, and the army.

The objective is also internal: to legitimize a form of ecclesiastical authority based on the model of the patriarchal household. By this means the Pastoral circles seek to combat heterodox and divisive tendencies. The major heresy under attack may indeed be the source of the earlier version of the Pauline literature. How and why their corpus could have been taken over and superseded by the Pastoral version is a question that will be addressed.

To summarize the thesis that will be defended: on the basis of a study of literary origins it is argued that the subjection material of the New Testament does not belong with the more primitive, eschatological strata of tradition, but that it was introduced later, it is suggested in the first half of the second century, as part of a later stratum extending across the Pauline corpus and 1 Peter.

The subjection material in light of New Testament scholarship

The problem of the subjection material in the New Testament epistles has presented itself in two ways. There is first the question of how it is that apparently extraneous material in the Pauline corpus has close parallels in 1 Peter, and secondly how it is that 1 Peter, which must be a document of the primitive, apostolic church if it in fact issues from the apostle Peter, has close parallels, not only with the blocks of subjectionist teaching in Rom 13: 1–7, Eph 5: 21 – 6: 9, and Col 3: 18 – 4: 1, but also with much else in the Pauline collection, as well as with Hebrews, James, and other New Testament writings.

The Petrine authorship of 1 Peter is difficult to uphold even if all the letters involved are primitive, for the Pauline corpus is obviously a post-Pauline construction, whatever the dating of the letters within it. Hence knowledge of its different parts supports sub-apostolic origin. The tendency to regard Ephesians, Hebrews, and James as later than A.D. 70 adds to the problem, unless some explanation other than literary dependence is forthcoming.

The code and catechetical theories

Here the idea of common use of an oral or written source or similar sources has proved useful, though not always put forward in order to establish authenticity. The designating of certain New Testament passages as 'household tables' (*Haustafeln*) seems to be derived from Martin Luther's use of the term as a sub-title above Eph 5: 21 – 6: 9 and Col 3: 18 – 4: 1 in his translation of the scriptures, and as a designation for such teaching in his Small Catechism to which K. Weidinger referred in *Die Haustafeln ein Stuck urchristliche Paränese*.[3]

Some time before, K. von Weizsäcker wrote concerning the 'household table of duties' to be discerned in 1 Peter as also in Colossians and Ephesians. He regarded 1 Pet 2: 13 – 3: 1 as a post-primitive insertion in the body of the letter, with some adaptation, and 5: 1ff and 5: 5ff as following the plan of the 'household tables',[4] but it is not clear whether he considered this the work of the writer of the epistle as a whole or an addition by a later writer. Either way he considered the passages later than the primitive period, for he took Col 3: 18 – 4: 1 as a sign that Colossians belongs to a later period than genuine Pauline epistles.[5]

M. Dibelius, also assuming their non-primitive character, applied the methods of form criticism to Eph 5: 21 – 6: 9 and Col 3: 18 – 4: 1, and connected the material with similar passages in the Pastorals, 1 Peter, the Didache, Barnabas, 1 Clement, Polycarp's epistle, the epistles of Ignatius, and with the popular moral teaching of the Stoics.[6]

Though building on Dibelius' ideas, Weidinger assumed that the passages are primitive.[7] At this point he was in agreement with A. Seeberg, to whom he made acknowledgement for his recognition of specific forms in the New Testament, including the *Haustafeln*, but he considered Seeberg mistaken in postulating a fixed Christian catechism of which the 'household tables' were part.[8]

Seeberg's idea of such a catechism has continued, however, to exert far-reaching influence. Taking as his starting-point the phrase τύπον διδαχῆς (a form of teaching) in Rom 6: 17, he sought to identify a substratum of oral tradition which, in his view, followed the pattern of the 'two ways' manifested in lists of vices and virtues in the New Testament and other early Christian literature.[9] Unlike von Weizsäcker, Dibelius, and Weidinger, Seeberg stressed the Jewish background of the material in question, including the *Haustafeln*, and in this he was followed by G. Klein, who put such teaching in the context of Jewish proselytism among the Gentiles, where it appeared to him to be a substitute for the observance of the Torah.[10]

P. Carrington developed the idea of a more extensive primitive catechism, used in preparing candidates for baptism, underlying the epistles of the New Testament and including the subjection material.[11] He too stressed the Jewish origins of the presumed substratum on the assumption that the catechism was based on the holiness code of Lev 17–20.[12] His suggested pattern was taken up and developed further by E. G. Selwyn,[13] and adopted also by W. D. Davies.[14]

Following the form-critical approach, Selwyn postulated four different sources in 1 Peter: hymnic material, *verba Christi*, a persecution form, and a catechism such as Carrington proposed. In this way he accounted for the similarities and parallels that exist between 1 Peter on the one hand, and on the other the Pauline corpus, James, Hebrews, the synoptic gospels, the Acts, and the Johannine writings.[15]

To realize the extent of these affinities one has only to review the evidence for some form of relationship as set out by O. D. Foster,[16] A. E. Barnett,[17] and C. L. Mitton,[18] as well as Carrington[19] and Selwyn[20] themselves. Whereas the former interpreted the data as indicating literary influence and dependence, the latter two scholars considered that they supported use by different writers of common traditional material, though Carrington did not extend his explanations beyond the hypothetical catechism.

In attempting to reconstruct its main outlines, he set out four main divisions: (*a*) the new creation, or new birth; (*b*) *deponentes*, concerning the renunciation of heathen idolatry and vice, and thought to be based on the Levitical holiness code; (*c*) the worship of God; and (*d*) *subiecti*, concerning the law of humility and consisting for the most part of the subjection material. Selwyn preferred to include two further divisions which Carrington itemized only in single versions of the catechism, termed *vigilate*, concerning the duty of watchfulness and prayer, and *state*, concerning the duty of steadfastness. These Selwyn included in a fifth division, which he characterized as 'teaching called out by crisis' and connected with the persecution form.[21]

Selwyn identified the subjection material as part of an earlier substratum which circulated orally but also perhaps in writing in various versions.[22] He also distinguished three strata within the 'code of subordination' itself. Uppermost he found a superstructure of theology which he ascribed to the apostles Peter and Paul. Below this he pointed to elements of common Christian teaching, and basic to all versions were certain fundamental principles which suggested to him a fusion of Jewish and hellenistic concepts such as might have come into being within circles of hellenistic Judaism.[23]

At the same time, Selwyn gave emphasis to Jewish precedents by the inclusion in his commentary of a piece of Rabbinic scholarship by D. Daube, in the form of an appended note on 'Participle and Imperative in 1 Peter'.[24]

Daube also placed the subjection material in a wider context of catechetical instruction, and considered that this, like the 'household code', arose directly from Jewish models.[25] He reconstructed from a variety of sources what he considered was the characteristic pattern of instruction recommended by the Tannaim for proselytes in preparation for baptism. He identified five categories of teaching for this purpose: (1) the test, warning would-be converts of the trials and afflictions that await them,

(2) the commandments, concerning rituals, duties and moral obligations, including the subjectionist teaching, (3) charity, mainly in the sense of almsgiving, (4) the penalties of transgressing or falling away, and (5) the reward and the world to come. The categories listed do not tally exactly with those of Carrington, Selwyn, and Davies, but Daube suggested that the New Testament catechism accorded more closely with his postulated outline than other scholars had indicated.[26] He noted, however, that the Tannaite plan, while assigning a special place to charity, said nothing about humility and subordination. He tried to solve the difficulty by suggesting that one version emphasized love and another, humility and subordination.[27]

Views on the first epistle of Peter

Whatever version of the catechetical theory is preferred, however, it does not solve the major problems bearing on the primitive and apostolic character of 1 Peter. Among them are the fluent Greek of the epistle, its freedom from Aramaisms and Hebraisms, and the intimate knowledge of the LXX which it displays. All this Selwyn explained by assuming that the Silvanus mentioned in 1 Pet 5: 12 was the cultivated writer, acting as amanuensis, behind whom stood the apostle Peter as the ultimate source of the contents.[28]

In addition the Silvanus mentioned at the end of 1 Peter was identified with the Silvanus who was linked with Paul and Timothy as joint author of 1 and 2 Thessalonians (1 Thess 1: 1; 2 Thess 1: 1) and the Silas mentioned as one of the messengers who conveyed the letter concerning the apostolic decree of Acts 15.[29] Thus Silvanus served also to explain the similarities between 1 Peter and the Thessalonian epistles, for which Carrington and Selwyn accounted in part by postulating an earlier version of the catechism connected with the requirements of the apostolic decree of Acts 15: 29 and the Levitical holiness code.[30] Selwyn suggested too that the 'persecution form', in which he included for the most part parallels between 1 Peter and 1 and 2 Thessalonians,[31] is largely his work.[32]

The Sylvanus hypothesis in combination with the catechetical theory has gained considerable support for dating the letter before the death of Peter. Writing just before the first edition of Selwyn's work appeared in 1946, F. W. Beare could refer to 'the thesis, now widely accepted, that First Peter is a pseudonymous work of the post-Apostolic age'.[33] In a supplement to the second revised edition, Beare indicated that the situation had changed considerably, though a number of scholars had raised serious, and in some instances decisive, objections to Selwyn's defence of the primitive and apostolic character of the epistle.[34]

The most vulnerable aspect of Selwyn's complicated hypothesis is his depiction of Sylvanus, which Beare effectively demolished. First, he pointed out, there is no evidence whatever to suggest that the prophet Silas who hailed from the primitive church in Jerusalem was any better equipped than the Galilean fisherman Peter to produce polished Attic prose.[35] Secondly, the connection with the Silvanus of the Thessalonian letters fares little better for, as W. L. Knox observed, the Greek style of the Pauline corpus is considered to descend to a 'low-water mark' in these two epistles.[36]

As for Selwyn's form-critical explanations for the numerous parallels with the rest of the New Testament in 1 Peter, literary critics have remained unconvinced. C. L. Mitton's case for the deutero-Pauline nature of Ephesians,[37] prepared before Selwyn's book was available, also involved the conclusion that 1 Peter is dependent on Ephesians and is therefore even later. His subsequent article on the subject,[38] which takes account of Selwyn's work, seems to establish even more securely that the writer of 1 Peter knew Ephesians. Beare himself concurred with M. S. Enslin[39] in finding that Selwyn's evidence for discerning similar forms in different epistles actually confirmed his view that 1 Peter is dependent on earlier writings, and in particular the Pauline epistles. As in the gospels, Beare correctly indicated that the presence of forms does not eliminate the possibility of literary dependence.[40]

Similarly, the presence of traditional material in identifiable forms does not render questions of date and authenticity redundant. It is significant that scholars whose approach to 1 Peter is form-critical do not necessarily regard the epistle as primitive. For instance, W. G. Kümmel[41] and R. H. Fuller,[42] while accepting the code hypothesis and the common use in the epistles of catechetical and liturgical material, nevertheless regard 1 Peter as sub-apostolic.

Other theories concerning the nature and composition of 1 Peter are either neutral as regards date, or else assume a post-Petrine dating. The variety of views is conveniently summarized elsewhere.[43] Hence this discussion will do no more than survey the main alternatives to the catechetical approach.

There is first the view of R. Perdelwitz[44] that the major part of 1 Peter, 1: 3 – 4: 11, is a baptismal homily to which the author added 1: 1-2 and 4: 12 – 5: 12 to put it into the form of a letter. As an adherent of the 'history of religions' school, Perdelwitz found much affinity with the mystery cults, concluding that the composition must be a pseudonymous work of the second century. W. Bornemann[45] followed A. Harnack in suggesting that 1: 3 – 4: 11 is an address on Psalm 34 by Silvanus in his old age, while B. H. Streeter[46] thought the letter was originally a baptismal sermon by the elder Aristion, mentioned by Papias, who he concluded was identical with Ariston, named in the Apostolic Constitutions as first bishop of Smyrna.

H. Windisch[47] accepted Bornemann's view, adding that the homily contains traditional paraenesis, an introductory hymn in 1: 3-12, and Christ-hymns in 1: 18-21 and 2: 21-5. R. Bultmann also took up the idea of hymnic material in 1 Peter and identified a series of rhythmic stanzas in 1: 18-21, 2: 21-5, and 3: 18-22.[48]

In a revision of Windisch's commentary H. Preisker took the opportunity to present the theory that 1 Peter is a baptismal liturgy put together by Silvanus, a second- or third-generation Christian, and sent out in the form of a letter from Rome.[49] The liturgy, he maintained, extends from 1: 3 to 5: 11 and on the basis of style he differentiated between the following elements: 1: 3-12, a prayer psalm; 1: 13-21, a teaching discourse, after which the baptism takes place; 1: 22-5, a baptismal dedication; 2: 1-10, a hymn attributed to pneumatics; 2: 11 - 3: 12, a paraenetic homily by a new preacher, with the congregation joining in a christological hymn in 2: 21-4; 3: 13 - 4: 7a, a discourse by an apocalyptic preacher; 4: 7b-11, a closing prayer which has been changed to an exhortation; 4: 12-19, an apocalyptic discourse in an open service after the baptism; 5: 1-9, a paraenetic discourse like that in 2: 11 - 3: 12; 5: 10, a blessing; and 5: 11, a doxology.

Fanciful and implausible as Preisker's proposal may sound, it does recognize and attempt to deal with the disjointed nature of 1 Peter, and the distinct variations in style. E. Lohse[50] acknowledged the basic validity of Preisker's divisions, except in the concluding section of the epistle, but he put forward the view that they represent different kinds of traditional material incorporated into a pastoral letter. Thus he also rejected literary dependence, and tended to align himself with such scholars as Seeberg, Dibelius, Carrington, and Selwyn. He considered it unfortunate, however, that Selwyn had linked his form-critical view with the question of genuineness. He too concluded the compilation was made in sub-apostolic times and, like Dibelius and Weidinger, he viewed the paraenetic (mainly *Haustafel*) material as thoroughly hellenistic. He also found Jewish connections, of a hellenistic rather than a Palestinian kind, as manifested by use of the LXX, and the affinity with certain passages in Tobit, the Testament of the Twelve Patriarchs, Sirach, and Pseudophocylides. By contrast, the psalm-like passage in 1: 3-12 seemed to Lohse to have some affinity with Palestinian texts and the Damascus document of the Qumran sect. Here then is a view that comes close to the concept of different strata in the same document, though Lohse presented the sources as oral rather than literary. The redactor, he suggested, was a Paulinist of Rome, thus accounting for the similarities between 1 Peter and the Pauline corpus, and the close links with 1 Clement through the use of common *Traditionsgut*.

Another variation on Preisker's theory came from F. L. Cross.[51] He related 1 Peter to second-century paschal and baptismal procedures as evidenced in The Apostolic Tradition, generally ascribed to Hippolytus, and in Melito's Homily on the Passion. Cross thought the traditional material could be much earlier, but left the matter of date open. As T. C. G. Thornton has pointed out, however, there is no evidence for any connection between the words πάσχειν and πάθημα and the Passover in Egypt (πάσχα), on which Cross's theory largely depends, before the second century.[52] The citations Cross made from Philo, he argued, indicated no explicit connection. It can be added that if there is a connection between 1 Peter and the interpretation of the passion words in Hippolytus, Melito, and Irenaeus as Cross maintained, this serves to support a later rather than an earlier date for the epistle.

One further approach to the problem of the origins of 1 Peter should be mentioned. Recently E. Best replied to revived attempts to establish its primitive and apostolic character on the basis of resemblances between the epistle and the gospels.[53] Subjecting the evidence to careful analysis, Best found no reason for thinking there is any contact between the writer of 1 Peter and either the historic teaching of Jesus or the tradition behind the fourth gospel, and no special links with Mark. He indicated that such contact as there is exists with the tradition in its developed, rather than its original, form. He demonstrated too that the connections are not haphazard, as one would expect if they issued from the apostle Peter, but are confined to two blocks of Lucan material (chs. 6 and 12), and two isolated sayings in Matthew and one in Mark. Such a result actually suggests literary dependence, either on Luke itself or some Lukan source.[54]

There seems, then, to be no acceptable answer to the arguments advanced against regarding 1 Peter as primitive. It follows that the occurrence in the epistle of subjectionist teachings by no means indicates that they were current in the Christianity of the apostolic era.

The subjectionist teaching in the Pauline corpus

As for the subjectionist teaching in the Pauline corpus, most of the passages concerned occur in epistles which it can be concluded were written later than Paul, or which contain much non-Pauline material, and the remaining passages are recognized to be problematic. The present investigation proceeds on the premises that neither the three Pastoral epistles nor Ephesians is the work of Paul, and also that Ephesians is prior to the Pastorals and later than Colossians, from which it is largely derived. The survey that follows is intended only to show that there is sufficient scholarly consensus to forego establishing these assumptions afresh.

While R. H. Fuller characterized 2 Thessalonians and Colossians as 'disputed' and Ephesians as 'more widely disputed',[55] he classified the Pastorals as later than Paul in the judgement of the great majority of scholars, though he acknowledged significant disagreement.[56] The Pastorals, then, are the most obvious instances in which the subjectionist teaching appears in material that is not primitive and apostolic.

The Pastoral epistles

The authenticity of the Pastorals has been called into question ever since the beginning of the nineteenth century.[57] 1 Timothy was assailed by F. Schleiermacher on grounds of language and historical discrepancies,[58] and by F. C. Baur as belonging in the anti-gnostic struggle of the second century.[59] In 1812 J. G. Eichhorn extended rejection to all three on the basis of language.[60] The Pastorals became widely regarded as post-Pauline after the publication of H. J. Holtzmann's study of these epistles.[61]

In 1897 Bernhard Weiss wrote that criticism in general assumed their inauthenticity to be 'definitely settled',[62] a state of affairs he deplored. He mentioned too the attempts of some scholars to distinguish Pauline from non-Pauline material in the Pastorals.[63]

In 1921 P. N. Harrison, building on Holtzmann's analysis of vocabulary and style, applied statistical criteria to the measuring of literary differences.[64] By such means he distinguished the Pastorals sharply from the other letters of the Pauline corpus and showed a close relation to the early patristic and apologetic literature of the second century. He also isolated certain biographical portions as genuinely Pauline.[65] Though his methods have been criticized, his statistical findings still stand.[66]

Since then A. Q. Morton and J. McLeman[67] have subjected all the letters of the corpus except the shortest (2 Thessalonians, Titus, and Philemon) to computer analysis for use of commonly used short words, with the result that 1 and 2 Timothy manifest similar characteristics, diverging from all other letters in the corpus, particularly Romans, 1 and 2 Corinthians, and Galatians, the only four which emerge as genuinely Pauline.

Another development in the argument has come from J. Jeremias[68] who, from a close examination of the beginnings and endings of the letters of the Pauline corpus, found that, while the wording in the Pastorals differs somewhat, it corresponds with a progressive development from 1 Thessalonians to Colossians, and from there to the Pastorals. It may be answered, however, that the development is not of a kind that necessarily involves only one writer.

Three positions thus emerge: first, the traditional view of apostolic authorship, with or without an amanuensis,[69] secondly, the idea of Pauline fragments in largely non-Pauline letters,[70] and thirdly, the complete rejection of Pauline origin.[71]

The case for the second and third positions rests on both external and internal evidence. Regarding the former, while there appears to be knowledge of the Pastorals in Polycarp's letter, and Irenaeus cites them, this proves no more than that early catholic circles approved them in the second century. They do not appear in the earliest New Testament manuscript, the Chester Beatty papyrus ($\mathfrak{P}^{46}$), but since Philemon is also missing, additional pages containing the Pastorals may be lost.[72] In the Muratorian canon, usually dated the end of the second century,[73] they are listed after Philemon, which gives them the appearance of an addendum, but no certain conclusion can be drawn from this. More substantial is the fact that Tertullian criticized Marcion for omitting the Pastorals from his version of Paul's letters (*Ad Marc* 21). Instead of excising them, however, Marcion could have dealt with them less drastically by making only a few omissions to suit his views, particularly since they contain far less Old Testament material than a letter such as Romans.[74] It seems more probable that the version of Paul's epistles on which Marcion based his own edition did not include the Pastorals, whether or not he knew of their existence.

The internal evidence is historical, theological, linguistic, and stylistic. Historically the Pastorals present a problem for, if authentic, they must belong to a period of Paul's life after his imprisonment in Rome, of which nothing is known other than that he may have journeyed to Spain.[75] Also, the form of church government described in the Pastorals appears quite different from that reflected in earlier epistles, whether or not it was yet mon-episcopal.[76] Baur's view that the Pastorals are anti-gnostic is not very useful, for the heresy attacked in these epistles does not tally with any known gnostic system of the second century.[77]

There is certainly significant theological difference from the earlier epistles, in particular in the understanding of faith and the relation between faith and works.[78] Most convincing of all, however, are the measurable differences in vocabulary and style, quite apart from the results of computerized research. First there is the relatively high proportion of words peculiar to an epistle (mistakenly referred to as *hapax legomena* by Harrison) in the Pastorals as compared with other epistles of the corpus, however they are measured.[79] Secondly there is the absence in the Pastorals of many shorter words which are common in the rest of the corpus,[80] thirdly the predilection of the Pastorals for certain types of compound words, especially those beginning with φιλο- and α-privative,[81] and fourthly the repeated use of phrases which do not appear in the other letters of the corpus,[82] and the absence of common Pauline phrases.[83]

The hypothesis of a secretary or amanuensis, which those adhering to the traditional view have often adopted, is an acknowledgement of the validity of the linguistic and stylistic, and to some extent also the theological arguments against Pauline authorship of the Pastorals. It fails, however, to account for the very different outlook and point of view in the latter. Taken cumulatively, the evidence is as decisive as one can reasonably expect in any instance of pseudonymity.

The matter of dating will be considered later. For the present it is sufficient to conclude that the Pastorals were written after the publication of the ten-letter corpus for, as Harrison has shown, apart from non-Pauline words and phrases, they are a veritable mosaic of phrases suggesting acquaintance with every letter within it.[84] This evidence is strong enough to justify the conclusion that the ten letters were gathered together into a unified collection before the Pastorals were written. Thus the Pastorals must have been added to the corpus at a later stage, as the data from Tertullian concerning Marcion's version and in the Muratorian canon seem to indicate. As an important corollary it follows that the Pastorals must be later than any deutero-Pauline letters in the ten-letter corpus.

The epistle to the Ephesians. As already mentioned, the most widely disputed letter among the ten is Ephesians, which happens also to contain the longest continuous 'household' passage in the pre-Pastoral collection.

The authenticity of Ephesians was called into question even earlier than that of 1 Timothy, before the end of the eighteenth century.[85] Recognizing its internal problems, Schleiermacher suggested that Tychicus, mentioned in Eph 6: 21, wrote the letter under Paul's direction, while Baur and his disciples, finding it reflected gnosticism and Montanism, located it in the second century.[86] Its close correspondence with Colossians led H. J. Holtzmann[87] to put forward the theory that Ephesians is a revision of an earlier version of Colossians, whish was subsequently inter--polated with material similar to that in Ephesians. This explanation has however proved too complicated to win support.

While many German scholars rejected Ephesians as Pauline, it was almost universally accepted as authentic among English scholars.[88] A notable exception was J. Moffatt, who considered Ephesians dependent on Colossians in view of the close parallels between the two.[89] Next E. J. Goodspeed developed the notion that Ephesians is an encyclical letter written by the collector of the Pauline letters to introduce the ten-letter corpus,[90] an idea suggested earlier by J. Weiss.[91] Goodspeed's theory received support from the studies of J. Knox and C. L. Mitton to the effect that Ephesians was originally probably the opening letter of the ten-letter corpus.[92] In addition Mitton built on Goodspeed's view that Ephesians is not only based on Colossians, but is a mosaic of material conflated from the rest of the collection.[93] Not only did he marshal the evidence for concluding that Ephesians is dependent on the other letters, and particularly Colossians, but he also devised means to test this hypothesis.[94] The results, taken in conjunction with the linguistic, stylistic, literary, historic, and doctrinal arguments advanced previously on both sides of the issue,[95] appeared to decide the question decisively in favour of post-Pauline authorship, though the verdict of scholars was by no means unanimous.[96]

Perhaps the most impressive defence of Ephesian authenticity is that of E. Percy, whose strongest argument is probably that most of the stylistic peculiarities of Ephesians are found in liturgical-type material which could have a different origin.[97] This approach has gained ground more recently. G. Schille explored the possibility that liturgical elements are present,[98] and N. A. Dahl argued that the epistle contains oral–traditional material in the setting of a circular baptismal letter from Paul.[99] J. C. Kirby elaborated the theory that Ephesians is a prayer and discourse put into letter form, and that it reflects liturgical material pertaining to the Jewish festival of Pentecost and early Christian baptism.[100] J. P. Sampley followed Dahl and E. Käsemann in viewing the document as a mosaic of early Christian tradition.[101] Käsemann, however, unlike Dahl, thinks the epistle is post-Pauline and dependent on Colossians as well as hymnic material.[102] Similarly W. Marxsen accepted the use in Ephesians of traditional and hymn-like sources, but concluded that a post-Pauline author is much to the fore in its treatment.[103]

As for the 'household table' in Ephesians, scholars assume it is an integral part of the paraenetic section of the epistle (Eph 4: 1 – 6: 20), though some have found a disjunction between Eph 5: 21 – 6: 9 and the rest of the letter.[104] There has been no recently published exploration of the problem except for an article by the present investigator.[105] Sampley has attempted to bring the passage into alignment with the strong Jewish background others have identified in the epistle in general. His approach is to trace the affinities between Eph 5: 21–3 and the Old Testament theme of Israel as the bride of YHWH.[106] Whether or not the passage was included in the original version of the document, however, there is clearly good reason to conclude that the occurrence of 'household' or subjection material in the New Testament literature at this point is post-Pauline, since Ephesians as a whole appears to be later than Paul.

The epistle to the Colossians and Col 3: 18 – 4: 1. Col 3: 18 – 4: 1, which parallels Eph 5: 21 – 6: 9, also occurs in a disputed epistle, but the evidence is less clear than for Ephesians. It was rejected by the Tübingen school mainly on the now untenable ground that it contains gnostic terminology.[107] It is not proposed to survey the varying views. Suffice it to say that the un-Pauline style, vocabulary, and theology found in the epistle[108] can be explained by assuming that Colossians is an augmented version of a genuine Pauline letter.[109] The investigations of E. P. Sanders substantiate this possibility.[110] Following one of Mitton's tests for literary dependence in Ephesians[111] he found that, excluding stock phrases, the degree of verbatim agreement with, and conflation of phrases and sentences occurring in other letters of the Pauline corpus, is significantly greater in Colossians than in Philippians, up to Col 3: 11. He concluded that all or most of the letter till this point is non-Pauline, and suggested reconsideration of Holtzmann's hypothesis that there has been considerable interpolation by the writer of Ephesians.[112] Mitton's work seems, however, to establish quite securely that Colossians is largely prior to Ephesians, whoever the second writer may have been, or whether or not Colossians is genuine. For present purposes it will be assumed that the immediate surroundings of Col 3: 18 – 4: 1 are Pauline. Whether or not this is the case, however, the passage is contextually problematic.

According to the code theory of Dibelius and Weidinger, it is the earliest and least-Christianized form of the early Christian *Haustafel.*[113] That is tantamount to asserting that it is manifestly un-Pauline, and that the writer of Colossians, whether Paul or another, merely quoted it from another source with the addition of certain characteristic phrases. It is also clearly unintegrated into the context, as is commonly observed. K. E. Kirk remarked on the fact that this part of Colossians would read more easily without 3: 18 – 4: 1, and that the same applies to the Ephesian parallel.[114] E. Lohse mentioned that the passage is introduced without any connection with what precedes it, that it is a self-contained entity, and that 4: 2 would follow smoothly from 3: 17.[115]

J. E. Crouch observed that 'no awkward break would be noticed if the entire section were omitted', and remarked the differences in style, as also

the concentration of *hapax legomena*, but took all this as confirming its
pre-Colossian nature. He dismissed as 'not warranted by the evidence' the
suggestion of D. Bradley that the passage is an interpolation. His own view
is that it is a probably post-primitive Christian development from hellenistic Judaism, included here to counteract the assertion of equality by
enthusiastic slaves and women in the syncretistic movement opposed in
the epistle as a whole.[116] This motivation, however, has no basis in the text
and scarcely solves the contextual problem.

1 Cor. 14: 33b-35. Very similar problems surround 1 Cor 14: 33b-35,
clearly a subjectionist passage, though not included among the *Haustafeln*.
It has raised questions on three counts. First, there is its apparent conflict
with 1 Cor. 11: 2-16, which implies the right of women to pray and
prophesy in public, whereas the former seems to silence women totally in
the assemblies of churches. Secondly, 1 Cor 14: 33b-35 appears to interrupt its context, which flows more easily without it. Thirdly, there is a
discrepancy in the textual evidence concerning the position of vss. 34-5.
Whereas Codex Bezae, G, 88, some Latin manuscripts, Ambrosiaster, and
Sedulius Scotus place it after 1 Cor 14: 40, other authorities, including
$\mathfrak{P}^{46}$, include it after 1 Cor 14: 33.
  Most scholars have accepted the passage as Pauline without apparent
difficulty. Others have recognized the problems to varying degrees, but
have explained them to their own satisfaction. A common explanation for
the apparent conflict with 1 Cor 11: 5 is that while the former has to do
with relatively private or family gatherings, the latter refers to church
assemblies.[117] Another suggestion is that the ruling does not affect utterances inspired by the Spirit, such as prophesying,[118] and yet another that
the fragment is related to its context by the fact that order and decorum
are under discussion in 1 Cor 14.[119]
  Many scholars have, however, either doubted the genuineness of this
section, or rejected it outright. Special weight attaches to the study of
G. Zuntz, in which 1 Cor 14: 33b-35 is judged to be one of many brief
intrusions into the text of the Pauline epistles. Zuntz judged it was
originally a marginal gloss, the position of which was altered to improve
the continuity of the text.[120] M. E. Thrall took account of Zuntz's view,
but thought the style is Pauline, and hence that it could have been incorporated later from an independent message from Paul.[121] T. B. Allworthy
rejected the passage, mentioning the tendency for manuscripts to be
altered to minimize the importance of women in the primitive church.[122]
From a careful assessment of the evidence C. K. Barrett concluded that
there is a strong likelihood that the passage is an interpolation, but left the

matter open due to the absence of definite textual evidence to this
effect.[123] A number of scholars have gone on record as definitely rejecting
the passage.[124] In addition, an impressive number of nineteenth-century
scholars reached similar conclusions.[125]

As for views on the source of 1 Cor 14: 34–5, if it is an intrusion into
the text, Barrett suggested a post-Pauline writer, such as the author of
1 Timothy,[126] and while Wendland related it to the time of the Pastorals,
Loisy, the present investigator, and now also Jewett have argued that it is
part of a larger, over-all editing of the same character as the Pastorals.[127]

Rom 13: 1–7. What, then, is to be said concerning Rom 13: 1–7, which
Dibelius and Weidinger did not classify as a *Haustafel* passage, for obvious
reasons, but which Carrington and Selwyn included as an integral part of
their 'code of subordination'? The Pauline origin of Rom 13: 1–7 is
seldom challenged explicitly, yet questions frequently arise concerning its
relation to Paul's thought as a whole, as well as to its immediate context,
and a few have gone so far as to reject it.

What has caused perplexity is how to reconcile subjection to the
ἐξουσίαι (authorities) and ἄρχοντες (powers or rulers) with a world view
that assumed the existence of hostile angelic powers standing behind
earthly rulers and nations. Most scholars have taken the view that the
sense of words depends on their context, and since there is no sign in
Rom 13: 1–7 of a supernatural sense for the terms in question, there is no
reason to assume it.

Others, notably O. Cullmann, have found a dual reference.[128] He used
as his basis 1 Cor 2: 6, 8, which describes the powers as passing away, and
as the perpetrators of Jesus' crucifixion, and 1 Cor 6: 1–7, where Christians
are enjoined to avoid litigation before 'the unrighteous', since the saints
are destined to judge the world, including the angels. The presumed reference to both spiritual and earthly authorities in 1 Corinthians Cullmann
tried to transfer to Rom 13: 1–7, arguing that Christ's victory over the
powers has subjected them to his authority and made them his servants.

Plausible as the theory may sound, it has elicited considerable negative
reaction which Cullmann himself documented.[129] C. Morrison pointed out
that critics had noted that only in Rom 13: 1–7 does ἐξουσία, apart from
its abstract use, appear independently of a catalogue of at least two powers,
and without an immediate relation to ἄρχων.[130] Furthermore, he indicated, in other contexts in the New Testament the former clearly refers to
supernatural powers,[131] and only three times quite clearly to civic and
political authorities,[132] the typical sense in pagan writings. Similarly the
latter generally applies to civic authorities, and in the New Testament refers

to spiritual powers only where there is a modifying phrase that indicates this sense. Another difficulty in Cullmann's theory, Morrison observed, is that in other contexts references to spiritual powers are christological, whereas Rom 13: 1-7 is not. Moreover, there is no evidence for the recommissioning of the authorities.[133]

Concluding that in Rom 13: 1-7 ἐξουσία carries the usual secular meaning, Morrison investigated the Graeco-Roman view of the state. He found that it is somewhat like the Hebrew view in that both regard ruling authority as part of the divine order. Translated into Christian categories, the state belongs to the order of creation, which Morrison thought Paul assigned to the Father. Thus he concluded that in Paul's mind Christ's work of redemption had nothing whatever to do with secular authorities, but affected only the church.[134] This argument, apparently the last resort of exegesis to incorporate Rom 13: 1-7 into Paulinism, also fails. It is surely a dubious construction which implies that the writer of Rom 8: 18-25, concerning the redemption of the whole of creation, could have limited its implications to the church.

Käsemann also rejected the 'demonic' explanation of Rom 13: 1-7, and considered that 'the exegetical battle came to a decisive end'[135] with an article by A. Strobel showing 'conclusively' that the Jewish doctrine of the angels of the nations is not to be imported into this passage, since its terminology coincides throughout with that of secular government in the Graeco-Roman world.[136] Käsemann therefore took issue with the view of Cullmann, Barth, and others that Rom 13: 1-7 has to do with the present lordship of Christ in the world, pointing out that there is no christological and eschatological patterning in the passage. 'To ignore this is to build castles in the air', he observed. His own explanation is that the injunctions to obey the state are a matter of expediency in dealing with eschatological enthusiasts who anticipated the new age prematurely.[137]

The evidence for this conclusion is slender,[138] but even assuming its correctness, it is difficult to understand how Paul could have changed his attitude to the state as expressed in 1 Cor 2: 6-8 and 6: 1-7 so radically in response to a local situation. Quite obviously, the problem remains unsolved.

A similar impasse exists on the question of the relation of Rom 13: 1-7 to its immediate context. Many find a lack of connection between what precedes and follows it, in particular between Rom 12: 21 and 13: 1, and attempts abound to identify some logical sequence or underlying unity.[139]

Others regard the exercise as futile, and accept the disjointed character of the text as it stands.[140] O. Michel advanced compelling reasons for regarding the passage as a self-contained entity. He pointed to the repetition of μηδενί in Rom 12: 17 and 13: 8 as a difference in style, and to the absence of connection with the teaching on love before and after Rom 13: 1-7. He also found it surprising that the teaching on subjection to the state followed the exhortation in Rom 12: 2 not to be conformed to this age, and that it preceded the explicitly theological content of Rom 13: 11-14.[141]

Cranfield, in replying to Michel's points, mentioned the verbal connection provided by ὀφειλάς and ὀφείλετε in Rom 13: 7 and 8, and while Michel considered Rom 13: 1-7 to be Jewish-hellenistic wisdom teaching, Cranfield replied that Rom 12: 9-21 also show signs of such influence.[142]

Käsemann's response to contextual difficulties was to discount the 'laborious attempts' to relieve Rom 13: 1-7 of its character of a 'foreign body' (*Fremdkörper*). Instead, he referred to the structure of Pauline paraenesis in general, which he maintained is not constructed logically by 'subordination and deduction', but by 'co-ordination' and 'association of ideas'.[143]

A more developed version of such an approach was put forward by D. G. Bradley,[144] who, using the form-critical method, identified four *topoi* strung together in Rom 13: vss. 1-5 on authority, 6-7 on paying tribute, 8-10 on love, and 11-14 on the eschatological hour, each having its key word. A *topos*, he maintained, can stand by itself, but the series is strung together by means of *Stichwörter*, as in the Sermon on the Mount. He was unable, however, to find any connecting words to link vss. 8-10 and 11-14.

Finally, the view that the passage is a non-Pauline insertion has found recurring expression. H. Windisch characterized it as a foreign pericope in 1913, and M. Dibelius as an interpolation in 1956. A. Pallis (1920) and A. Loisy (1936) both saw it as belonging to the time of the Antonines and the early Christian apologists in the second century.[145]

E. Barnikol (1961), though pointing to the break between Rom 12: 18-21 and 13: 1-10, to the un-Pauline use of terminology, and to the decretal-like style, based his argument mainly on the unqualified acceptance of the authority and goodness of government in Rom 13: 1-7. He found that it goes even further in this respect than the trito-Pauline Pastoral epistles or 1 Clement. He mentioned too that Epiphanius' and Tertullian's versions of Marcion's text both seem to omit it. Indeed, he could find no external evidence for the passage before a fragment quoted by Origen from the gnostic Heracleon, who wrote between 145 and 180 A.D. Irenaeus, he pointed out, was the first church father to cite it. He concluded that it was added to the text towards the end of the second century on episcopal authority.[146]

J. Kallas, with his stress on the 'demonism' of the apocalyptic world view from which Christianity arose,[147] saw a similar outlook in the references to the principalities and powers in the Pauline letters. Thus he could not conceive of Paul as exalting Rome in the manner of Rom 13: 1–7. Otherwise Kallas' arguments for regarding the passage as a separate entity[148] coincide with Michel's.

The rejection of the passage by these critics cannot be too easily discounted in view of the general recognition that it is problematic, both in its immediate and wider context, and the fact that a number of others came very close to the same conclusion, but left the question open as to whether Paul himself or someone else placed the passage where it is.

The subjection material and the concept of a Pastoral stratum

It seems, then, that not one of the passages in the Pauline letters identified as of the subjectionist or 'household' type is definitely primitive. It can be no coincidence that of those located in material assumed to be Pauline, not one is free from obvious contextual difficulties, and each is to some degree at odds with the sense and continuity of its literary surroundings. Thus there is no firm evidence, either in 1 Peter or in the Pauline collection, that any of this teaching was current in primitive Christian communities. What is more, there is a distinct tendency, where it is doubted or rejected as apostolic, for scholars to align it, not with the period and writers immediately following Paul, but with the Pastorals and the earlier part of the second century.

The hypothesis of redactional overworking of the Pauline letters is by no means new. It is implicit in the idea of their deliberate compilation for publication, as also in the numerous theories concerning the piecing together of different letters and letter fragments. As H. Gamble has stated:[149]

> These judgements and suspicions are occasioned by the literary difficulties with which Paul's letters are rife: anacolutha, repetitions, abrupt shifts of subject matter and tone, seemingly distinct situations presupposed within what is presented as the text of a single letter, etc. Theories of redaction have sought to make these phenomena intelligible as the consequences of secondary editorial reworking, a surmise which may be correct.

That such extensive redactional activity could take place with impunity makes it highly unlikely that it would have proceeded without editorial additions. It strains credulity to assume they would have been confined to brief connections and minor improvements.

Some have associated Ephesians with the collecting of the ten letters,[150] and the idea of Pastoral-type redaction has also been suggested from time to time. P. N. Harrison identified Rom 1: 19 – 2: 1 as a Pastoral intrusion and, as already indicated, some scholars have discerned the hand of a Pastoral reviser in 1 Cor 14: 33b–35. W. O. Walker and the present investigator, quite independently of each other, have gone on record to the same effect as regards 1 Cor 11: 2–16.[151] In addition, J. Weiss pointed to catholicizing amendments to 1 Corinthians in the process of editorial revision, and G. Zuntz identified numerous glosses in the ten letters, which he interpreted as issuing from an over-all editing for canonization.[152]

Going further than any others, A. Loisy claimed to find three successive literary layers corresponding with three kinds of 'catechesis' or teaching belonging to different stages of the early church: the 'eschatological', taught by the first apostles and teachers, including Paul; the eschatological intermingled with gnostic themes; and the 'antignostic' period of institutionalization corresponding with the Pastoral epistles as well as James, 1 and 2 Peter, Jude, and the Johannine epistles. A weakness in Loisy's approach is that, like F. C. Baur, he imposed a pre-determined historical construction upon the text. As a result he distinguished between one stratum and another according to content and tendencies, without sufficient attention to other criteria. Nevertheless, his concept of successive strata extending across the epistles and coexisting in the same epistle provides a useful framework for an investigation such as the present one.

Loisy's third strain is obviously the one corresponding most closely to that under investigation here. It certainly has affinity with what has been referred to as 'early catholicism' (*Frühkatholizismus*). In raising the question of its presence in the New Testament, E. Käsemann has described it as differing significantly from Paulinism in that it replaced charismatic communities, in which all exercised their gifts freely, with circumscribed ecclesiastical office.[153] Nevertheless, he thinks that Paul anticipated it in his attempts to establish authority for various kinds of ministry. One of the ways in which he tried to do this, according to Käsemann, was through the teaching of the 'household tables' and similar material. Such instruction, he thinks, served to counter hellenistic enthusiasts,[154] corresponding with the gnostics whom W. Schmithals has found everywhere in opposition to Paul in the original form of the corpus.[155]

R. H. Fuller considers that codes of this kind developed in the process of institutionalization in the sub-apostolic age, and are an aspect of 'early catholicism'.[156] The stratum of 'early catholicism' which he identifies in the New Testament is, however, far broader than that under investigation here, for it incorporates all sub-apostolic redaction and writing in the New

Testament excluding the Johannine gospel and epistles, and Revelation. The later stratum to be identified in this study, by contrast, will be differentiated from deutero-Pauline material such as predominates in Ephesians and ascribed to redaction subsequent to the writing of this epistle.

Method and criteria for critical study

Since the Pastoral stratum is held to be later than the primitive and deutero-Pauline writings in which it occurs, the critical task is that of applying criteria for establishing or rejecting dissociation from immediate context, and also for association with other material.

The aim is not to establish common authorship of all that is associated together in a common stratum, but rather that it issues from a common circle or school of tradition. This course is adopted owing to the difficulty, and perhaps even the impossibility, of proving common authorship of material in different documents, such as the epistles of the New Testament. So for instance, H. von Campenhausen, having advanced various kinds of arguments for his view that the writer of Polycarp's Epistle to the Philippians is also the writer of the Pastorals, concluded with the observation that if Polycarp is not the author of the Pastorals, then at least they emanate from the same thought world and surroundings, and must have been composed under his direction.[157] Literary dissociation obviously involves denial of authorship. In the present study it also carries the implication of a milieu different from that of earlier strata. The arguments to be used for the former correspond with three kinds of criteria which Robert Fortna identified as applicable in distinguishing an earlier source from later redaction in the Fourth Gospel.[158] They are what he terms the 'ideological' or *sachlich* kind, concerning tendencies and content; the stylistic, concerning vocabulary and linguistic characteristics; and the contextual, which has to do with the relation of material to its immediate literary surroundings.

Important as each is, Fortna indicated, none can stand by itself. First, though no two writers have exactly the same views and are bound to betray differences to some degree, the ideological type of argument can easily be a circular one.[159] The perception of a writer's point of view depends on what he is taken to have written. Thus to decide in advance what he thinks can predetermine the judgement as to what he has or has not written. Also, there may be inconsistencies in a writer's thought, or inner tensions which have the appearance of contradictions. In regard to epistolary writing, it may be added, apparent inconsistency may appear because of a difference in the situation to which the writer addresses himself.

Though this criterion requires other kinds of analysis to confirm it, it will prove useful in the present study in identifying passages which call for examination, and in determining whether material is to be associated with the subjectionist teaching in a later stratum. It will be an important means also of establishing affinity with the Pastoral epistles and certain other early Christian writings.

Stylistic criteria also involve certain difficulties.[160] Again, as Fortna observed, the argument can be circular for, to determine which stylistic characteristics do or do not pertain to a certain writer, a prior judgement is required as to what he has written.[161] Next, a later writer or editor may change the style of earlier material, or may attempt to imitate it,[162] something which may, however, betray itself through exaggeration or distortion. In addition it is possible for a writer to vary his style in accordance with his purpose and subject matter. In the Pauline epistles, for instance, the sentences in the opening, usually a thanksgiving, are very different in structure from those in the closing admonitions and greetings. Also to be considered is the possibility that stylistic difference may be due to citation from an earlier source rather than the interpolation of a later source. Nevertheless, stylistic unity tends to confirm authenticity, while stylistic diversity strengthens the possibility that more than one hand has been at work in the text. Stylistic similarities in different writings also obviously tend to support a theory that they issue from a common source.

In order to draw attention to certain stylistic characteristics which recur throughout the material identified as belonging to a later stratum, their occurrence will be set out numerically and their frequency calculated per page or according to the number of lines to each occurrence and compared with material assumed to be earlier. Such data, however, are intended to describe recurring differences which tend to confirm dissociation on other grounds. They will not be put forward as statistical proof for different authorship, but only indications of characteristics to be taken into account.

Similarly, calculations showing a tendency to conform with the linguistic habits of the Pastorals rather than the rest of the Pauline letters are not offered as decisive proof of Pastoral authorship, but simply to indicate certain significant affinities that do in fact exist. The high occurrence of New Testament *hapax legomena*, or words found nowhere else in the Pauline writings, may confirm that a passage is a later insertion, but their use may be due to the nature of the subject matter. They have greater force if found, not in extra-biblical writings contemporary with the primitive period, but somewhat later than that time. Also, it should be noted, the occurrence of rare New Testament words is not a *sine qua non* for interpolated material. An inserted imitation of an earlier writer may be singularly devoid of uncharacteristic words because of a deliberate intention to draw on the characteristic terminology and phraseology of the earlier material.

Differences in the use and meaning of words are relevant, though a single writer may employ a term in varying ways from one context to another. Such analysis will bear in mind the cautions of J. Barr[163] against imposing theological structures upon individual words, the meaning of which, he pointed out, depends on their use in sentences as well as larger complexes. Applying Barr's approach, R. Jewett[164] attempted to account for the differences in the sense of certain anthropological terms in the Pauline letters by reference to Paul's polemical purposes in dealing with different groups of opponents, and by reference also to the kind of writing in which Paul is engaging. Without undertaking here to evaluate the validity of Jewett's distinctions, however, it can be assumed that differences in the way words are used do tend to confirm rather than to deny the presence of another hand in the text, but taken in isolation this factor is relatively useless.

Obviously, as Fortna maintained, ideological and stylistic analyses can correct and complement each other.[165] In addition this study follows him in attaching special importance to contextual factors.[166] The disjointed nature of 1 Peter and many parts of the Pauline letters have been explained in a variety of ways. Here as in the Fourth Gospel they lead to the question whether they indicate the juxtaposition of different strata which has given rise to *aporiae* in the text. An *aporia* Fortna defined as the outcome of a clash between materials containing different ideological and stylistic elements.

A seam joining a later insertion to earlier material, he pointed out, may be indicated by the repetition of a catch-word or phrase,[167] with the insertion usually beginning with the first occurrence and continuing till immediately before the second, or beginning after the first and concluding with the second. This is a phenomenon which proves on occasion to be a clue to portions of the later stratum cohering with the subjection material.

It may be added that another sign of a seam may be the repetition of a word very soon after its first occurrence, so that it serves to link originally separate material in the manner of *Stichwörter*, or link words according to form-critical analysis.

Yet another clue which Fortna mentioned is the occurrence of variant readings in manuscripts at certain points in the text where there have been attempts to smooth an awkward transition.

However identified, contextual evidence proves indispensable in determining whether deviant material was incorporated from an earlier source by the original writer, or inserted by a later writer. It is quite obvious that citations from known sources such as the Old Testament scriptures in the Pauline corpus and 1 Peter do not interrupt the thought sequences of their contexts, but on the contrary carry them forward.[168] Thus when a supposedly quoted or adapted code or catechetical excerpt does the opposite, it is questionable whether it was an original part of the text.

In particular, such an interruption may be assumed to be an interpolation if, in addition to other confirming factors, there is continuity of sense, style, and possibly form and rhetorical patterning between what immediately precedes and follows it. That this is a recurring phenomenon in the contexts of the subjection material is an added reason for regarding it as later rather than earlier than the original.

Yet another criterion to be applied is that of literary dependence. If a piece of writing draws on other writing, it was obviously written later than the other writing. The problem of how to determine literary dependence has no better solution than that put forward by C. L. Mitton, who demonstrated the dependence of Ephesians on the rest of the ten-letter corpus by showing that it repeatedly conflates parts of sentences from different contexts in the other letters, and that it does so far more frequently than Philippians.[169] In addition he applied the criterion that if a yet later writer is dependent on an earlier imitator, the latter will manifest closer adherence to the original than the former. In this way he indicated that 1 Peter is later than Ephesians.[170] The validity of this criterion depends both on its recurring nature, and on confirmation from other kinds of evidence, since a single writer may repeat his own phrases, and two writers may use similar turns of phrase because they share a common milieu.

The case for dissociation is considerably strengthened if it can be argued that an alleged interpolation coheres with material belonging to another milieu. In the present study such corroborating evidence is found by reference to the Pastoral epistles. That the later stratum in the ten-letter corpus and 1 Peter is to be associated with them will be established by a comparison of tendencies and points of view, style, and vocabulary. Further confirmation will be forthcoming from comparison with the ideological characteristics of early patristic writings already mentioned. Positive results from such analysis will lessen the possibility that the insertions identified as making up the Pastoral stratum are actually parts of disparate Pauline letters which a redactor has pieced together.

In sum, the judgement as to whether any passage is interpolated depends on a variety of factors and depends on no one infallible criterion.

It is a matter of taking into account the cumulative effect of converging lines of evidence.

As for the hypothesis as a whole, the ultimate tests for its validity will be the range of problems it solves, whether it simplifies and clarifies the understanding of the text, and whether it proves fruitful for future scholarship in that it opens the way for the resolution of further questions. It is predictable that while scholars will take issue with the specific locations and extent of Pastoral-type redaction, its presence in some form to some degree will prove undeniable.

Procedure

Chapter 2, 'The identification of a later stratum in the Pauline corpus and 1 Peter', will proceed to apply critical criteria to the investigation of relevant parts of the text of the Pauline corpus and 1 Peter. The resulting dissociation of the relevant passages from their immediate literary contexts will involve additional material both in the Pauline collection and 1 Peter manifesting similar characteristics and also to be detached from its literary surroundings. It will be argued that all these passages cohere in a literary stratum representing a common strain of Christian tradition to be distinguished from primitive and deutero-Pauline strata.

The starting-point for the investigation of the text will be the parallel subjectionist passages in Colossians and Ephesians, where the trito-Pauline character of the material will be established. In view of the close connections between Ephesians and 1 Peter, the study assumes that these three epistles may be treated as a roughly homogeneous complex. The study will therefore move to 1 Peter before returning to the Pauline letters. Here it will become evident that the subjection material is part of a redaction which incorporates a short, earlier letter in 1 Peter as one of its sources. Rom 13: 1–7 will be examined next, due to its affinity to 1 Pet 2: 13–17. Thereafter there will be investigation of 1 Cor 14: 33–6, which will lead also to consideration of 1 Cor 11: 2–16. The latter will be shown to be connected with Eph 5: 21–2, and at the same time will reveal the presence of material cohering with the later stratum in 1 Cor 10 and the rest of 1 Cor 11, 1 Cor 8, Rom 14 and 15, and in 1 and 2 Thessalonians.

Chapter 3, 'The later stratum and the Pastoral epistles', will apply criteria pertaining to tendencies, style, and vocabulary to determine to what extent the later stratum is to be associated with the Pastorals. It will be concluded that the affinity is such that the later stratum and the Pastoral epistles are to be associated together in a common tradition to be distinguished from earlier strata. At the same time, it will transpire that the later material in 1 Peter is probably closer in time to the Pastoral epistles, and the equivalent material in the ten-letter corpus is somewhat earlier. Here Rom 1: 19 – 2: 1 will emerge as an additional part of the later stratum, but as closer in time to the Pastoral epistles than the rest of the later stratum in the ten-letter corpus. All the material associated with the Pastoral epistles will thereafter be referred to as the 'Pastoral' stratum.

In chapter 4, 'The literary and historical context of the subjectionist material', the inquiry will be extended to take into account the marked affinities of the Pastoral stratum to 1 Clement, Polycarp's Epistle to the Philippians, and the Ignatian letters, as also some parts of the Didache and Barnabas. It will be demonstrated that these too are to be accounted part of the context of the subjection material of the New Testament epistles. From the evidence furnished by all the writings associated together in this manner, it will be concluded that the Pastoral circles tend toward Rome in their political and ecclesiastical leanings, and that they are to be placed in the first half of the second century.

Consideration of Pastoral revision of the Pauline corpus and 1 Peter in the context of their redactional history will lead to the conclusion that they were probably taken over from Jewish-oriented, possibly Qumran-type opponents who disappeared with their version of Paul and other scriptures in the wake of the second Jewish war.

The final chapter will summarize the study, review the findings, and discuss their implications.

2   THE IDENTIFICATION OF A LATER STRATUM IN THE PAULINE CORPUS AND 1 PETER

The later stratum in Ephesians and Colossians[1]

There is quite obviously an intimate relation between Eph 5: 21 - 6: 9 and Col 3: 18 - 4: 1, as the code theory assumes. It has generally been held that the shorter Colossians passage is earlier, and that the longer version in Ephesians is a later expansion of it.[2] While this appears to be true of Ephesians as a whole in relation to Colossians,[3] the parallels which Mitton collected[4] provide evidence that Col 3: 18 - 4: 1 is dependent on, and therefore subsequent to, Eph 5: 21 - 6: 9, as will be shown. In addition, it will be argued that Eph 5: 21 - 6: 9 is later than the rest of Ephesians, and so must be accounted an interpolation.

These two conclusions may be drawn in the first instance by applying Mitton's method of determining dependence and priority. He argued that 1 Peter must be later than Ephesians, on the ground that where both parallel or echo the same earlier material, Ephesians is invariably closer to it. Thus he concluded that 1 Peter made use of Ephesians and so was written after it.[5]

Similarly the dependence of Col 3: 18 - 4: 1 on Eph 5: 21 - 6: 9 appears from the fact that where both passages echo earlier letters of the Pauline corpus in slightly different ways, the Ephesians version is invariably closer to the original, as the following comparisons show:

Eph 6: 8: ἕκαστος, ἐαν τι ποιήσῃ ἀγαθόν, τοῦτο κομίσεται παρὰ κυρίου, εἴτε δοῦλος εἴτε ἐλεύθερος. [6:9] Καὶ οἱ κύριοι, τὰ αὐτὰ ποιεῖτε πρὸς αὐτούς, ἀνιέντες τὴν ἀπειλήν, εἰδότες ὅτι καὶ αὐτῶν καὶ ὑμῶν ὁ κύριός ἐστιν ἐν οὐρανοῖς, καὶ προσωπολημψία οὐκ ἔστιν παρ' αὐτῷ.

2 Cor 5: 10: ἵνα κομίσηται ἕκαστος τὰ διὰ τοῦ σώματος πρὸς ἃ ἔπραξεν, εἴτε ἀγαθὸν εἴτε φαῦλον. 1 Cor 7: 13: εἴτε δοῦλοι εἴτε ἐλεύθεροι Rom 2: 11: οὐ γάρ ἐστιν προσωπολημψία παρὰ τῷ θεῷ.

Col 3:25: ὁ γὰρ ἀδικῶν <u>κομίσεται ὃ</u>
ἠδίκησεν, καὶ οὐκ ἔστιν προσωπολημψία. [4:1] <u>Οἱ κύριοι, τὸ δίκαιον</u>
<u>καὶ τὴν ἰσότητα τοῖς δούλοις</u>
<u>παρέχεσθε, εἰδότες ὅτι καὶ ὑμεῖς ἔχετε</u>
<u>κύριον ἐν οὐρανῷ.</u>

First it is evident that both Eph 6: 8f and Col 3: 25 make contact with
Rom 2: 11, but the Ephesians version is closer to it in that it includes παρ'
αὐτῷ which corresponds with παρὰ τῷ θεῷ, while Colossians omits it. It is
unlikely that such a detail was acquired by accident in the course of
enlarging on Colossians; it seems more probable that it was omitted in the
course of abbreviation. As for the occurrence in Colossians of κομίσεται
where Ephesians has ἀγαθόν . . . εἴτε . . . εἴτε in common with 2 Cor 5: 10,
it is not impossible for the Ephesians writer to have made a mental connection between a single word in Colossians and its use in another part of the
Pauline corpus, enlarging on it accordingly. The previous evidence for con-
traction strengthens the probability, however, that it has taken place here
also, and that the Ephesians version is prior.

This probability receives further support from the following:

Eph 6: 5: Οἱ δοῦλοι, ὑπακούετε τοῖς   Phil 2: 12: πάντοτε ὑπηκούσατε, . . .
<u>κατὰ σάρκα κυρίοις μετὰ φόβου καὶ</u>   μετὰ φόβου καὶ τρόμου
<u>τρόμου.</u>
Col 3:22: Οἱ δοῦλοι, <u>ὑπακούετε</u> κατὰ
<u>πάντα</u> τοῖς <u>κατὰ σάρκα κυρίοις</u>, . . .
<u>φοβούμενοι τὸν κύριον.</u>

Since Col 3: 22 has two points of contact with Phil 2: 12, one might
suspect some connection quite apart from Eph 6: 5. The latter is, however,
clearly directly dependent on Phil 2: 12, while the Colossians version
could have been derived from that in Ephesians. The likeness between
πάντοτε in Phil 2: 12 and κατὰ πάντα in Col 3: 22 is not close enough to
outweigh the evidence pointing here to the priority of the Ephesians
wording.

The next instance suggests not only that the Colossians passage is derived
from Ephesians, but also that this part of Ephesians is dependent on, and
therefore later than, the rest of Ephesians:

Eph 6: 5: <u>ἐν ἁπλότητι τῆς καρδίας</u>   Gal 1: 10: ἢ ζητῶ ἀνθρώποις
<u>ὑμῶν ὡς τῷ Χριστῷ.</u> vi. 6 <u>μὴ</u> κατ'   ἀρέσκειν; εἰ ἔτι ἀνθρώποις ἤρεσκον,
<u>ὀφθαλμοδουλίαν ὡς ἀνθρωπάρεσκοι</u>   Χριστοῦ δοῦλος οὐκ ἂν ἤμην.
<u>ἀλλ' ὡς δοῦλοι Χριστοῦ ποιοῦντες τὸ</u>   Eph 1: 18: πεφωτισμένους τοὺς

θέλημα τοῦ θεοῦ ἐκ ψυχῆς, 6:7 μετ᾽   ὀφθαλμοὺς τῆς καρδίας [ὑμῶν] εἰς τὸ
εὐνοίας δουλεύοντες, ὡς τῷ κυρίῳ καὶ   εἰδέναι ὑμᾶς
οὐκ ἀνθρώποις, [vi. 8] εἰδότες ὅτι ...
Col 3: 22: μὴ ἐν ὀφθαλμοδουλίᾳ ὡς
ἀνθρωπάρεσκοι, ἀλλ᾽ ἐν ἁπλότητι
καρδίας, ... 3: 23 ὃ ἐὰν ποιῆτε, ἐκ
ψυχῆς ἐργάζεσθε, ὡς τῷ κυρίῳ καὶ
οὐκ ἀνθρώποις. 3: 24 εἰδότες ὅτι ...
τῷ κυρίῳ Χριστῷ δουλεύετε

Here the Ephesians version is nearer to Gal 1: 10 in that it parallels
Χριστοῦ δοῦλος with δοῦλοι Χριστοῦ, whereas Col 3: 24 has τῷ κυρίῳ
Χριστῷ δουλεύετε, which is closer to Eph 6: 7. It may be concluded then
that it is the Ephesians passage that has conflated Gal 1: 10 with Eph 1: 18
and produced the compound word ὀφθαλμοδουλία, indicating its use, not
only of the rest of the Pauline corpus, but also of the main body of
Ephesians. Nor is this an isolated instance of apparent dependence on
Ephesians on the part of Eph 5: 21 - 6: 9, as will be seen from four
further comparisons:

Eph 5: 2: καθὼς καὶ ὁ Χριστὸς   Gal 2: 20: τοῦ υἱοῦ τοῦ θεοῦ τοῦ
ἠγάπησεν ἡμᾶς καὶ παρέδωκεν   ἀγαπήσαντός με καὶ παραδόντος
ἑαυτὸν ὑπὲρ ἡμῶν   ἑαυτὸν ὑπὲρ ἐμοῦ.
Eph 5: 25: Οἱ ἄνδρες, ἀγαπᾶτε τὰς
γυναῖκας, καθὼς καὶ ὁ Χριστὸς
ἠγάπησεν τὴν ἐκκλησίαν καὶ ἑαυτὸν
παρέδωκεν ὑπὲρ αὐτῆς

The similarity between Eph 5: 2 and 5: 25 is so striking that it is hard
to believe it is merely accidental. The more feasible explanation is that it
is deliberate. The possibility that Eph 5: 2 draws on an oral source which
is also used in Eph 5: 25 is to be rejected, for both seem to be dependent
on Gal 2: 20, besides sharing some material not found in this source. Eph
5: 2 is, however, close to Gal 2: 20 in that while it changes the personal
pronouns με and ἐμοῦ to plural, Eph 5: 25 replaces them with the words
τὴν ἐκκλησίαν and αὐτῆς. It is therefore more likely that Eph 5: 2 is prior,
and that Eph 5: 25 is dependent upon it.

Next, in the following parallels ἐστιν ἡ κεφαλή in Eph 4: 15 tallies
exactly with Col 1: 18, whereas Eph 5: 23 omits the article. Taking into
account the other instances cited, it may be assumed that this is not sheer
chance, but yet another sign that Eph 5: 21 - 6: 9 is dependent on the rest
of the epistle. The phrase τῆς ἐκκλησίας in Col 1: 18 is evidently a gloss
added under the influence of Eph 1: 22f, 5: 22.[6]

Eph 1: 22: καὶ πάντα ὑπέταξεν ὑπὸ τοὺς πόδας αὐτοῦ, καὶ αὐτὸν ἔδωκεν <u>κεφαλὴν ὑπὲρ πάντα τῇ ἐκκλησίᾳ</u> 1: 23 ἥτις ἐστὶν τὸ σῶμα αὐτοῦ, τὸ πλήρωμα τοῦ τὰ πάντα <u>ἐν πᾶσιν</u> πληρουμένου.

Col 1: 18: <u>καὶ αὐτός ἐστιν ἡ κεφαλὴ τοῦσ ὡματος, τῆς ἐκκλησίας</u>· ὃς ἐσ ἀρχή ... ἵνα γένηται <u>ἐν πᾶσιν αὐτὸ</u> πρωτεύων

Eph 4: 15: ἀληθεύοντες δὲ ἐν ἀγάπῃ αὐξήσωμεν εἰς αὐτὸν τὰ πάντα, ὃς <u>ἐστιν ἡ κεφαλή</u>, Χριστός, ἐξ οὗ πᾶν τὸ σῶμα συναρμολογούμενον

Eph 5: 23: ὅτι ἀνήρ ἐστιν <u>κεφαλὴ</u> τῆς γυναικὸς ὡς καὶ ὁ <u>Χριστὸς κεφαλὴ τῆς ἐκκλησίας</u>, αὐτὸς σωτὴρ <u>τοῦ σώματος</u> 5: 24 ἀλλὰ ὡς ... <u>ἐν παντί</u>

Evidence for the dependence of Eph 5: 21 - 6: 9, both on Ephesians and Colossians, is contained in the following:

Eph 1: 4: <u>εἶναι ἡμᾶς ἁγίους καὶ ἀμώ-μους κατενώπιον αὐτοῦ ἐν ἀγάπῃ.</u>

Eph 5: 27: <u>ἵνα παραστήσῃ</u> αὐτὸς ἑαυτῷ ἔνδοξον τὴν ἐκκλησίαν, μὴ ἔχουσαν σπίλον ἢ ῥυτίδα ἤ τι τῶν τοιούτων, ἀλλ' ἵνα ᾖ ἁγία καὶ ἄμωμος. 5: 28 οὕτως ὀφείλουσιν καὶ οἱ ἄνδρες ἀγαπᾶν τὰς ἑαυτῶν γυναῖκας

Col 1: 22: <u>παραστῆσαι ὑμᾶς ἁγίους καὶ ἀμώμους καὶ ἀνεγκλήτους κατενώπιον αὐτοῦ</u>

Col 1: 28: <u>ἵνα παραστήσωμεν</u> πάντι ἄνθρωπον τέλειον ἐν Χριστῷ.

2 Cor 11: 2: ἡρμοσάμην γὰρ ὑμᾶς ἑ ἀνδρὶ παρθένον ἀγνὴν <u>παραστῆσα</u> τῷ Χριστῷ

Eph 5: 27f appears to combine Eph 1: 4 with Col 1: 22, using ἀγαπᾶν to echo ἐν ἀγάπῃ in Eph 1: 4. It is also possible, however, that the writer of Eph 5: 21 - 6: 9 takes direct notice of 2 Cor 11: 2f in elaborating the theme of the bride as betrothed to her 'one husband'. Nevertheless, his wording is clearly influenced by the precedents in Colossians and the rest of Ephesians.

That the literary dependence to which this evidence points applies to Eph 5: 21 - 6: 9 as a whole and not merely to that which is not shared with Col 3: 18 - 4: 1 is clear from the distribution of the parallels in the former: Eph 5: 21, 23, 25, 27f, 6: 5, 8f. Of these, four instances involve parallels with the rest of Ephesians, Eph 5: 21, 23, 25, 27f, which is to say, they occur in the material in Eph 5: 21-3, likening the relation between husband and wife to that between Christ and the church.

It is of course possible for a single writer to repeat his own terminology and turns of phrase in different contexts, re-using material borrowed from other sources in slightly different ways. This is not however an adequate explanation for the series of parallels identified as between Eph 5: 21 - 6: 9 and the rest of the epistle for, though the latter tends to be repetitive in its language, what one finds is not comparable in general to what occurs in Eph 5: 21 - 6: 9.[7]

To review the findings based on examination of verbal parallels it has been shown, first, that Col 3: 18 - 4: 1 is probably dependent on Eph 5: 21 - 6: 9, which seems therefore to be prior. It has been shown, secondly, that the latter is probably dependent on the rest of Ephesians as well as Colossians. If these conclusions are correct, the order of writing was as follows: Colossians, Ephesians, Eph 5: 21 - 6: 9, Col 3: 18 - 4: 1. Confirmation that Col 3: 18 - 4: 1 is later than both Ephesians and Eph 5: 21 - 6: 9 is to be found in Col 3: 20, which has the appearance of a conflation combining Eph 5: 10 with 6: 1, as shown below:

Col 3: 20: <u>Τὰ τέκνα, ὑπακούετε τοῖς</u> <u>γονεῦσιν</u> κατὰ πάντα, <u>τοῦτο γὰρ</u> <u>εὐάρεστόν ἐστιν ἐν κυρίῳ</u>.

Eph 6: 1: <u>Τὰ τέκνα, ὑπακούετε τοῖς</u> <u>γονεῦσιν</u> ὑμῶν ἐν κυρίῳ, <u>τοῦτο γὰρ</u> <u>ἐστιν</u> δίκαιον.

Eph 5: 10: δοκιμάζοντες τί ἐστιν <u>εὐάρεστον</u> τῷ <u>κυρίῳ</u>.

Dependence cannot be on the side of Eph 5: 10, since, as Mitton has shown,[8] this part of Ephesians is to be explained as a conflation of Rom 12: 2, εἰς τὸ δοκιμάζειν ὑμᾶς τί τὸ θέλημα τοῦ θεοῦ, τὸ ἀγαθὸν καὶ εὐάρεστον καὶ τέλειον, and Phil 4: 18, εὐάρεστον τῷ θεῷ. In taking over the sentence structure and most of the wording of Eph 6: 1, Col 3: 20 substitutes εὐάρεστον ἐστιν ἐν κυρίῳ for ἐστιν δίκαιον, apparently under the influence of Eph 5: 10.

Confirmation that Col 3: 18 - 4: 1 is an interpolation is to be found also in the context of the passage. It is not unusual for commentators to observe that it interrupts the flow of thought in Col 3 and 4, and that Col 3: 16f, containing exhortations to praise and thanksgiving, finds a more natural and logical sequence in Col 4: 2f, urging watchfulness, prayer, and thanksgiving, than in the catalogue of duties in 3: 18ff. The lack of continuity has, however, been ascribed to the apostle's having made an addition himself at this point.[9]

If then Col 4: 2f be joined to Col 3: 16f, leaving out the intervening material, a continuum, not only in sense but also in style and rhythm, results. Added to the proliferation of ἐν phrases in 3: 16f and 4: 2 is the repetition of rhyming participles in both; compare 3: 16 διδάσκοντες καὶ νουθετοῦντες . . . ᾄδοντες . . . εὐχαριστοῦντες (3: 16f), γρηγοροῦντες . . . (4: 2).

If this was the form of the text before the insertion of Col 3: 18 - 4: 1, why, it may be asked, did the interpolator select Col 3: 17 as the place at which to break into the epistle, when a more felicitous joining-point could have been found without much difficulty somewhere else, for instance, before Col 4: 7? The position of the passage no longer appears arbitrary, however, if one assumes that he had before him the text of Ephesians with Eph 5: 21 attached to Eph 5: 20, εὐχαριστοῦντες τῷ Θεῷ καὶ Πατρί, which closely resembles εὐχαριστοῦντες τῷ Θεῷ Πατρί δι 'αὐτοῦ in Col 3: 17b, a parallel that may be ascribed to the dependence of the earlier form of Ephesians on the earlier form of Colossians.

Was this the cue that prompted a yet later scribe or editor to insert in Colossians a short passage summarizing Eph 5: 21 - 6: 9, in order to make good what appeared to be an omission at this point? This would explain why Col 3: 18 has ὑποτάσσεσθε, whereas Eph 5: 21 employs the participle in the introductory phrase to the pericope. That copyists found the latter awkward is evident from the number of variations in the manuscripts in order to include an imperative form of the verb in Eph 5: 22.[10] Also, the tendency for the text of Ephesians to influence Colossians appears in the variant Θεῷ καὶ Πατρί in some manuscripts, uncials, minuscules, and lectionaries at Col 3: 17.[11]

At the same time it is obvious that Col 3: 18 - 4: 1 is no chance accretion, but manifests studied and deliberate efforts to bring it into alignment with the context. Besides the two ἐν κυρίῳ phrases in 3: 18 and 20 which are additional to ἐν ἁπλότητι (Col 3: 22) and ἐν οὐρανῷ (Col 4: 1) following Eph 6: 5 and 9, the Colossians passage has changed κατ' ὀφθαλμοδουλίαν in Eph 6: 6 to ἐν ὀφθαλμοδουλίᾳ in Col 3: 22. The Colossians version thus has five ἐν phrases compared with eight in Eph 5: 21 - 6:9, which is actually a proportional increase, since Col 3: 18 -4: 1 is only half the length of its equivalent in Ephesians. This stylistic characteristic accords with the ἐν phrases noted in Col 3: 16 - 4: 2, but it also diverges from it in that these phrases do not follow euphoniously one upon another as in the surrounding context.

This still leaves unexplained, however, why Eph 5: 21 - 6: 9 begins with a present participle, whereas Col 3: 18 - 4: 1 avoids the usage. As in the case of the ἐν phrases in the Colossians passage, adaptation to the immediate context is the answer. Despite the protracted discussion of the so-called unattached participial imperative,[12] there appears to be no reason for thinking ὑποτασσόμενοι is intended as other than the continuation of the sentence in 5: 18ff, taking its place in the series of present participles to be found here. That there is an *aporia* is evident. It is not syntactical, however, but rather one of sense, mood, and rhythm, as between 5: 18ff and 5: 21ff.

As for 5: 22, αἱ γυναῖκες τοῖς ἰδίοις ἀνδράσιν ὡς τῷ κυρίῳ, though it
appears as a fresh sentence in printed texts, it is not syntactically impossible for it to be a continuation of the sentence to which the opening
participle is attached. The participle does not agree with αἱ γυναῖκες in
gender, but this noun refers to only one of the groups who are addressed
in a generalized way. The clumsiness of the result may be ascribed to an
unsuccessful attempt on the part of the interpolator to bring his material
into alignment with Ephesian style, marked as it is by prolonged periods
abounding in participles.

One has only to compare this awkward sequence with that which results
if 6: 10ff is read directly after 5: 18–20 to realize how rudely 5: 21 – 6: 9
interrupts the rhythmic flow of the original. It is noteworthy that
πληροῦσθε ἐν πνεύματι, λαλοῦντες . . . εὐχαριστοῦντες finds a rhyming
sequence in ἐνδυναμοῦσθε ἐν κυρίῳ, which is characteristic of the
Ephesian use of assonance and repetition.[13]

Signs of stylistic adaptation of the rest of Ephesians are to be found not
only in the frequent use of participles (nine times in all, a rate practically
identical to that in the rest of the epistle), but also in the frequent pairing
of words either synonymous or closely related in meaning. There are five
such instances in 5: 21 – 6: 9, averaging one pair to every 6.4 lines, compared with nineteen in the rest of Ephesians, averaging one pair to every
12.7 lines,[14] suggesting exaggerated imitation of the trait by 5: 21 – 6: 9.
In addition, the passage differs from the epistle as a whole in that the
frequency of its use of ἐν (eight times, averaging one occurrence to every
four lines or just over eight to a page) represents a rate that is markedly
lower than the rest of Ephesians. The latter employs the word on an
average of 13.4 times to the page, with variations ranging between 11 and
21, and with a relatively even distribution on every page. This then is a
distinction that clearly demarcates 5: 21 – 6: 9 from the epistle as a whole.

If Eph 5: 21 – 6: 9 is an expanded version of material such as occurs in
Col 3: 18 – 4: 1, one would expect the writer to manifest the stylistic
peculiarities of the rest of the epistle, especially in Eph 5: 22–33, very
little of which appears in Col 3: 18 – 4: 1. Such a trait is the repeated use,
except in 5: 21 – 6: 9, of the adjectival genitive to express peculiarly close
identity in sense or content.[15]

Also distinguishing the passage from the rest of Ephesians are the
differences in the use of certain key concepts of the epistle. Commentators
have remarked on the confusion in the understanding of κεφαλή, σῶμα,
and ἐκκλησία in Ephesians. That it is quite impossible to make logical
sense of the figurative language used was implied by H. Schlier in charac-
terizing the 'body' in this epistle as actually a 'torso', and Christ as at one
and the same time the κεφαλή alone and the σῶμα plus κεφαλή of the

anthropos and the ἐκκλησία.[16] If however exegesis proceeds on the premise that 5: 21 - 6: 9 was added later, two distinct views are to be discerned: the first, that Christ is the 'head' of the universe as the 'man' or 'son of man' to whom all things have been subjected *for the church* (a dative of advantage) which is the 'body' (Ps 8: 4, 6; Eph 1: 22f). The whole body is already proleptically in the position of the 'head' that exercises world dominion (2: 5f), who, far from being distinguishable from the body, is the unifying principle that holds all parts together (2: 15, 21; 4: 4, 16). The second view, found in 5: 21ff, clearly demarcates the 'body' from the 'head' (the genitive in 'head of the church' is evidently partitive, and in 'saviour of the body' objective, 5: 23), with the latter acting as the authority principle that provides the prototype for the pattern of authority and subjection in human relations. Here there is no room for growth into a common dominion.

Then too, while in the epistle as a whole 'flesh' is found on both sides of the divide between light and darkness,[17] Eph 5: 21 assumes it to be intrinsically evil until purified 'by the washing of water' (probably a reference to baptism)[18] 'in the word' (Eph 5: 26).

In addition, μυστήριον in vs. 32 has a meaning quite distinct from its use elsewhere in the epistle and the New Testament, as is often observed. While in the rest of Ephesians it occurs five times over in the same sense of hidden truth that is made known concerning God's plan of salvation in Christ (1: 9; 3: 3, 4, 9; 6: 19), in vs. 32 it seems to refer to a sign or symbol, translated *sacramentum* by Jerome.[19] Justin, significantly, uses the word interchangeably with παραβολή, σύμβολον, and τύπος,[20] the meaning the word acquired later than the immediate sub-apostolic period.

Yet another sign suggesting that Eph 5: 21 - 6: 9 is to be dissociated from its surroundings is the finding of K. G. Kuhn that the paraenesis of Eph 5: 1 - 6: 20 bears a marked likeness throughout to what is to be found in the Qumran texts, with the exception of Eph 5: 21 - 6: 9, which is alone in showing no trace whatever of any relationship.[21]

It may be concluded, then, that Eph 5: 21 - 6: 9 and Col 3: 18 - 4: 1 are roughly contemporary insertions into the text from the same or closely connected sources. In addition, certain other short insertions cohering with the two passages seem to have been made elsewhere in the two epistles.

First, Eph 5: 15-18 bears a marked similarity in sentence structure to Eph 5: 21 - 6: 9 in that both make regular use of antithetic parallels bound together by negative particles, as well as ὡς and ἀλλά. Both the last-mentioned occur in Eph 5: 21 - 6: 9 to a degree that bears no relation to the rest of the epistle as a whole. The first occurs nine times in the slightly more than one page of the passage, or once in every 3.9 lines, compared with six uses in the rest of the epistle, that is, under one (0.8) to the page, or once every forty lines. Similarly ἀλλά occurs five times or once to every seven lines of Eph 5: 21 - 6: 9, compared with the eight uses, averaging once per page or once to every thirty lines in the rest of Ephesians. Significantly, Eph 5: 15-20 contains three antithetic parallels, each making use of ἀλλά, and in the first ὡς is used twice. The sentence structure in Eph 4: 28f also resembles that in Eph 5: 21 - 6: 9, for here there are two antithetic parallels. The second contains ἀλλά, and both employ ἵνα, which is another conjunction used with relative frequency in Eph 5: 21 - 6: 9. It occurs five times in this page-long passage, as compared with the rate of 2.3 uses to the page in the rest of the epistle.

Other factors also support the view that these two short passages are later additions to Ephesians. Eph 4: 28f interrupts the sequence between 4: 26f and 4: 30ff, which warns of the danger of allowing anger and enmity to continue overnight till the next day, which may be the 'day of redemption', and exhorts the saints to 'put away' wrath and slander in favour of kindness and forgiveness. The subjects of larceny and idleness in 4: 28f have no obvious connection with this train of thought. These verses also obscure the antithesis between 'the devil' in 4: 27 and 'the holy spirit of God' in 4: 30, which accords with the strong dualistic tendencies in the epistle.

Eph 5: 15-18 also represents an abrupt change of mood, in that the lyrical climax to the preceding paraenesis (5: 13f) suddenly gives place to banal exhortations on wisdom (vss. 15-17), work (vs. 16), and sobriety (vs. 18*a*).

Secondly, αἱ ἡμέραι πονηραί in 5: 16, while superficially resembling ἐν τῇ ἡμέρᾳ τῇ πονηρᾷ in 6: 13, differs in that while the latter refers to the expected eschatological crisis, which will also be the 'day of redemption', the former refers to the ongoing present. Thirdly, Eph 5: 15f appears to be a conflation of two parts of the rest of Ephesians, such as is not to be expected from the main writer, or alternatively combines elements of Ephesians and Colossians, as shown below:

Eph 5: 15 Βλέπετε οὖν ἀκριβῶς πῶς περιπάτειτε, μὴ ὡς ἄσοφοι ἀλλὰ
 ὡς σοφοί, 16 ἐξαγοραζόμενοι τὸν καιρὸν ὅτι αἱ ἡμέραι πονηραί εἰσιν.
Eph 5: 8 ὡς τέκνα φωτὸς περιπατεῖτε . . .
Eph 6: 13 . . . ἐν τῇ ἡμέρᾳ τῇ πονηρᾷ καὶ ἄπαντα κατεργασάμενοι
 στῆναι.
Col 4: 5 Ἐν σοφίᾳ περιπατεῖτε πρὸς τοὺς ἔξω, τὸν καιρὸν
 ἐξαγοραζόμενοι.

All that Eph 5: 15 has in common with Col 4: 5 points to dependence one way or the other. Assuming Col 4: 5 is prior, Eph 5: 15 has conflated it with Eph 6: 13, with the similarity of κατεργασάμενοι to ἐξαγοραξόμενοι suggesting that the two might have been combined, and the similarities with Eph 5: 8 might be sheer chance, since περιπατεῖν occurs with relative frequency in Ephesians. If, however, Eph 5: 15 combined Eph 5: 8 and 6: 13 independently of Col 4: 5, as is quite feasible, Col 4: 5 must be accounted an addition to Colossians of the same kind as Col 3: 18 - 4: 1, under the influence of Ephesians, with ὡς σοφοί changed to ἐν σοφίᾳ to accord with the context. A factor that decides the issue in favour of the second possibility is that Col 4: 5 interrupts a series of rhyming parallels, as the following indicates:

Col 4: 3 ... λαλῆσαι τὸ μυστήριον τοῦ Χριστοῦ, δι' ὃ καὶ δέδεμαι,
    4 ἵνα φανερωσω αὐτὸ ὡς δεῖ με λαλῆσαι. ...
    6 ὁ λόγος ὑμῶν πάντοτε ἐν χάριτι, ἅλατι ἠρτυμένος, εἰδέναι
    πῶς δει ὑμᾶς ἑνὶ ἑκάστῳ ἀποκρίνεσθαι.

Here Col 4: 5, with its very different rhythm, sounds a jarring note in the musical sequence of the context.

So too Eph 5: 15-18a seems to interrupt a sequence from a hymnic citation in 5: 14b to a call for the manifestation of pneumatic gifts in 5: 18b-20. There is no syntactical discontinuity in the sentence in 5: 18, but the warning against intoxication seems rather to be an implied criticism of pneumatic enthusiasm than a supporting contrast. The original version of the text probably read as follows:

Eph 5: 14b ῎Εγειρε, ὁ καθεύδων,
    καὶ ἀνάστα ἐκ τῶν νεκρῶν,
    καὶ ἐπιφαύσει σοι ὁ Χριστός.
5: 18b-20 πληροῦσθε ἐν πνεύματι,
    λαλοῦντες ἑαυτοῖς
    [ἐν] ψαλμοῖς καὶ ὕμνοις
    καὶ ᾠδαῖς πνευματικαῖς
    ᾄδοντες καὶ ψάλλοντες
    τῇ καρδίᾳ ὑμῶν τῷ κυρίῳ,
    εὐχαριστοῦντες πάντοτε ὑπὲρ πάντων
6: 10f Τοῦ λοιποῦ ἐνδυναμοῦσθε ἐν κυρίῳ
    καὶ ἐν τῷ κράτει τῆς ἰσχύος αὐτοῦ.
    ἐνδύσασθε τὴν πανοπλίαν τοῦ θεοῦ.

Finally, there seems to be an insertion at Eph 4: 32c, 5: 1, 2a, which emphasizes the idea of the imitation of deity in following the example of

Christ (cf. γίνεσθε οὖν μιμηταὶ τοῦ Θεοῦ) as if in preparation for the imitation of Christ urged in 5: 22-33. The repetition of καθὼς καὶ in 4: 32*b* and 5: 2*a*, and the similarity between the ensuing words in each instance (cf. ὁ Θεὸς ἐν Χριστῷ ἐχαρίσατο ὑμῖν in 4: 32*b* and ὁ Χριστὸς ἠγάπησεν ἡμᾶς in 5: 2*a*) suggests that the material after the first καθὼς καὶ and up until the second has been inserted. If the suspected words are omitted the text reads as follows: χαριζόμενοι ἑαυτοῖς καθὼς καὶ ... ὁ Χριστὸς ἠγάπησεν ἡμᾶς καὶ παρέδωκεν ἑαυτόν ... (4: 32*b*, 5: 2*b*).

It is concluded then that Eph 4: 28f, 32*c*, 5: 1, 2*a*, 14*b*-18*a*, 21-6: 9, along with Col 3: 18 - 4: 1, 5 belong with a later stratum extending across Ephesians and Colossians.

The later stratum in 1 Peter

The subjection material in Ephesians and Colossians finds its closest parallels in the New Testament in 1 Peter, an epistle acknowledged to bear a close relation to Ephesians in other respects as well.[22] On the basis of the generally agreed assumptions of the code theory, it can be assumed that the parallels to Eph 5: 21 - 6: 9 and Col 3: 18 - 4: 1 in 1 Peter (2: 13-20, 3: 1-7, 5: 1-5), are from the same or a similar source as the later stratum in Colossians and Ephesians. The question to be answered is whether the subjection material in 1 Peter coheres with 1 Peter as a whole, whether it issues from an earlier source incorporated by the writer or redactor of the final version of the epistle, or whether it is part of a later stratum extending across the epistle. It will be shown that the third possibility is most probable, and furthermore, that the later material in 1 Peter extends so far beyond the subjection material, that the earlier version of the document may actually be regarded as a source incorporated into a later, expanded epistle.

Earlier and later material in 1 Pet 1: 3 - 2: 10

1 Pet 1: 3-12 forms a highly organized syntactical unity which does not seem to have been disturbed by later intrusions. There is a distinct likeness to the opening chapter of Ephesians in style, vocabulary, thought, tone, and mood,[23] which is all the more remarkable in view of the slight nature of any verbal correspondence denoting literary dependence.[24] The least that must be said is that they emanate from the same circle of Christian tradition. Since the later stratum in Ephesians was differentiated from the rest of the epistle with the exception of two short additional interpolations, it follows that 1 Pet 1: 2-12 must have a different origin from the subjection material in 1 Pet 2: 13-20, 3: 1-7.

The first positive sign of material akin to the subjection material in

1 Peter and the later stratum in Ephesians and Colossians appears after
1 Pet 1: 13. In the first place 1 Pet 1: 14-19 manifests the same pattern of
antithetic parallelism, as compared with the synthetic parallelism in much
of Ephesians and in 1 Pet 1: 3-12, that occurs in the later stratum in
Ephesians and its parallels in 1 Peter,[25] involving the use of the words
ἀλλά and ὡς. Also to be observed is the use of εἰδότες ὅτι in 1 Pet 1: 18
as in Eph 6: 8, 9, and the same tendency to employ present participles in
exhortations. In addition the use of the compound word πατροπαράδοτος
in 1 Pet 1: 18 recalls the compounds ὀφθαλμοδουλία and ἀνθρωπάρεσκος
in Eph 6: 6 and Col 3: 22, as also the similar compounds in the subjection
material in 1 Peter.[26] There is the same exhortation to 'fear', as essential to
right conduct, as in the subjection material,[27] and the same appeal to the
impartiality of divine judgement (cf. 1 Pet 1: 17, Eph 6: 9, Col 3: 25).
None of these features figure, however, in 1 Pet 1: 20f. There is no obvious
seam between 1: 19 and 20. Nevertheless, it is significant that if 1: 13 and
20f are read continuously, leaving out 1: 14-19, they form a syntactical
unity, with the participles προεγνωσμένου and φανερωθέντος in 1: 20
agreeing with Ἰησοῦ Χριστοῦ in 1: 13. If this analysis is correct, the insertion has been made by breaking into an earlier source after Χριστοῦ in
1: 13, and by so constructing the intervening material that this word is
repeated in the same case before 1: 20, where the source is resumed.[28]

As for content, without 1: 14-19, the theme of the revelation of Jesus
Christ continues from 1: 13 to 20, whereas the intervening material
digresses to draw a moral concerning holy living, and the worthlessness
of silver and gold, which perhaps relates to the condemnation of orna-
mental display in 3: 3ff and avarice in 5: 2.

The later stratum seems to appear again at 1: 22f. Here one may
observe the use of the compound word φιλαδελφία and a resumption of
antithetic parallelism involving a negative statement followed by a positive,
virtually identical in meaning, introduced by ἀλλά (vs. 23). The LXX
citation from Isa 40: 6-9 in 1: 24f obviously continues from 1: 22f, and
1: 24b - 2: 3 is clearly commentary upon it. Moreover, the material after
the citation also resembles the later stratum stylistically. 1 Pet 2: 1f is an
antithetic parallel employing the ὡς ... ἵνα sequence that is characteristic
of the later stratum, though there is no negative particle, and ἀλλά is
absent. The compound word ἀρτιγέννητα also recalls the later stratum.

As for contextual considerations, there is a sudden change of subject at
1: 22, which Preisker recognized in postulating an act of baptism after the
teaching discourse in 1: 13-21, and before a 'baptismal dedication' in 1:
22-5.[29] The sentence which proceeds from 1: 13 to 1: 20f, omitting vss.
14-19, ends so weakly, however, that it is very probable that it was

interrupted at δόξαν αὐτῷ δόντα and that ὥστε . . . εἰς Θεόν was added to ease the abruptness of the transition. The sentence finds a more fitting sequence at 2: 4, for not only does πρὸς ὃν προσερχόμενοι follow syntactically from 1: 21a, but the phrase is characteristic of an opening to a psalm,[30] such as 2: 4-10 is acknowledged to be. In addition,[31] the hypothesis that 2: 4 did not originally follow from 2: 3 explains the lack of obvious connection between the concept of the 'milk of the word' (2: 2f) and of 'living stone(s)' and 'spiritual house' (2: 4f).[32]

There is also positive gain for the exegesis of 1 Pet 2: 4-10 if the idea of living stone(s) is brought into close relation to that of the resurrection in 1: 21. The erection of the new temple described in the passage may thus be interpreted as identical with a process of continuous resurrection, beginning with Jesus Christ.[33] His resurrection may then be understood as equivalent to the laying of the first stone in the building of the 'spiritual house' (vs. 5). Its metaphorical position is at the base of the construction, and not at the top as much exegesis assumes in regard to ἀκρογωνιαῖος (2: 6), and κεφαλὴν γωνίας (2: 7).[34]

Then too, unlike the household code of subjection, 1 Pet 2: 4-10 resembles the main body of Ephesians in that it has marked links with the thought of the Qumran sect, in particular in its use of the temple to apply to the community of the faithful.[35]

At 2: 8b, however, concerning the stumbling of those who disobey the 'word', there is probably interference from the later stratum. The thought accords closely with that in 1: 22-5 regarding obedience to the 'living and abiding word'. Moreover there is an otherwise inexplicable change from condemning the 'unfaithful' as opposed to the 'faithful' (2: 7) to warning those presumably within the Christian community who do not heed the teaching given them.

It may be concluded, then, that the later stratum is present in 1 Pet 1: 14-19, 22f, 25b, 2: 1-3, 8, and that 1: 3-13, 20-21b, 2: 4-8a, 9f, belong to the earlier source.

Earlier and later material in 1 Pet 2: 11 - 3: 22

After 1 Pet 2: 10, vss. 11f introduce the main body of paraenesis for which the later material has prepared the way earlier in the epistle. The later stratum predominates from 2: 11 till the end of the third chapter, with an intermingling of no more than a few fragments from the original epistle.

It is evident that the later stratum extends beyond the subjection material in 3: 1-7, for 3: 8f is continuous with what precedes it. There is stylistic continuity in the use of seemingly unattached present participles with an imperative force (cf. ὑποτασσόμενοι in vss. 1, 5, and ἐποπτεύσαντες in vs. 2, which is, however, not directly imperative in sense; ἀγαθοποιοῦσαι and φοβούμεναι in vs. 6; and συνοικοῦντες and ἀπονέμοντες in vs. 7). As in Eph 5: 21 - 6: 9, it seems that they are intended to emulate the very frequent use of participles in the earlier material in both epistles, with clumsy results.

Then too, since there are no signs of discontinuity, as between 3: 8f and the LXX quotation in 3: 10-12, and the exposition of its content in vss. 13-17, it may be assumed that it too is to be associated with 3: 1ff and the material in 2: 11ff and 5: 1-5. This finds confirmation in the fact that 3: 13-17 draws on Ps 34 (LXX 33) in ways that indicate continuity with the catalogues of duties in both 1 Peter and Ephesians, as also the parallel to 1 Pet 2: 13-16 in Rom 13: 1-7.

Expressions in the psalm that recur in the subjection material are the following: ἀγαθός and κακός, usually in contrast to each other (1 Pet 3: 10, Ps 33: 13f); the combination of both these words with ποιεῖν either in compound form or separately (1 Pet 3: 11f, Ps 33: 15, 17); and forms of φόβος and φοβεῖσθαι (Ps 34: 8, 10).[36] The latter have explicit attention drawn to them in the quotation from Is 8: 12-13 woven into the text of 1 Pet 3: 14. Similarly, the word κύριος, which occurs both in this citation and the psalm (34: 4, 5, 7, 9, 10, 11, 12, 17, 18, 19, 21) is used with great frequency in some parts of this material.[37]

While all these words are exceedingly common in the New Testament, the same cannot be said of their use in combination with one another,[38] which is to be accounted a mark of close association or even identical origin.

At 3: 18 there is a sign of a possible break into an earlier source, in that ὅτι καὶ Χριστὸς ἅπαξ περὶ ἁμαρτιῶν (ὑπὲρ ὑμῶν) ἀπέθανεν . . . ἵνα closely resembles the words joining the injunctions to slaves in 2: 18-20 to the adaptation of Is 53: 4-9 in 3: 22-5: εἰς τοῦτο γὰρ ἐκλήθητε, ὅτι καὶ Χριστὸς ἔπαθεν ὑπὲρ ὑμῶν . . . ἵνα (2: 21). In 3: 9 ὅτι εἰς τοῦτο ἐκλήθητε ἵνα serves a somewhat similar purpose in forming a bridge with the quotation from Ps 33 (34).

The repetition of εἰς τοῦτο γὰρ ἐκλήθητε and ὅτι καὶ Χριστὸς ἔπαθεν, both of which appear in 2: 21, suggests that they were present in combination in the original letter, and are utilized in the later stratum to establish continuity with earlier material separated from its original context. It is significant that ἐκλήθητε in 2: 21 makes contact with ἐκλεκτόν and καλέσαντος in 2: 9. In contrast to the hiatus between 2: 10 and 2: 11, the two clauses cited above from 2: 21*ab* form a natural sequence to 2: 9f.

At the same time the material which follows after 2: 21*ab* (2: 21*c*-25) accords perfectly with the paraenesis of the later stratum. The theme of the imitation of Christ harks back to the exhortation to emulate the holiness of God in 1: 14–19. The idea of Christ as silently suffering injustice without resistance accords exactly with the behaviour which slaves are called upon to adopt in 2: 18–20.

In addition, ὑπογραμμός in 2: 21c has a meaning very close to that ascribed in this study to μυστήριον in Eph 5: 21 – 6: 9.[39] It could be said indeed that the passion theme in 1 Peter serves the same kind of purpose, as does that of the head–body relation in Eph 5: 21 – 6: 9, in providing the pattern or example which is set up for emulation in the catalogues of duties. A further likeness to the later stratum is to be found in 2: 23b, which points to God as judge of present wrongs, as does also Eph 6: 9, Col 3: 25, and 1 Pet 1: 17.

Stylistically the manner of the later stratum is to be observed in the combination of ἵνα, ὡς, and ἀλλά with present participles in 2: 24f. Also, the use of σῶμα for the fleshly being of Christ in vs. 24 is what one might expect from the later stratum, considering the use of the word as an alternative for σάρξ in Eph 5: 28.

If then 1 Pet 2: 21ab did in fact originally follow after 2: 10, its sequel must lie elsewhere. The most likely place is in 3: 18–22. Since ὅτι καὶ Χριστὸς ἅπαξ περὶ ἁμαρτιῶν ἀπέθανεν in 3: 18–19a roughly parallels 2: 21ab, it is possible that the latter was originally attached to material that follows it. Here Bultmann's reconstruction of what he took to be a christological hymn or confession underlying this part of the text[40] is a useful basis for distinguishing two strata.

He excluded 3: 18b, δίκαιος ὑπὲρ ἀδίκων, ἵνα ὑμᾶς προσαγάγῃ τῷ Θεῷ, as obviously prose and as not fitting into the hymnic pattern. This however is not necessarily so, as will be shown. He also rejected 3: 20f, which bears the characteristic marks of the later stratum. There is first the same sacramental interest in baptism as in Eph 5: 21 – 6: 9 (cf. λουτρῷ τοῦ ὕδατος in Eph 5: 26, ὕδατος ... οὐ σαρκὸς ἀπόθεσις ῥύπου in 1 Pet 3: 20f). There is also a very similar use of typology. In the Ephesians passage it relates to marriage, termed a 'mystery' symbolizing the relationship of Christ and the church (Eph 5: 32).[41] In 1 Pet 2: 21–5 it relates to Christ and his passion, termed a ὑπογραμμός to be imitated,[42] in 1 Pet 3: 20f it relates to Noah and the primeval flood, termed an ἀντίτυπος of salvation through baptism. Then too the antithetic parallel containing οὐ ... ἀλλά together with the phrase συνειδήσεως ἀγαθῆς[43] tends to associate 3: 21 with the later stratum.

As in Bultmann's reconstruction, then,[44] 3: 20f is to be dissociated from the earlier material. In addition 3: 19 appears to be part of the later material, though Bultmann included it in his hymn. First, the repetition of πορευθείς in vss. 29 and 22 suggests it may be connected with the break in the material. Secondly, the phrase πορευθεὶς εἰς οὐρανόν follows the rhyme and rhythm of θανατωθεὶς μὲν σαρκί and ζῳοποιηθεὶς δὲ πνεύματι in 3: 18c so closely that the conclusion that it originally followed immediately after is hard to resist. Thirdly, ἐν ᾧ in vs. 19 forms a connection with πνεύματι in vs. 18 that is clumsy both grammatically and in sense.[45]

On the basis of this analysis 1 Pet 2: 4–10 is taken to continue from 2: 10 to 2: 21ab, 3: 18c, 22. The earlier material is taken to have proceeded as follows:

1 Pet 2: 9	Ὑμεῖς δὲ γένος ἐκλεκτόν,
	βασίλειον ἱεράτευμα,
	ἔθνος ἅγιον
	λαὸς εἰς περιποίησιν
	ὅπως τὰς ἀρετὰς ἐξαγγείλητε
	τοῦ ἐκ σκότους ὑμᾶς καλέσαντος
	εἰς τὸ θαυμαστὸν αὐτοῦ φῶς·
2: 10	οἵ ποτε οὐ λαός
	νῦν δὲ λαὸς Θεοῦ,
	οἱ οὐκ ἠλεημένοι
	νῦν δὲ ἐλεηθέντες.
2: 21ab	εἰς τοῦτο γὰρ ἐκλήθητε,
	ὅτι καὶ Χριστὸς ἔπαθεν
3: 18c	ἵνα ὑμᾶς προσαγάγῃ τῷ Θεῷ·
3: 18ab	ἀπέθανεν περὶ ἁμαρτιῶν
	δίκαιος ὑπὲρ ἀδίκων[46]
3: 18de	θανατωθεὶς μὲν σαρκί
	ζῳοποιηθεὶς δὲ πνεύματι,
3: 22bc	πορευθεὶς εἰς οὐρανόν
	ὑποταγέντων αὐτῷ ἀγγέλων
	καὶ ἐξουσιῶν καὶ δυνάμεων.

It will be observed that ὑπὲρ ὑμῶν (3: 18b) and ἅπαξ (3: 18a) are omitted. The first is a stock phrase which could have been added editorially, and the second does not find a natural place in the rhythmic sequence. It could have been added editorially for emphasis. Otherwise the text remains undisturbed, except that the word order in 3: 18 has been rearranged to accord with the context, and 3: 18c is placed before instead of after 3: 18ab, as the sense seems to follow more logically after 2: 21ab.

The material left by the stripping away of the later stratum falls into three seven-line stanzas. 1 Pet 2: 7b–8a can be arranged in the same way, but this does not apply with clarity to any material following 3: 22. The main concern here however, is to establish the original continuity of the earlier material 2: 10 to 2: 21*ab* to 3: 18, 22*bc*. The later stratum thus probably includes 2: 11-20, 21*cd*, 23-5, 3: 1-9, 13-17, 19-22*a*, omitting the LXX citations at 2: 22 and 3: 10-12.

Earlier and later material in 1 Pet 4: 1-11

There is nothing decisive to connect the next block of material, 1 Pet 4: 1-11, with earlier or later material in the epistle. It appears rather to be an amalgam of both such as may be beyond certain recovery. The following, however, attempts a tentative reconstruction of both strata on the basis of such evidence as is discernible.

The catalogue of vices in 4: 3f tells one nothing in itself, for such listings occur in both strata in Ephesians,[47] and in both earlier and later New Testament writings.[48]

Some of the vices listed occur also in Ephesians in a scattered manner (cf. ἀσελγείαις, Eph 4: 19; ἐπιθυμίαις, Eph 4: 22; εἰδωλολατρίαις, Eph 5: 5; εἰδωλολάτρης, βλασφημοῦντες, Eph 4: 31 βλασφημία). The first two of these, however, together with κώμοις, are found together within the short space of Rom 13: 13f, which is part of a passage that bears a close resemblance to the thought of Ephesians in its darkness–light dichotomy (Rom 13: 12), its expectation of the coming 'day', the 'putting off' and 'putting on' image combined with the idea of arming for a conflict with evil (13: 12-14), and its condemnation of fleshly lusts (13: 13f).

If one takes into account the conclusion that 1 Pet 3: 22*bc* was originally preceded directly by 2: 9f, 21*ab*, 3: 18, it appears probable that the darkness–light dichotomy in 1 Pet 2: 9 was in relatively close proximity to what follows in chapter four.

What is more, all these elements are shared with 1 Thess 5: 1-11, which contains an eschatological warning practically identical to that found in 1 Peter (cf. 'Let us be vigilant and sober' in 1 Thess 5: 6 and 'Be sober, be vigilant' in 1 Pet 5: 8).

At the same time other elements in the category of vices in 1 Pet 4 tally with the corresponding category in the later stratum in Ephesians (cf. οἰνοφλυγίαις ... πότοις ... ἀσωτίας ἀνάχυσιν in 1 Pet 4: 3f, and μὴ μεθύσκεσθε οἴνῳ ἐν ᾧ ἐστιν ἀσωτία in Eph 5: 18*a*. Οἰνοφλυγία and πότος, both of which relate to the condemnation of drunkenness, are *hapax legomena.* Ἀσώτια is used nowhere else in the New Testament but in Tit 1: 6, where, significantly, the word is paired with ἀνυπότακτα, the exact opposite of the participial form of the verb ὑποτάσσεσθαι. Another connection between the two passages is the occurrence of ἀλλὰ συνίετε τί τὸ θέλημα τοῦ κυρίου in Eph 5: 17 and ἀλλὰ θελήματι Θεοῦ in 1 Pet 4: 2.

A later writer could, of course, have combined various elements from different parts of the Pauline letters, or could have incorporated a version in which they were already combined. It appears, however, that the earlier material probably did have some sequel in this passage, for in vs. 1 the theme of the suffering Christ is continued in conjunction with use of battle imagery (cf. ὁπλίσασθε). The idea of arming the mind obviously corresponds with the concluding part of the body of Ephesians (cf. Eph 6: 10-20). It is postulated then that the earlier material may have continued as follows:

4: 1*a*   Χριστοῦ οὖν παθόντος σαρκὶ καὶ ὑμεῖς τὴν αὐτὴν ἔννοιαν
           ὁπλίσασθε·
4: 3   Ἀρκετὸς γὰρ ὁ παρεληλυθὼς χρόνος τὸ βούλημα τῶν ἐθνῶν
          κατειργάσθαι, πεπορευμένους ἐν ἀσελγείαις, ἐπιθυμίαις . . .
          κώμοις . . . καὶ ἀθεμίτοις εἰδωλολατρίαις.

It is assumed that 1 Pet 4: 1*b*, 2, οἰνοφλυγίαις . . . πότοις in vs. 3, and vss. 4–6 probably belong to the later stratum. Reason has been shown for connecting vss. 2, 4, and parts of vs. 3 with the later stratum. There is evidently a sequel in vs. 6 to the preaching to the dead mentioned in 3: 19–21, which it was concluded should also be associated with the later material. The immediately preceding verse, with its reference to the judgement of the living and the dead, contains a formula which occurs nowhere else in the New Testament except in 2 Tim 4: 1. It may therefore be regarded as later rather than earlier. 1 Pet 4: 2 also seems to issue from a somewhat later period in that it speaks of life 'for the rest of the time in the flesh', which implies an expectation that the lives of those who are addressed will continue uninterrupted until death, without the intervention of the *parousia*. This version of the eschatological hope obviously differs from the sense of its imminence in the earlier material (cf. 1: 6). Also, the view of the flesh appears to correspond with that which was found in Eph 5: 21 - 6: 9.[49] Taken with 1 Pet 4: 2, 4: 1*b*, ὅτι ὁ παθὼν σαρκὶ πέπαυται ἁμαρτίας may be understood to refer to the release of the soul from the evil body through death, since Christ's suffering (Χριστοῦ οὖν παθόντος, 4: 1*a*) obviously involved death.[50] The same body-soul dualism is evident in 4: 6, where the dead, though imprisoned for their sins while in the flesh, are said to live to God in the spirit. Here, as in 3: 19, πνεῦμα is used in the sense of ψυχή, and as in the later stratum at 2: 11 (ἀπέχεσθαι τῶν σαρκικῶν, αἵτινες στρατεύονται κατὰ τῆς ψυχῆς) the ethical dualism of Ephesians and, it may be assumed, the earlier stratum in 1 Peter, is displaced by a dualism of body and soul, which is to say, between the material and the spiritual in the sense of the non-material.[51]

The later material appears, then, to continue from 1 Pet 4: 4 to 4: 6. The next few verses 4: 7-11, appear to parallel 5: 8-11 as a possible closing section to the letter body before the concluding greetings in 5: 12-14. Not only does 4: 7b contain the word νήψατε which is used in 5: 8, but also σωφρονήσατε, which is roughly equivalent in meaning to γρηγορήσατε, found directly after νήψατε in 5: 8. In addition, 'the end of all things is at hand' in 4: 7a is reminiscent of 'the day is at hand' in Rom 13: 12.[52] As already shown, Rom 13: 11-13 bears a close resemblance to 1 Thess 5: 1-11, which, significantly, contains the words γρηγορῶμεν καὶ νήφωμεν (1 Thess 5: 6) with reference to the imminent expectation of the sudden coming of 'the day' in vs. 4.[53] Then too, the concluding words of 1 Pet 4: 11, ἡ δόξα καὶ τὸ κράτος εἰς τοὺς αἰῶνας τῶν αἰώνων are very similar to the words in 5: 11, αὐτῷ τὸ κράτος εἰς τοὺς αἰῶνας ἀμήν. In addition the phrase εἰς τὴν αἰώνιον αὐτοῦ δόξαν occurs in 5: 10.

As will be shown presently, 5: 8-11 probably belongs to the original letter. Thus it is more likely that 4: 7 is based on 5: 8-11 than the other way round. As for the possibility that the earlier writer is responsible for both passages, it is difficult to see why he should have repeated his own terminology and phrases, or why he should have ended the letter body in these two different ways for two different sets of recipients. Thus it is assumed here that the later writer incorporated and rephrased certain elements from the original concluding section with the initial intention of excluding 5: 8-11, for the concept in the latter of Christian suffering as inevitable (5: 9) runs counter to the view expressed in the later stratum that it may be avoided (cf. 3: 13).

In this case it is very probable that 'the end of all things is at hand' was originally joined to 'be sober, be vigilant' at the beginning of 5: 8a and that 4: 7b and the latter half of 4: 11 are imitative variations on 5: 8a and 5: 10f.

As for the rest of 1 Pet 4: 7-11, vs. 8 does not accord with the outlook to be expected of a letter in the same tradition as Ephesians, for the idea of love as covering a multitude of sins conflicts with that of salvation by grace through faith, and not by works (cf. Eph. 2: 8f). Moreover the opening thanksgiving passage in 1 Peter, judged here to belong to the original version of the epistle, also gives expression to the doctrine of salvation by faith (cf. 1: 9). By contrast the subjection material clearly regards good works as a means of earning the approval of God and heavenly reward.[54] In addition 4: 8a contains a loosely attached participle with imperative force as elsewhere in the later stratum.[55] It also contains the phrase ἀγάπην ἐκτενῆ ἔχοντες, which finds a parallel in the later stratum at 1: 22; cf. ἀγαπήσατε ἐκτενῶς. Were it not for the signs that 4: 8 probably belongs to the later stratum it could be surmised that 1: 22

had borrowed from 4: 8. It appears more likely, however, that both issue
from the hand responsible for the later material in 1 Peter. The same
appears to apply to 4: 9, for φιλόξενοι is the kind of compound that
abounds in the later stratum in 1 Peter.[56] Regarding 4: 10, 11a, the teaching on the use of charismata contrasts with the idea of office and authority
present in 5: 1-5. It is therefore assumed that 4: 10, 11a was the original
sequel to 4: 1a, 3, and that 4: 7a has been displaced from just before 5: 8.
The rest of 4: 1-11 is ascribed to the later stratum.

Earlier and later material in 1 Pet 4: 12 – 5: 14

As already mentioned, it seems that the later redactor intended to bring
the letter or letter body to a close at 1 Pet 4: 11.[57] It is as if he had second
thoughts, however, due to a change of circumstance, for while the discussion of persecution in 3: 13-17 implies that it is only a possibility, in
4: 12-19 it is actual.[58] Some of the language and thought in the passage
resembles what one finds in the earlier stratum, in particular in vss. 12f
and 17. There appears, however, to be a mingling of strata, for there are
signs also of the presence of the later stratum.

First, the passage resembles the later stratum in that it contains a
number of compound words formed from adjectives, and/or nouns, and/or
adverbs; compare κανοποιός, ἀλλοτριεπίσκοπος (4: 16), and ἀγαθοποιΐα
(4: 19).[59] It is to be noted that two of these compounds, κακοποιός and
ἀγαθοποιΐα, happen to relate to the kind of combinations issuing from
Psalm 34 in the later stratum.[60] Dependence one way or the other is
unlikely, since there is no precise correspondence in wording, and ἀγαθοποιΐα is a New Testament *hapax legomenon* besides differing in form from
similar compounds in this epistle.

In 4: 12f one finds the typical sentence structure of the subjection
material in the μή . . . ὡς . . . ἀλλά . . . ἵνα sequence. This similarity is not
sufficient in itself to associate the material with the later stratum. At the
same time the resemblance to the earlier stratum could be due to dependence on 1: 6-11.[61] Moreover, since 4: 13f makes unmistakable contact
with one of the Matthean beatitudes,[62] vs. 14 was probably originally
joined to vs. 13. The former manifests a view of persecution different from
that in the earlier stratum for, instead of accepting it as intrinsic to the
role of the elect community,[63] it vests suffering 'in the name of Christ'
with the special blessings of the divine glory and spirit. Here then one finds
the same martyrological outlook as earlier in the later stratum[64] where
μακάριοι also occurs (cf. 4: 14, 3: 14). The next two verses (4: 15f)
amplify the thought by emphasizing the importance of righteous suffering,
as in the later stratum at 3: 16. The same may be said of 4: 19, which brings

the section to a lame close, at the same time serving as a bridge connecting 4: 12-19 with the subjection material in 5: 1-5. The material in 4: 12-16, 19, seems then to belong to the later stratum.

As for 4: 17f, the language and thought accord better with the earlier stratum. The idea of the judgement as beginning with the 'household of God' is not obviously relevant to the train of thought in 4: 12-16, but forms a plausible sequel to the earlier material in 4: 1-11 (4: 1*a*, 3, 10, 11*a*), concerning the preparation for the conflict against evil and the use of charismata 'as household stewards of the varied gifts of God' (vs. 10). The theme accords with that of the Christian community as 'built up into a spiritual house' and as a holy priesthood called upon to render spiritual sacrifices (2: 10).

In 5: 1-5 one finds a combination of characteristics which is typical of the later stratum as identified in Ephesians, Colossians, and the first three chapters of 1 Peter. There are three negative-positive antithetic parallels involving negative particles, ἀλλά and ὡς (vss. 2f). There are also three compound words other than those formed through the addition of standard prefixes: αἰσχροκερδῶς (vs. 2), ἀρχιποίμενος (vs. 4), and ταπεινοφροσύνην (vs. 5). Then too, as in the 'household' codes in Ephesians and Colossians, and as in 1 Pet 3: 1-7, exhortations are addressed to both sides in a relationship of superior and subordinate. The elders (πρεσβύτεροι) are instructed in the proper exercise of authority (vss. 1-4), and the younger in the duty of subjection to elders (vs. 5). Clearly the elders who are addressed are not merely those who are older in years, but those who bear responsibility for the governance of congregations. In other words, they are ecclesiastical office-holders. It seems then that 1 Pet 5: 1-5 applies the household pattern of subjection by children to parents, and more specifically to the father, to the sphere of the church.

None of these characteristics occurs in the remainder of the epistle. Confirming the impression of a change in the type and source of the material is the fact that while in 5: 6 humility has to do with the relation of the elect to God, in 5: 5*a* it concerns the relation of superior to subordinate within the Christian community. Yet both verses appear to be commentary upon the citation from Prov 3: 34 concerning God's opposition to the proud and elevating of the humble.

1 Pet 5: 5*b*-7 finds a close parallel in Jas 4: 6-8, 10, where Prov 3: 34 is also cited (cf. Jas 4: 6*b*). Hence it can be assumed that 1 Pet 5: 5*b*-8 was joined together from the onset of its incorporation into the epistle, whether the parallel with the similar passage in James is due to dependence one way or the other, or to use of a common source. It is unlikely that the writer of the later stratum in 1 Peter borrowed from James at this point,

for in that case he would most probably have taken over ὑποτάγητε immediately after the quotation from Proverbs in Jas 4: 7*a* instead of employing ταπεινώθητε in 1 Pet 5: 6*a*, for the former obviously accords more closely with the theme of subjection to authority in 1 Pet 5: 5*a*.

If this analysis is correct, 1 Pet 5: 5*b* must have followed directly after 4: 18 in the original letter. The sequence receives confirmation from the fact that the citation from Prov 3: 34 and the ensuing comment upon it relate to the theme of elevation and vindication in the judgement, as Christ was elevated (3: 18, 22*bc*).[65] Since in 4: 17 καιρός seems to refer to the time of the final judgement, it can be assumed that ἐν καιρῷ in 5: 6 has the same significance. The use of the word at 4: 17 and 5: 6 also strengthens the supposition that 'the end of all things is at hand' in 4: 7*a* was originally joined to 5: 8 but has been displaced.

The earlier material seems to continue until at least as far as 1 Pet 5: 11, for vss. 8-11 obviously forms a unity. There is, furthermore, no reason to think 1 Pet 5: 12-14 is anything other than the close to the original letter. By the same token it can be assumed that the opening to the letter in 1: 1f is original.[66] Whether it was ascribed to Peter in the first place may be questioned, since the final greetings are what one would expect of a Pauline letter or a letter written as from Paul, but the resolution of this question is beyond the scope of the present enquiry.

Further confirmation for dissociating of the subjection material from 5: 5*a*-14 is to be found in the nature of the content. The image of the devil as a lion (5: 8) in combination with that of 'Babylon', in all probability a symbol for 'Rome' (5: 13),[67] tends to associate the closing material with apocalyptic thinking such as finds expression above all in Revelation, where such imagery is prominent.[68] It is hard to believe that such thinking issued from the same source as the subjection material in 1 Peter, which enjoins implicit obedience to the emperor and governors (2: 13-17), which is to say the Roman imperium, or that such symbolism was used in ignorance of its hostile implications in much Jewish and Christian tradition.[69] On the other hand, it is conceivable that the teaching on subjection to authority was attached to a brief letter containing such language in order to neutralize its effects, for though 5: 8-11 would have been omitted if the expanded letter body at first ended at 4: 11, it is probable that the closing greetings in 5: 12-14 were retained, and with them the reference to Babylon.

By contrast there is no difficulty in associating 1 Pet 4: 17f, 5: 5*b*-14 with the earlier material. According to 5: 9, suffering is to be undergone by the brotherhood of the elect throughout the world (ἐν τῷ κόσμῳ ὑμῶν ἀδελφότητι ἐπιτελεῖσθαι). According to 1: 7 it is an inevitable necessity for testing the genuineness of faith. Both passages assert that the time will be short (ὀλίγον, 1: 6, 5: 10). In 1: 6 the faithful are warned that this time may be upon them now (ἄρτι), which accords with the imminence of the judgement according to 4: 17. In both passages too the suffering referred to is evidently scattered and sporadic, for the 'various trials' mentioned in 1: 6 correspond with the uncertainty implied in the figure of the lion attacking at random (5: 8f).

The original letter is assumed, then, to have consisted of 1 Pet 1: 1-13, 20, 21*ab*, 2: 4-8*a*, 9f, 21*ab*, 3: 18, 22*bc*, 4: 1*a*, 3, 10, 11*a*, 17f, 7*a*, 5: 5*b*-14.[70] The rest of the epistle is taken to belong to the later stratum of redaction. Excluding the citations from the LXX in 1 Pet 1: 24, 25*a*, and 3: 10-12, it is assumed to consist of 1 Pet 1: 14-19, 21*c*-23, 2: 1-3, 8*b*, 11-20, 21*c*, 22-5, 3: 1-9, 3: 17, 19-22*a*, 4: 1*b*, 2-6, 7*b*, 8f, 11*b*-16, 19, 5: 1-5*a*.

Distinctions between the earlier and later strata in 1 Peter

Though the later stratum as identified above takes up about two-thirds of the final version of the epistle, it is the earlier material that provides epistolary continuity. Its length of just over two pages fits the description of brevity in 1 Pet 5: 12.

Both strata are confronted with the possibility and actuality of persecution, but, while the first writer calls for steadfast faith in expectation of speedy deliverance, the second is concerned to refute the calumnies directed against Christians (2: 12) and to win their accusers over to a good opinion of the new faith. This he thinks may be done first by ensuring that the accusations are false and by living in a way that commends itself to outsiders, in particular those in authority (2: 11ff, 3: 1f), and secondly, by gently persuasive argument and explanation (3: 15).

A major accusation which the later stratum apparently attempts to refute is that Christians undermine the social order. To submit to the state and patriarchal family head is enjoined, not only as a matter of prudence, but also of conscience. It is brought into relation with Christian teaching to love, bless, and do good to enemies (3: 8f). It is also intrinsic to the teaching based on Ps 33 LXX that God preserves those who 'do good' (3: 10-13).

Considering the specific content the later stratum gives to doing good in the subjectionist teaching, it follows that its opposite which it seeks to eradicate or avoid must be, or include, insubordination and sedition. Its condemnation is perhaps present in 4: 12-17, which is addressed to a situation in which Christians are liable for reprisals simply for the name of

Christian (4: 16). This the later stratum distinguishes sharply from suffering 'as a murderer, thief or evildoer' or ὡς ἀλλοτριεπίσκοπος (4: 15). The fourth offence is particularly serious, for repetition of ὡς gives it emphasis at least equal to the other three crimes in combination. It must therefore have a far weightier meaning than the petty trouble-making of a busybody, as many exegetes interpret the word.

Since the term does not occur anywhere else in available ancient literature until the fourth century,[71] it seems that the later stratum has coined it. The most likely source is the kind of philosophical language which occurs in Epictetus III 22: 97, οὐ γὰρ τὰ ἀλλότρια πολυπραγμονεῖ, ὅταν τὰ ἀνθρώπινα ἐπισκοπῇ, ἀλλὰ τὰ ἴδια. Here the opposite of τὰ ἀλλότρια is τὰ ἴδια, which could also be expressed by the phrase τὰ ἑαυτοῦ. Significantly, τὰ ἑαυτοῦ πράττειν is a hellenistic ideal consisting in the performing of one's own function and not another's within the body politic, according to one's true nature.[72]

That this has direct bearing on the subjection material is obvious. The function of wives, according to the later stratum, is to submit to their 'own' (τοῖς ἰδίοις) husbands (1 Pet 3: 1, Eph 5: 22), and of husbands to love and care for their own (τὴν ἑαυτοῦ) wives (Eph 5: 22). The implications for the other duties categorized according to station are self-evident.[73] In each case to follow these injunctions is to do what pertains to oneself (τὰ ἑαυτοῦ πράττειν). Conversely, it can be inferred, to go beyond one's assigned role is to presume to take on the functions that belong to others and are alien to oneself (τὰ ἀλλότρια). Since ἐπίσκοπος can have the sense of a person with a definite function within a group,[74] an ἀλλοτρι-επίσκοπος may be understood as one who seeks to take over the position of another, thereby disrupting good order. In the context of 1 Peter this must mean stepping outside the bounds of subjection and thus rebelling against the authority set over one.[75] It applies not only to the spheres of the state and the household, but also to the church, since 5: 1–5*a* applies the household pattern of authority to the ecclesiastical sphere.

Here authority is evidently vested in a group of πρεσβύτεροι, with some degree of leadership exercised by a συμπρεσβύτερος over the rest, for he undertakes to instruct his fellow elders (5: 1–4). In the stage represented by the later stratum in 1 Peter, then, it seems that a chief elder speaks as if in the person of an apostle. At the same time all the elders have considerable authority over the flock, such that they are warned not to abuse it by lording it over the rest (5: 2f).

By contrast the earlier material gives the impression of a non-hierarchical and charismatic form of ministry. All members of the community are represented as God's predestined elect (1: 1f, 20; 2: 4, 9; 5: 13).

They are called to the royal authority Christ has won over the principalities and powers (3: 22*b*). They are to be a body of priests (2: 9)
offering spiritual sacrifices (2: 5) as Christ offered himself (2: 21*ab*,
3: 18), and exercising varied charismata according to divine distribution
(4: 10, 11*a*).

Then too, the idea of suffering differs from one stratum to the other.
According to the earlier material it is intrinsic to the role of the elect to
undergo suffering with the near approach of the *eschaton.*[76] It is seen
essentially as a test of the genuineness of faith (1: 7). To stand fast in the
trial of suffering is to prove that one is indeed among the elect to whom
the inheritance kept in heaven is rightly due (1: 4, 7-10). In this sense
suffering represents judgement, for it differentiates between those who are
vindicated and elevated, and those whom God rejects (4: 17f, 5: 5*b*, 6).

For the later stratum, however, good fortune and adversity correspond
in general with reward and punishment, since God is a righteous judge who
constantly surveys human actions (3: 9-13). How then does this material
accommodate the suffering of Christ and of the righteous in general? The
answer is that such suffering is regarded as intrinsically meritorious. It falls
into the category of good works which receive their due reward. The later
stratum insists, however, that such suffering be devoid of any wrong-doing
which may render it deserving of punishment instead of a cause for gaining
God's approval or grace (2: 20), blessing and glory (3: 14, 4: 14f). The
premise of the later stratum, that good and bad fortune are generally
deserved, has evidently led to the conclusion that the ordeals that come
upon Christians may surprise them (4: 12). The saints of the earlier
stratum, by comparison, need only to be reminded that suffering is
intrinsic to their calling (5: 9f) and to be exhorted to readiness and
patience (4: 1*a*, 3, 10, 17*b*, 5: 8-10). Both strata regard it as a trial or test
(cf. 1: 6f, 4: 12). For the earlier it is faith and faithfulness that are at stake
(1: 7, 5: 9 with 4: 3, 4: 10, 11*a*, 17). For the later it is important for
suffering to be wholly innocent, so that its only genuine cause is the bearing of the name of Christian (2: 12, 4: 14f). Thus it is essential to refrain
from retaliating under provocation or in any way offending against
propriety and morality. Hence the subjection material in 2: 13-20, 3: 1-7
has special relevance.

The eschatological motif features in both strata, but here too there are
differences. For the earlier material the end time coincides with an intensification of the conflict (4: 1*a*, 5: 9) that serves to distinguish the faithful
from the unfaithful (1: 7, 2: 7f, 10, 4: 17f). The later stratum also looks
ahead to the *parousia* (4: 13, 5: 1), though with less sense of its immediacy
if one takes into account the expectation that those addressed will

probably die before it arrives (4: 2).[77] The preoccupation of the later stratum with harmonious relations with existing society has similar implications.

Another significant difference between the two strata is that while the earlier distinguishes sharply between believers and the realm of light on the one hand, and on the other unbelievers and the realm of darkness (2: 6f, 9), the later stratum tends to blur such distinctions. Thus in the later material the pagan state is represented as the agent of God to whose representatives submission, honour, and respect are due (2: 13–17), masters (presumably either Christian or pagan) as just or unjust (2: 18), the sufferings of Christians as not always undeserved (3: 14, 16f, 4: 15f), and even the elders of the church as in danger of forfeiting their final reward through overbearing behaviour and avarice (5: 2–4).

The two strata diverge also in the way each regards good works. Indeed, the first does not think in terms of such a category, but rather of the community of faith as living in accordance with its true nature. Being a holy priestly body, it offers spiritual sacrifices (2: 5), which may be taken to refer to its total life as activated by the Spirit.[78]

The later writer, by contrast, urges good works and the avoidance of evildoing as means of attaining a desired state in relation to God and other people. The aim is essentially the winning of credit, recognition, favour, praise, and blessing,[79] both from God and from other people. The object is also to avoid shame and disgrace, which is the eventual outcome for those who slander Christians unjustly (3: 16), whereas innocent suffering, it is asserted, is no cause for shame (4: 16).

There is some degree of correspondence in the ideas of the good life or good works in the earlier and later strata and the typically Jewish and Greek ideas which W. C. van Unnik found in combination in the epistle.[80] The former, he pointed out, consisted in commendable actions over and above those which the law required, such as the study of the Torah, and works of mercy and charity toward the afflicted. Such acts, he explained, were related to the concept of a treasury in heaven.[81] There may be a suggestion of this symbolism in the reference at 1: 4 in the earlier stratum to the treasure or inheritance kept safe in heaven, though, as already indicated, the earlier material thinks in terms of the good life as expressing the true character of the Christian community, rather than of specific good deeds.

By contrast, the socially directed hellenistic ethic looked for the treasure of a grateful person, as van Unnik expressed it,[82] and the Greek idea of καλὰ ἔργα concerned benevolence that went out to all without exception. This has obvious relevance to the idea of social and political duty which is present in the term ἀγαθοποιεῖν in the later stratum.[83] It fully accords with hellenistic ideas of citizenship to find the state referred to as giving recognition and credit to those who do good.[84]

Clearly two sets of tendencies are present in 1 Peter, corresponding with two main strata, with the later incorporating the second in an expanded version of the original letter. The original letter was evidently one of warning and encouragement in the face of threatened and sporadic persecution. The suffering involved is interpreted as the beginning of the eschatological trials and judgement signalling the imminence of the 'end'. The later stratum faces the actuality of calumny against Christians, and the possibility of persecution, but considers appropriate behaviour can earn the goodwill of the surrounding society and its rulers, and even win recognition for Christian virtue. In accordance with this point of view it may be surmised that the later stratum at first omitted the closing part of the original body (4: 17f, 5: 8–11). With the onset of actual persecution, it seems it was restored with additional later material from 4: 12, accepting suffering as a part of the Christian calling, but with even stronger insistence that it be innocent. In drawing nearer to the earlier stratum and including the material descriptive of the intense conflict in which Christians are involved, the later stratum at the same time adds a passage on the authority of church elders and the need to submit to them (5: 1–5).

Despite the close affinity of the later stratum in 1 Peter with the later material in Ephesians and Colossians, there are certainly differences, but even these mask basic similarities.

There is first the fact that unlike Eph 6: 5–9 1 Peter has no injunction to masters to match those to slaves in 1 Pet 2: 18–22. The reason becomes clear if one accepts the finding that the subjectionist teaching in both Ephesians and 1 Peter was adapted to earlier writing. Thus while the head–body symbolism in Ephesians lent itself to the pattern of paired relationships, the theme of suffering in 1 Peter is applicable only to the submissive role of inferiors. In 1 Peter the teaching on subjection to the state is accommodated alongside that concerning the submission of slaves to masters (1 Pet 2: 13–16, 18–20), whereas it finds no place in the reciprocal structure of the subjectionist teaching in Ephesians. Then too in Ephesians the instructions to wives and husbands are prior to those to slaves and masters (Eph 5: 21–33, 6: 5–9), while in 1 Peter the order is reversed (1 Tit 3: 1–7, 2: 18–20). Again the explanation appears to be the context to which the material was attached in 1 Peter. Even so, there is an awkwardness in the transition to the teaching addressed to wives, which has no obvious connection with the immediately preceding material on the passion of Christ in 2: 22–5. The words to husbands prefaced by ὁμοίως also lack any connection with 2: 22–5. Another difference is that whereas the later material in Ephesians contains directions to children and parents (Eph 6: 1–4), 1 Peter 5: 1–5, as mentioned previously, appears to apply this aspect of the subjectionist teaching to church order, with the pattern of paired relationships again in evidence.

Then, though the parallel sets of subjection material in Ephesians and 1 Peter differ in the way they are elaborated, the method in each case is very similar. Each addresses exhortations to specific groups within the congregation, and follows with an appeal to scripture and/or an aspect of Christian teaching to reinforce the paraenetic motif.[85]

The two sets of material resemble each other also in that their exhortations consist largely of appeals to conform to or imitate a pattern or type. In 1 Peter Christ is the ὑπογραμμός whose submissive suffering is to be emulated (2: 21–5). In Ephesians the relation between Christ and the church is a μυστήριον which marriage partners are called upon to imitate (5: 32 with 5: 21–33). As already indicated, this word is probably used with the same sense as παραβολή, σύμβολον, and τύπος in Justin, which are close in sense to ὑπογραμμός.[86]

Similarly Sarah's relation to her husband is put forward as an example for emulation by wives (1 Pet 3: 5f). So too, in the exhortations to elders, the apostle from whom the letter purports to come refers to himself as a model for the shepherding of the flock (5: 1f). In the same way the elders are to serve as τύποι for the flock to follow (5: 3), a word that has the same significance as ὑπογραμμός in 2: 21. Then too the reference to Christ as the ἀρχιποίμην in 5: 4 not only harks back to Christ as 'shepherd and bishop' in 2: 25, but also suggests that he is regarded as the original pattern or archetype for all to follow. Thus the passage appears to assume a descending order of types, from Christ the leader or chief (another implication of ἀρχι-)[87] to the apostolic eyewitness and fellow elder (συμπρεσβύτερος), to elders, and to the congregation. Ultimately imitation is to be of God himself, if one takes into account the inclusion of 1:14–19 in the later stratum.

This way of thinking in the later stratum corresponds with its characteristic style. Its injunctions are attached to earlier tradition and its themes by means of comparisons which often involve the use of such words as ὡς, οὕτως, and ὁμοίως. In almost all parts of the later material identified thus far one finds the call for imitation of a certain pattern or mode of conduct expressed in such terms, and at the same time often placed in contrast to its opposite. Thus sentences frequently contain both negative and positive parts which form antithetic parallels.

In Ephesians and Colossians the average occurrence of antithetic parallels sharply differentiates the material assigned to the later stratum from the rest of each epistle. There are eleven such parallels in the forty-five lines of Eph 4: 28f, 4: 32*c*, 5: 1, 2*a*, 5: 15–18*a*, 5: 21–6: 9, which is to say, 4.1 lines to each occurrence. This result compares with fifteen antithetic parallels in the rest of Ephesians, yielding a rate of 14.0 lines to each occurrence. In Col 3: 18–4: 1, 5 there are four occurrences in 16.1 lines, or 4.0 lines to each occurrence. There are nine antithetic parallels in the rest of Colossians, or 20.0 lines to each occurrence.[88]

In 1 Peter very similar results emerge for the material assigned to the later stratum as compared with the rest of the epistle. There are thirty antithetic parallels in the 114.8 lines assigned to the later stratum, which is to say, 3.9 lines to each occurrence. The characteristic is, moreover, fairly evenly distributed throughout the later material, with scores ranging between two and five lines to each occurrence for each part. By contrast the earlier stratum contains seven antithetic parallels in the 79.4 lines of its total length or 11.3 lines to each occurrence, with most corresponding with the darkness–light contrast in 1: 4–10.

This then is a trait that distinguishes the two strata in 1 Peter from each other, and at the same time confirms a close association with the later material in Ephesians and Colossians.

Also differentiating the two sets of material in 1 Peter is the relatively frequent use in the later stratum of compound words other than those involving prepositions employed as prefixes. Such words are used thirty-one times in the 122.6 lines of the later stratum, or once to every 3.9 lines. By contrast there are eight occurrences in the 79.4 lines of the earlier material, or one to every 9.9 lines. That is to say, these compound words are twice as frequent in the material assigned to the later stratum as in the rest of 1 Peter.[89]

Another differentiating feature is the fact that the later material contains many more New Testament *hapax legomena* in proportion to its length than the earlier material. While the whole epistle averages 10.0 such words to the page, the rate for the later stratum is 13.0 per page as compared with 5.2 per page for the earlier stratum, including repetitions. Excluding repetitions the score for the later material is 12.4. Distribution is fairly even in each stratum, though one portion of the later stratum, 3: 13–17, contains no such words. It coheres so unmistakably with the later material in other respects, however, that its reassignment is scarcely feasible. In the earlier stratum 5: 8–14 contains four *hapax legomena*, yielding a score of 11.6 to a page, but here too other factors weigh against reassignment.[90]

The identification of a later stratum in 1 Peter cohering with the later stratum in Ephesians and Colossians provides important clues for the further identification of such material in the Pauline corpus. The fact that the later material in 1 Peter includes teaching on duties to the state in close conjunction with other subjectionist instructions strongly suggests that the parallel injunctions in Rom 13: 1-7 are continuous with Eph 5: 18 - 6: 9 and Col 3: 18 - 4: 1. To this passage then the investigation will now turn.

Two strata in Rom 12 and 13

The reason why the subjection material in Ephesians and Colossians does not contain a section on duties to the state, whereas the later stratum in 1 Peter does, is not far to seek. Such teaching obviously cannot be adapted to the Ephesian theme of Christ's relation to the church, used to join the subjection material in Ephesians to the rest of the epistle. It can be expected, then, that teaching on subjection to the state has been inserted elsewhere in the Pauline corpus, probably in a paraenetic context such as surrounds Eph 5: 21 - 6: 9 and Col 3: 18 - 4: 1, and this is exactly what one finds in Rom 12 and 13.

Like Eph 5: 21 - 6: 9 and Col 3: 18 - 4: 1, Rom 13:1-7 is acknowledged to be a distinct and self-contained unit.[91] It is difficult to reconcile it with some elements in its immediate context, yet it coheres to a considerable degree with others. Here too, it will be shown, the later stratum extends beyond the subjection material, and a mingling of strata has taken place.[92]

J. Kallas' argument that the passage interrupts material that is commentary on synoptic-type teaching[93] loses some of its force when one takes into account the points of contact between the Lukan version of the pericope concerning the payment of taxes to Caesar (Luke 20: 20-6) and Rom 13: 1-7.[94]

There is certainly a hiatus between Rom 12: 21 and 13:1ff. The same applies, however, to Rom 12: 21 and 13: 8, for there is no obvious connection between the thought of overcoming evil with good in the former and owing no one anything but love in the latter, unless one subsumes both under the theme of love. This theme, however, also takes in the teaching on non-resistance to evil in 12: 14–21. The latter could conceivably be intended to prepare the way for teaching on submission to the state and the performance of duties toward the state and its representatives, particularly in an historical context in which the state is actually or potentially an instrument of persecution. If, however, the material at the end of chapter twelve is intended to pave the way for 13:1-7, it has a contrived appearance, for the subjectionist passage presents the state and its actions as characteristically good, which conflicts with the idea of the state as an agent of persecution. It is as if a redactor resorted to whatever material he could find in Jewish and Christian tradition to forge links with an extraneous unit of teaching.

There is a significant connection too between Rom 13: 1–7 and what immediately follows it. Rom 13: 8–10, the portion preceding the eschatological climax in 13: 11–14, concerns the law. The words ὁ γὰρ ἀγαπῶν τὸν ἕτερον νόμον πεπλήρωκεν in 13: 8*b* echo Matt 5: 17 (τὸν νόμον . . . πληρῶσαι), while Rom 13: 9, with its citation in summary form of the decalogue as well as the Levitical law of love may be intended to allude to a version of the synoptic teaching that appears in the episode of the rich young ruler.[95] The question concerning the great commandment may also be in the writer's mind.[96]

The use of the decalogue in Rom 13: 9 may well be related to its occurrence in the subjection material in Ephesians (cf. Eph 5: 31, 6: 2). This would explain why Rom 13: 9 omits the command to obey parents, for it appears in Eph 6: 2. Whether or not the two facts are related, however, the decalogue is a factor supporting the association of Rom 13: 8f with the subjection material,[97] and therefore also with the later stratum.

At the same time ὀφειλάς in 13: 7 and ὀφείλετε in 13: 8 have the appearance of link words connecting originally separated units. While the former occurs in a sentence enjoining the payment of what one owes, the second is found in an exhortation which seems to exclude the existence of debt in any formal sense. This may, however, be an over-literal understanding of 13: 8, which is perhaps no more than a piece of advice to Christians not to borrow from one another and to be financially self-supporting, and not necessarily in conflict with 13: 7.

While it is possible to argue that ὀφειλάς in 13: 7 is an adaptation to 13: 8, it is no less likely that ὀφείλετε in 13: 8 is intended to provide a connecting link for 13: 7, and so also the whole pericope, or that each of the two words has been included with the purpose of making contact with the other.

The case is very different, however, in regard to 13: 11–14.[98] Its sharp eschatological dualism and exhortations to dissociate from the realms of darkness accord perfectly with 12: 1f, which urges those who offer themselves to God not to conform to the present age or world order (12: 2*a*). By contrast, considerable exegetical ingenuity is needed to bring 13:11–14 into alignment with 13: 1–7. The darkness–light dichotomy of 13: 11–14 is inapplicable in 13: 1–7, since the latter assumes that Christians could well find themselves categorized as evildoers if they defy rulers of the present

age. The authorities of the present world, by contrast, are automatically identified as God's agents, and thus, in terms of 13: 11–14, as representatives of light versus darkness.

Moreover, καὶ τοῦτο at the beginning of 13: 11 would seem to require an immediately preceding phrase or clause which is explicated in what follows it.[99] There is no connection of this kind, however, between 13: 10 and 13: 11. In addition, 13: 11 lacks a predicate, unless one assumes that at καὶ τοῦτο there is an ellipsis for a finite verb such as, for instance, ποιεῖτε.[100]

If then a break in the original version has occurred before 13: 11, the question arises to what part of the text it was originally joined. The abruptness of the transition between 12: 21 and 13: 1 has been noted, but 13: 11 is not a convincing sequel to 12: 21 and what directly precedes it. Within Rom 12, however, there is marked discontinuity.

First, Ἡ ἀγάπη ἀνυπόκριτος in 12: 9 appears to stand alone syntactically, having no explicit grammatical connection with what precedes or follows it. Next, there follows a series of apparently unattached adjectives and present participles, often cited as instances of the special imperative use of the present participle, either in the koine Greek, or as a direct reflection of corresponding Hebrew idiom to give expression to secondary or less than absolute injunctions.[101]

Then, though the result is clumsy and cumbersome, it is syntactically possible, by omitting 12: 9a, to read from 12: 4 to 12: 13 as a single sentence, with the participles and adjectives in 12: 6–13 agreeing with the first person plural subject implied in ἐσμεν in 12: 5. Does this mean that an originally viable sentence has been augmented with additional phrases, in somewhat the same way that the opening words of the subjection material in Ephesians, ὑποτασσόμενοι ἀλλήλοις ... (Eph 5: 21) are attached to a preceding sentence?[102]

Significantly, the material both before and after the first phrase in 12: 9 falls into fairly regularly patterned groups of phrases that could bear some relation to each other. In the earlier passage the 'gifts given to us differently according to grace' (12: 6a) fall naturally into the following series:

12: 6b   εἴτε προφητείαν κατα τὴν ἀναλογίαν τῆς πίστεως
12: 7   εἴτε διακονίαν ἐν τῇ διακονίᾳ,
         εἴτε ὁ διδάσκων ἐν τῇ διδασκαλίᾳ
         εἴτε ὁ παρακαλῶν ἐν τῇ παρακλήσει
12: 8   ὁ μεταδιδοὺς ἐν ἁπλότητι,

ὁ προϊστάμενος ἐν σπουδῇ
ὁ ἐλεῶν ἐν ἱλαρότητι.

The repetition of the εἴτε . . . ἐν sequence four times over in 12: 6b–8a, and the series of singular present participles with the article and followed by ἐν in 12: 7b–8 produce a tightly organized unity with a definite series of rhythms.

By comparison 12: 9–13 is in disarray, unless one assumes that ἡ ἀγάπη ἀνυπόκριτος in 12: 9a was intended to form a pair with the last of the three phrases in 12: 8. It is scarcely a convincing parallel to ὁ ἐλεῶν ἐν ἱλαρότητι, however, for it begins with a feminine article, whereas the articles in the preceding three phrases are masculine. Also, what follows in each instance in 12: 8 is a singular present participle that serves as a noun, while in 12: 9a ἀγάπη is a noun which shares a common root with the verb ἀγαπᾶν. Similarly each phrase in 12: 8 ends with a qualifying prepositional phrase introduced by ἐν, to which the adjective ἀνυπόκριτος corresponds only roughly in that it begins with the prefix ἀν-. It is difficult, moreover, to believe that the finely balanced rhythms of 12: 6b–8 originally included the clumsy dissonance of 12: 9a. It seems more probable that the latter is an intrusion into the original. That it probably represents more than a minor gloss will be shown presently.

The next two phrases, ἀποστυγοῦντες τὸ πονηρόν and κολλώμενοι τῷ ἀγαθῷ, are parallel in sense and structure, resembling the pattern of the 'two ways' of evil and good[103] which is in evidence more prominently in the negative-positive contrasts of 12: 16–21 and 13: 1–7 than in what follows in 12: 10ff.

C. H. Talbert has set out the latter in the following pairs of phrases in 12: 10–13:

τῇ φιλαδελφίᾳ εἰς ἀλλήλους φιλόστοργοι – τῇ τιμῇ ἀλλήλους προηγούμενοι
τῇ σπουδῇ μὴ ὀκνηροί – τῷ πνεύματι ζέοντες
τῷ κυρίῳ δουλεύοντες – τῇ ἐλπίδι χαίροντες
τῇ θλίψει ὑπομένοντες – τῇ προσευχῇ προσκαρτεροῦντες
ταῖς χρείαις τῶν ἁγίων κοινωνοῦντες – τὴν φιλοξενίαν διώκοντες[104]

It is to be observed that only the second pair falls into the pattern of the 'evil-good' contrast, but the phrases that follow τῇ σπουδῇ ὀκνηροί have much closer resemblance to one another in structure than do the two phrases in this pair and the first. Also, the first three phrases in Talbert's construction are just as dissonant a sequel to 12: 8 as ἡ ἀγάπη ἀνυπόκριτος in 12: 9a. What is more, the vocabulary in 12: 9f is of the kind that is typical of the later stratum. The two words ἀνυπόκριτος (12: 9a) and φιλαδελφία (12: 10) appear in combination with each other in 1 Pet 1: 22, which was associated with the later material in that epistle. The latter, along with φιλόστοργοι in 12: 10 and φιλοξενίαν in 12: 13, is a compound of an adjective and noun, which is also characteristic of the later stratum.[105] If then one assumes that everything in 12: 9f and the first phrase in 12: 11 belongs to a different strain from the rest, one is left with seven phrases in 12: 11b–13. The first four fall into the following euphoniously balanced pairs:

τῷ πνεύματι ζέοντες - τῷ κυρίῳ δουλεύοντες
τῇ ἐλπίδι χαίροντες - τῇ θλίψει ὑπομένοντες
(12: 11b–12ab)

These phrases form a credible sequence to 12: 6–8, if one assumes that after the exhortation concerning the exercising of particular gifts in 12: 6–8, the passage turns to those of a more general nature that should characterize the Christian community as a whole, and therefore changes from singular to plural participles.

As for the sequel to these two pairs, τῇ προσευχῇ προσκαρτεροῦντες in 12: 12c and ταῖς χρείαις τῶν ἁγίων κοινωνοῦντες in 12: 13a resemble the structure of the two pairs of phrases in 12: 11b–12ab, but they also differ in that the participles προσκαρτεροῦντες and κοινωνοῦντες consist of five and four syllables respectively, while those in the two pairs of phrases in 12: 11b–12ab consist of three and four syllables. In addition, 12: 13a departs from the pattern of a singular dative noun before the participle and has instead the words ταῖς χρείαις τῶν ἁγίων. While a writer may of course vary a pattern which he is repeating a number of times over, this will, if he is reasonably skilled, enhance rather than detract from the rhythmic effect as a whole. Such, however, is not the case here, for the two phrases in question tend rather to disrupt the cadences of 12: 6–8, 11b–12ab.

What is more, the remaining participial phrase in 12: 13, τὴν φιλοξενίαν διώκοντες, serves no better as a sequel to 12: 6–8, 11b–12ab, either in itself or in combination with either of the two phrases in 12: 12c and 12: 13a. It comes under suspicion too because it contains the word διώκοντες, which serves as a link word[106] forming a connection with 12: 14, εὐλογεῖτε τοὺς διώκοντας, εὐλογεῖτε καὶ μὴ καταρᾶσθε, which echoes the synoptic sayings, or versions of them, in Matt 5: 44, ἀγαπᾶτε τοὺς ἐχθροὺς ὑμῶν καὶ προσεύχεσθε ὑπὲρ τῶν διωκόντων ὑμᾶς, and in Luke 6: 28, εὐλογεῖτε τοὺς καταρωμένους ὑμας. Since it is scarcely possible that διωκόντων owes its presence in Matt 5: 44 or the Matthean source to the occurrence of the same verb in Rom 12: 13, it may be concluded that whatever accommodation has taken place must be on the side of the material preceding Rom 12: 14. But 12: 14 is close enough in sense and structure to the synoptic material cited above[107] to say that it marks the beginning of the synoptic-type teaching which appears to cohere with Rom 13: 1-7. If then the hypothesis that Rom 13: 1-7 is part of the later stratum is to be sustained, it follows that the same applies to 12: 14, as also 12: 13*b*, since the latter evidently owes its presence in the passage to the need to provide a point of attachment for 12: 14.

But if the later stratum emulated the repeated participial phrases of the original, why are they abandoned in 12: 14 but resumed in 12: 16-19*a*? The clue is probably to be found in 12: 19f, where 'for it is written' and 'says the Lord' (12: 19) are formulae indicating citations from scripture recognized as authoritative, and where the same kind of change is in evidence. Though 12: 14 is probably not an accurate citation from a synoptic source, it is possible that its association with Jesus himself leads to the use of the imperative instead of the less authoritative participial usage.[108]

The next exhortation, χαίρειν μετὰ χαιρόντων, κλαίειν μετὰ κλαιόντων (12: 15), has the acceptable Greek use of the infinitive in an imperative sense. It accords neither with the pattern of antithetic parallelism in 12: 14 and 12: 16-19, 21 nor with the pairs of present participles in 12: 11*b*-12*ab*. It probably belongs with the later stratum, however, for it can be understood as an elaboration of the thought of 12: 14.[109] That is to say, it concerns conciliatory behaviour toward those outside the Christian community, a theme which receives emphasis throughout 12:16-21 and 13:1-7.

What seems to decide the issue, however, is that the most feasible point of attachment to 13: 11 presents itself not at 12: 15 but at 12: 12*ab*. First, if one assumes that 13: 11 originally followed directly after τῇ ἐλπίδι χαίροντες, τῇ θλίψει ὑπομένοντες in 12: 12, there is no need to assume that a finite verb such as ποιεῖτε is to be understood,[110] for εἰδότες at the beginning of 13: 11 falls into place as a present participle parallel to ἔχοντες (12: 6), ζέοντες, δουλεύοντες (12: 11), χαίροντες, and ὑπομένοντες (12: 12*ab*). These words and the phrases of which they are part may be regarded as original components of a sentence which proceeded from 12: 4 to 12: 8, and thereafter from 12: 11*b* to 12: 12*b*, finally concluding with 13: 11.

Though somewhat prolonged, this period is by no means cumbersome or inherently improbable in terms of syntax or sense. Indeed, to turn to a second consideration, καὶ τοῦτο at the beginning of 13: 11 now makes quite specific reference to preceding content and is no longer problematic. The phrase quite clearly points back to the hope which is cause for rejoicing, and the tribulation which is to be endured (12: 12*b*), both of which relate to the 'time' or 'hour' which calls for special readiness, for the eschatological salvation is nearer now than ever before (13:11). That the night is far advanced (προέκοψεν, 13: 12*a*) and the 'day' on the verge of arrival (13: 12*b*) refers, it is suggested, not to the mere lapse of time, but to an intensification of the situation,[111] so that it appears that the final woes expected to attack the elect and engulf the world are in the initial stage of their onset. It seems from 12: 12*ab* that the affliction viewed in the light of the eschatological hope is a present reality.

Since then 13: 11 was very probably originally joined to 12:12*b*, Rom 12:1-11*a*, 12*c*-21, 13:1-10, may be peeled away as belonging to a later stratum, leaving Rom 12: 1-8, 11*b*-12*b*, 13: 11-14. The latter is set out below from 12: 4 in such a way as to indicate the stylistic device of rhythmic repetition which the earlier writer has used to great effect:[112]

Rom 12: 4 καθάπερ γὰρ ἐν ἑνὶ σώματι πολλά μέλη ἔχομεν -
τὰ δὲ μέλη πάντα οὐ τὴν αὐτὴν ἔχει πρᾶξιν.

12: 5 οὕτως οἱ πολλοὶ ἕν σῶμά ἐσμεν ἐν Χριστῷ -
τὸ δὲ καθ᾽ εἷς ἀλλήλων μέλη

12: 6 ἔχοντες δὲ χαρίσματα κατὰ τὴν χάριν
τὴν δοθεῖσαν ἡμῖν διάφορα
εἴτε προφητείαν (ἐν τῇ προφητείᾳ)[113] -

12: 7 εἴτε διακονίαν ἐν τῇ διακονίᾳ
εἴτε ὁ διδάσκων ἐν τῇ διδασκαλίᾳ -

12: 8 εἴτε ὁ παρακαλῶν ἐν τῇ παρακλήσει
ὁ μεταδιδοὺς ἐν ἁπλότητι -
ὁ προϊστάμενος ἐν σπουδῇ[114]
ὁ ἐλεῶν ἐν ἱλαρότητι

12: 11*b* τῷ πνεύματι ζέοντες -
τῷ κυρίῳ δουλεύοντες

12: 12 τῇ ἐλπίδι χαίροντες -
τῇ θλίψει ὑπομένοντες

13: 11 καὶ τοῦτο εἰδότες τὸν καιρόν -
ὅτι ὥρα ἤδη ὑμᾶς ἐξ ὕπνου ἐγερθῆναι
νῦν γὰρ ἐγγύτερον ἡμῶν ἡ σωτηρία
ἢ ὅτε ἐπιστεύσαμεν.

13: 12 ἡ νὺξ προέκοψεν -
ἡ δὲ ἡμέρα ἤγγικεν.
ἀποθώμεθα οὖν τὰ ἔργα τοῦ σκότους -
ἐνδυσώμεθα δὲ τὰ ὅπλα τοῦ φωτός.

13: 13 ὡς ἐν ἡμέρᾳ εὐσχημόνως περιπατήσωμεν -

μὴ κώμοις καὶ μέθαις
μὴ κοίταις καὶ ἀσελγείαις -
μὴ ἔριδι καὶ ζήλῳ,
13: 14   ἀλλὰ ἐνδύσασθε τὸν κύριον Ἰησοῦν Χριστόν -
καὶ τῆς σαρκὸς πρόνοιαν μὴ ποιεῖσθε εἰς ἐπιθυμίας.

The stylistic unity of this material is to be perceived in the series of two-line parallels linked together by similarities in sentence structure. Its interruption by other material indicates that it is the earlier of the two strata in Rom 12 and 13.

That which has been associated together as belonging to the later stratum also tends to follow a certain patterning, but of a different kind. It very often falls into the antithetic parallelism found to be characteristic of the later stratum in Ephesians, Colossians, and 1 Peter, though these may or may not include μή . . . ἀλλά constructions. From the table given below it can be seen to what extent this material manifests the characteristic as compared with the material which appears to be earlier, all data relating to the later stratum being underscored:

Passages in Romans	No. of antithetic parallels	No. of lines	No. of lines to each occurrence
12: 1-3	1	6	6
12: 3-8*bd*, 11*bc*, 12*ab*	1	13.5	13.5
12: 8*c*, 9-11*a*, 12*b*-21	7	18.5	2.6
13: 1-7	5	16	3.2
13: 8-10	3	6.4	2.1
13: 11-14	1	8	8

The LXX citations in 13: 8-10 have been included, because they are woven into the sentence structure in such a way as to be essential to the parallelism. This does not apply, however, to the explicit quotations from the LXX versions of Lev 19: 18 in Rom 12: 19, and from Prov 25: 21f in Rom 12: 20. If they are omitted, the number of lines to each occurrence for Rom 12: 8*c*, 9-11*a*, 12*b*-21 is 2.2. If one takes into account the revised figure, the earlier stratum scores 8.0 lines to each occurrence, and the later stratum 2.5. That is to say, the trait is present more than three times as often in the material identified as later as compared with the other material in Rom 12 and 13.

At the same time it is to be observed that antithetic parallels are extremely common in most chapters of Romans.[115] They coincide for the most part, however, with the dialectic style of argument of the epistle, and not with the type of contrast reminiscent of the two ways as in the later stratum.[116]

Both layers in Rom 12 and 13 make significant contact with other parts of the ten-letter corpus. Thus Rom 12: 1f echoes Rom 6: 11, 13; Rom 12: 3-8 is strongly reminiscent of 1 Cor 12: 4-14, 27-31, and Rom 13: 11-14 of 1 Thess 5: 1-10, while Rom 12: 11b-12ab makes slight contact with 1 Thess 5: 16-19. It is outside the scope of the present enquiry to determine the nature of these parallels in the material identified as earlier. As for those in the material identified as later, the similarities can be ascribed either to use of common paraenetic patterns, or to literary dependence. Assuming the correctness of the analysis differentiating earlier original material from that which appears to have been inserted later, however, literary dependence is as plausible an explanation as use of common patterns.

Realizing that the exposition on love in 1 Cor 13 follows that on varying gifts in 1 Cor 12,[117] the interpolator could quite easily have shaped his material accordingly. Thus ἡ ἀγάπη ἀνυπόκριτος in Rom 12: 9a both forges a link with the preceding material, and serves to introduce the over-all theme. The phrase τὴν φιλοξενίαν διώκοντες in Rom 12: 13b may be a deliberate echo of Διώκετε τὴν ἀγάπην in 1 Cor 14: 1, and Rom 13: 8-10 may be intended to recall the structure and rhythm of 1 Cor 13 as a whole,[118] at the same time incorporating elements of Gal 5: 13f.

So too, noticing the occurrence of πνεῦμα and χαίρειν in both Rom 12: 11b, 12a and 1 Thess 5: 16, 19, the interpolator could have decided to augment the similarity to render the interpolation more plausible.[119]

As for the resemblances between 1 Thess 5: 12-22, Rom 12: 9-21, and 1 Pet 3: 8f, there is nothing in the last-mentioned that could not be derived from Rom 12: 9-21. That there is direct contact between the two passages is evident from the presence in each of a key word (εὐλογοῦντες in 1 Pet 3: 9, εὐλογεῖτε in Rom 12: 14) not found in 1 Thess 5: 12-22. In addition they share a stylistic trait, the loosely attached participle with imperative force, whereas 1 Thess 5:12-22 uses ordinary imperatives.[120]

By distinguishing two strata of tradition in Rom 12 and 13 it is possible to perceive how they differ from each other, not only stylistically, but also in emphasis and point of view.

One may discern the sharpness of the dualistic contrast between the Christian body (12: 4) and the present age or world order to which the elect are bidden not to conform (12: 2). They are urged instead to offer themselves to God (12: 1) and to serve him according to their several gifts (12: 5ff). They are to be aglow with the spirit (12: 11b), to rejoice in hope, and to don the armour of light so as to withstand the tribulation that must come before the new day finally dawns (12: 12ab with 13: 11-14).

In this eschatological catechesis there is no room for positive acceptance of the life and society that lies without, for it is doomed to be set aside.[121] As for secular authority, it is disregarded in favour of the new alternative the Christian community offers, rather than being actively opposed, as far as can be construed from the Pauline letters.[122]

In the later stratum, by contrast, the same kind of socially directed ethic is in evidence, as appears in the later material in 1 Peter. Here 'doing good' (κολλώμενοι τῷ ἀγαθῷ in 12: 9, τὸ ἀγαθὸν ποίει in 13: 3) is subsumed under the theme of love (Rom 12: 9, 13: 10), and supported with allusions to synoptic teaching as well as quotations from the LXX. It encompasses not only relations within the Christian community, but extends outward to society at large in an all-encompassing way.

Thus Rom 12: 17b contains an exhortation to see that one's conduct takes account of what 'all people' consider noble. The addition of 'all' to the citation from Prov 3: 4 in 12: 17b, as also the repetition of the phrase 'all people' in 12: 18, has special significance at this point. As in the later stratum in 1 Peter, with its injunction in 2: 17 to 'honour all', this universalism encompasses persecutors (cf. Rom 12: 16, 1 Pet 3: 13–17) as well as all instituted authority. According with such tendencies are exhortations aimed at winning the good will of those without, as for instance the encouraging of benevolence (Rom 12: 13a) and hospitality (φιλοξενία, 12: 13b), a virtue highly prized in the ancient world.[123] Synoptic-type teaching on blessing instead of cursing persecutors, refraining from retaliation, and returning neighbourly goodness for evil (Rom 12: 14f, 17–21; cf. Matt 5: 38–48, Luke 6: 27–36) also proves serviceable. Most important, if space be any indication, are the instructions in Rom 13: 1–7 on rendering deference and obedience to the state.

Essential to the teaching on subjection to authority is a readiness to accept a lowly position for oneself and to respect certain others as superiors, which appears to be the import of Rom 12: 10b and 12: 16, if taken in conjunction with 13: 1–7.[124] The teaching on humility in the earlier material (cf. 12: 3–5) involves, as in 1 Cor (cf. vs. 23) the honouring of each in the Christian community for some particular gift. In 12: 16, by contrast, τοῖς ταπεινοῖς συναπαγόμενοι, which may be rendered literally as 'associating with the lowly', means for most Christians, in the context of the later stratum, acquiescing in one's own social station. Similarly, μὴ τὰ ὑψηλὰ φρονοῦντες in the same verse, which means literally 'not thinking lofty things', may be interpreted in the sense of not presuming to rise above oneself, advice supported by an allusion to Prov 3: 7 not to be wise in one's own estimation (Rom 12: 16).[125] The phrase τῇ τιμῇ ἀλλήλους προηγούμενοι in Rom 12: 10b may be translated literally as 'going before one another as to honour'. In the context of the later stratum it may be rendered as 'excelling one another in showing respect', an interpretation that has the support of very early translations.[126] The word $\tau\iota\mu\tilde{\eta}$ would seem, accordingly, to point forward to the use of the same word in 13: 7 to indicate the proper attitude to superiors. Here, as in the later material in 1 Peter, the sense of $\tau\iota\mu\dot{\eta}$, $\tau\iota\mu\tilde{\alpha}\nu$ is more strongly expressed by $\varphi\acute{o}\beta o\varsigma$, $\varphi o\beta\epsilon\tilde{\iota}\sigma\vartheta\alpha\iota$. Both involve the obligation of subjection to superior authority and obedience as to God himself, for all authority is divinely instituted, and whoever resists it resists God and incurs his judgement (13: 2).

In the view of the later stratum God has indeed conferred upon prevailing authority his own prerogative of judgement, so that it acts as the servant ($\delta\iota\acute{\alpha}\kappa o\nu o\varsigma$, 13: 4) of God in praising and rewarding good and punishing evil (13: 3f), whereas the Christian community is to leave judgement to God (12: 9). At first sight this is contradictory, but so closely does the later stratum associate authority with the divine that there is probably no dichotomy between judgement by human and divine authority in its thought. The same combination of ideas occurs in the later stratum in 1 Peter, where there is also teaching on non-retaliation (3: 9), on the state in its role of judge (2: 14f), and on God as supreme judge (2: 23, 4: 5f, 19).

It is unlikely that the mention of the law in Rom 13: 8-10, immediately after Rom 13: 1-7, is fortuitous. Though it refers specifically to the decalogue and thus in some sense to the Mosaic law, the word could be intended to bear also upon Graeco-Roman concepts of law.[127] The clause 'if there be any other law' after the citations from the decalogue and before the quotation of the law of love (13: 9) is sufficiently ambiguous to make contact with the teaching of the Jewish scriptures as well as the requirements of civic law referred to in general terms in 13: 1-7.

In sum, it may be said that the portions of material assigned to each stratum in Rom 12 and 13 for a variety of reasons cohere together thematically in each case without difficulty. The major difference between the two is that the eschatological dualism of the earlier stratum virtually disappears in the later. The darkness–light dichotomy may be deliberately echoed in the 'two-ways' type contrast of the later stratum. The latter, however, does not necessarily correspond with the difference between the Christian community and the present age, for pagan authorities are ranged automatically on the side of good, and Christians possibly on the side of evil if they disobey them.

Concerning the two chapters as a whole, it can be assumed that the interpolator first prepared or adapted the unit of teaching in Rom 13: 1-7, and attached to it the portion in Rom 13: 8-10, and that he then detached

Rom 12: 11*bc*, 12*ab* from 12: 8 and 13: 11, weaving this fragment into the series of exhortations in 12: 9–21 to form an introduction to 13: 1–7. Despite these elaborate efforts the hiatus remains, for it is one not merely of thought sequence, but of a different outlook and world view from that of Paul and primitive Christianity in general.

The later stratum in 1 Cor 10, 11, 14, and 7[128]

Of the passages in the ten-letter corpus associated with the so-called 'household code' or 'code of subjection' only 1 Cor 14: 33*b*-35 remains. The textual problems surrounding the passage have been mentioned, as also the suggestion that it may be a marginal gloss incorporated in two different places, and that it is often found to be in conflict with 1 Cor 11: 2–16.[129] In what follows here it will be maintained that the two passages are closely connected, and both cohere with the later stratum, together with additional material in 1 Cor 10, 11, and 14.

The later stratum in 1 Cor 14

The conclusion that Eph 5: 21 - 6: 9 is an insertion belonging to a later stratum means that the same probably applies to 1 Cor 14: 33*b*-35, because of the very obvious similarities in vocabulary, style, and thought. Not only does the οὐ γὰρ . . . ἀλλὰ . . . καθὼς καί construction in vs. 34 resemble Eph 5: 29, but the passage recalls Eph 5: 21-33 in its combination of the terms ὑποτασσέσθωσαν, αἱ γυναῖκες . . . τοὺς ἰδίους ἄνδρας (cf. Eph 5: 21f). Such similarities taken in conjunction with each other cannot be merely accidental, but are best explained as due to some form of direct contact.

The possibility that Eph 5: 21 - 6: 9 is dependent on 1 Cor 14: 33*b*-35 is unlikely, for the thought of the latter is more probably derived from the former than the other way round. Just as 1 Pet 5: 1-7 appears to apply to church order the household pattern of subjection by children to parents,[130] so 1 Cor 14: 33*b*-35 seems to do with the pattern of subjection by wives to husbands. Indeed, the instruction in 1 Cor 14: 35 that wives receive instruction from their husbands at home perhaps finds a parallel in the requirement in Eph 5: 29 that husbands 'nourish and cherish' their wives, for the word for 'nourish' (ἐκτρεφεῖν) is used in Eph 6: 4 of the parental duty to rear children in the 'discipline and instruction of the Lord' (ἐκτρέφετε . . . ἐν παιδείᾳ καὶ νουθεσίᾳ κυρίου).

Moreover if one assumes that the original version of 1 Cor 14 did not contain 14: 33*b*-35, the difficulty of reconciling this small pocket of material with the rest of the chapter is solved. 1 Cor 14 speaks with evident approval of 'each' member of the congregation as exercising a gift involving oral expression, such as a 'hymn', a 'teaching', a 'revelation', a 'tongue', or an 'interpretation' (14: 26). That ἕκαστος in this sentence refers to all without exception is evident from 14: 5, which indicates the desire of the apostle that 'all' should give expression to such gifts. As in the case of the personal pronoun, one may assume that ἀδελφοί in 14: 6 incorporates both genders, since the word is a common Pauline mode of addressing a whole congregation.[131] Indeed, the fact that women are directly addressed in the subjection material (cf. Col 3: 18, Eph 5: 22) bears testimony to the assumption that they would be present in the congregation at the reading of apostolic letters and are among those addressed.

The silencing of women in 1 Cor 14: 33*b*-35 is often explained as due to special circumstances in the Corinthian church,[132] but this is unconvincing, for the injunction lays claim to universality in its application, not only in the words 'as in all the churches of the saints' (14: 33*b*), but also in the appeal to 'the law' in vs. 34, though as it stands the reference is obscure.[133]

To consider next the question of context, though the passage echoes some of the wording of the preceding material,[134] it interrupts the course of a discussion on the ordering of the gifts of prophecy, speaking in tongues, and interpreting (14: 26-33*a*). At the same time the thought in 14: 33*a* that God is not a God of ἀκαταστασία (disturbances, disorders, or acts of unruliness) but of peace, suggests that it may be intended to prepare the way for 14: 33*b*-35, and so that it proceeds from the same source.[135] Tending to confirm the possibility is the fact that vs. 33*a* forms an antithetic parallel following the οὐ γὰρ . . . ἀλλά construction that is common in the later stratum, as is the case in vs. 34 as well. The word ὑποτάσσεται in 14: 32 is also characteristic of the later stratum, though its implications are rather different, for it seems to refer to the control of spirits inducing prophecy, in a way that resembles the use of the same verb for the subjection of the spirits to Christ in Luke 10: 17.[136]

It is possible that 14: 32 was added to provide a link with the key term ὑποτασσέσθωσαν in 14: 34, and so to connect the subjectionist teaching with the exhortations on pneumatic gifts. That the clause in 14: 32 follows weakly and without obviously logical sequence as the concluding part of the sentence in 14: 31 confirms the possibility that the later stratum was introduced into the earlier version of the text at this point.

If then it is assumed that the later material begins at 14: 32, where, must it be concluded, is the original sequel to 14: 31? The rhetorical question in 14: 36 is scarcely a convincing joining-point. It actually follows more fittingly after the injunction that women remain silent in assemblies, for the implied accusation that those addressed presume to determine for themselves what is 'the word of God' accords with the claim that the ruling reflects the practice that prevails in 'all the churches of the saints' (14: 33*b*).

Furthermore, it is by no means evident that 14: 37 is the true sequel to 14: 31 either. First, it seems that the singular reading ἐστιν ἐντολή is to be preferred to the plural of some manuscripts and other authorities.[137] It follows that 14: 37 applies more probably to the one major requirement in 14: 33-5 that women be silent in assemblies, repeated as it is three times over, than to the series of exhortations in the immediately preceding part of the chapter. Secondly, the claim made in vs. 37 that anything written by Paul has the same authority as a divine command suggests a lapse of time in which his written words have come to be regarded in a way that approaches canonicity.

If, however, 14: 37 is to be associated with 14: 32-6, the same would seem to apply to 14: 38, for its most obvious sense is a threat of non-recognition (cf. ἀγνοεῖται) against anyone who does not recognize the validity of the claim in vs. 37.

There is a return to the subject of prophesying and glossolalia in 14: 39f, which summarizes the discussion in 14: 1-31. Here then is the most fitting sequel to 14: 31. It may therefore be concluded that 14: 32-8 is an insertion cohering with the later stratum. As for the appearance of 14: 34f after 14: 40 in some manuscripts,[138] this can be ascribed to a yet later attempt to deal with the clumsiness of the thought sequence and to achieve a smoother result.

Two strata in 1 Cor 10 and 11

If the subjectionist injunction in 1 Cor 14 is to be accounted part of the later stratum, what then of 1 Cor 11: 2-16, which seems to accept certain forms of oral expression by women in cultic assemblies as normal practice?

The position taken here is that, far from contradicting 1 Cor 14: 32-8, this passage actually coheres with it in its underlying thought and intention and, like it, has close links with Eph 5: 21 - 6: 9, Col 3: 18 - 4: 1, and the later stratum as a whole. W. O. Walker has reached similar conclusions, arguing that 1 Cor 11: 2-16 is a Pastoral-type interpolation connected also with Colossians and Ephesians,[139] but this study differs from him in regard to context. The later stratum will be shown to begin before 11: 2 and to extend beyond 11: 16.

Regarding the relation of the passage to 14: 32-8, there are a number of obvious similarities. In both there is an appeal to apostolic authority (11: 2; 14: 37f), to standard practice in all the churches (11: 16; 14: 33*b*), and to notions of propriety in society at large.[140] That in 11: 2–16 there is affirmation of masculine authority and priority over woman as strong as in the subjectionist passages already discussed will transpire as the argument proceeds.

Though 11: 2–16 may appear to countenance praying and prophesying by women (vs. 5) while 14: 32–8 silences them completely in gatherings of the church, the intention of the former is not necessarily in conflict with the latter. This possibility emerges if it is taken into account that the head-covering which 11: 2–16 requires women who participate verbally in cultic activities to wear is in all probability the traditional veil (κάλυμμα), which evidently served both as a supposed protection against exposure to evil[141] and as a mark of a woman's subjection to a husband, with the implication that she should remain silent in the presence of men.[142] The result is that she is deemed unfit to make herself heard if she wears no veil, and obliged to remain silent if she does.

The intention for the inclusion of 11: 2–16 could indeed be to prepare the way for the prohibition in 14: 32–8.[143] Both passages assume a similar situation, that women are expressing themselves verbally in Christian assemblies, with implications of violating proper order, and both have the effect of silencing them, the former by implication, the latter explicitly.

Furthermore, 11: 2–16 resembles 14: 32–8 in the close ties it appears to have with Eph 5: 21–33, the section of the Ephesian 'household' code which concerns wives and husbands. In the first place an analysis of literary relations indicates that if Eph 5: 21 – 6: 9 is accounted part of a later literary stratum, the same probably applies to 1 Cor 11: 2–16.

It will be recalled that in the analysis of Eph 5: 21 – 6: 9 and Col 3: 19 – 4: 1, one line of evidence for their being later additions emerged on applying Mitton's method of determining the priority of Ephesians to 1 Peter, which was to compare their respective closeness to an earlier shared source. In setting out the parallels with Eph 4: 15 and 5: 23, Mitton assumed dependence in each case also on 1 Cor 11: 3.[144] The analysis given below of the passages involved leads, however, to a very different conclusion:

1 Cor 11: 3: θέλω δὲ ὑμᾶς εἰδέναι ὅτι παντὸς ἀνδρὸς ἡ κεφαλὴ ὁ Χριστός ἐστιν, κεφαλὴ δὲ τοῦ Χριστοῦ ὁ Θεός

Eph 5: 23f: ὅτι ἀνήρ ἐστιν κεφαλὴ τῆς γυναικὸς . . . ὁ Χριστὸς κεφαλὴ τῆς ἐκκλησίας, αὐτὸς σωτὴρ τοῦ σώματος. ἀλλὰ ὡς . . . ἐν παντί

Eph 4: 15f: ἀληθεύοντες δὲ ἐν ἀγάπῃ αὐξήσωμεν εἰς αὐτὸν τὰ

πάντα ὅς ἐστιν ἡ κεφαλή, Χριστός,
ἐξ οὗ πᾶν τὸ σῶμα συναρμολογούμενον καὶ συμβιβαζόμενον διὰ
πάσης ἀφῆς
Col 1: 18: καὶ αὐτός ἐστιν ἡ
κεφαλὴ τοῦ σώματος (τῆς ἐκκλησίας) ὅς ἐστιν ἀρχή . . . ἵνα
γένηται ἐν πᾶσιν
Col 2: 19: τὴν κεφαλήν, ἐξ οὗ
πᾶν τὸ σῶμα, διὰ τῶν ἀφῶν . . . καὶ
συνβιβαζόμενον

The verbal contact between 1 Cor 11: 3 and Eph 5: 23 is so close that some direct connection between the two seems to be an inescapable conclusion. Assuming the correctness of the hypothesis that Eph 5: 21 – 6: 9 is later than the main body of Ephesians, a possible explanation for the similarities of Eph 5: 23 to both 1 Cor 11: 3 and Eph 4: 15 is that it is a conflation of both, and possibly also Col 1: 18, though, as mentioned before, τῆς ἐκκλησίας in the latter is probably a gloss inserted under the influence of Ephesians.[145]

It can also be argued, however, that 1 Cor 11: 3 is a conflation of Eph 5: 23 and 4: 15 and that Eph 4: 15 is earlier than 1 Cor 11: 3, because it is clearly closer to Col 1: 18[146] as well as to Col 2: 19.[147]

It appears, then, that while there is evidence suggesting that both Eph 5: 23 and 1 Cor 11: 3 are later than the main body of Ephesians, it is by no means clear which of these two is earlier than the other. Indeed, a reasonable inference would seem to be that they issue from the same source and make use of the same earlier material. Unfortunately there are no other similar parallels between 1 Cor 11: 2–16 and Ephesians to test this possibility.

Another line of evidence tending to confirm the suggestion is to be found, however, in the varying uses of the head (κεφαλή) symbol in the Pauline collection. Given the deutero-Pauline character of most of Colossians and of the main body of Ephesians, and assuming the correctness of the conclusion that Eph 5: 21 – 6: 9 is a later addition to Ephesians, one may trace a series of related but differing versions ranging from the primitive Pauline conception to that which appears in the trito-Pauline material in Ephesians.

Excluding 1 Cor 11: 2–16 from consideration, chronologically speaking the first use of the symbol is in 1 Cor 12: 21. Here there is nothing whatever to identify Christ with any one part of the 'body' rather than another,

or even to elevate the 'head' over other parts. All are viewed as inter-
dependent members of the one 'body of Christ' (cf. 1 Cor 12: 27).

Next the term for head is used symbolically in Col 1: 18 and 2: 10.
Here Christ is represented as the 'head' of the 'body' in the sense of the
cosmos (Col 1: 15-20). As such he is regarded as the unifying factor
holding all things together (vs. 17), and as pre-eminent over the principalities and powers (1: 16, 2: 10). In 1: 24 'body' refers to the church,
but there is no mention of a 'head'.

Thereafter 'head' occurs with symbolic significance in Eph 1: 22 and
4: 15, again in close relation to 'body'. In the main body of Ephesians the
word has an exclusively ecclesiastical reference, but combined with the
christology of Col 1: 15-20 this makes of Christ the pre-eminent 'head'
over the cosmos on behalf of the church (Eph 1: 22f).[148] According to
Eph 4: 15f Christ is the 'head' in the sense of the one who has ascended to
the heights of the heavens, once again, for the benefit of his body, the
church, to whom gifts of various kinds are distributed (4: 10-12). Since
the churchly body consists of those who have been raised up with Christ
and sit with him in the heavenly places (2: 5f), it would seem to follow
that the entire church shares the role and status of the 'head' of the
cosmos. The original Ephesian writer is evidently aware, however, of a
tension between the church as proleptically in the exalted situation of the
'head' and its actual present situation. Thus according to 4: 15f Christ is
the 'head' into which the rest are yet to grow. The implication is that he
is at its 'head' in that he leads the way to the position of exaltation over
the principalities and powers. At the same time, far from there being any
separation between Christ and the church, he is regarded as the one who
holds together its varying parts in unity (4: 16).[149]

Finally, in Eph 5: 21 - 6: 9 a quite distinctive christology and ecclesiology appear. In 5: 23 Christ as the head is clearly distinguishable from
and elevated over the church. He represents the principle of ruling authority over the church following the hierarchical pattern of the marriage
relationship as depicted in the Ephesian 'household' code.[150]

Where if anywhere in this spectrum should the use of κεφαλή in 1 Cor
11: 3 be assigned? Here there is no mention of a body, but man is
characterized as 'head' of woman as Christ is 'head' of every man, and as
God is 'head' of Christ. The same sense of authority over a subordinate
seems to be present in 1 Cor 11: 3 as in Eph 5: 23, despite the strenuous
efforts of exegetes to relieve the word of this connotation. To argue, as
does R. Scroggs, that the possible metaphorical meaning of 'source' makes
of the passage merely a requirement concerning sexual distinction in
dress,[151] with no thought of subordination, is evasive. Scroggs sets aside

the instances in the LXX where the word denotes superior rank, on the grounds that ἄρχων and ἀρχηγός are the more usual terms to render the Hebrew for head in the sense of chief or leader.[152] If, however, 'head' is intended to mean 'source' in vs. 3, then the implication of authority over woman is, if anything, intensified, for it means not merely that man is prior in a temporal sense, but that her very being is derived from him, as his is from God and Christ, and that he therefore stands in the place of Christ in relation to her. Once again the passage recalls Eph 5: 21ff, where woman is urged to subject herself to her husband 'as to the Lord' (vss. 21f). There is no explicit instruction in 1 Cor 11: 2-16 that woman submit to and obey man, or her husband, but what the passage does is to extend the superior status of husband over his wife to all men over all women, so that it can be applied to ecclesiastical order. As will be shown, the rest of the pericope reinforces this motif.

Parallel to the God–Christ–man–woman hierarchy connected with the 'head' symbolism is the God–man–woman–hair series connected with δόξα. While man is the 'glory of God' and has woman as his 'glory' (vs. 7), woman is in the lesser position of the 'glory of man' and has her hair as her 'glory' (vss. 7, 15). Then too, with an evident reference to the prior creation of man in Genesis 2 as in 1 Tim 2: 13, it is argued that woman was originally derived from man and not the other way round, and so was created for man, though man is now born of woman (vss. 8f).

These contentions are connected with the sentence in 11: 10 by means of διὰ τοῦτο. The use of this preposition with the accusative means that the phrase most probably points back to what has gone before as the reason or purpose for what follows.[153] It is therefore unlikely that the words 'a woman ought to have authority (ἐξουσίαν) over her head' (11: 10) contradict or nullify the preceding arguments concerning the secondary nature of woman and the priority and superiority of man. Hence it is more likely that the one who should exercise authority over woman's head according to 11: 10 is man rather than woman herself. Furthermore it can be concluded that the wearing of a veil is regarded as a recognition of this masculine authority.[154] Such a conclusion accords with the ordinary Greek use of the term ἐξουσία for the authority or right of one over another, especially in relations between parents and children, husbands and wives, masters and slaves, and owners in relation to their property, in accordance with the various laws and institutions determining these rights.[155]

Similarly the expression διὰ τοὺς ἀγγέλους at the end of 1 Cor 11: 10 may be taken to underscore the theme of woman's subjection by reason of her inferiority to man, whatever interpretation one favours: the more common view, held here, that the angels are potentially malevolent spirits to whose attack woman is prone unless protected by a veil;[156] or that they are angels of the created order for whom the veil is a mark of respect,[157] that is, presumably a sign of deference to the original secondary nature and status of woman; or as Fitzmyer maintains, that they are good angels present in worship, before whom it is disrespectful for unveiled women to appear, because they are equivalent to defective men, who were excluded from Qumran worship.[158]

While 11: 11f concedes that man and woman are not apart from each other and that the woman is derived from man as man comes through (διά) woman, it does not by any means alter the subordination of woman. On the contrary, it implies a purely instrumental role for women in procreation, at the same time affirming marriage, probably over against ascetics who rejected marriage, as in the Pastorals (1 Tim 4: 1-3).

Not only does the passage cohere in giving expression to or implying male superiority and female subordination, but in addition the God- or Christ-man-woman hierarchy connected with both κεφαλή and δόξα spans the two major pericopes (vss. 3, 8f, 11f; and 4-7, 10, 13, 16) into which Walker divides the whole. Moreover the δόξα series extends to vs. 14, which is to say, into Walker's third pericope, vss. 14f. Whether or not the passage is an amalgam of originally separate entities, his theory does point up the somewhat rambling and disjointed nature of 11: 2-16. This characteristic is, however, shared by the surrounding material, which can also be divided into loosely connected instructions, bound together by the broad common theme of church order.

Walker effectively demonstrates the un-Pauline character of 11: 2-16, in its thought, tone, and use of vocabulary.[159] At the same time there is a very marked coherence in thought and style between this passage and its *immediate* surroundings.[160] Despite the abrupt transition from 11: 1 to 11: 2, there is a close correspondence between the idea of imitating the apostle as he imitates Christ in vs. 1, and the idea of remembering in the sense of observing the traditions which the apostle has received and passed on. The resemblance in mode of thought accords too with the linear and hierarchical patterns present in 11: 2-16 in its entirety. There is a similarity between the God- or Christ-man-woman sequence in 11: 3-16 and the Christ-apostle-apostolic follower succession in 11: 1f. Significantly, the latter extends also to 11: 23 in the idea of the apostle having received from the Lord what he has delivered to others. In addition in 10: 23 - 11: 1 and 11: 2-16 there is a common appeal to behave in such a way as to please society and obey propriety (see 10: 32f and 11: 6, 13f). This motif is probably present also in the injunctions concerning abuses in observing the Lord's supper in 11: 17ff. In all three sections there is deference to 'the church (or churches) of God'. There is also stylistic unity in the use of antithetic parallels, as will be shown.

As one moves backward in 1 Cor 10, however, one encounters a sharp break in continuity between 10: 22 and 10: 23, very often ascribed to the insertion of part of another Pauline letter.[161] As is often observed, the point of view in 10: 23–33 seems to differ distinctly from that expressed in the earlier part of the chapter. The material preceding 10: 23 condemns, not only idolatry as such, but also the eating of what has been sacrificed to idols, because this is to commune with demons and conflicts with sharing in the body and blood of Christ (10: 16, 21). The material following after 10: 22, by contrast, is less rigorous, advising that one eat without question unless another raises the issue (10: 25–9). Here too there is a shift in the basis for ethical judgement from the unity and distinctiveness of the body of Christ (10: 16–21) to neighbourly relations with those within and outside the Christian community (10: 24, 28f, 23f), and to the scruples of individual conscience (10: 25, 28f).

Furthermore, if one examines the way the language is structured in 10: 14–22, it seems that a break has occurred in the original text. The pattern may be set out as follows:

1 Cor 10: 14–17

Vss. 14f	Exhortation	Therefore, my beloved, flee from idolatry. I speak as to prudent people. Judge you what I say.
Vs. 16	Questions	The cup of blessing which we bless, is it not a sharing in the blood of Christ? The bread which we break, is it not a sharing in the body of Christ?
Vs. 17	Explanation	For we (though) many are one bread, one body, for all share in the one bread.

1 Cor 10: 18–20

Vs. 18a	Exhortation	Observe Israel according to the flesh.
Vss. 18b, 19	Questions	Are not those who eat the sacrifices sharers in the altar? What then do I say? That what is sacrificed is anything? Or that an idol is anything?
Vs. 20	Explanation	But that which (pagans) sacrifice is to demons and not to God: I do not want you to commune with demons.

1 Cor 10: 21f

Vs 21	Exhortation	You cannot drink the cup of the Lord and the cup of demons. You cannot share in the table of the Lord and the table of demons.[162]
Vs 22	Questions	Or shall we provoke the Lord's anger? Are we stronger than he?

The predilection for the repetition of regular patterns of the dialogue type is to be observed in many parts of the Pauline corpus, as R. Bultmann has pointed out.[163] Here one may observe three times over a piece of instruction, teaching, or exhortation followed by two or more rhetorical questions. What is surprising is to find that though in the first two such sequences each continues with some form of explanation which comes as a direct response to what has gone before (cf. 10: 14–16 and 10: 17, 10: 18f and 10: 20), this does not apply to 10: 21f. Instead the last-mentioned section ends with two dangling rhetorical questions without any succeeding response which relates quite distinctly to their import. Very similar material, following the same rhetorical patterning and corresponding in subject matter, occurs in 1 Cor 6: 12–20 and 2 Cor: 6: 14 – 7: 1, such that some partition theories link the three passages together as parts of a single letter.[164] The close similarity between 1 Cor 10: 23 and 6: 12 suggests that 6: 12–20 originally followed after 10: 22. Yet the lack of an appropriate sequel to 10: 22 remains.

There is a not dissimilar series of comments and questions in 11: 20–2, on the subject of the Lord's supper, but there is nothing here that could be construed as a direct response to and explanation of 10: 21f. Not indeed until 11: 30 does a convincing sequel appear to the questions: 'Or shall we provoke the Lord's anger? Are we stronger than he?' (10: 22). In the comment: 'Because of this many among you are weak and ill, and some have fallen asleep' in 11: 30 the adjectives ἀσθενεῖς (weak, powerless, sick),[165] and ἄρρωστοι (powerless, ill)[166] provide a contrast to ἰσχυρό-τεροι (stronger, more powerful)[167] that suggests a connection with 10: 22. Moreover, 11: 30 provides exactly the kind of explanatory response to 10: 21f which the patterning of the language in 10: 17–22 leads one to expect.

If then it is assumed that 1 Cor 11: 30 was originally attached to 10: 22, the phrase διὰ τοῦτο at the beginning of 11: 30 appears to point back quite specifically to the statement in 10: 21 concerning the impossibility of communion with both the Lord and demons. This in turn relates what 11: 30 says concerning those who have 'fallen asleep' or died with the thought of 10: 6–11, which refers to the account in Num 25: 1–9 of the participation by the Israelites in sacrifices to the Moabite Baal, and at the same time in cultic prostitution. The ensuing plague, interpreted as a judgement, is reported to have resulted in the death of 24,000 (23,000 according to 1 Cor 10: 8). If 1 Cor 11: 30 is taken to have followed 10: 22, the connection between Christian participation in pagan practices and the reference to Num 25: 1–9 is obvious. The latter serves not only as a warning, but as an interpretation of what is already taking place in the Christian community.

Assuming then that 1 Cor 11: 30 has been detached from 10: 22, it is very probable that the same applies to 11: 31f, which urges the saints to judge themselves so as not to be condemned along with the world. A detail which tends to confirm the possibility is the use of the first person plural in 11: 31f, as in 10: 14–22, whereas there is no such identification between the writer and those addressed in the intervening material (10: 23 - 11: 29).

In 11: 33f, however, there is a return to the theme of 11: 17–29 in attacking disorder and heresy relating to the Lord's supper. It may be assumed, therefore, that this portion belongs with that which precedes 11: 30. It follows that the earlier stratum in chapters ten and eleven comprises 10: 1–22, 11: 30–2, and that the later material extends from 10: 23 to 11: 29, and continues at 11: 33–4.

The reason for the transference of 11: 30–2 to chapter 11 is feasibly to reinforce the instructions concerning the Lord's supper in 11: 17–26 and at the same time to weaken the stringency of 10: 1–22. Κρίμα and διακρίνων in 11: 29 and κρίμα in 11: 34 could be intended to serve as links with the displaced fragment.

1 Cor 10: 1–22, 11: 30–2 possibly continue in 1 Cor 6: 12–20a and 2 Cor 6: 14 - 7: 1,[168] which follow the same rhetorical patterning as the earlier material in 1 Cor 10 and 11. However, the continued explanation, leading into exhortation in 1 Cor 6: 12ff, follows logically from the thought in 10: 33, 11: 30–2. The thought that 'all things are lawful for me, but not all are helpful . . . but I will not be enslaved by anything' in the former can be connected with the idea of judgement and of the power of demonic possession through cultic prostitution in the latter. It is understandable that the redactor responsible for the later stratum would have broken up this material to modify its import. The idea of complete separation from the surrounding society, expressed in 2 Cor 6: 14 - 7: 1, would have been particularly objectionable to the socially oriented ethic of the later stratum. Its placement in 2 Cor 6 seems to be an act of editorial burying of something which could not be discarded, because of its reputed

apostolic origin. It is difficult to conceive of any use it could have served anywhere in the corpus in the view of the later stratum. Jewett has, however, suggested that its insertion after 2 Cor 6: 13 by a Pastoral redactor is to counter the words 'broaden yourselves also', which could encourage too wide a tolerance toward paganism.[169] Whether this earlier stratum is in fact Pauline, or belongs to the sub-apostolic period prior to the stratum under examination is outside the scope of this study. For present purposes what is important is its dissociation from the later stratum.

To return to the ramifications of the latter, it is to be observed that 1 Cor 8 expresses the same point of view on food offered to idols as 1 Cor 10: 23 – 11: 1, evidencing the same concern for individual conscience and for weaker, more scrupulous Christians. Present findings tend to confirm the views of those who consider that 1 Cor 8 and 10: 23ff cohere together in the midst of material of a different character. While scholars taking this view have associated them with a different Pauline letter,[170] the present line of evidence and argument points to their being deposits of a later stratum.[171] As for Rom 14: 1 – 15: 6, it coheres with the later stratum in its tendencies and outlook.[172]

Stylistic confirmation for the above analysis of 1 Cor 10 and 11 is to be found in the regular occurrence of antithetic parallels throughout the material ascribed to the later stratum.[173] The frequency of the trait in various parts of 1 Cor 10 and 11 is as shown in the table, the data for material assigned to the later stratum being underscored:

Passages in 1 Corinthians	No. of antithetic parallels	No. of lines	No. of lines to each occurrence
10: 1–13	1	23	23.0
10: 14–22; 11: 30–32	2	17.6	8.8
10: 23 – 11: 1	4	17	4.25
11: 2–16	6	25	4.2
11: 17–22	3	11	3.7
11: 23–25	0	9	-
11: 27–29, 33f	2	8	4.0

It will be observed that all parts of the material assigned to a later stratum exhibit the trait with similar frequency (between 3.7 and 4.25 lines to each occurrence) excepting 11: 23–5, which, it is claimed within the text itself, issues from another source (cf. παρέλαβον ἀπὸ τοῦ κυρίου in 11: 23). The characteristic is by contrast far less frequent in the material not included in the later stratum. If the test is extended to the chapters preceding and following 1 Cor 10 and 11, the results given in the table emerge:

Passages in 1 Corinthians	No. of antithetic parallels	No. of lines	No. of lines to each occurrence
Chap. 6	3	36.5	12.2
Chap. 7	24	75	3.1
Chap. 8	6	25	4.1
Chap. 9	7	51	7.3
Chap. 12	2	51	25.5
Chap. 13	3	51	17.0

It can be no coincidence that 1 Cor 8, which resembles the material assigned to the later stratum in its outlook, accords with it in this respect too. Similarly the rate for Rom 14: 1 – 15: 6 is 4.1 lines to each occurrence.[174] An exception to these results appears in 1 Cor 7, where the rate is 3.1 lines to each occurrence. The possibility that this part of 1 Corinthians belongs to the later stratum is, however, to be excluded, for it runs counter to Col 3: 18 – 4: 1, Eph 5: 21 – 6: 9, and 1 Cor 11: 2–16, both in its egalitarian view of the marriage relationship and in its discouragement of marriage (cf. 1 Cor 7: 2-4, 8f, 26ff, 32ff), whereas the passages mentioned above take it for granted. The requirement that women wear a head-covering in 1 Cor 11: 2ff probably assumes it.

A possibility that suggests itself is that 1 Cor 7 serves as a model for the emulation of Pauline style by the redactor responsible for the later layer, in particular because he seeks to neutralize its import. This receives support from the fact that 1 Cor 11: 2–16 seems to echo 1 Cor 7 at certain points; cf. 11: 8, where the οὐ ἀλλά and γυνή . . . ἀνήρ . . . ἀνήρ . . . γυνή sequences occur as in 1 Cor 7: 4, and 11: 10, where ἐξουσίαν ἔχει seems to echo the same words in 1 Cor 7: 36f, a word-play that perhaps provides the explanation for the rather awkward and unusual use of ἐξουσία in this context.[175] There are no fewer than eight points of convergence between 11: 2–16 and the nine lines of 7: 36–40 (see besides the above mentioned εἰ δέ τις in 7: 36 and 11: 16, ϑέλει in 7: 36, 39 and ϑέλω in 11: 3, and γυνή and ἀνήρ with ἐν κυρίῳ in 7: 39 and 11: 11), an accumulation which speaks loudly for literary dependence.

It is concluded then that material cohering with the later stratum is present in 1 Cor 10: 23 – 11: 29, 33f and as a corollary that 1 Cor 8 and Rom 14: 1 – 15: 6 are probably of the same character. Conversely 1 Cor 10: 1-22, 11: 30-2 is taken to be earlier material, since its original course appears to have been interrupted.[176]

The motive of the redactor in inserting material in 1 Cor 10 and 11 was first, evidently, to counter the position taken in the earlier material on food sacrificed to idols with a more flexible view. Since the earlier material contains a description of a community meal which differed from that approved by the redactor and his circle, he included his own version of the Lord's supper, and related injunctions. The subject thus became that of the proper ordering of cultic practices, which in turn provided opportunity to broach the matter of women's vocal participation, with a view to curbing it. Like Rom 13: 1-7, 1 Cor 11: 2-16 has the appearance of an independent, previously prepared unit for which an appropriate context was sought. The words 'I praise you . . .' in 11: 17 were used to introduce the unit and at the same time to attach it to the rest of the insertion. Proximity to 1 Cor 14, where the explicit silencing of women occurs, made it an advantageous point at which to include the pericope concerning the wearing of the traditional veil.

1 Cor 7

Additions from the later stratum relevant to the subjectionist theme appear to be present also in 1 Cor 7: 17-24. A puzzling feature of the passage is the apparent contradiction between vss. 20 and 21. While the former instructs each to remain in the station ($\kappa\lambda\acute{\eta}\sigma\epsilon\iota$) in which he was called, the latter seems to advise slaves to make use of the opportunity to become free if at all possible.[177] Increasing the difficulty is the fact that vs. 24 repeats the import of vs. 20, as if to emphasize it. In addition vs. 17 strengthens the injunctions in vss. 18-24 by insisting that the teaching to follow, on living in the state in which one was called, represents what the apostle commands ($\delta\iota\alpha\tau\acute{\alpha}\sigma\sigma\omega\mu\alpha\iota$) in all the churches. This verb, however, together with the expression $\grave{\epsilon}\nu$ $\tau\alpha\~i\varsigma$ $\grave{\epsilon}\kappa\kappa\lambda\eta\sigma\acute{\iota}\alpha\iota\varsigma$ $\pi\acute{\alpha}\sigma\alpha\iota\varsigma$, recalls the later stratum.[178]

Then too the concept of calling in vss. 20 and 24 resembles that in the later stratum in 1 Peter. That is to say, the calling of Christians is determined by their position within the social structures of existing society, so that the slave is to fulfil the calling of obedience to his master and a wife to her husband (1 Pet 2: 18-20; 3: 1-6). In the earlier material in 1 Peter, by contrast, the Christian calling is out of the darkness of the world and into the light of the new life (2: 9).[179]

The fact that $\grave{\epsilon}\nu$ $\tau\~\eta$ $\kappa\lambda\acute{\eta}\sigma\epsilon\iota$ $\~\eta$ $\grave{\epsilon}\kappa\lambda\acute{\eta}\vartheta\eta$ in 1 Cor 7: 20 bears a close resemblance to $\grave{\alpha}\xi\acute{\iota}\omega\varsigma$ $\pi\epsilon\rho\iota\pi\alpha\tau\~\eta\sigma\alpha\iota$ $\tau\~\eta\varsigma$ $\kappa\lambda\acute{\eta}\sigma\epsilon\omega\varsigma$ $\~\eta$ $\grave{\epsilon}\kappa\lambda\acute{\eta}\vartheta\eta\tau\epsilon$ in Eph 4: 1 suggests that Ephesians may be dependent on 1 Cor 7 at this point. The stylistic device of using a verb form of a word in close combination with the corresponding noun is, however, a characteristic of the main body of Ephesians.[180] The possibility that the main Ephesian writer is responsible for 1 Cor 7: 20 is also to be excluded, for the Christian calling in

Ephesians, as in 1 Peter, consists in separation from the present age and all that pertains to it in order to take one's place in the closely knit unity of the body of Christ.[181]

The more likely alternative is that 1 Cor 7: 20 issues from the later stratum and that it draws on Eph 4: 1 for its wording. The same also probably applies to ἕκαστον ὡς κέκληκεν ὁ Θεός, οὕτως περιπατείτω in 1 Cor 7: 17 in view of the use of the verbs καλεῖν and περιπατεῖν here as in Eph 4: 1, but in a sense that accords with the later stratum rather than with Ephesians.

If then it is concluded that 1 Cor 7: 17f, 20 are additions from the later stratum, vs. 24 must also be included in this category, since it simply repeats the import of vs. 20 in very similar words. If then 7: 17f, 20, 24 are peeled away, the following remains:

> 1 Cor 7: 18 Was anyone called having been circumcised? Let him not be uncircumcised. Was anyone called in uncircumcision? Let him not be circumcised. 7: 19 Circumcision is nothing, and uncircumcision is nothing, but keeping the commandments of God. 7: 21 Were you called as a slave? Let it not matter to you; but if you are able to become free, rather use it. 7: 22 For the one called as a slave is the Lord's freedman; he is the slave of Christ. 7: 23 You were bought with a price. Do not become the slaves of people.

Not only does the passage now read more smoothly and coherently, but it harmonizes with the stance of chapter seven as a whole, that freedom from the ties of the present world order is preferable to attachment (vss. 8, 27–31, 32ff). Thus slaves are advised to obtain their freedom if the opportunity presents itself though assured that whether one is a slave or freeman is immaterial (vss. 14, 16). The material added from the later stratum in vss. 17–24 evidently attempts to apply to slaves the injunctions to wives and husbands not to abandon the marriage bond. In this way the advice to slaves in vss. 21–3 is brought into accord with the view of the later stratum that one's social station is divinely assigned and normative for the Christian calling.

Conclusion

In 1 Cor 10, 11, and 14 it has become evident, as in 1 Peter, that the later stratum extends well beyond specific subjectionist passages. In particular the association of 1 Cor 11: 2–16 with the later stratum has important implications for the ten-letter corpus as a whole, for it implicates not only its immediate surroundings, but also other material in 1 Corinthians as well as a fairly large section in Romans. Furthermore, if the findings thus far are to be sustained, it is necessary to investigate connections with parts of 1 and 2 Thessalonians, where similar material is in evidence.

The later stratum in 1 and 2 Thessalonians

While each of the Thessalonian epistles contains material bearing a distinct resemblance to the later stratum as thus far identified, 2 Thessalonians presents the less complicated problem. It will therefore be given prior consideration, which will facilitate examination of 1 Thessalonians.

The later stratum in 2 Thessalonians

Though usually accepted as genuine, the Pauline origin of 2 Thessalonians has been seriously questioned.[182] The issue does not, however, affect the present inquiry, for no more than a small amount of material appears to cohere with the later stratum, while the rest is evidently earlier, whether or not it is the work of Paul.

The major portion appearing to belong to the later stratum is 2 Thess 3: 6–15, a self-contained unit of paraenesis.[183] Stylistically the passage is to be distinguished from the rest of the epistle and associated with the later stratum for its use of antithetic parallelism. There are six occurrences in the nineteen lines of the passage, a rate of 3.2 lines to each occurrence, compared with only one in the 77.5 lines of the rest of the epistle (cf. 2: 12). What is more, this characteristic is combined with sentence structure very similar to that found in the later material.[184]

Also reminiscent of the later stratum is the use of the compound word καλοποιοῦντες in 3: 13, recalling the occurrence of ἀγαθοποιεῖν, ἀγαθοποιός, and ἀγαθοποιία in the later stratum of 1 Peter (cf. 2: 14f, 20, 3: 6, 17, 4: 19); ἔχομεν ἐξουσίαν in 2 Thess 3: 9, which like ἐξουσίαν ἔχειν in 1 Cor 11: 10 seems to echo οὐκ ἐξουσίαν μὴ ἐργάζεσθαι in 1 Cor 9: 6, particularly since here the expression also occurs in close proximity to ἐργάζεσθαι (cf. 2 Thess 3: 8f);[185] and τύπος in close conjunction with the idea of imitation in 2 Thess 3: 9 as in 1 Pet 5: 3.[186]

As for the content of the passage, here again the thought and interests are exceedingly close to those of the later stratum. The concern that members of the Christian community should work for a living, as did the apostles, recalls Eph 4: 28, which it was concluded is part of the later stratum.[187] While, however, Eph 4: 28 urges manual work as an alternative to theft and in order to have the means to contribute to help the needy, 2 Thess 3: 6–15 seems to aim at eliminating dependence on the church for the means of subsistence. What the latter seeks to combat, however, is not the distribution of charitable gifts but, it is suggested here, support for what is regarded as unauthorized leadership in Christian congregations.

Those who conduct themselves in a manner described as ἀτάκτως (vss. 6, 11) are not castigated for sheer idleness as opposed to work as is commonly concluded.[188] From the word περιεργαζόμενος in 3:11 it is clear that they are by no means inactive, but on the contrary busy themselves to a greater degree than they should in ways of which the writer disapproves. The term has the sense of being over-active, wasting one's efforts, being officious and meddling in affairs which do not concern one.[189] In keeping with these senses, ἀτακτεῖν (vs. 7) and ἀτάκτως have the connotations of being undisciplined, irregular, insubordinate, lawless, and even rebellious and riotous. In military contexts the words refer to troops who are not in battle order or at their assigned post.[190] These meanings are particularly relevant to the description of the people involved as 'not walking according to the tradition received from' the apostles (μὴ κατὰ τὴν παράδοσιν ἣν παρελάβοσαν παρ' ἡμῶν, vs. 6). Such an interpretation accords with the connection drawn between the passing on of tradition and the observance of church order in 1 Cor 11.[191] Then too in 1 Clement the word ἀτάκτως is used in a context which concerns the ordering of varying functions in the church, compared to the Roman army with its officers who are praised amongst other things for their 'good order' (cf. εὐτάκτως in 37:11f). That is to say, each discharges his duty according to his rank (τάγμα) in perfect submission to superiors (cf. 37:2ff). In 1 Clem 40:2, ἀτάκτως is used of those who are disorderly in the celebration of sacrifices and services, not observing the times, places, and persons fixed by God's will. The passage goes on to distinguish between the 'proper' (ἴδιος) ministrations of the high priest in Jerusalem, the 'proper' place of the priests, and the 'proper' services of the Levites. Similarly the laity have their particular functions (cf. vs. 5). Here then the person who behaves ἀτάκτως disturbs this order by doing what he has no business to do.

It is suggested that the implications of the terms ἀτάκτως and ἀτακτεῖν in 2 Thess 3:6–15 are of a similar nature and are aimed at doing away with material support for unauthorized persons who exercise charismata which conflict or overlap with the duties assigned to church officials.[192] Instead of expecting to receive their means of subsistence from Christian congregations, they are to desist from their disorderly activities and work for a living, as did the apostle Paul and his companions (vss. 7f). If they do not wish to work in this sense they must do without (vs. 10) and if they do not heed these instructions, they are to be excluded from the fellowship (vss. 6, 14).

This interpretation accords with the attitude to ecclesiastical assemblies and observances expressed in 1 Cor 11. The exclusion of disorderly and schismatic elements which is implicit in that context (cf. vss. 18f) is quite explicit in 2 Thess 3: 6–15. The same kind of thinking is evidently present also in 1 Cor 14: 33–8, which warns that anyone who disregards or fails to recognize the rule silencing women in assemblies will be disregarded or denied recognition (ἀγνοεῖται, vs. 38).

Then too, there is an appeal to the tradition passed on by the apostles, as in 1 Cor 11, again in close association with the ideas of remembering and imitating.[193] Though there is no specific term for remembering in 2 Thess 3: 6–15, it is implied in the use of the word οἴδατε instead of μεμνῆσθαι for the calling to mind of the apostolic example.

It is to be observed too that as in 1 Cor 14: 37, what the apostle is purported to have written has absolute authority (2 Thess 3: 14), which means it has a status akin to canonicity.[194] This, like the exhortations to remember and to imitate the apostle and his fellow workers, would seem to indicate a time somewhat later than the lifetime of Paul.

At the same time, 2 Thess 3: 6–15 also resembles parts of the Pauline corpus that are evidently not to be included with the later material. In the first place, as already mentioned, there is the use of the expression ἔχομεν ἐξουσίαν in close conjunction with ἐργαζόμαι in vss. 8f as in 1 Cor 9: 6, where the same words occur in the rhetorical question, οὐκ ἔχομεν ἐξουσίαν μὴ ἐργάζεσθαι. It is evident, however, that the surface similarity in wording overlies a distinct difference in thought and intention, for in the context of 1 Cor 9 and the epistle as a whole, the apostle is engaged in a defence of his status as an apostle alongside Cephas and others (cf. 1 Cor 9: 5 with 3: 22, 4: 6), and seeks amongst other things to establish his right to similar privileges, including material support, even though he did not demand such support in Corinth, but worked for a living.

In 2 Thess 3: 6–15, however, it is not the status of Paul and his fellow apostles that is at issue, but rather the position of the ἄτακτοι. That the apostles worked for a living is explained as due, not to their lack of authority, but in order to provide an example of hard work and industry (3: 8f).[195]

There is evidence for thinking that 2 Thess 3: 6–15 conflates elements from different parts of the corpus, as the following parallels show:

2 Thess 3: 8f ἐν κόπῳ καὶ μόχθῳ νυκτὸς καὶ ἡμέρας ἐργαζόμενοι πρὸς τὸ μὴ ἐπιβαρῆσαί τινα ὑμῶν· . . . εἰς τὸ μιμεῖσθαι ἡμᾶς.

2 Cor 11: 27 κόπῳ καὶ μόχθῳ, ἐν ἀγρυπνίαις πολλάκις,

1 Thess 3: 10 νυκτὸς καὶ ἡμέρας ὑπερεκπερισσοῦ δεόμενοι εἰς τὸ ἰδεῖν ὑμῶν

The fact that 2 Thess 3: 8 echoes not only the wording but also the sentence structure of both 2 Cor 11: 27 and 1 Thess 3: 10 weighs against the points of contact being mere chance, and in favour of deliberate conflation, which in turn points to the possibility that the former passage is later than the two other texts.

Viewing the passage next in its immediate context, it is evident that the continuity of the closing exhortations, prayers, and blessing before the farewell greetings is markedly improved if read without 3: 6-15. The prayer in 3: 5 that the Lord might direct the hearts of the recipients 'to the love of God and the endurance of Christ' finds a more natural sequence in the prayer in 3: 16 that the Lord of peace might give them peace than in the extended instructions in 3: 6-15.[196]

In the broader context of the epistle as a whole, the unity and clarity of the letter are considerably improved if one assumes that 3: 6-15 is a later accretion. The intention of the letter as stated in the opening to the body[197] in 2: 1f is to urge the recipients not to be excited by reports that the 'day of the Lord' has come. The material in 3: 6-15, however, makes no explicit contact with the theme of the *parousia*. The assumption that it has to do with people who were refraining from working because of the illusion that the *parousia* has arrived or is on the verge of doing so[198] finds no confirmation whatever within this passage.

The injunctions in 3: 6-15 do however seem to be anticipated at two points earlier in the letter, 2: 15 and 3: 4. The first, in urging firm adherence to any word or letter from the apostles, makes contact with the reference to apostolic teaching and tradition by word and letter in 3: 6-15 (cf. vss. 6, 10, 14). The second (3: 4) expresses confidence that those addressed 'are doing and will do the things that we command'. Occurring as it does immediately before the prayer preceding 3: 6ff, the use of the word παραγγέλλομεν in 3: 4 as in 3: 6 has the appearance of a conscious attempt to provide some link between 3: 6-15 and the material that precedes it. Though 2: 15 occurs a little earlier in the text, it could well have the same intention. It is noteworthy that neither 2: 15 nor 3: 4 is integral to the thought sequence of its immediate context, and 3: 4 has relevance only in relation to 3: 6-15, for the rest of the letter is not concerned with instructions as to what the congregation is to do, but with expectations and states of mind. It is suggested that both these verses are to be regarded as redactional additions issuing from the same source as 3: 6-15.

It is concluded, then, that 2 Thess 2: 15, 3: 4, and 3: 6-15 are to be accounted part of the later stratum.

The later stratum in 1 Thessalonians

Turning next to 1 Thessalonians, it appears that here too there is an intermingling of different strata. The first passage to attract attention for its resemblance to the material cohering together in the later stratum is 4: 1–12.

The passage resembles material included in the later stratum, specifically 2 Thess 3: 6–15 and Eph 4: 28, in that it exhorts Christians to 'work with their hands' (ἐργάζεσθαι ταῖς χερσὶν ὑμῶν, 1 Thess 4: 11), giving as a motive that they should be self-supporting instead of depending on others (probably the rest of the Christian community) for the means of subsistence (cf. ἵνα . . . μηδενὸς χρείαν ἔχητε in 1 Thess 4: 12). By this means they will behave with decorum and propriety before[199] those without (vs. 12). Here then there is the same concern for good relations with the surrounding society as has appeared in various parts of the later stratum.[200]

What is more, the expression πράσσειν τὰ ἴδια in 1 Thess 4: 11 embodies what is probably the underlying concept in the injunction μὴ . . . ὡς ἀλλοτριεπίσκοπος in 1 Pet 4: 15,[201] which occurs in material judged to belong to the later stratum in 1 Peter. That is to say, it implies the idea that each should be employed in that which pertains to his own nature and position in society, fulfilling his own role. This notion is present too in 2 Thess 3: 6–15, in that it is directed against the disorderly who evidently go beyond their recognized roles and trespass on the duties and affairs of others.[202]

In addition the passage has significant links with Eph 5: 21–3 in its teaching on sexual relations, whether the word σκεῦος (literally a vessel) in 1 Thess 4: 4 is taken to mean 'wife' or 'body'. In the context of the later stratum the latter is the more probable,[203] but then the body referred to is evidently a man's own (τὸ ἑαυτοῦ σκεῦος) as distinct from that which belongs to others. In the same way Eph 5: 21–33 refers to men's own bodies (τὰ ἑαυτῶν σώματα, vs. 28) and a man's own flesh (τὴν ἑαυτοῦ σάρκα, vs. 29). Clearly in the Ephesian passage the body or flesh referred to is a man's wife (cf. τὰς ἑαυτῶν γυναῖκας, vs. 28). Similarly, if 1 Thess 4: 1–12 is viewed as part of the later stratum, and κτᾶσθαι is taken in its usual sense,[204] the expression τὸ ἑαυτοῦ σκεῦος κτᾶσθαι may be understood to mean to acquire a body (i.e., a wife) of one's own, which is to say, to marry. This conclusion receives confirmation from the exhortation not to wrong one's brother (vs. 6), presumably a reference to adultery.[205] It accords also with the expression ἀσθενεστέρῳ σκεύει τῷ γυναικείῳ (the weaker feminine vessel or body) in the later stratum in 1 Peter (3: 7). Here, though σκεῦος means body rather than wife, it is clear that the word is used of a man's wife. Here as in 1 Thess 4: 1-12 there is mention of 'honour' (τιμή) in the relationship (1 Pet 3: 7, 1 Thess 4: 4). In 1 Thess 4: 1-12 as in Eph 5: 21-33 there is also mention of holiness (cf. ἁγιασμός in 1 Thess 4: 2, 4, 7, and ἁγιάσῃ in Eph 5: 26 and ἁγία in Eph 5: 27). It seems then that 1 Thess 4: 1-12 is urging each man in the Christian community to acquire a wife (vs. 4) as a safeguard against immorality (vss. 3-5)[206] in opposition, perhaps, to a type of gnostic rigorism which eschews marriage.[207]

1 Thess 4: 1-12 is reminiscent of the later stratum also in its use of compound words from nouns and/or adjectives and/or verbs (cf. φιλαδελφίας and θεοδίδακτοι in vs. 9, and φιλοτιμεῖσθαι in vs. 11). Then too the expression πρὸς τοὺς ἔξω in vs. 12 occurs elsewhere in the New Testament only in Col 4: 5[208] which was included in the later stratum.[209]

As for contextual factors, it is evident that material giving expression to intense eschatological expectations is interrupted to voice very different concerns. Immediately before 1 Thess 4: 1-12 there is mention of 'the *parousia* of our Lord Jesus with all his saints', and immediately after 4: 12 there is the assurance that 'God will bring with him those who have fallen asleep' so that those who are left alive till the *parousia* of the Lord will not precede those who have 'fallen asleep' (4: 14f). A description of the expected event follows (4: 16-18), after which there is a call to readiness lest the *parousia* come upon the elect unawares (5: 1-11). In 4: 1-12, by contrast, there is no reference or allusion whatever to the *parousia*.

Some manuscripts, versions, and early fathers include the word ἀμήν after αὐτοῦ in 3: 13, immediately before 4: 1,[210] as if attempting to round off the preceding section in view of the sudden change of subject. This is to be rejected as the original reading, however, since it is easier to account for it as a subsequent addition to smooth the abruptness of the transition between 3: 13 and 4: 1 than as something omitted by chance in the process of transmission.

Stylistically the passage resembles the later stratum in its frequent use of antithetic parallelism, in particular in its combination of the negative with ἀλλά and a comparative word or phrase; cf. μὴ . . . καθάπερ καὶ . . . τὰ μὴ . . . τὸ μὴ . . . καθὼς καί in vss. 5f, and οὐ γὰρ . . . ἀλλ' . . . οὐκ . . . ἀλλά in vss. 7f. In the twenty-seven lines of 1 Thess 4: 1-12 there are six antithetic parallels, or 4.5 lines to each occurrence. In this respect the passage differs from the rest of the epistle, with certain exceptions, as shown in the table:

Passages in 1 Thessalonians	No. of antithetic parallels	No. of lines	No. of lines to each occurrence
1: 1 – 2: 2	2	28.7	14.4
2: 1–16	8	34	4.3
2: 17 – 3: 13	1	36.5	36.5
4: 13–18	0	14	–
5: 1–11	3	18.5	6.2
5: 12–28	2	21	10.5

It will be observed that the trait occurs with some frequency in 2: 1–16 and 5: 1–11. It is unlikely, however, that the latter belongs to the later stratum, for its concepts and vocabulary are far closer to the earlier paraenetic material in Ephesians, and the earlier material in Rom 12, 13 and in 1 Peter.[211]

Then too, like the earlier material in Rom 12 and 13, the antithetic parallels in 1 Thess 5: 1–11 arise from the sharp eschatological dualism expressed in the day–night, light–darkness contrast, and the accompanying distinctions (cf. vss. 5, 6, 9). In 4: 1–12, however, as in the later material in Rom 12, 13,[212] the antithetic statements concern the contrast between that which Christians are to avoid and the good they are to follow.

By contrast, the two antithetic parallels in 1 Thess 5: 12–28 are not of the eschatological kind, but rather resemble what was found in 4: 1–12 (cf. 5: 15, 21f). In 5: 15, 21b, 22 the parallels are clearly of the 'two ways', good-evil kind, such as is typical of the later stratum, in particular in Rom 12.[213] In addition, 1 Thess 5: 15 closely corresponds with the wording of Rom 12: 17.[214] Similarly 1 Thess 5: 16–19 makes contact with the wording of Rom 12: 11–15.[215] At not all points, however, are the resemblances confined to the later stratum in Rom 12. The exhortations to rejoice, pray, and give thanks are typical of the conclusions to Pauline letters.[216] Then too the encouragement of the spirit and prophecy, albeit with the proviso that prophets be tested (1 Thess 5: 19f, 21), accords with earlier Paulinism.[217] The most obvious solution is that a mingling of strata is present in 5: 12–28. The material in 5: 12–15 appears to belong to the later stratum, for it contains the compound words ὀλιγόψυχος and μακροθυμεῖτε in vs. 14. The term ἀτάκτους in the same sentence recalls the admonitions against disorder in 2 Thess 3: 6–15.[218]

Contextually considered, the passage does not contain obvious interruptions in the flow of thought. Additional material could, however, have been inserted with minimal disruption into a loosely connected series of exhortations. The sequence from 5: 11, concerning mutual upbuilding among community members, to 5: 16–21a enjoining them to rejoice, pray, give thanks, and not to quench the spirit or despise prophesying, is plausible, as is also the transition from these brief injunctions to the theme of 5: 23 urging a state of sanctity in expectation of the *parousia*.

It is concluded then that 5: 12–15, 21*b*, 22 are to be assigned to the later stratum. The scores for the use of antithetic parallels may accordingly be adjusted as in the table:

Passages in 1 Thessalonians	No. of antithetic parallels	No. of lines	No. of lines to each occurrence
5: 12–15, 21*b*, 22	2	9.5	4.8
5: 17–21*a*, 23–28	0	11.5	–

What is to be said then of 1 Thess 2: 1–16, which manifests the same use of antithetic parallelism?[219] The passage also resembles the later stratum in general in its language and thought, and accompanying the antithetic parallelism already mentioned is a similarity in sentence structure, as may be seen from the οὐ . . . ἀλλά sequences with ὡς, καθώς, and οὕτως; cf. vss. 1f, 3f, 6f, 8 and 13.

There is a distinct change of subject at 2: 1, but this is to be expected, since at 1: 10 the letter reaches an eschatological climax, as is customary at the close of the introductory thanksgiving in the Pauline epistles.[220]

On this basis White has pointed tentatively to 2: 1–4 as the body-opening section of the epistle, which is introduced by a body-opening formula in 2: 1. In identifying the structural elements of such formulae, White judged that 1 Thess 2: 1 follows the pattern of a 'disclosure formula' such as he found also in Gal 1: 11, Rom 1: 13, Phil 1: 12, and 2 Cor 1: 8, for it consists of a verb of disclosure (οἴδατε), a vocative of address (ἀδελφοί), and the subject disclosed, introduced by ὅτι.[221]

It is to be observed, however, that 1 Thess 2: 1 does not accord as easily with the disclosure pattern White identified as do the equivalents in the other instances he cited. In the first place, while each of the others consists of a verb of desiring in the first person, together with a verb of knowing[222] (with the exception of Gal 1: 11, where there is only a verb of revealing, γνωρίζειν), 1 Thess 2: 1 uses only a verb of knowing, in the second person, not the first. Thus the sentence is a statement about what those addressed already know, and not what the writers intend to disclose to them. The structure then is somewhat less than that of a typical disclosure formula.[223]

As for the function of 2: 1–4, the material resembles the equivalent passages in the Pauline letters to which White referred in that it establishes 'a basis for mutuality'.[224] It certainly leads into the subject matter of 2: 5–16, which concerns the teaching role of the apostolic group in exhorting their hearers to holy living and providing models for conduct that is pleasing to God. It also makes contact with the teaching in 4: 1–12 on living so as to please God (4: 1). In addition the emphasis on the exemplary character of the apostle and his companions relates to their example of self-supporting work (2: 9), which in turn anticipates the teaching to this effect in 4: 11f. So too the apostolic character and role described in 2: 1–13 can be connected with the exhortation to give recognition to ecclesiastical leaders in 5: 12f. Significantly, however, 1 Thess 2: 1–4 makes no obvious contact with the main interests of the rest of the epistle, which has to do with the apostolic desire to return to the Thessalonians, and their relation to the *parousia* (cf. 2: 17 – 3: 13, 4: 13 – 5: 11).

This discontinuity receives emphasis from the fact that 2: 1ff proceeds without interruption until 2: 16, where there is an abrupt break. Yet the sentence in 2: 1f resembles 2: 17 in a number of ways. Each contains the vocative of address, ἀδελφοί, with a participial construction (προπαθόντες καὶ ὑβρισθέντες in 2: 2, ἀπορφανισθέντες in 2: 17) and an ἐν phrase containing the adjective πολύς at the end of the sentence (ἐν πολλῷ ἀγῶνι in 2: 2, ἐν πολλῇ ἐπιθυμίᾳ in 2: 17). In addition, 2: 1f contains the phrase πρὸς ὑμᾶς twice over, while the same phrase occurs also in 2: 18. Then too, Αὐτοὶ γὰρ οἴδατε in 2: 1 could be borrowed from 3: 3.

If 2: 1–16 is in fact a later addition to the epistle, it follows that the resemblances between 2: 1f and 2: 17ff are due to efforts to model the former on the latter, in order to achieve a convincing transition. That would mean that 2: 17 was originally joined to 1: 10.

Assuming that Sanders and White are correct in taking 1: 10 to be the close to the thanksgiving section, there should be a body opening at 2: 17, falling into the pattern of a body-opening formula. The material in 2: 17f does not follow any of the Pauline body-opening formulae identified by White,[225] but it resembles the most frequent disclosure type in that it contains a vocative of address (ἀδελφοί), a verb of desiring (ἐσπουδάσαμεν) followed by an infinitive (ἰδεῖν), a reference to those addressed (τὸ πρόσωπον ὑμῶν) which establishes mutuality, and the conjunction διότι, which has the same force as ὅτι when used causally.

If this does in fact represent a body-opening formula, it departs from the usual disclosure type in that the infinitive is not a verb of disclosure, but of seeing. This can, however, be explained as due to the fact that the letter is in a very immediate sense a substitute for the presence in particular of Paul. His desire to be present in person with the Thessalonians receives the strongest possible emphasis through the expansion of Ἡμεῖς by the phrase ἀπορφανισθέντες ἀφ’ ὑμῶν πρὸς καιρὸν ὥρας, προσώπῳ οὐ καρδίᾳ, and of ἐσπουδάσαμεν by means of the words περισσοτέρως … ἐν πολλῇ ἐπιθυμίᾳ. What remains if these expansions are set aside is very close to the characteristic disclosure formula, and actually closer to it than 2:1.

On this basis the body-opening section to the body of the epistle is probably 2:17–20, which establishes mutuality in the strongest possible fashion, and relates Paul's eagerness to be present to the expectation of the *parousia* of 'our Lord Jesus' (2:19). That is to say, 2:17–20 points to the major theme of the epistle as elaborated in 4:13 – 5:10, which is precisely what 2:1–4 does not do.

Alternatively, to follow Schubert, the opening thanksgiving includes 2:17 – 3:13,[226] with the eschatological climax occurring at 3:13, and the opening to the body of the letter at 4:13. In 4:13 there are all the typical elements of a disclosure formula, a verb of desiring in the first person (θέλομεν), a verb of knowing (οὐ ἀγνοεῖν), a vocative of address (ἀδελφοί) and the subject disclosed (περί ... ἵνα). Nevertheless, the thanksgiving section (1:1–5a, 6b, 8–10, 2:17 – 3:13) is still unwieldy in relation to the rest of the epistle. Thus the body opening is more probably to be located at 2:17.

In contrast both to 2:17–20 and 4:13, 2:1–4 points forward quite specifically to the content of those passages assigned to the later stratum, as already indicated.[227]

Indeed, 2:1–16 as a whole has unmistakable affinity with them. In 2:2f the 'gospel of God' is clearly identified with παράκλησις, which is the substantive form of παρακαλοῦμεν, used in 4:1. While 2:3 dissociates this teaching from 'uncleanness' and 2:10 points to the apostolic group as examples of holy, righteous, and blameless living, 4:3–7 speaks of the necessity for holiness as opposed to fornication and uncleanness (vs. 7). While 2:9 recalls the unceasing toil and labour of the apostles to avoid burdening their converts, 4:11 instructs the congregation to 'work with their hands' as the apostle charged them. In 2:12 there is reference to the apostolic charge to 'walk' worthily of God, while 4:1 and 4:12 use the same terminology of proper conduct. Moreover, 4:1–12 appears quite consciously to build on and develop the idea of imitation of the apostolic example in 2:1–16, which is bound up with the concept of transmission of right tradition from God himself through the apostolic group to those who come after them (cf. 2: 2, 4, 13, 4:1f). This receives emphasis from the father-son imagery (2:11), which is traditionally related to the notion of transmission as well as imitation.[228]

At the same time the imitation theme pervading 2:1–16 and 4:1–12 connects these parts of the epistle with 1:5–7 in what has been characterized as the thanksgiving section. Here too one finds the idea of imitation of the apostolic example, and of the church as a τύπος for those who come after them, corresponding with the imitation of earlier believers according to 2:14.

Here too, however, there are signs of an insertion into the earlier version of the text. First, an indication of a possible seam appears in the fact that the phrases ἐν δυνάμει καὶ ἐν πνεύματι ἁγίῳ καὶ (ἐν) πληροφορία πολλῇ in vs. 5 find a sequel in ἐν φλίψει πολλῇ in the second half of vs. 6. The similarity between (ἐν) πληροφορία πολλῇ and ἐν θλίψει πολλῇ suggests that an insertion may begin with the former and continue till immediately before the latter, or begin after the former and end immediately after the latter. The first possibility appears more likely, since ἐν θλίψει πολλῇ forms a balancing contrast to μετὰ χαρᾶς πνεύματος ἁγίου which follows immediately after it.

Then too, there is stylistic awkwardness in the repetition of ἐν τῇ Μακεδονίᾳ καὶ (ἐν) τῇ Ἀχαΐᾳ in 1:7 and 1:8, giving the impression of yet another seam. In this instance the first occurrence of the words seems to mark the clause that has been inserted, for it contains the word τύπος which is one of the elements connecting this part of the thanksgiving section with 2:1-16, 4:1-12.

The material underscored in the reproduction of 1:5-8 given below indicates that which appears to have been added, and the rest that which is judged to be the original:

1 Thess 1:5 ὅτι τὸ εὐαγγέλιον ἡμῶν οὐκ ἐγενήθη εἰς ὑμᾶς ἐν λόγῳ μόνον ἀλλὰ καὶ ἐν δυνάμει καὶ ἐν πνεύματι ἁγίῳ καὶ [ἐν] πληροφορία πολλῇ, καθὼς οἴδατε οἷοι ἐγενήθημεν [ἐν] ὑμῖν δι' ὑμᾶς. 6 καὶ ὑμεῖς μιμηταὶ ἡμῶν ἐγενήθητε καὶ τοῦ κυρίου, δεξάμενοι τὸν λόγον ἐν θλίψει πολλῇ μετὰ χαρᾶς πνεύματος ἁγίου, 7 ὥστε γενέσθαι ὑμᾶς τύπον πᾶσιν τοῖς πιστεύουσιν ἐν τῇ Μακεδονίᾳ καὶ ἐν τῇ Ἀχαΐᾳ. 8 ἀφ' ὑμῶν γὰρ ἐξήχηται ὁ λόγος τοῦ κυρίου οὐ μόνον ἐν τῇ Μακεδονίᾳ καὶ [ἐν τῇ] Ἀχαΐᾳ, ἀλλ' ἐν παντὶ τόπῳ ἡ πίστις ὑμῶν ἡ πρὸς τὸν θεὸν ἐξελήλυθεν,...

The fact that this brings the phrases ἐν πνεύματι ἁγίῳ and μετὰ χαρᾶς πνεύματος ἁγίου in close association suggests that one or the other is part of the suggested insertion in 1:5f. The regular patterning evident in the οὐκ ... ἐν ... μόνον ἀλλὰ καὶ ἐν ... καὶ ἐν ... καὶ ἐν sequence in 1:5f, followed by the very similar οὐ μόνον ἐν ... καὶ (ἐν) ... ἀλλα' ἐν sequence in 1:8 suggests, furthermore, that they are designed to form stylistic parallels. The rhythm of the pattern is improved, however, if an ἐν phrase is eliminated in 1:5f; hence it is concluded that καὶ ἐν πνεύματι ἁγίῳ is additional to the original.

Again, it seems, the later stratum has interrupted earlier material where there is mention of suffering undergone by Christians.[229] Here it is brought into relation with the imitation theme which receives elaboration in 2:1–16. In the latter there is evidently an attempt to neutralize the references in 2:17–3:8 to the affliction suffered by the apostles and the Thessalonian church. As if to counter any adverse impressions, it is explained that the apostles did not suffer because of any evil-doing, for they were righteous and blameless (2:3, 10), that they spoke not to please men but God (2:4), and that they did not use words of flattery or seek glory from men (2:5f). Similarly those who heeded their words accepted them not as the word of men but of God (οὐ λόγον ἀνθρώπων ἀλλά ... λόγον Θεοῦ, 2:13), and suffered in like manner. The opposition and affliction they endured is ascribed to the perversity of the local inhabitants, who are placed in the same category as the Jews 'who killed both the Lord Jesus and the prophets', who drove out Paul and his companions, and 'displeased God and opposed all men' (Θεῷ μὴ ἀρεσκόντων, καὶ πᾶσιν ἀνθρώποις ἐναντίων, 2:15) and hindered the apostles from preaching to the Gentiles, but 'wrath has come upon them' at last or 'to the uttermost' (εἰς τέλος).[230] By these means it seems, the later stratum attempts to dissociate the church and its past leaders from the odium attached to the Jews.[231] Though this passage rejects ingratiation in theory, it apparently aims at winning the good will of Graeco-Roman society, as does also the rest of the later stratum.[232]

On the basis of these findings the later stratum seems to appear in 1 Thess 1:5b, 6a, 7, 2:1–16, 4:1–12, 5:12–15, 21b, 22,[233] while 1 Thess 1:1–5a, 6b, 8–10, 2:17–3:13, 4:13–5:11, 16–21a, 23–8 appears to be earlier.

Conclusion

It is concluded then that the later stratum extends across 1 and 2 Thessalonians, where it deals in particular with ecclesiastical office, and seeks to eliminate the unauthorized activites of charismatics. While the former are to be honoured for their labour in the congregation, the latter are to be cast out unless they desist and find self-supporting work elsewhere. The apostles serve as a model of physical work to the disorderly, and of diligent labour in teaching the word for recognized leaders.

Conclusion

From examination of the subjection material in the ten-letter Pauline corpus and 1 Peter, it is concluded, first, that it represents later additions to the text and, secondly, that it coheres with other material in a fairly extensive post-Pauline stratum. The passages identified in the Pauline

ten-letter collection are Rom 12: 9–11*a*, 12*c*–21, 13: 1–10, 14: 1 - 15: 6;
1 Cor 7: 17*b*, 20, 24, 8: 1–12, 10: 23 – 11: 29, 33f; Eph 4: 28f, 32*c*, 5: 1,
2*a*, 15–18*a*, 21 – 6: 9; Col 3: 18 - 4: 1, 5; 1 Thess 1: 5*b*, 6*a*, 7, 2: 1–16,
4: 1–12, 5: 12–15, 21*b*, 22; 2 Thess 2: 15, 3: 4, 6–15. In 1 Peter the later
stratum is judged to consist of 1: 14–19, 21*c*–23, 2: 1–3, 8*b*, 11–20, 21*c*,
22–5, 3: 1–9, 17, 19–22*a*, 4: 1*b*, 2–6, 7*b*, 8f, 11*b*–16, 19, 5: 1–5*ab*.

Yet other amendments and additions are probably involved in the
Pauline letters,[234] but enough has been associated with the later stratum
to indicate that it belongs to a major revision of the corpus to bring Paul
into alignment with the point of view of the later stratum. The revision of
1 Peter evidently seeks to do the same for the apostle Peter in order to
place him alongside Paul in support of the point of view the later stratum
seeks to promote.

Where this stratum belongs in early Christian history and the redactional history of the epistles will become clearer when its literary affinities
have been determined. Association with material belonging to a milieu and
stage of development later than the primitive will, moreover, provide
significant confirmation for the foregoing textual analysis. To this kind
of consideration the study will now turn with reference to the Pastoral
epistles.

3 THE LATER STRATUM AND THE PASTORAL EPISTLES

The subjection material in the context of the Pastorals

The identification of a later stratum in the ten-letter Pauline corpus and 1 Peter raises the question of its relation to the Pastoral epistles. There is a strong likelihood that the stratum belongs to roughly the same stage of Christian history for, like the Pastorals, it is evidently subsequent to Ephesians.[1] Moreover, the later stratum differs to such a degree from earlier material in tendencies and outlook that it cannot be supposed that it issued from the same circles at a slightly later time. On the other hand, it is not necessary to assume that it is a distinctive strain in the Pauline corpus to be differentiated from all others. As will be shown, the later stratum in the ten letters and in 1 Peter is close enough to the Pastorals to assume that it emanates from the same circle or school of tradition.

There is obviously some close connection between the Pastorals and much that has been assigned to the later stratum. According to the code and catechetical theories, some parts of the Pastoral epistles draw on or reflect the same or a similar earlier oral source included in the stratum in the present study. Dibelius assumed that 1 Tim 2: 8ff, 6: 1, and Tit. 2: 1-10 are to be categorized as belonging to the same genre as the *Haustafeln*,[2] and K. Weidinger regarded them, along with the whole of 1 Tim 2, and, indeed, the entire middle part of 1 Timothy, as reminiscent of the *Haustafeln*.[3]

P. Carrington's more extensive parallels have no place for the Pastorals.[4] Selwyn, on the other hand, included 1 Tim 2: 1-3 and Tit 3: 1 among the passages in his postulated 'code of subordination' which has to do with civic obedience, 1 Tim 6: 1f among those relating to slaves and masters, and 1 Tim 2: 9-15 and Tit 2: 4f among those relating to wives and husbands.[5]

To apply here the same kinds of considerations used elsewhere, it could be said that the similarities are of a kind to suggest the possible presence of

the later stratum in the Pastorals. Contextual examination of the passages
involved does not, however, reveal sufficient reason to dissociate them
from their immediate surroundings because they interrupt otherwise continuous material, or because they differ in thought and outlook from the
rest of each epistle involved.[6] On the contrary, they are integral to the
thought and intention of the Pastorals as a whole, as will be shown. It is
true that the transitions between 1 Tim 1: 20 and 2:1, 2:15 and 3:1ff,
5: 25 and 6: 1, and 6: 2 and 6: 3 are somewhat abrupt, but nothing is
gained in terms of coherence or continuity by assuming they represent
interpolations.[7]

Moreover, there is underlying continuity in that 1 Tim 1: 18 - 6: 20
is concerned throughout with the ordering of authority and practice in
the church. Indeed, the interconnected themes of church order and
opposition to heresy go hand in hand in unifying the loosely connected
series of instructions and exhortations making up 1 Timothy. Its rambling
character may be regarded as a stylistic trait, such as occurs also in certain
continuous blocks of the later stratum in the ten-letter collection and in
1 Peter.[8]

The injunction in Tit 3: 1 to remind the Christian community to subject
themselves to rulers and authorities (ἀρχαῖς ἐξουσίαις ὑποτάσσεσθαι) contains the same terminology as the direct instruction to the same effect in
Rom 13:1 (cf. ἐξουσίαις ὑπερεχούσαις ὑποτασσέσθω). Similarly 1 Tim
2:1f, requiring the community to pray and give thanks for kings and rulers
(βασιλέων καὶ πάντων τῶν ἐν ὑπεροχῇ ὄντων, vs. 2), uses much the same
words for these persons as does the injunction to obey them in 1 Pet 2:13
(cf. βασιλεῖ ὡς ὑπερέχοντι).

In the same way, the phrase ὑποτασσομένας τοῖς ἰδίοις ἀνδράσιν in Tit
2: 5, concerning the duty of wives to submit to husbands, comes close to
ὑποτασσόμενοι . . . αἱ γυναῖκες, τοῖς ἰδίοις ἀνδράσιν in Eph 5: 21f, and
γυναῖκες, ὑποτασσόμεναι τοῖς ἰδίοις ἀνδρασιν in 1 Pet 3: 1.

Then too 1 Tim 2: 9–15 makes contact with no fewer than three parts
of the later stratum that have to do with women. Its regulation of
feminine attire and adornment in vss. 9f closely resembles 1 Pet 3: 3–5
(cf. κοσμεῖν . . . χρυσίῳ . . . ἱματισμῷ πολυτελεῖ, 1 Tim 2: 9; χρυσίων . . .
ἱματίων . . . πολυτελές ἐκόσμουν, 1 Pet 3: 3–5). The same can be said of
the silencing of women in vss. 11f as in 1 Cor 14: 24f (cf. γυνὴ ἐν ἡσυχίᾳ
μανθανέτω ἐν πάσῃ ὑποταγῇ, 1 Tim 2:11; αἱ γυναῖκες . . . σιγάτωσαν . . .
ὑποτασσέσθωσαν . . . μαθεῖν, 1 Cor 14: 34f). In addition, the reference to
the creation of Adam before Eve according to Gen 2: 21f in 1 Tim 2: 13
recalls the use of the same Old Testament passage in 1 Cor 11: 8f to
establish the pre-eminence of man over woman.

As for the instructions concerning the subjection of slaves to masters in 1 Tim 6: 1 and Tit 2: 9, though they are close in sense to Col 3: 22, Eph 6: 5, and 1 Pet 2: 18, there is no correspondence in wording in the last three, except for the use of δοῦλος as in Col 3: 22 and Eph 6: 5, and of ὑποτάσσειν as in 1 Pet 2: 18.

In none of these passages, however, is there any clear sign that either 1 Timothy or Titus quotes from or adapts an earlier form, though the similarities in wording and sense to the subjection material in the ten-letter corpus and 1 Peter cannot be ascribed to mere accident. What then is the relation of the later stratum to the Pastoral epistles, if material that most obviously resembles their content neither underlies them nor has been interpolated into them? Unless the similarities are due to literary dependence, the only alternative is that such teaching is the product of a single circle or school of Christian tradition. Put differently, it is suggested that the subjectionist passages, and the later stratum as a whole, cohere with the Pastorals as a whole in a single trito-Pauline stratum, with the possible exception of certain fragments.[9] This hypothesis will now be tested with reference to tendencies and points of view, style, and vocabulary.

Tendencies and points of view

The contents of the Pastorals, like the later stratum, consist almost wholly of paraenesis, except in 2 Timothy, which includes a considerable amount of biographical material as well. Titus contains some biography, as does the later stratum in the ten-letter corpus also to some extent.[10] The teaching on duties in the household and the state is not set out in a systematic fashion in the Pastorals as in Rom 13: 1-7, Col 3: 18 - 4: 1, Eph 5: 21 - 6: 9, and 1 Pet 2: 13-20, 3: 1-7. Nevertheless, this material provides basic assumptions and patterns which pervade Pastoral paraenesis, just as in the later stratum in the ten-letter corpus and 1 Peter.[11]

Patriarchal authority and the church

In essence one finds that the patriarchal character of the household is transferred to the church, which is evidently regarded as a household of households.[12] Thus according to 1 Pet 5: 1-5, the younger (νεώτεροι) are required to submit themselves to the elder (πρεσβύτεροι). The latter, by virtue of the naturally derived authority they are deemed to have, have the right to take charge of 'the flock of God' and to be obeyed, though at the same time they are enjoined to avoid misuse of their power. Their position also receives sanction as from the apostle Peter, who at the same time is placed in the same category, for he is termed a 'fellow elder'

($\sigma\nu\mu\pi\rho\epsilon\sigma\beta\acute{\nu}\tau\epsilon\rho\sigma\varsigma$, vs. 1). His pre-eminence over the $\pi\rho\epsilon\sigma\beta\acute{\nu}\tau\epsilon\rho\sigma\iota$ addressed is evident, however, from the mention of his having been a witness of Christ's sufferings (vs. 1) and from the fact that he has authority to issue instructions to those who come after him.

Similarly Paul is represented in the later stratum in the ten-letter collection as a 'father' over the churches to which he writes. This is an image which the apostle himself seems to have used to describe the relation of affectionate regard and concern toward his converts (cf. 2 Cor 12: 14ff, Phm 10). In the later material, however, it also has specific implications for the apostle's authority. So according to 1 Thess 2:11ff 'like a father with his children' he, together with his fellow workers, exhorts, encourages, and charges the Christian community, which in turn receives his teaching, not merely as the word of men, but of God (vs. 13). He is also represented as the 'father' of Timothy, his 'beloved and faithful child in the Lord' (4: 17), whom he sends in order to remind the congregation of his ways in Christ.[13]

As if continuing where the later material in the ten-letter corpus leaves off, the Pastoral epistles are addressed to Timothy as the apostle's 'true child in faith' (1 Tim 1: 2), and to Titus as his 'true child according to a common faith' (Tit 1: 4). Timothy is referred to as the apostle's 'child', who has received from his father Paul that which he is to entrust to 'faithful men' who in turn will pass it on to others (2 Tim 1:13f, 2:1f). That this is considered to involve appointment to a specific office is clear from the reference to the charge committed to Timothy by prophetic utterances (1 Tim 1:18) and the laying on of hands by the apostle for the reception of the spirit (2 Tim 1: 6).

In 1 Cor 10: 23 – 11: 29, 33f the transmission theme appears without mention of the father–son sequence (cf. 11: 2, 23, 24b, 25b), but its tacit presence is suggested by the combination of the *paradosis* concept with that of imitation and remembering. As already pointed out, this motif is commonly associated with patriarchal lineage and transmission of tradition.[14] Similarly in the later stratum in 1 Peter, the apostle is represented as giving instructions to elders in tending the flock and providing an example for emulation by those who are younger (1 Pet 5: 1-5).

The imitation concept appears also in the Pastorals, though the words $\mu\iota\mu\acute{\epsilon}\sigma\mu\alpha\iota$ and $\mu\iota\mu\eta\tau\acute{\eta}\varsigma$ are absent. Timothy as successor to the apostle is to adhere to the 'pattern' ($\acute{\upsilon}\pi\sigma\tau\acute{\upsilon}\pi\omega\sigma\iota\nu$) of 'sound words' or correct doctrine heard from Paul himself (2 Tim 1:13). The term $\acute{\upsilon}\pi\sigma\tau\acute{\upsilon}\pi\omega\sigma\iota\varsigma$ has a sense here which corresponds closely with the meaning of $\tau\acute{\upsilon}\pi\sigma\varsigma$ in the later stratum (cf. 1 Thess 1: 7, 2 Thess 3: 9, and 1 Pet 5: 3). Timothy has the same obligation as the apostle to guard the truth entrusted to him

(2 Tim 1: 12, 14). He is to take his share of suffering without being ashamed (2 Tim 1: 8), just as the apostle suffers without being ashamed (2 Tim 1: 12). In contrast to evil men and impostors, he has followed the teaching, practice, purpose, faith, patience, love, endurance, persecutions, and suffering of the apostle, knowing from whom he has learnt this way of life (2 Tim 3: 10-14). That is to say, the apostle serves as his model.

In commanding and teaching these things, the apostle's successor in turn is to provide a model for imitation to others (1 Tim 4: 11f, Tit 2: 7). But how can 'Timothy' be the 'son' who imitates his 'father' the apostle Paul, and at the same time the 'elder' who sets an example to those who are subordinate to him and in this sense younger? The Pastoral writer apparently attempts to resolve the dilemma by the suggestion that his youth is not to be despised, for he is endowed with the appropriate qualities and authority through the laying on of hands by the apostle (2 Tim 1: 6) and a group of elders (1 Tim 5: 22). Here then the writer resorts to the Pauline idea of special gifts, but they are mediated, not by the direct action of the spirit of God, but by institutionalized practice, following the leading of prophetic utterances (προφητείας, 1 Tim 4: 14, 1: 18).

Both Timothy and Titus are given criteria, furthermore, for the selection of an elder or bishop (1 Tim 3: 1-7, Tit 1: 6-9). From each set of instructions it is clear that the office is confined to the patriarchal heads of households, for it is open only to the husbands of one wife (1 Tim 3: 2, Tit 1: 6). They are also to be fathers of children and efficient household managers who have shown that they can keep their children submissive (1 Tim 3: 2, 4f, Tit 1: 6b).[15]

From Tit 1: 5-7 it appears that the term πρεσβύτερος is interchangeable with ἐπίσκοπος. In 1 Timothy, however, elders are mentioned separately from the bishop (1 Tim 3: 14, 5: 17-20). Since the latter is mentioned in the singular, there may be a distinction between them.[16] The bishop possibly acts as a chief elder, just as in 1 Pet 5: 1-5 Peter is represented as a συμπρεσβύτερος who is in some sense prior to or pre-eminent over a group of elders.[17] In this case both 1 Timothy and 1 Pet 5: 1-5 probably represent a somewhat later stage in the development of church order toward the monarchical episcopate than Titus.[18]

However this may be, the elders, like the bishop, have the authority to preside over or manage (προεστῶτες) the church (1 Tim 5: 17), just as the patriarchal family head manages (προϊστάμενον) the household (1 Tim 3: 4). The same appears to apply to the elders' role in the church according to 1 Pet 5: 1-5. That is to say, their function within the family unit as set forth in the 'household tables' is determinative also for their role in the church.

Exemplary heads of households who are husbands of one wife are eligible also for selection as deacons (1 Tim 3: 12), though it is by no means clear from this context how their functions differ from those of the bishop, or whether they are included among the elders mentioned in 1 Tim 5: 17.

At the same time age is not an automatic qualification for church office. An older man (πρεσβυτέρῳ) is subject to pastoral oversight like younger men (νεωτέρους, 1 Tim 5: 1). Thus the word πρεσβύτερος does not necessarily imply church office, but can also refer exclusively to age and sex.[19] Similarly Tit 2: 2ff instructs Titus to urge old men (πρεσβύτας) to behave fittingly, without reference to ruling, preaching, or teaching. By contrast old women (πρεσβύτιδας) are to be instructed, in addition, to 'teach what is good'(καλοδιδασκάλους) and to train (σωφρονίζωσιν) the young women in appropriate virtues. It appears then that whereas the older women automatically have teaching functions, albeit only in relation to younger women, older men do not, unless, presumably, they are among the πρεσβύτεροι chosen for this purpose.

Criteria for their selection also follow the household pattern. Thus bishops and deacons must not only be heads of households but must, in addition, display qualities appropriate to household management. They must be sober, serious, sensible, dignified, hospitable, not drunkards or aggressive, but humble, gentle, even-tempered, and self-controlled (cf. 1 Tim 3: 2–10, Tit 1: 6–8). These virtues obviously befit the patriarch who commands respect in society at large. They also tally to a considerable degree with the kind of character the 'household tables' require of the family head. Husbands are instructed to be loving, gentle, and thoughtful in their treatment of their wives (Col 3: 19, Eph 5: 25, 28f, 33, 1 Pet 3: 7), fathers to avoid harsh and provocative behaviour toward their children (Eph 6: 4, Col 3: 21), and masters to refrain from threats and to be just and equitable to their slaves (Eph 6: 9, Col 4: 1). Similarly, the elders addressed in 1 Pet 5: 1–4 are to be controlled in the application of their power so as to avoid being tyrannical (vs. 3). So too in the later stratum in the ten-letter corpus the apostolic officeholder seeks to admonish with gentleness and affection (1 Thess 2: 7f, 11), though he has authority to discipline with harsh punishment if necessary (2 Thess 3: 14f).[20]

In the Pastorals other requirements for church office have to do more specifically with the particular demands of the position in question. Thus teaching ability (διδακτικόν) is needed in the bishop (1 Tim 3: 2) and elder (Tit 1: 9), along with orthodoxy (Tit 1: 9), and freedom from love of money (1 Tim 3: 3, 8, Tit 1: 7). The function of teaching, however, also has a place in the duties of the household head, for husbands are to instruct wives (Eph 5: 29, 1 Cor 14: 35), and fathers to instruct children (Eph 6: 4). Indeed, in the household as in the church, authority involves the right and duty to instruct.

Limitation of the role of women

The Pastoral epistles resemble the later stratum also in its tendency to limit the role of women. The provision that bishops and deacons must be the husbands of one wife would have rendered them ineligible. Also, they are by definition ineligible for the office of elder for the purpose of ruling or teaching, though the prohibition in 1 Tim 2: 12 against women's teaching or having authority over men implies that this could and did actually happen in earlier stages or in other Christian circles, or both.[21] The only exception is that older women (πρεσβύτιδας) have the responsibility of training younger women in domestic virtues (Tit 2: 4f).

In addition the Pastorals place stringent limitations on the order of widows that apparently existed at the time of writing in Christian communities within their purview. In the first place, they are to be honoured only if they really are widows (1 Tim 5: 3), and the recognition this implies appears to be withheld if they have children or grandchildren who have a claim on their services (1 Tim 5: 4). It is extended only if they are completely alone, without other ties, and devote themselves wholly to prayer night and day (1 Tim 5: 5). If a widow has relatives, they must provide for her, so that the church is not burdened (1 Tim 5: 8, 16). What is more, further enrolment in the order of widows is restricted to those over sixty years of age, who have been the wife of one husband, and are deemed to have displayed appropriate virtues (1 Tim 5: 9f). Younger women are excluded, partly on the ground that they will desire to marry in due course, thereby violating their pledge presumably taken at the time of enrolment not to remarry (1 Tim 5: 12). All this, if implemented, would have led to the eventual elimination of the order.[22]

Clearly, for the Pastorals as for the later stratum, women's only legitimate sphere of activity is within the family structure. In the church setting their proper role is taken to be one of almost totally passive submission. Here the Pastoral writer accords with 1 Cor 14: 32–8, in explicitly silencing women in Christian assemblies, rather than with that of 1 Cor 11: 2–16, which does so by implication.[23] According to the Pastorals women are to learn in silence with all submissiveness, and are not allowed to teach or have authority over men (1 Tim 2: 11f). Significantly, the justification for these prohibitions closely resembles that in 1 Cor 11: 2–16 for the wearing of a head-covering, in that both appeal to the creation of woman from and after man according to Gen 2: 21ff (cf. 1 Cor 11: 8f,

1 Tim 2: 13). In addition the Pastorals regard woman as responsible for the original transgression, since she was 'deceived' whereas Adam was not (1 Tim 2: 14).[24] She may, however, compensate by fulfilling the role of wife and mother, for she is said to be 'saved through childbearing if she continues in faith and holiness with modesty' (1 Tim 2: 15).

Similarly the later stratum seems to associate women with moral weakness. Eph 5: 21 - 6: 9 implies it in the teaching that the female, identified with the fleshly body ($\sigma\tilde{\omega}\mu\alpha$, $\sigma\acute{\alpha}\rho\xi$) over against the male 'head' is cleansed by marriage as the church is by baptism (Eph 5: 22-7). So too 1 Cor 11: 2-16 possibly assumes that woman is prone to demon-possession unless she wears a veil indicating her subjection to a male authority or head.[25] In her designated married state according to the later material in 1 Peter, she receives honour, but only as 'the weaker vessel', though husband and wife are termed 'joint heirs of the grace of life' (1 Pet 3: 7).

In the same way the Pastorals consider women, even in their proper domestic setting, as lesser beings (cf. the diminutive $\gamma\upsilon\nu\alpha\iota\kappa\acute{\alpha}\rho\iota\alpha$, 2 Tim 3: 6), and as an easy prey to heretics who enter and subvert households (2 Tim 3: 6f). Outside the married state women are regarded as especially prone to evil. Unless they engage in ceaseless prayer the Pastoralist thinks they are liable to become voluptuous ($\sigma\pi\alpha\tau\alpha\lambda\tilde{\omega}\sigma\alpha$, 1 Tim 5: 5f), and if younger to become alienated from Christ by sensual desire ($\kappa\alpha\tau\alpha\sigma\tau\rho\eta\nu\iota\acute{\alpha}\sigma\omega\sigma\iota\nu$ $\tau o\tilde{\upsilon}$ $X\rho\iota\sigma\tauo\tilde{\upsilon}$, 1 Tim 5: 11). He considers they become idlers, wandering about from house to house, gossiping, meddling in affairs that do not concern them ($\pi\epsilon\rho\acute{\iota}\epsilon\rho\gamma o\iota$), and saying things they have no right to say ($\lambda\alpha\lambda o\tilde{\upsilon}\sigma\alpha\iota$ $\tau\grave{\alpha}$ $\mu\grave{\eta}$ $\delta\acute{\epsilon}o\nu\tau\alpha$, 1 Tim 5: 13). The two last-mentioned errors suggest the unauthorized activities of heretics, such as, it seems, are under attack in the later material in 2 Thessalonians (2 Thess 3: 6-15, cf. $\pi\epsilon\rho\iota-$ $\pi\alpha\tauo\tilde{\upsilon}\nu\tau\alpha\varsigma$ ... $\grave{\alpha}\tau\acute{\alpha}\kappa\tau\omega\varsigma$ $\mu\eta\delta\grave{\epsilon}\nu$ $\grave{\epsilon}\rho\gamma\alpha\zetao\mu\acute{\epsilon}\nuo\upsilon\varsigma$ $\grave{\alpha}\lambda\lambda\grave{\alpha}$ $\pi\epsilon\rho\iota\epsilon\rho\gamma\alpha\zetao\mu\acute{\epsilon}\nuo\upsilon\varsigma$, vs. 11).

That the Pastorals associate feminine aberrations and insubordination with heresy appears very probable if 2 Tim 3: 6-8 is taken in conjunction with the accusation in Tit 1: 11 that heretics are 'overturning' whole households by teaching for dishonest gain what they have no right to teach. The use of the words $\delta\iota\delta\acute{\alpha}\sigma\kappao\nu\tau\epsilon\varsigma$ $\grave{\alpha}$ $\mu\grave{\eta}$ $\delta\epsilon\tilde{\iota}$ recalls the similar expression $\tau\grave{\alpha}$ $\mu\grave{\eta}$ $\delta\acute{\epsilon}o\nu\tau\alpha$ quoted above from 1 Tim 5: 13 concerning feminine chatter. Indeed, if all three passages are considered together, it appears very possible that women are among those who actually dis-seminate forbidden teaching, and are not merely its victims.[26]

In this case the restrictions on women in 1 Tim 2: 11f and 5: 3-16 are to be viewed as aimed in part also at the silencing of heretics. Tending to confirm this possibility is the fact that the implicit curbing of women in 1 Cor 11: 2–16 occurs in the same context as the criticism of factionalism and heresy in the Christian community (1 Cor 11: 18), and that 1 Cor 14: 32–8 threatens that those who do not recognize the prohibition on feminine expression will not be recognized, which is to say, will be denied legitimacy and excluded (cf. vs. 38), thereby being placed in the position of schismatics and heretics.

The Pastorals also have a common factor with the later stratum in that they seek to regulate feminine attire and adornment. In that part of the 'household table' addressed to wives in 1 Peter the avoidance of braided hair, gold ornaments, and sumptuous robes is connected with the quietness and submissiveness of Christian wives in proper subjection to their husbands (1 Pet 3: 3–5). In the Pastorals the same kind of requirements are linked not only with feminine submissiveness (cf. 1 Tim 2: 9–12) but also with the attire thought to befit women professing religion (vs. 10).[27] Once again, then, it is possible to discern a close connection between the 'household' material and church order as set out in the Pastorals.

Conciliation with society

The subjectionist teaching on the state has also affected certain Pastoral instructions on church order. First, it is evident that the kind of teaching on submission to and honouring of secular authority, particularly that of the state, found in Rom 13: 1–7 and 1 Pet 2: 13–17 is to be an essential part of church instruction (Tit 3: 1). It is also to be presented in the same context as in the later material in Rom 12, 13 and 1 Peter. That means it is intrinsic to instruction on conciliatory behaviour toward 'all men' (Tit 3: 2), which is to say, the surrounding society in general (cf. Tit 3: 2–5, Rom 12: 14–21, 1 Pet 2: 12, 3: 9, 13, 15).

Similarly the requirement in 1 Tim 2: 1f that prayers, intercessions, and thanksgiving be offered for all people, including kings and all in authority, corresponds with the teaching in Rom 13: 1–7 and 1 Pet 2: 13–17 that authorities be honoured (cf. ἀπόδοτε πᾶσιν τὰς ὀφειλάς . . . τῷ τὴν τιμὴν τὴν τιμήν in Rom 13: 7, and πάντας τιμήσατε . . . τὸν βασιλέα τιμᾶτε in 1 Pet 2: 17). The purpose of such prayers is evidently that the relations between rulers and subjects should be such that peace, quiet, godliness, and respect prevail (1 Tim 2: 2), which implies obedience on the part of subjects as well as right action on the part of rulers.[28]

In all its teaching on social and civic duties the obvious intent of the later stratum in the ten-letter corpus and 1 Peter, and also in the Pastorals, is to make a good impression on outsiders. According to the latter, younger women are to marry, bear children, and manage their households

so as not to provide the adversaries of the faith with occasion to revile it
(1 Tim 5: 14). Older women are to behave appropriately themselves and
also teach the younger women to love their husbands and children, cultivate
domestic virtues, and to be submissive to their husbands, so that the word
of God is not 'blasphemed' (Tit 2: 3–5). Slaves likewise are to regard their
masters as worthy of honour, 'so that the name of God and the teaching is
not blasphemed' (1 Tim 6: 1). They are to obey and please their masters,
not to be impertinent or steal, and to be completely faithful, so that they
may 'adorn' or bring credit to the doctrine of God (Tit 2: 9f).

So too anyone chosen to be a bishop must have the good opinion of
those without so that he does not fall into disgrace and the snare of the
devil (1 Tim 3: 7). Not only is the motive evidently to create a favourable
view of the church among those outside the Christian community, but it
seems too that their opinion is accepted as a valid measure of worth and a
guide to future behaviour, 'so that an adversary may be put to shame,
having nothing evil to say about it' (Tit 2: 7f, cf. 1 Pet 3: 16).[29]

'Conscience' and good works

Related to the ethical motivation to gain a favourable reaction from out-
siders is the understanding of 'doing good' ($\dot{\alpha}\gamma\alpha\vartheta o\pi o\iota\epsilon\hat{\iota}v$) and 'good works'
($\kappa\alpha\lambda\dot{\alpha}\ \check{\epsilon}\rho\gamma\alpha$). Both involve the discharge of social and political duty and
the winning of credit from God and society. This tendency is quite clearly
present both in the later material in 1 Peter[30] and the ten-letter corpus,[31]
and in the Pastorals.

In the Pastorals the expression $\kappa\alpha\lambda\dot{\alpha}\ \check{\epsilon}\rho\gamma\alpha$ occurs with far greater
frequency than in any other New Testament tradition. In almost every
instance the phrase has the connotations mentioned above, either for
individuals, or the Christian community, or God himself. A reputation for
good deeds qualifies a widow for enrolment (1 Tim 5: 10), recalling the
requirement that to be well thought of by outsiders is necessary in order
to be chosen as a bishop (1 Tim 3: 7). As already mentioned, Titus is to be
a model of good works performed to counter outside criticism (Tit 2: 7f).
He is also to see that all believers engage in good works as profitable to
humanity (Tit 3: 8), and to provide help where there is need so as not to
be unfruitful (Tit 3: 14). This recalls the exhortation in 1 Pet 2: 12 to
maintain good conduct among the gentiles or pagans so that, instead of
speaking against Christians as evildoers they will observe their good works
and glorify God.

The concept of 'good works' in the Pastorals and the later stratum is
related also to that of $\sigma vv\epsilon\acute{\iota}\delta\eta\sigma\iota\varsigma$, usually translated 'conscience'. It may
possibly be more accurately rendered by the alternative translation

'consciousness' in the sense of a state of mind[32] in the Pastorals, particularly since the word is syntactically parallel to καρδία in 1 Tim 1: 5, and to νοῦς in Tit 1: 15. In the latter one finds the Pastoral view that: 'All things are pure to the pure, but to the defiled and unbelieving nothing is pure, but their νοῦς and συνείδησις are defiled.' So too according to 1 Tim 4: 4: 'Everything God has created is good, and nothing is to be rejected if it is received with thanksgiving, for it is hallowed through the word of God and prayer.' What is evil is the 'seared' conscience or consciousness (1 Tim 4: 2) of those who regard what God has created as evil.

In 1 Tim 4: 1-5 the reference is specifically to the marriage relationship and to food. From the context of Tit 1: 15, however, it appears that the issue goes far beyond asceticism, encompassing the social order along with the natural creation as that which is to be received as good. In contrast to those with a defiled consciousness, Titus is to teach 'sound doctrine', which, it appears from what follows, obviously refers to instruction in the ways in which different categories of people – the old and young, men and women, as also slaves – are to live, according to their sex, age, and social station (cf. Tit 2: 2-10). In addition all are to be reminded to be submissive (ὑποτάσσεσθαι) to rulers and authorities.

By implication, then, the entire social structure is included in 'all things' which are 'pure' to the 'pure' (Tit 1: 15). Thus what the Pastorals term a 'good' or 'pure' συνείδησις evidently refers to a harmonious acceptance of the world and the way it is ordered as the creation of God. A bad or defiled conscience or consciousness, it may be inferred, is one that rejects and rebels against the world and the social order, or certain aspects of it, and so sets itself against and denigrates God himself.[33] This, it seems, is precisely what the Pastorals have in mind in their castigation of heretics. Not only do these heretics adhere to food taboos and reject marriage, but they are characterized as disobedient (Tit 1: 16) and insubordinate (Tit 1: 10). They are accused of overturning whole houses, which probably means that they disturb and disrupt the ordering of the household and undermine proper authority. They are condemned also as speculative, quarrelsome, the cause of controversy (1 Tim 1: 6, 2 Tim 2: 14, 23, Tit 3: 2, 9), and as guilty of blasphemy (1 Tim 1: 20, 6: 4).

It is significant that in the later stratum in the ten-letter corpus there is relatively frequent use of the term συνείδησις (nine times in all),[34] and that here too the word relates to a concern to avoid the kind of conscience or consciousness that rejects the good God has created. The basis of the argument in favour of eating without question meat that has been sacrificed to idols is the assertion cited from the LXX Pss 23: 1, 49(50): 12, and 88(89): 11 that 'the earth is the Lord's and all within it' (1 Cor 10: 26).

This reasoning is clearly close to the point of view expressed in 1 Tim 4: 4 that 'everything created by God is good, and nothing is to be rejected if it is received with thanksgiving'. In common with 1 Tim 4: 4, moreover, 1 Cor 10: 30 speaks of partaking with thanks and of giving thanks for such food.

1 Cor 10: 25 differs from the Pastorals, however, in that it attempts to be conciliatory toward the weak whose scruples cause them to reject food sacrificed to idols. It advises those whose sense of liberty allows them to partake, to refrain if it could possibly affect the conscience or conscious-ness of another adversely (vss. 28f), that is to say, if it could cause a fellow Christian to 'blaspheme' (βλασφημοῦμαι, vs. 30).[35] In the Pastorals, however, the tone is one of uncompromising opposition to those who err in this way. The explanation is possibly that the Pastorals represent a later stage in the controversy, when there is no longer any hope of holding the different factions together, and an open breach has occurred.[36] In other words, it is suggested that the difference is one of time and situation rather than of outlook and point of view.

For this reason too 1 Cor 10: 23ff may avoid qualifying συνείδησις as either 'pure' and 'good' or bad and 'defiled', as do the Pastorals,[37] and the blasphemy involved is referred to in the passive voice (cf. 1 Cor 10: 30). According to the Pastorals, by contrast, blasphemy is a positive offence warranting expulsion from the Christian community (1 Tim 1: 20). From the case of Alexander and Hymenaeus it is evident that it is understood as the antithesis of good consciousness, such as describes the apostle's faith-ful child Timothy (1 Tim 1: 18f). It apparently involves the defaming and rejection of God himself through rejecting and regarding as defiled and evil that which he has made or which pertains to himself. Whereas 1 Cor 10: 23-31 is concerned to prevent fellow Christians from falling into this state of mind, the Pastorals express similar solicitude, lest outsiders defame and reject the word and being of God through disorderly and insubordinate behaviour among believers, and thereby blaspheme (cf. 1 Tim 6: 1, Tit 2: 5).

To turn to 1 Cor 8, which it was suggested earlier coheres with 1 Cor 10: 23-33,[38] the same interpretation of συνείδησις is found to apply. Here the word is qualified by the adjective ἀσθενής (weak, 1 Cor 8: 7, 10, 12). In one instance it is the subject of the present passive form μολύνεται (is defiled, vs. 7). Here the use recalls the occurrence of the word with μεμίανται (are defiled) in Tit 1: 15. In 1 Cor 8 the concern is to take care lest liberty in the matter of food offered to idols cause the person of weak συνείδησις to partake of what he does not approve because he thinks τοῦ εἰδώλου (that belonging to or connected with an idol, i.e. idol meat) is in fact εἰδωλόθυτον (an idolatrous sacrifice, vs. 7).[39] By so doing he would wound his συνείδησις so that he falls and is destroyed (vss. 11, 13). The outcome follows logically if we assume that the defiled consciousness rejects and is alienated from the good which it condemns, in this instance, not merely the food itself, but its very self, hence its self-destruction.[40]

The same view of food taboos and ascetic practices as finds expression in 1 Cor 8 and 10: 23–33 appears in Rom 14: 1 – 15: 6, which it has been suggested also belongs to the later stratum,[41] though the word συνείδησις does not occur. Here too, as in 1 Cor 10: 26, there are words reminiscent of Tit 1: 15. According to Rom 14: 14, 'nothing is common (κοινόν) of itself; but it is common to that one who thinks it is common',[42] and according to Rom 14: 20, 'everything is clean (καθαρά) but it is evil for the man who eats with offence'. Here too the one who condemns the good is regarded as guilty of blasphemy and once again, as in 1 Cor 10: 30, the form of the verb involved is passive (cf. μὴ βλασφημείσθω, Rom 14: 16). Here again one finds a desire to be conciliatory toward those who have scruples, and to promote peace and harmony within the church (cf. Rom 14: 1-3, 19; 15: 1f, 1 Cor 10: 32).

Other uses of συνείδησις in the later stratum also correspond with what has been found in the Pastorals. There it was observed that the concept applies by implication to the social order, something which is quite explicit in the subjection material of the ten-letter corpus and 1 Peter. In Rom 13: 5 subjection to rulers is enjoined, not only because it is the function of the ruling authority to punish wrong-doers, but also because of conscience (διὰ τὴν συνείδησιν, Rom 13: 5).[43]

The phrase is usually thought to refer to the guilt that would be incurred in disobeying authority sanctioned by God. It becomes more comprehensible, however, if it is understood in the broader sense found in the Pastorals of consciousness that would become defiled, and alienated from God and the world by rejecting and opposing what belongs to God's good ordering of his creation. This possibility receives support from the fact that the argument is based on the concept of God as the origin of the ruling powers and their authority (vs. 1), which is to say, their Creator.

In the later material in 1 Peter the same sense is present. Slaves are urged to continue in submission to their masters even when mistreated, διὰ συνείδησιν Θεοῦ (1 Pet 2: 19). The implication is possibly that it is important to maintain a consciousness that is godly or good,[44] instead of falling into a state of opposition and rebellion toward what God has ordained and therefore also toward God himself. In this way one gains and retains God's approval and favour (vss. 19f), and maintains a harmonious relation with him and his ordering of the world.

Similarly those who suffer for righteousness' sake are exhorted to maintain a good conscience or consciousness (συνείδησιν ἔχοντες ἀγαθήν, 1 Pet 3: 16) in meekness and fear. In the context of the later stratum this means continuing in the virtues of submission to authority, gentleness, and love as set out in the subjection material (1 Pet 2: 13ff, 3: 1ff, 3: 8f). It means too that persecuted Christians are to avoid the error of turning against the society and its ordering, by offering resistance to authority in retaliation for wrongs suffered (cf. the injunction to refrain from returning evil for evil and reviling for reviling in 3: 9). A rebellious reaction would presumably bring Christians into a state of bad συνείδησις, justifying the calumnies of enemies. Their detractors would otherwise be put to shame for abusing their good way of life (3: 16).

Finally, in material that appears to belong to the later stratum, baptism is referred to as a request, appeal or, as appears most likely, a pledge (ἐπερώτημα)[45] of a good conscience or consciousness (συνειδήσεως ἀγαθῆς) toward God (1 Pet 3: 21). That is to say, it is an occasion, not for setting aside the uncleanness of the flesh, but for undertaking to maintain accord with God.[46] The pledge taken thus probably involves the determination to honour and obey the authorities in accordance with the will of God, as enjoined in 1 Pet 2: 13ff and 3: 1ff, and to live in harmony, love, and humility, as counselled in 1 Pet 3: 8f. It also evidently implies the acceptance of the surrounding society and its institutions as ordained by God.

The Pastoral concept of συνείδησις seems then to apply with ease to all uses of the word in the later stratum. Apart from the Acts,[47] almost all other uses in the New Testament diverge quite clearly from the sense in the Pastorals. In the ten-letter corpus all instances outside of the later stratum point to a concept of συνείδησις as the individual's faculty of judging both the self and others.[48] In the Epistle to the Hebrews it concerns the consciousness of guilt, or freedom from it, through the cleansing efficacy of Christ's atonement for sin (Heb 9: 9, 14, 10: 2, 22). In Heb 13: 18, however, καλὴν συνείδησιν ἔχομεν recalls the expression συνείδησιν ἔχοντες ἀγαθήν in 1 Pet 3: 16, as well as the occurrence of the noun in combination with the adjective in 1 Tim 1: 5, 19, and 1 Pet 3: 21, and with the adjective καθαρός in 1 Tim 3: 9 and 2 Tim 1: 3. Moreover, in Heb 13: 18 the context is one in which there is considerable material which is reminiscent of the later stratum and the Pastorals.[49]

It seems, then, that the concept of συνείδησις in the later stratum and the Pastorals identifies the good and moral with behaviour that accords harmoniously with the present forms and structures of the world as part of the natural order.

The 'approved' and the 'disapproved'

While the primary target of the teaching described above seems to be a form of gnostic dualism which exalts asceticism, the later material and the Pastorals also negate the eschatological dualism of earlier layers of tradition.[50] This means that instead of differentiating between the elect as representative of the new era of light and the present era of darkness, the later stratum and the Pastorals distinguish between diverging groups in some sense within the sphere of the church.

The acceptance of the pagan state as an instrument of divine judgement in Rom 13: 1–7 and 1 Pet 2: 13–17 clearly cuts across the sharp distinction between the Christian community and the world in earlier strata. It also involves a potential distinction between Christians who are submissive and deemed worthy to receive praise from the governing authorities on the one hand and, on the other, those who are disobedient and subject to wrath and punishment from this source.[51]

1 Peter distinguishes also between Christians who suffer innocently and for doing right, and those whose suffering is deserved punishment.[52] The later stratum in the ten-letter corpus distinguishes in addition between the worthy and approved (δόκιμοι) and the unworthy who are to be denied recognition (ἀδόκιμοι)[53] and excluded from the fellowship.[54] Here the grounds for distinction are deviations from church order as laid down by recognized authority within the church.

Like the later stratum in the ten-letter corpus, the Pastoral epistles distinguish between those who are approved and rejected within the church sphere, but more particularly in relation to heresy and the activities of heretics.[55] The word δόκιμος is used in 2 Tim 4: 15 to describe the ideal of orthodoxy required of a successor to the apostles. He is 'approved' if he handles correctly (ὀρθοτομοῦντα) 'the word of truth', avoiding the profane and futile talk of those who have turned away from the truth by maintaining that the resurrection has already come (vss. 16–18). Here again there is probably a reference to gnostic-type teaching. The word ἀδόκιμος, as one may expect, is used to describe those who deviate from the truth and are unsound as to the faith (ἀδόκιμοι περὶ τὴν πίστιν, 2 Tim 3: 7f). In Tit 1: 16 it is used of the disobedient who are unfit (ἀδόκιμοι) for any good work, who are to be disciplined for heeding 'Jewish myths' and the ascetic prohibitions of those who turn away from the truth.

As is evident from the last-mentioned instance, heresies are viewed as forms of insubordination (cf. Tit 1: 10). The heretical person disregards instruction, and so is to be rejected and avoided (Tit 3: 10). Thus it can be concluded that here too the central issue distinguishing the approved from the unworthy is adherence to church order and authority, and rebellion against it is regarded as moral evil of the worst kind.[56]

A respect in which the Pastorals differ from the later stratum in the ten-letter corpus is in their attitude to the Jews and Judaism. The later stratum, as already shown[57] takes a conciliatory view of those who adhere to food taboos, probably among Jewish or Jewish-oriented Christians (1 Cor 10: 32f). At the same time 1 Thess 2: 14–16, which this study has assigned to the later stratum,[58] is vehement in its denunciation of the Jews of Judaea along with the local inhabitants of Thessalonica.[59] Just as the Thessalonian Christians are distinguished from other local inhabitants, so also are members of the churches of Judaea from the Jews (vs. 14).

The Pastorals make no such distinctions. All Cretans without distinction are described as 'habitual liars, evil beasts, idle gluttons' (Tit 1: 12) in the course of invective against heretics in the church (vss. 10: 14). In the same passage the condemnation of the disobedient or rebellious ($\dot{\alpha}\nu\upsilon\pi\acute{o}$-$\tau\alpha\kappa\tau\sigma\iota$) includes 'especially those of the circumcision party' (Tit 1: 10), and those who disseminate 'Jewish myths' (vs. 14).

There is also dissociation from a certain understanding and use of 'the law', which can be none other than the Jewish law (1 Tim 1: 7-10). The concept of law in 1 Timothy is moral and perhaps juridical rather than ceremonial. The Pastoral use recalls that found in Rom 13: 8-10, where it has associations simultaneously with the decalogue and the injunctions for subordination to the state. So too 1 Timothy relates the concept to the decalogue[60] and to actions deemed criminal such as murder, kidnapping, and perjury (1 Tim 1: 9f).

In sum, while the Pastoral epistles show a far clearer separation from Judaism than the later stratum in the ten-letter corpus, the two actually agree significantly on the issues involved in the conflict with Jewish gnosticism. The difference can, however, be ascribed to the intensification of the disagreement with the passage of time. Contributing factors may well have been the growing strength of gentiles in proportion to Jews and Jewish influence in the church, or an external climate of anti-Jewish feeling, or both. It could also have to do with efforts to avoid persecution through the association of the church with the Jews and Jewish insurrection.

On the basis of tendencies and points of view as well as the use of key terms then, it can be concluded that there is a significantly close relation between the later stratum and the Pastoral epistles.

Style and vocabulary

Some important similarities between the later stratum and the Pastorals
are to be observed also in regard to style and vocabulary.

There is first the fact that the μή (or μόνον) ... ἀλλά ... (ὡς) (ἵνα)
construction which recurs in the later stratum is prominent also in the
Pastorals.[61] Here the test for antithetic parallels which proved useful in
identifying the later stratum yields very similar results. The scores range
from approximately four to eight lines to each occurrence in each chapter
of the Pastoral epistles,[62] as compared with three to six lines to each
occurrence in the later stratum.[63] In 1 Timothy the number of lines to
each occurrence ranges from 4.5 to 7.8 from one chapter to another, the
average score being 5.6. In 2 Timothy the range is from 4.9 to 6.7, the
average being 5.9, and in Titus the range is from 5.2 to 5.8, with an
average of 5.5.[64] The average number of lines to each occurrence in the
later stratum in the ten-letter corpus is 4.1, and in the equivalent material
in 1 Peter, 4.1.

Though the trait is slightly less frequent in the Pastorals than in the
later stratum, the closeness of the respective average scores can be no
coincidence. At the least it bespeaks similar use of a common paraenetic
mode of expression. That the characteristic pertains more particularly to
paraenesis is evident from the fact that it occurs far less frequently in the
purely biographical parts of the epistles which Harrison identified as
genuine Pauline fragments.[65] If these passages are excluded from the
calculations, the results for 2 Timothy and Titus are even closer to those
for the later stratum. The average for 2 Timothy is now 3.7, and for Titus
5.1. For other reasons, however, the Pauline origin of Harrison's fragments
is to be rejected.[66]

Secondly, there is a close correspondence between the Pastorals and the
later stratum in 1 Peter as regards the occurrence of *hapax legomena*, and
words used more than once in given material, but nowhere else in the New
Testament. The average rate of 13.1 such words per page in the later
material in 1 Peter compares favourably with Harrison's scores of 15.2
for 1 Timothy, 12.9 for 2 Timothy, and 16.1 for Titus.[67] If one eliminates
the words that occur in more than one of the Pastoral epistles the figures
are 12.3, 10.4, and 11.5 respectively.[68] This provides a more satisfactory
basis for comparison, since the higher figures include words that are distinctive to material 13.3 pages in length, whereas the later material in
1 Peter consists of only 3.5 pages. This compares with lengths of 6.1 pages
for 1 Timothy, 4.1 for 2 Timothy, and 2.6 for Titus.

By contrast the passages assigned to the later stratum in the ten-letter corpus tend to a far less frequent use of distinctive words on the whole than the rest of the material in these epistles. If one includes words these passages share with one another the average score is 3.3 words per page, as compared with a rate of between 3.3 and 6.2 for these epistles, according to Harrison's calculations.[69] This figure for the total 12.2 pages making up the later stratum in the ten-letter corpus is misleading, however, for it masks the fact that the passages involved are far less typical of the epistles in which they are placed than the average score suggests. They usually fall well below the score for the epistles in which they are placed. Were it not for a few passages which exceed the average per page for the epistles in which they occur, it could be said that the later stratum in the Pauline corpus is characterized by the use of very few distinctive words, as compared with the rest of the ten-letter corpus.

A possible explanation is that the later stratum in the ten-letter corpus belongs to the earlier stages of development of the tradition from which it came, and the Pastorals, along with the later material in 1 Peter, belong to a somewhat later stage, when there was increased acquaintance with Greek literature, and command of a wider range of Greek vocabulary. That some or most of the later stratum in the ten-letter corpus is probably earlier than the Pastorals has emerged in the consideration of attitudes to the Jews and the ascetic practices of Jewish-oriented gnosticism.[70]

That the difference in vocabulary under consideration has to do with the earlier dating of the later stratum in the ten-letter corpus as compared with the Pastorals receives possible confirmation from the presence in Rom 1:19 – 2:1 of sixteen words peculiar to this passage in the New Testament. This passage yields a rate of 15.1 per page, which is actually a higher frequencey than the score of 12.8 for the Pastorals as a whole, or the score of 11.5 for the 2.6 pages of Titus only, which corresponds more closely with Rom 1:19 – 2:1 in length.

Harrison has put forward the view that the passage is a Pastoral insertion,[71] partly on the basis of the lexical data mentioned above. He also pointed to the presence of thirty words which do not occur elsewhere in the Pauline corpus, as compared with a third of this number per page for the rest of Romans. These include three words shared only with the Pastorals in the New Testament. In addition he mentioned the accentuation in Rom 1:19 – 2:1 of the tendency to use words beginning with *a*-privative.

Such factors confirm Harrison's argument that the passage was not missing from Marcion's Apostolicon because he excised it, as some have maintained,[72] but that it was not in the text which he copied. He argued that there is no reason why Marcion should have excluded Rom 2: 1, particularly since, on Tertullian's showing, he retained the very similar words in Luke 6: 37: 'Do not judge, and you will not be judged, do not condemn, and you will not be condemned.'[73]

Reinforcing this argument is the occurrence of ὦ ἄνθρωπε ὁ κρίνων in both Rom 2: 1 and 2: 3. Harrison suggested the phrase was intended to form a link with the end of the interpolation and the original text.[74]

Harrison's view has not attracted the support of scholars, but he was able to cite Carrington's review of *The Problem of the Pastoral Epistles*[75] to the effect that if his analysis of the vocabulary of the Pastorals is extended to this passage, the results are similar. Carrington suggested, however, that Paul cited the diatribe from another source, which accords with his view of many of the paraenetic passages in the corpus as part of an earlier construction.[76]

The application of the methods used in the present study confirms Harrison's conclusions regarding Rom 1: 19 – 2: 1. Not only is it to be dissociated from its context in Romans and associated with the Pastorals, as he maintained, but it also bears a close relation to the later stratum in the ten-letter corpus.[77] It differs from the latter both in its exceptionally frequent use of words found nowhere else in the New Testament, and in that it was evidently missing in Marcion's Apostolicon. There is positive evidence that most of the later stratum in the ten-letter corpus found a place in Marcion's version.[78] If then Harrison's view of Rom 1: 19 – 2: 1 is accepted, it follows that this part of the stratum did not feature in the version of the corpus which Marcion used, and the most obvious way of accounting for the omission is that the passage had not as yet been added. It must then have been inserted later at approximately the same time as the writing of the Pastoral epistles. Thus Rom 1: 19 – 2: 1 manifests a tendency to use non-New Testament words to the same degree as the Pastorals, and the same evidently applies to the later material in 1 Peter for the same reason.

Further vocabulary tests indicate that words lacking in the Pastorals tend to be absent also in the later stratum. Harrison listed 112 particles, prepositions, and pronouns found in the ten-letter corpus but not in the Pastorals.[79] Of the seventy which occur in no more than three epistles of the corpus, only four appear in the later stratum (ὁμοίως, πάντως, ἐπεί, πλήν) as compared with twenty-three in Galatians and Philippians. Of the total 112 words, twenty-six appear in the later stratum seventy-six times counting all repetitions, that is to say, at a rate of 5.8 per page. This compares with a total of 856 in the rest of the Pauline corpus, yielding a rate of 9.4 per page, which is close to twice as frequently. These figures may be compared with the results for Galatians and Philippians in combination, the total 14.13 pages of which is close to the 13.0 pages of the later stratum in the ten letters. Here fifty-six of the words under consideration occur 143 times counting all repetitions, which means at a rate of 10.1 per page.

The difference gains in significance when it is taken into account that a number of the words are used with disproportionate frequency in the later stratum, which is approximately one-seventh as long as the rest of the ten-letter corpus.[80]

More frequently used and characteristic words in the ten-letter corpus yield similar results. Of the 1053 that are found elsewhere in the New Testament but not in the Pastorals, Harrison lists eighty nouns, verbs, adjectives, and adverbs which occur in five or more of the ten letters.[81] Of these, forty are used also in the 13.0 pages of the later stratum. Counting all repetitions, they occur 106 times, or 7.7 times per page, as compared with 112 times in the 91.5 pages of the ten letters, or 12.2 uses per page, which is close to twice the frequency. Galatians and Philippians, by comparison, use seventy of these words for a total of 179 occurrences, which is to say, 12.7 per page.

The difference gains in significance when it is taken into account that a number of the eighty typically Pauline words are even more typical of the later stratum which is approximately one-seventh as long as the rest of the ten-letter corpus.[82]

In addition, Harrison combined the scores for all words which occur in at least five Pauline epistles but not in the Pastorals, which procedure yields scores of between 13.8 and 20.3 per page for the ten letters, and an over-all average of seventeen per page.[83] The total 153 occurrences of such words in the later stratum yields a score of 11.7 per page, which is significantly lower than the lowest scores for the various letters of the corpus: 14.5 for Ephesians, and 13.8 for Romans. Moreover, if the total figures are adjusted by subtracting those for the later stratum, the rest of the corpus is found to contain 1638 such words in 91.5 pages, raising the average to 17.9 per page.

It appears, then, that the later stratum in the ten-letter Pauline corpus and in 1 Peter is to be associated with the Pastoral epistles, not only on grounds of tendencies and perspectives, but also on grounds of style and vocabulary. The study will therefore proceed on the assumption that the material in question issues from the same school or circle of tradition though not, apparently, at exactly the same time. Together with the Pastorals it will now be referred to as 'the Pastoral stratum'. The next chapter will attempt to determine its time, context, and place in the history of the text.

4 THE LITERARY AND HISTORICAL CONTEXT OF THE PASTORAL STRATUM

Literary relations

The enquiry thus far has led to the conclusion that the subjection material in the New Testament epistles is an integral part of an extensive layer of redaction in 1 Peter and the fourteen-letter Pauline corpus, including all or most of the Pastoral epistles, now to be termed 'the Pastoral stratum'. Not only is the subjection material integral to this stratum, but it also distinguishes it from all other strains in the New Testament, in that only here does advocacy of submission to human authority find explicit expression.

The gospels

According to a saying of Jesus in the Gospel of John the Roman governor, Pilate, has no authority over him unless it has been given 'from above' (John 19: 11). On the other hand, the words could be intended as an expression of non-recognition because on this basis Pilate's authority has no true legitimacy. Moreover, the claim of the chief priests to have no king but Caesar (John 19: 15) signifies rejection of Jesus as the Christ, and not approved obedience and loyalty to a divinely appointed ruler.

Similarly the pericope in the synoptic gospels concerning the payment of taxes to Caesar[1] is ambiguous in that it is capable of interpretation either as enjoining obedience and service to pagan authorities in all matters pertaining to their spheres of jurisdiction, or as a statement of non-recognition and dissociation from the things or realm of Caesar as opposed to the things or realm of God.[2] The latter is a stronger possibility in the Matthean and Markan versions, for both make quite clear that Jesus has no Roman denarius in his possession, since the questioners are obliged to bring him one (Matt 22: 19, Mark 12: 15f). In this way, possibly, their dealing in the currency carrying the objectionable image of Caesar is exposed, and at the same time also their tacit acceptance of the obligation to pay tribute to Rome.[3] The point, if intended, is clearer in Matthew, where Jesus' reference to 'the money of the tribute' (τὸ νόμισμα τοῦ κήνσου, Matt 22: 19) suggests currency regarded as foreign. It is least clear in Luke, where there is no mention of the questioners' bringing a coin to Jesus after his request to be shown one (Luke 20: 24).

Luke–Acts

The outlook of the subjection material may also be implied in the pericope concerning the boy Jesus in the temple (Luke 2: 41–52), for verse 51 refers to his subjection to his parents (καὶ ἦν ὑποτασσόμενος αὐτοῖς), immediately after the dialogue in which he claims to have been engaged in the affairs of his father, meaning his heavenly Father, as he ought to be (vs. 49).

Verses 51 and 52 may, however, issue from a later revision of Luke, for elsewhere in this gospel Christian discipleship takes precedence over family loyalties, even to the point of their repudiation, and is seen as a cause of division and strife. Such material is admittedly shared with Matthew or with Matthew and Mark, but the Lukan versions in some instances actually accentuate this tendency.[4]

In the Acts the earlier chapters represent the Christian movement in Jerusalem as obliged to defy the orders of the Jewish rulers to desist from its proclamation on the grounds that it must obey God rather than men.[5] The latter part of the book seems, however, to be at pains to show Paul as obedient to Jewish law (Acts 6: 3, 21: 20–6, 22: 3), though conflict with the Jews is a continuing theme.[6] There is mention of the accusation of sedition against Paul and his companions, but this is accounted for either as a Jewish slander (Acts 17: 5–9), or as a false charge by local inhabitants arising from their Jewish identity (Acts 16: 20f), or as due to mistaken identity (Acts 21: 37). Paul and Silas are represented as proud possessors of Roman citizenship who can strike fear into Roman officials on this account (Acts 16: 37–9, 22: 25–9), and Paul as acknowledging the superior authority of the Roman imperium by his appeal to Caesar (Acts 25: 8–11). Moreover, the Roman system of justice is depicted as a protection against the hostility of Jews and local inhabitants. In spite of the weakness and neglect of certain individual officials, Roman authority appears to ensure a fair hearing for accused Christians.[7] Above all, the Roman army has the appearance of a friendly ally of the emerging Christian movement, serving as a rescuing bodyguard to Paul rather than as a force that takes him captive and confines him as a dangerous criminal.[8]

It seems then that while the Acts shows the early church as respecting Jewish law, it appears here to have enjoyed far better relations with Rome. Though this is not enough to align the work with the subjection material, it can be said that the Paul presented here is entirely compatible with the Paul of the Pastoral stratum in the ten letters, who enjoins subjection to existing governing authority, which can be none other than Rome or those whose authority has Roman sanction. The defiance of Jewish rulers by Peter and John runs counter to this tendency, but the earlier chapters in which this is recounted may well be from a pre-Lucan source.[9] Its retention, moreover, strengthens the impression of cleavage and conflict between Christianity and Judaism, culminating in the rejection of the Jews in favour of the Gentiles in the final chapter (cf. Acts 28: 23-8).

Then too the Areopagite speech of Acts 17: 22-31 shares the basic assumptions of Stoic philosophy with Rom 1: 19 - 2: 1, which has been associated in this study with the Pastoral stratum.[10] Both assert that the knowledge of God is natural to humanity, the first because of the kinship between God and his offspring man (Acts 17: 28), the second because the nature of God is to be perceived in his works (Rom 1: 19f). Both then view God primarily as Creator. They differ however in that Acts 17: 22 regards idolatry as excusable because it arises from ignorance (vs. 30), whereas according to Rom 1: 19 - 2: 1 it is wilful and culpable (Rom 1: 20-2, 28, 32).[11] Also, while Acts 17: 22-31 ascribes idolatry to the ignorance of the past (vs. 3*b*), Rom 1: 19 - 2: 1 argues that God has been known from the beginning but rejected (vss. 19f).

These differences may be explained in part as due to differences in purpose. Acts 17: 22-31 clearly seeks to align the Christian preaching with hellenistic philosophy as an apologetic stratagem,[12] while Rom 1: 19 - 2: 1, it is suggested, seeks also to rebut accusations of sexual licence and perversion and other vices.[13] In this case the tactic adopted is to join the accusers in vehement condemnation of such practices, at the same time ascribing them to idolatrous cults from which dissociation is sought.

Even apart from this explanation, however, it is evident that the two passages share a common circle of ideas and are at one in their acceptance of Stoic thought. Taken in combination with the other points of contact between the Acts and the Pastoral stratum, they strengthen rather than weaken the evidence for some degree of association between the two sets of material.

Like the Pastorals, Acts 20: 18-35 is concerned to combat heretical teachers,[14] compared in Acts 20: 29f to wolves that ravage the flock. That they belong to a time somewhat later than that of the apostle is evident from the words 'after my departure' (vs. 29). So too 2 Timothy refers to all manner of evils, including heretical teachers (2 Tim 3: 6-9) that will come 'in the last days' (2 Tim 3: 1), which is to say, in the future from the standpoint of the apostle's lifetime.

The Acts accords with the Pastoral stratum in general also in the kind of church government it depicts as prevailing in the primitive church. In the earlier stages of the Gentile mission there is mention of the apostles and elders in Jerusalem presiding over the church,[15] whereas on Paul's final return he is shown meeting with the elders and there is no mention of apostles (Acts 21: 18). Outside Jerusalem Paul, represented as subject to the church in Jerusalem,[16] appoints elders in every church (Acts 14: 23), which tallies with the instruction to Titus in the Pastoral epistles to make good a lack in this respect in Crete (Tit 1: 5). It also tallies with the view of succession as handed on from apostle to elder or bishop according to the Pastoral stratum,[17] though there are no clear signs of mon-episcopacy.

Most significant is the resemblance between the charge Paul delivers to the elders of Ephesus (Acts 20: 18–35) and the exhortations to elders in the later layer in 1 Peter (cf. 1 Pet 5: 1–4). Both use the metaphor of the shepherd tending the flock to describe the function of the elders in caring for the church (1 Pet 5: 2). Whereas Acts 20: 28 speaks of guardians, overseers, or bishops (ἐπισκόπους) who are obviously synonymous with the elders referred to in Acts 20: 17, 1 Pet 5: 2 uses the verb of the same root (ἐπισκοποῦντες) to describe the proper activity of elders of the church. Also, both passages oppose the evil of avarice among elders. 1 Peter warns elders not to labour for 'shameful gain', while in Acts 20: 33f Paul claims that he has not coveted silver or gold or clothing, but has served his needs with his own hands. Reminiscent of these concerns are the references to the apostle's self-support and the exhortation to work with one's own hands in the Pastoral material of the ten-letter corpus.[18]

This by no means exhausts the similarities between the Pastoral epistles and the Acts, as indeed Luke–Acts in general.[19] Yet, J. C. O'Neill pointed out, there are no signs that the writer of the Pastorals made direct use of Luke–Acts. He therefore concluded that they must be roughly contemporary.[20] It is not claiming too much to say, in addition, that Luke–Acts in its final form must issue from a circle or milieu that is either identical with or closely related to that from which the Pastoral stratum proceeds. It is difficult, indeed, to conceive of these two developments as taking place in complete independence or ignorance of each other. The possibility that they are intended to supplement each other in presenting an acceptable picture of Paul cannot be too easily dismissed.

In contrast to the New Testament apart from the Pastoral stratum, subjectionist teaching occurs quite clearly to some degree in most early patristic writings, and in some instances is all-pervading.

The Didache

First, Did 4: 9–11 contains injunctions to parents to discipline and teach their children (vs. 9), to slave-owners not to command their slaves harshly (vs. 10), and to slaves to subject themselves to their master as a type of God. The reciprocity of the instructions to masters and slaves resembles Eph 5: 21 – 6: 9 and Col 3: 18 – 4: 1. So too do the references to the fear of God as well as superiors (Did 4: 9, 10, 11; Eph 5: 33, 6: 5, Col 3: 22), the obligation to instruct the young (Did 4: 9; Eph 6: 4), and the impartiality of God (cf. οὐ . . . κατὰ πρόσωπον, Did 4: 10; προσωπολημψία οὐκ ἐστιν, Eph 6: 9, Col 3: 22).

Though some close relation evidently exists between Did 4: 9–11 and the subjection material in the Pastoral stratum, the outlook of the subjection material and the Pastoral stratum does not pervade the Didache as a whole. Significant differences appear in the injunction against eating what has been sacrificed to idols in Did 6: 3, as in earlier Pauline material, and the Didache recognizes the ministrations of itinerant apostles and prophets or teachers and the obligation to support them (Did 10: 7, chs. 11, 13), something which has no parallel in the Pastoral stratum.

The Didache does, however, resemble the epistle to Titus in that there is an instruction to appoint bishops and elders (Did 15: 1f), just as there is in Tit 1: 5 to appoint elders to remedy what is amiss or lacking. Did 15: 1f makes significant contact with the vocabulary of the Pastoral stratum; hence here too some relationship can be assumed.[21] This too could be a later Pastoral-type addition, for it conflicts with the implications of Did 13: 4 that if no prophet resides with a congregation available funds are to go to the poor. Thus it appears that there is no other local leadership to be supported. In addition, the strong eschatological tone of Did 16, and its evident sense of the imminence of the *parousia* (cf. vs. 1), has more in common with earlier strata of the Pauline corpus than the Pastoral stratum.[22] It is therefore assumed that the Didache probably contains some redactional material from the same or a similar source as the Pastoral stratum, but that in the main it issues from different and earlier (apparently Jewish–Christian) circles.[23]

The epistle of Barnabas

Subjectionist teaching of a kind almost exactly similar to that in Did 4: 9–11 appears in Barn 19: 5b, 7, in the course of injunctions following the two ways pattern of Did 1–6, except that here the contrast is between the ways of light and darkness instead of the ways of life and death (cf. Barn 18–20). This part of the epistle of Barnabas appears to be a shortened form of Did 1–6,[24] attached to a homily which interprets the Jewish law and temple cult typologically as referring to moral teaching and to Christ and the church (Barn 2–17).

This material resembles the Pastoral stratum in that it repudiates Jewish food taboos,[25] typologically interpreted as referring to the avoidance of the ungodly (Barn 10: 1-10), and to the knowledge of God and his ways (Barn 10: 11f). As in the later stages of the Pastoral stratum there is repudiation of Judaism, and as in the final chapter of the Acts, the Jews are displaced by the Gentiles.[26]

The situation from which this epistle arises is evidently similar to that of the later stages of the Pastoral stratum, as is also its point of view in relation to the Jews, but there is not sufficient evidence to conclude that a close relationship exists between them. The presence of subjectionist injunctions could be due to their presence in the Didache, which the Epistle of Barnabas may have utilized.

The first epistle of Clement

A far closer relationship appears to exist between the Pastoral stratum and 1 Clement, a work which not only contains material very similar to the subjectionist code in the Pauline corpus and 1 Peter, but which can be described as a homily based throughout on the subjectionist theme as it applies to the church and society.

At the same time, though the epistle clearly knows and uses 1 Corinthians, it does not cite any of the material within it which has been assigned to the Pastoral stratum. Also, though it contains the same terminology and teaching as the subjectionist passages, there is nothing that has the appearance either of literary dependence or incorporation of a subjectionist code. Rather, like the Pastoral epistles, it shares similar tendencies and terminology, indicating that it issues from the same circles at approximately the same time.

This is evident from the outset, for after preliminary greetings and references to calamities and internal disturbances which have delayed the epistle, the writer proceeds to commend the Corinthian church for observance of the rules of subjection to ruler, elders, and to husbands on the part of wives (1: 3, 2: 1). He thereby provides the basis for his main concern, to legitimize and uphold the authority of those in ecclesiastical office. To reject this authority is to be guilty of rebellion ($\sigma\tau\acute{\alpha}\sigma\iota\varsigma$, 1: 1, 3: 2), motivated by 'jealousy and envy' ($\zeta\tilde{\eta}\lambda o\varsigma$ $\kappa\alpha\grave{\iota}$ $\varphi\vartheta\acute{o}\nu o\varsigma$, 3: 2), the primary sins which lead to all others (3: 4).

The Jewish scriptures are then pressed into service to furnish examples, not always very apt, of those who have been victims of this evil, and who can be placed alongside Peter, Paul, and their followers, the persecution of whom is ascribed to the same source (5, 6: 1f). There is also a contrasting catalogue of the obedient, from Enoch to Rahab (9-12), culminating in the assertion that it is right and holy to obey God rather than to follow the initiators of detestable 'jealousy' into strife and sedition (14: 1f).

Supporting the pleas for obedience are appeals for humility (13, 16), love and peace (14: 3-5, 15: 1-4) as in the Pastoral stratum.[27] Here too, as in the Pastoral stratum, there is use of the imitation motif. 1 Clem 16: 3-14 like 1 Pet 2: 21-5 holds up the suffering of Christ for emulation, citing Isa 53. While, however, the former points to the humility of Christ to reinforce the exhortations to obedience, the latter emphasizes his patient endurance of unjust punishment. Biblical figures such as the prophets (17:1), Abraham (17: 2), Job (17: 3), Moses (17: 5f), and David (whose prayer of repentance in Ps 51 is quoted in 1 Clem 18) serve as examples of humility and submission, just as 1 Peter cites Sarah as a model of wifely submission (1 Pet 3: 5f).

1 Clement appeals too to the natural order as an example of submission to God and his decrees (1 Clem 20). The movements of the heavenly bodies (vs. 3), the regular succession of day and night (vs. 2) and of the seasons (vss. 4, 9), the movement of the oceans, waters (vss. 6f, 10b) and winds (vs. 10a) are all cited as instances of obedience to 'the master of the universe' (vs. 11, cf. ch. 33). There is mention also of human creation in God's image (1 Clem 33: 4f, Gen 1: 26f), which supports an exhortation to take the example of the righteous as a pattern for emulation (ὑπο-γραμμόν,[28] 1 Clem 33: 8). These references to the natural world and to creation resemble the tendency of the Pastoral stratum to base ethical injunctions on the created order and on nature understood to include human society.[29]

The good works urged after chapter 20 include injunctions to reverence for Jesus Christ, to honour rulers or officials (προηγουμένους), to respect the aged, or possibly also the presbyters (cf. πρεσβυτέρους), to instruct (παιδεύσωμεν) the young in the teaching of the fear of God (τὴν παιδείαν τοῦ φοβου τοῦ Θεοῦ), and to direct wives in what is good (1 Clem 21: 6), with elaboration on the instruction to be given to wives and the young in vss. 7f. Then too, in 1 Clem 22, as in the Pastoral stratum, more particularly in 1 Peter, there is use of Ps 34 to support the subjectionist teaching and moral instruction in general.[30]

Exhortations in chapters 34-7 culminate in an appeal to serve God as members of an army, in constant readiness and submissiveness to discharge the orders of their generals (37: 2). 'Not all are prefects, or tribunes, or centurions, or leaders of fifty men, and so forth, but each in his own rank (ἐν τῷ ἰδίῳ τάγματι) performs the commands of the king and his generals' (37: 3), the writer goes on to declare. Here there is a distinct correspondence with the teaching of the Pastoral stratum in 1 and 2 Thessalonians.[31]

Alongside the analogy of the army the epistle utilizes that of the body, evidently drawing on 1 Cor 12: 12–26 (1 Clem 37: 4 – 38: 4). As in the subjection material of Eph 5: 21 – 6: 9 submission is represented as mutual (cf. 1 Clem 38: 1, Eph 5: 21). Just as the household head is to care for, instruct, and discipline wife, children, and slaves, and each of these are to render him honour and obedience according to the Ephesians passage, so according to 1 Clem 38: 2 the strong are to care for the weak and the weak to respect the strong, the rich are to help the poor and the poor are to thank God for their help, so that all are united in one subjection (1 Clem 37: 5).

After a digression urging humility, in particular among ascetics (1 Clem 38, 39) the epistle applies the concept of differences in position and function to the rites and services of the church (1 Clem 40). Just as the high priests, priests, and Levites have their own functions allotted to them (vs. 5), so each one in the church is to please God in his own rank (ἐν τῷ ἰδίῳ τάγματι) according to the rule of his ministry (1 Clem 41: 1). The hierarchical ordering of authority found throughout the Pastoral stratum is in evidence here too in that God is said to have sent Jesus Christ, who in turn sent the apostles (1 Clem 42: 1f), who in their turn went about from city to city appointing their first converts to be bishops and deacons (1 Clem 42: 4, cf. Tit 1: 5) to be succeeded by others when they die (1 Clem 42: 4).[32] This divinely ordained transmission of authority the Corinthians have evidently interrupted by ousting from their positions certain presbyters who have served blamelessly (1 Clem 44).

By a discursive argument, then, the writer finally arrives at his main purpose, which is to legitimize and uphold the authority of presbyters. The rest of the epistle serves for the most part to reinforce the concept of submission to ecclesiastical officials.

The epistle draws to a close with a prayer (1 Clem 59: 3 – 61: 3) which culminates in petitions for peace, concord on earth, and civil obedience (1 Clem 60: 4, 61: 1). There is also intercession for the well-being of rulers, that they may so govern as to please God (1 Clem 61: 1f), a feature reminiscent of the call for prayers for rulers in 1 Tim 2: 1f.

Thus the epistle ends where it begins, with a concern for concord in the church, regarded as dependent upon the maintenance of proper ecclesiastical authority. This in turn is based in 1 Clement, as in the Pastoral stratum, on an accepted pattern of authority and subjection in the family and society. The outlook of the subjection material therefore quite clearly pervades the entire epistle, and is by no means confined to certain subjectionist passages.

That there is a significantly close relationship between 1 Clement and the Pastoral stratum appears also from the various other tendencies and characteristics they have in common, mentioned in the course of this survey: appeals for humility, love, and peace in support of the subjectionist theme, use of the imitation motif, including the imitation of the sufferings of Christ, stress on the created order, the concept of reciprocal relations between superiors and subordinates, apostolic succession in the transmission of ecclesiastical authority, and the encouragement of prayer for rulers.

Strong connections between 1 Clement and the Pastoral stratum are evident too in the similarity between the catalogue of vices in 1 Clem 35: 5f and in Rom 1: 29–32, which could be ascribed to dependence one way or the other, or to use of a common source.[33]

The epistle appears to parallel earlier rather than later stages of the Pastoral stratum in that mon-episcopacy does not yet seem to have emerged, unlike 1 Timothy, Titus, and the later material in 1 Peter,[34] for there is no mention of a pre-eminent presbyter or bishop.[35]

In addition, 1 Clement is closer to the Pastoral stratum in the ten-letter corpus than to the Pastoral epistles in that there is no attempt to dissociate the Christian movement from the Jews. On the contrary, as in Luke–Acts, this epistle appears anxious to emphasize continuity not only with the Jewish past, as may be seen in the frequent citations from the LXX, and the use of scriptural characters to illustrate the argument for submission to authority, but also with the current Jewish cult in Jerusalem (1 Clem 40, 41).[36] At the same time there is strong identification also with Roman hegemony, as in the Pastoral stratum,[37] to be seen in the insistence on obedience to and prayers for rulers, and the evident pride in the Roman army and its discipline (1 Clem 37). It can therefore be said that 1 Clement accords with the positive attitude toward both Jews and Greeks expressed in certain parts of the Pastoral layer in the ten-letter corpus.

As in the Pastoral stratum there is a negative attitude toward asceticism (1 Clem 38: 2 – 39: 5). 1 Clement is not, however, as harsh as 1 Timothy in its condemnation of those who forbid marriage and abstain from certain foods (1 Tim 4: 1–3). As in the later stratum in the ten letters, there is mention of 'thanksgiving' for all God provides (1 Clem 38: 4),[38] alongside tolerance for abstainers. Here the abstainers are only warned against boastful elevation of themselves above others (1 Clem 38: 2; 39: 1), and against presuming to be pure before God because of their abstinence (1 Clem 39: 2–5). At the same time the series of derogatory adjectives directed against them (ἄφρονες, ἀσύνετοι, μωροί, ἀπαίδευτοι, 1 Clem 39: 1) approaches the kind of invective used in the Pastoral epistles against heretics (1 Tim 1: 35, Tit 1: 15f). The fact that this material immediately follows an exhortation for all to join in the common subjection of the body of Christ (1 Clem 37: 5, 38: 1) suggests that the ascetics are either identical with, or among, those who have rebelled against the presbyters. Like the later stratum in the ten letters, then, 1 Clement seeks conciliation and unity with those who differ on this issue (51f, 56-8), and not their exclusion as heretics as in the Pastorals.[39] In 1 Clement, however, an open breach is in evidence, which may indicate that it belongs to a slightly later stage in the conflict than the Pastoral stratum in the ten letters, but earlier than the Pastoral epistles.

The epistles of Ignatius

To consider next the epistles connected with Ignatius, and accepting the 'middle recension' for present purposes,[40] it is to be observed that there are no injunctions here corresponding with those directed to subordination in the household and the state in the Pastoral stratum and 1 Clement. In the epistle to Polycarp, however, Ignatius enjoins him to see that slaves do not become conceited or insolent, but serve to the glory of God. They are also not to desire their freedom at the expense of the common fund of the church so as not to be the slaves of desire (Ign Pol 4: 3). There are to be instructions also to wives to love God and their husbands, and to husbands to love their wives as the Lord loves the church, recalling the similar injunctions in Eph 5: 25, 29 (Ign Pol 5: 1).

It can nevertheless be said that the major emphasis of these epistles falls on the necessity for subjection to human authority for, excepting only the letter to the Romans, a constant theme of the collection is obedience to those holding ecclesiastical office, in the interests of unity and harmony in the church, as in 1 Clement.

Here there is no explicit dependence on the household pattern of authority and subjection for the concept of ecclesiastical authority, as in the Pastoral stratum and 1 Clement.[41] As in the Pastorals, however, the church is regarded as a household of which God himself is the head or master. The bishop whom he sends to undertake the management of his household is to be viewed in the same way as the Lord himself (Ign Eph 6: 1).[42] Moreover the immediately preceding verse, citing the saying from Prov 3: 34 that God resists the proud, equates a yielding attitude ($\mu\dot{\eta}$ $\dot{\alpha}\nu\tau\iota\tau\dot{\alpha}\sigma\sigma\epsilon\sigma\vartheta\alpha\iota$) to the bishop with subjection to God ($\Theta\epsilon\hat{\omega}$ $\dot{\upsilon}\pi\sigma\tau\alpha\sigma\sigma\acute{\sigma}\mu\epsilon\nu\sigma\iota$, Ign Eph 5: 3).[43] The bishop then is in a position akin to God in his relation to those properly subordinate to him.

Similarly, according to the household codes of subordination in the Pastoral stratum, wives are to be subject to their husbands as to the Lord (Eph 5: 21f). Slaves are to render obedience and service to their masters according to the flesh as to Christ (Eph 6: 5) and as to the Lord (Eph 6: 7), and not merely as men-pleasers (Eph 6: 6). So too rulers have authority that corresponds with that of God, according to Rom 13: 1-7 and 1 Pet 2: 13, and to resist them is to resist God himself (Rom 13: 2). Also, just as Ign Eph 6: 1 calls for fear of the bishop (cf. φοβείσθω), so too in the subjection material subordinates are instructed to 'fear' or respect superiors.[44]

Corresponding with the pattern of the 'household' code, the bishop, according to Ign Mag 6: 1, is to preside in place of, or as a type of God (depending on whether one accepts the manuscript reading εἰς τόπον or εἰς τύπον[45]), and the elders in the place of or as a type of the apostles. Such association of ecclesiastical authority with the divine appears also in Ign Trall 3, according to which the deacons are to be respected as Jesus Christ and the bishop as a type of the Father, while the elders as the council of God are as the apostolic band.

Ign Mag 13: 2 calls for subjection to the bishop and to 'one another', recalling ὑποτασσόμενοι ἀλλήλοις in Eph 5: 21 and ὑποτάγητε πρεσβυτέροις πάντες δὲ ἀλλήλοις in 1 Pet 5: 5, as Jesus Christ to the Father and the apostles to both. The words καὶ ἀλλήλοις can be construed as referring to various authorities within the community of the church, perhaps with tacit reference to the kind of teaching in the codes of subjection in the Pastoral stratum.

Then too the corpus viewed as a whole follows the same pattern of instruction as the codes of subjection in Eph 5: 21 - 6: 9, Col 3: 18 - 4: 1, and 1 Pet 3: 1-7, 5: 1-5, in that it contains exhortations to congregations to submit themselves to ecclesiastical authorities, and to Polycarp as a bishop concerning the discharge of his duties toward those in a position of subordination to him (Ign Pol, *passim*).

As in the Pastoral stratum, the position of bishop is not necessarily dependent on more advanced age. Just as Timothy's youth is not to be despised according to 1 Tim 4: 12, so Ign Mag 3: 1 urges that due respect be rendered to the bishop, regardless of his youthful appearance, as to the Father, the bishop of all.

Nowhere else in early patristic literature, nor in the Pastoral stratum, however, is there such emphasis on the identification of ecclesiastical office with divine authority. In addition, the threefold pattern of the episcopal ministry (bishop, deacons, presbyters) emerges more clearly here than in 1 Timothy and Titus or elsewhere in early patristic literature. It seems to reflect a more advanced stage of its development than 1 Clement,[46] where there is no sign of an office corresponding to that of the mon-episcopal bishop, either in its despatch from Rome or in the Corinthian church to which it is addressed.

In the Ignatian epistles subjection to such authority is enjoined in the interests of peace, harmony, and unity, over against heresy and schism,[47] the same motivation as is evident in the Pastoral stratum and 1 Clement.[48] While 1 Clem 20 points to the universe as a model of obedience and harmony, Ignatius uses the analogy of a choir which sings in harmony to the tune of a harp, the strings of which represent the presbytery in its close alignment with the bishop (Ign Eph 4: 1f).

Conversely, where there is division God is considered to be absent (Ign Philad 8: 1f). The heresy against which this teaching is directed, described as strange food or poison (Ign Trall 6: 1f), is evidently of the docetic kind, as in the Pastoral stratum, for its adherents deny that Christ suffered in the flesh (Ign Smyr 2) or was in the flesh after his resurrection (Ign Smyr 3), or was born or indeed lived at all in the flesh (Ign Smyr 4: 2 with Ign Smyr 1). That they abstain from the eucharist and do not recognize the flesh of Christ in the eucharistic elements recalls the schismatics of 1 Cor 11: 17–29 (associated with the later stratum[49]), who appear to observe a rite different from that described in 1 Cor 11: 23–6 and do not 'discern the body' in the bread and the cup (1 Cor 11: 29). From Ign Smyr 8 it seems that those attacked were baptising and holding a religious meal different from the recognized eucharist. In both contexts the alternative observance is characterized as invalid (1 Cor 11: 20, Ign Smyr 8: 1f). What makes the difference in Ignatius is the sanction and presence of the bishop (Ign Smyr 8: 2). In 1 Corinthians it is the tradition received from the Lord (1 Cor 11: 23), though Paul has the appearance of an ecclesiastical official akin to the bishop.

The heretical teachings rejected in the Ignatian corpus are also characterized as 'strange doctrines' and useless old myths, apparently connected with Judaism (Ign Mag 8: 1f). If this concerns the same heresy condemned in the epistle to the Smyrnians, that is to say, if it is a type of Jewish docetism, then there is a correspondence to be drawn with the 'Jewish myths' (Ἰουδαϊκοῖς μύθοις) and 'commandments of men', presumably ascetic practices, castigated in Tit 1: 14.

As in the Pastoral stratum (cf. 1 Thess 2: 14f) the Hebrew prophets are aligned with Christ as victims of persecution, over against Judaism (Ign Mag 8: 1f, 9: 2). Here, as in the Pastoral epistles (cf. 1 Tim 1: 3–20, 4: 1–3 with Tit 1: 14), a clear distinction is drawn between Christianity and Judaism. To accept Judaism means one has not received grace (Ign Mag 8: 1*b*). The Jewish Sabbath is to be rejected in favour of 'the Lord's day' (Ign Mag 9: 1). There is evidently still a form of contact with Judaism, among some at least, but it is to be repudiated (Ign Mag 10: 3, Ign Philad

6: 1). Once again, then, one finds a correspondence between the Ignatian epistles and the Pastoral stratum, with the former more explicit than the latter.

Here too as in the Pastoral stratum, in particular the Pastoral epistles,[50] heresy and schism are associated with blasphemy (Ign Eph 10: 2), and an impure conscience (οὐ καθαρός ἐστιν τῇ συνειδήσει, Ign Trall 7: 2). Similarly in the Ignatian letters as in the Pastoral stratum,[51] there is a sharp differentiation between those in good standing in the church and in subjection to the episcopate, and those who are in heresy and schism. Those within the sanctuary are characterized as pure, while those who separate themselves and are without are not (Ign Trall 7: 2). On this basis Ignatius draws a distinction between the church and the world that is not far distant from eschatological dualism (Ign Mag 3-7). Once again, then, Ignatius brings to a logical conclusion a tendency present with less clarity in the Pastoral stratum (Ign Mag 3, 4, 6, 7).

The same kind of relationship between the two sets of material appears in the intrinsic value attached in each to suffering as a Christian martyr. The beginnings of martyrology may be present in the biographical portions of 2 Timothy (cf. 1: 8, 2: 9f, 3: 10f, 4: 6-8), though there is nothing here to indicate that the apostle's suffering and death are considered meritorious in and of themselves. The concept does, however, find expression in the later material in 1 Peter (cf. 1 Pet 3: 14, 4: 14). Likewise 1 Clement furnishes examples of those who have won a reward through righteous suffering.[52] In Ignatius the tendency finds most extreme expression, however, in that he goes so far as to desire and to seek suffering and death, and writes to the church in Rome to refrain from any attempts to save him from this fate, for by this means he will 'attain to God' (Ign Rom 1: 2, 2: 1), become Christ's freedman, rise free from any desire (Ign Rom 4: 3), attain to Jesus Christ (Ign Rom 5: 3), receive pure light (Ign Rom 6: 2), and become a man (Ign Rom 6: 2). In this respect too, then, Ignatius accentuates and takes to its logical conclusion a trend in the Pastoral stratum and 1 Clement.

The Ignatian corpus resembles these writings also in its frequent use of the imitation theme. Ignatius observes or enjoins the imitation of God (Ign Eph 1: 1, Ign Mag 6: 2, Ign Trall 1: 2, Ign Rom 6: 3), of the Lord (Ign Eph 10: 3), of Christ (Ign Philad 7: 2, Ign Smyr 12), of individuals such as Onesimus (Ign Eph 1: 3), and Byrrhus (Ign Smyr 12), while he himself hopes to be found in the footsteps of Paul (Ign Eph 12: 2). Here too the concept of imitation involves that of a descending hierarchy of types. Thus Ign Philad 7: 2 exhorts to imitation of Jesus Christ as he imitates the Father, and Ign Smyr 12: 1 that all imitate Byrrhus, who is a model of the service of God. Similarly, as already shown, the bishop and elders are regarded as types of God and the apostles.[53]

It can be concluded, then, from examination of the tendencies of the Ignatian epistles, that their origin cannot be far removed from the circles responsible for the literary material associated with the subjectionist teaching in the Pauline corpus and 1 Peter.

Polycarp

The same applies to Polycarp's epistle to the Philippians, which assumes the subordinationist teaching, though it does not contain explicit injunctions for subjection to authority in the household and the state. It does, however, make contact with the Pastoral stratum and 1 Clement in the request for prayers for 'kings, rulers, and princes, and for those who persecute and hate you, and for the enemies of the cross' (12: 3).[54] The prayers for persecutors are reminiscent of the injunctions in Rom 12: 14–21, that is to say, in material associated with the subjectionist teaching in Rom 13: 1–7, to bless persecutors, to renounce vengeance, and to live peaceably with all.

The Latin portion of the text also contains instructions to all to be subject to one another (Pol Phil 10: 2), which, like Ign Mag 13: 2, recall Eph 5: 21 and 1 Pet 5: 5. Moreover the ethical motivation, 'having your conversation above reproach among the Gentiles that you may receive praise for your good works and that the Lord may not be blasphemed because of you' (Pol Phil 10: 2*b*), is precisely the same as that found in the Pastoral stratum, particularly in relation to the instructions to various categories of people to fulfil their duties according to their station.[55]

Though the subjectionist motif is muted in Polycarp's letter, this epistle resembles the Pastoral stratum in that in the course of general exhortations to all[56] there are instructions for wives to be taught to remain in the faith and in love and purity, to love their husbands and others in chastity, and to instruct their children in the fear of God (4: 2), for widows to pray continuously and avoid various evils (4: 3), for deacons to conduct themselves as servants of God (5: 2), for younger men to avoid immorality (5: 3), and for elders to care for the weak and needy and to avoid overbearing behaviour (6: 1).[57]

Also muted in Polycarp's letter is his position as mon-episcopal bishop. Were it not for the fact that Ignatius writes to him as bishop of Smyrna (Ign Pol Inscription) and instructs him in the fulfilment of this office (Ign Pol 1–5), it would not be clear whether he is to be regarded as a mon-episcopal bishop or not. His letter to the Philippians contains no reference to this office, though it can perhaps be inferred from the opening words, 'Polycarp and the elders with him', which suggest that he is probably the leader of the group of elders in Smyrna. This reticence may, however, be intended as a mark of humility, for in other respects his letter accords quite clearly with the kind of ecclesiastical organization emphasized in the Ignatian letters.[58] Not only does he mention deacons as well as elders (Pol Phil 5: 2, 6: 1), but he also calls for subjection to them as to God and to Christ (Pol Phil 5: 3), which is precisely the view of Ignatius concerning the obedience due to the bishop, deacons, and presbytery (Ign Eph 5–6).[59]

The lack of any mention of the bishop by Polycarp becomes more explicable if this epistle is regarded as an integral part of the Ignatian corpus completing the pattern of instruction, first to subordinates in their subjection to their superiors, and secondly to superiors in the use of their authority over subordinates. Ignatius' letters fulfil this pattern in the instructions to churches to subject themselves to the bishop, elders, and deacons, and in the instructions to the bishop in the person of Polycarp, from a fellow bishop who is in some sense prior and elder.[60] Polycarp in turn is to be seen instructing elders or presbyters and deacons in their duties, thereby completing the pattern of instruction in reciprocal duties.

Polycarp's letter coheres closely with the Pastoral stratum and the literature related to it in other respects also. It shares with it the tendency to use the theme of imitation. There is, for instance, its reference to 'the pattern' ($\tau \grave{a} \; \mu \mu \acute{\eta} \mu a \tau a$) of true love (Pol Phil 1: 1). There is also its exhortation to imitate Christ's endurance in suffering in a passage that bears a striking resemblance to that portion of the later material in 1 Peter which deals with the same subject (cf. Pol Phil 8: 1f, 1 Pet 2: 21–4).[61] In addition the letter points to the example of the apostles and other martyrs, including Ignatius, mentioned here as if he has already suffered and died (Pol Phil 9: 1f).

Here too, as in the Ignatian epistle to the Romans, and also 1 Clement and the Pastoral stratum, the sufferings of martyrdom are represented as having intrinsic merit or value for which a reward accrues (Pol Phil 9: 2).[62] Related to this is the idea of 'good works' (*bonis operibus*) as earning God's praise (Pol Phil 10: 2), as in the Pastoral epistles and the later material in 1 Peter.[63]

Like Ignatius' letter to the Smyrnians, Polycarp's letter condemns heresy which is evidently of the docetic kind (Pol Phil 7: 1, cf. Ign Smyr 2). There is no mention of any Jewish connections, but to maintain that none therefore exists would be a dubious argument from silence. It can be said, on the other hand, that the teaching condemned in Polycarp's letter is clearly similar to that castigated in Ignatius' letters and in the Pastoral epistles.

In arguing that Polycarp is the writer of the Pastoral epistles H. von Campenhausen pointed to similarities not only in tendency and content, but also in the use of language. First he mentioned that there are four words in Polycarp's letter found only in the Pastorals in the New Testament, which is more than appear anywhere else in the apostolic fathers.[64] He points also to the common use of the expression ὁ νῦν αἰών instead of the more usual αἰὼν οὗτος (Pol Phil 5: 2, 9: 2, 1 Tim 6: 17, 2 Tim 4: 10, Tit 2: 13),[65] the use of προάγειν and ἐπακολουθεῖν in close conjunction in Pol Phil 3: 3 and 1 Tim 5: 24,[66] and the occurrence of some common idioms in which the correspondence is not such that it can be ascribed to literary dependence.[67]

To add to the evidence for a close connection with the Pastoral epistles, as indeed the Pastoral stratum in general, it can be said that Polycarp's letter resembles them in its frequent use of words which are compounds formed from nouns and/or adjectives and/or verbs,[68] and also that it makes frequent use of antithetic parallels.[69]

Whether or not von Campenhausen was correct in identifying the author of the Pastorals with the author of Polycarp's epistle to the Philippians, it can be agreed that the three Pastoral epistles are to be associated with this letter and share the same ecclesiastical milieu.[70] For the present purpose, then, Polycarp's letter is accepted along with the Ignatian epistles and 1 Clement as part of a complex of writings forming the literary context of the Pastoral stratum and so also of the subjection material of the New Testament.

Conclusion

The conclusion of the literary and critical aspect of this study is that while the subjection material together with the passages associated with it in the Pauline corpus and 1 Peter is to be dissociated from the earlier layers or strata in which they are embedded, it bears a significant relation to Luke-Acts and coheres easily with literature of the early patristic period, in particular, 1 Clement, the Ignatian collection, and Polycarp's epistle to the Philippians.

How close the relationship is to each of these patristic writings is a matter which must await future, more exhaustive investigation. If the vocabulary analysis undertaken in respect of the Pastoral stratum and the various writings of the New Testament[71] were extended to the patristic writings, the results would very likely be positive. Even if they were inconclusive or negative, however, this would not be sufficient to outweigh the conclusions reached from examination of tendencies and points of view to the effect that the Pastoral stratum belongs with this literature in a common ecclesiastical development.

Time and place of the Pastoral stratum

Inasmuch as this stream represents that which came to be recognized as orthodoxy over against heresy, and valid order over against invalid and therefore schismatic activity, it is to be associated with what has been termed 'early catholicism', which came to be centred in Rome, whether or not it originated there.

Regardless of where the Pastoral stratum and the documents associated with it had their genesis, the geographical location which is of greatest significance within this tradition is Rome. Politically speaking this is quite obviously the case. The teaching on subjection to the state can have in mind none other than imperial Rome and those through whom its hegemony is exercised. The identification with Rome as opposed to the Jews and other subject peoples has already been observed in the Pastoral stratum,[72] and with the Roman army in 1 Clement,[73] while the Roman militia appears in a particularly favourable light in the Acts.[74]

From an ecclesiastical point of view the same applies. One of the purposes of the extended account of Paul's career in the Acts is evidently to span the distance between the primitive Christian community in Jerusalem and the church established in the capital city of the Roman empire. 2 Timothy is written as from the apostle during his imprisonment in Rome and directed to Asia Minor, since it appears to assume that Timothy is stationed in Ephesus.[75] 1 Clement represents an intervention in the affairs of a major church of the Aegean area by the Roman church. Ignatius' letters are not only written in the course of his journey to Rome where he faces martyrdom, but his letter to the church in Rome addresses it with such superlative praise as compared with the salutations to the churches of Asia Minor, that a primacy of honour but not of actual jurisdiction seems to be a tacit assumption. (Governing authority is evidently limited to the area surrounding Rome, Ign. Rom Inscription.) Moreover, this epistle, like 1 Clement, couples the two foremost apostles Peter and Paul together as standing in a special relation to the church in Rome (Ign Rom 4: 3, 1 Clem 5), and Ignatius disclaims any right to command it as did these two apostles. Instead he is a suppliant, beseeching the Roman Christians not to use their influence to prevent his martyrdom (Ign Rom 2–8). This in itself is a remarkable capitulation, considering that Antioch could have put forward similar claims concerning its relation to these two apostles.[76]

Ignatius, then, has ground for adopting the same tone of authority toward Rome as he does toward the other churches to which he writes.

Antioch's position vis-à-vis other churches is further weakened by the fact that Ignatius appeals for special help in the form of prayers for the church in Syria[77] as well as envoys to rejoice and glory with the church there in its restored peace.[78] In the context of the Ignatian letters this can mean none other than the restoration of good order, which is apparently presumed to have lapsed in Ignatius' absence, since no bishop has replaced him (Ign Rom 9: 1). It can be construed that the arrival of representatives from other churches would serve to strengthen the new episcopal leadership. However this may be, the impression is by no means that of a powerful eastern church extending its influence westward. Ignatius' voice is rather that of an eminent individual. In view of his virtual recognition of Roman pre-eminence, it may be said that his stance is Roman rather than Syrian.

Significantly, it is the Roman church that is reminded that Antioch lacks a bishop (Ign Rom 9: 1), and only the Roman church of all those to which Ignatius writes receives no exhortations on the subject of church order. Considering the priority given to this matter in the other letters, this must mean that no such exhortations are considered necessary, leading to the conclusion that Roman church government is viewed as firmly established, whereas that of the other churches is to some degree in jeopardy.[79] Thus the form of church government he advocates is presumably more typical of Rome than of any other centre which comes within the purview of his epistles. This conclusion receives confirmation from the apparent Roman origin of 1 Clement, which upholds the same kind of ecclesiastical authority, though mon-episcopacy is either absent or goes unmentioned.[80]

It is true that the Aegean area receives more attention than either Syria or Rome in the documents under consideration, yet this fact only serves to emphasize the extent to which it is subject to direction from without, from Rome via 1 Clement, and from Syria via Ignatius' letters. Polycarp's letter is of crucial importance for the validation and endorsement of the Ignatian letters, but he too is subject to Ignatius' directions, and the brevity of his letter is in striking contrast to the length of the other documents mentioned above.

Cumulatively, then, the literature connected with the Pastoral stratum has the effect of subordinating Achaea, Asia Minor, and Syria to Rome in terms of authority and importance. It can be said, too, that the writings in question, including the Pastoral stratum, represent a 'Roman' point of view, regardless of their place or places of origin.[81] The affinities of this stratum with 1 Clement point to Rome as the place of writing, while the close connections between the Pastoral epistles and Polycarp's epistle point to the Aegean area. If the latter is accepted as the venue for the Pastoral epistles, it must be concluded that the Pastoral stratum as a whole probably took shape there under strong 'Roman' influence, that is to say, in circles which were closely in touch with the Roman church and represented its point of view in those parts. These circles were also clearly in close touch with Rome in a cultural sense, if one takes into account the Latin character of the thought and language which F. R. Montgomery Hitchcock found in the Pastoral epistles.[82]

If Rome is their venue, then the question arises whether the same applies to Polycarp's letter to the Philippians, considering its close connections with the Pastoral epistles. In this case, however, it cannot be genuine and its date must be placed no earlier than A.D. 155, the probable year of Polycarp's martyrdom.[83]

As for the Ignatian letters, the question arises how the most developed version of early catholic tendencies in all early patristic literature came to be enunciated by a Christian martyr from the remote province of Syria. The normal isolation of the church in those parts from western orthodox circles appears from the appeals of Ignatius for the sending of envoys.

It is of course possible to resort to the theory of an amanuensis from Asia Minor who had excessive influence on content. A candidate for such a role exists in the person of Byrrhus, a deacon said to have been sent to Ignatius by the Ephesian and Smyrnian churches, and named as the one by whose hand he writes (Ign Eph 2: 1, Ign Philad 11: 2). In this case Ignatius has been enlisted by orthodox elements in Asia Minor in support of local bishops in their conflict with heresy.

A further difficulty presents itself in Polycarp's reference to Ignatius as among those who have suffered martyrdom and are 'with the Lord in the place due to them' (Pol Phil 9), whereas according to the latter part of the epistle his fate is not yet known (Pol Phil 13: 2). Harrison's two-letter hypothesis, however, provides an explanation which makes it possible to maintain the genuineness of the material ascribed to Polycarp in spite of this discrepancy.[84]

There the conclusion could rest, with the evidence weighing in favour of the Aegean area as the venue for Polycarp's epistle and the Pastoral stratum, were it not for the apparent Roman origin of 1 Clement. So close is its thought to that of the material just mentioned that it must be assumed either that Rome is in fact the place of origin of all the material in question, or that orthodox circles in or near Corinth or Ephesus wrote it as if from Rome, with the knowledge and support of ecclesiastical authority there, as reinforcement for their position in a local conflict.

The dating of the Pastoral stratum must needs be as fluid as its geographical location. Whatever the conclusion on this question, the Pastoral stratum could not have begun to appear in the ten-letter corpus much earlier than the end of the first century, given the conclusion that Col 3: 18 – 4: 1 and Eph 5: 21 – 6: 9 are subsequent to the main body of a deutero-Pauline epistle such as Ephesians.[85] A.D. 90 is therefore posited as a feasible *terminus a quo*.

A *terminus ad quem* for the earlier stages of the stratum may be determined by reference to Marcion's appearance in Rome in A.D. 138 or 139.[86] It is difficult to say with any certainty whether Marcion arrived in Rome from Asia Minor with his version of the Pauline epistles, or whether he produced it after his arrival, and in this case, whether he did so before or after his expulsion from the church in Rome. If the latter is correct, his canon probably did not appear much later than A.D. 145 or 146, and the version of the Pauline letters which he used must have been one issuing from early catholic circles at least a few years before this time, that is, not much later than A.D. 140. Since it appears that almost all of the later or Pastoral stratum in the ten-letter corpus was included in Marcion's version,[87] this date may be repeated as a *terminus ad quem* for most of the Pastoral material in the ten-letter corpus.

It is reasonable to conclude, then, that the Pastoral stratum began to find literary expression in the Pauline writings in Asia Minor and/or Rome between A.D. 90 and 140. Attempts to date it more exactly must needs be tentative, owing to the paucity of evidence.

The one event within this period which is more likely than any other to have left its mark on current Christian literature is the Jewish war of A.D. 132 to 135, culminating in the destruction of Jerusalem, the building of the city of Aelia Capitolina upon its ruins, the banishing of all Jews from the area, and the suppression of the practice of Judaism throughout the empire,[88] a state of affairs which continued for three years until some of the restrictions were relaxed during the reign of Antoninus Pius.[89]

C. Eggenberger rejected the usually accepted dating of 1 Clement (A.D. 93-6) in favour of the period of Hadrian's reign. He argued that it must have been written before the Jewish war of A.D. 132 to 135 because of its emphasis on the Jewish cult in the temple of Jerusalem as a valid model. This, he pointed out, was an impossibility for any writer friendly to the imperial power after the displacement of the Jewish temple by a temple to Jupiter.[90] Similarly, it can be argued that certain parts at least of the Pastoral material in the ten-letter corpus are more likely to belong to the period before this conflict than after it. Among these are the later stratum in 1 Cor 10 and 11,[91] since the conduct recommended here in regard to food sacrificed to idols aims at maintaining good relations with both Jews and Greeks (1 Cor 11: 32), and here as also in 1 Cor 8 and Rom 14: 1 - 15: 6 at maintaining unity with those who adhere to food taboos which are probably Jewish in character.[92] Significantly, much the same attitude is in evidence toward the ascetics referred to in 1 Clement.[93]

Quite a different reaction manifests itself, however, in 1 Thess 2: 14–16, which occurs in the course of material assigned to the Pastoral stratum[94] and which was also included in Marcion's corpus.[95] The import of this part of the text is that the wrath of God has come upon the Jews of Judaea 'finally' or 'to the uttermost' ($\varepsilon\grave{\iota}\varsigma$ $\tau\acute{\varepsilon}\lambda o\varsigma$, 1 Thess 2: 16) for killing the Lord Jesus and the prophets, persecuting the apostles and preventing them from preaching to the Gentiles, and opposing all people (vss. 15f). This catalogue of wrongs is evidently thought to lead up to and explain some culminating visitation of wrath.

The Pauline origin of the passage has seldom been challenged. Hence the possibility that it refers to one or other devastation of Jerusalem by the Romans has been precluded. The disaster of A.D. 70 would be the most likely event to have given rise to such a passage if it were deutero-Pauline in character or could be ascribed to the original Pauline redactor(s). The earlier version of the letter collection, however, evidences such strong and proud Jewish identification that it is unthinkable that the condemnation of Jews contained in this passage could have issued from the circles responsible for the original Pauline collection.[96]

Assuming that the association of 1 Thess 2: 1–16 with a trito-Pauline layer is correct, the earlier destruction would probably have been too remote for the immediacy implied by $\check{\varepsilon}\varphi\vartheta\alpha\sigma\varepsilon\nu$ in vs. 16. The event must needs be closer in time. Action against the Jews also took place during the reign of Domitian (A.D. 80–95), who gave orders for the execution of members of the family of David, which is to say, potential candidates for Jewish messiahship (Eusebius, *H. E.* III 19). It appears, however, from Eusebius' citation of Hegesippus' account of the questioning of the grandsons of Judas, described as the blood brother of Jesus and of the house of David (Eusebius, *H. E.* III 19), that the Christian defence was not at this stage to repudiate the Jews, for after their release the grandsons of Judas were honoured with leadership in Christian communities (*H. E.* III 20).

The occasion of the widespread upheavals among Jews in 115–17 is also to be rejected, for Palestinian Jewry does not seem to have been involved,[97] though Loukas, the leader of the Jewish rebels in Cyrenaica, is reported to have fled to Palestine where he was captured after some resistance and executed.[98]

The only remaining possibility for the dating of 1 Thess 2: 14–16, then, appears to be soon after the end of the Jewish war of A.D. 132–5. Significantly Justin wrote about this war in very similar terms in his Dialogue with Trypho,[99] represented as having taken place soon after the war. He wrote in a similar way too in his First Apology addressed to the emperor Antoninus Pius.[100]

In this case, however, it must be assumed that either 1 Thess 2: 14–16 or the entire passage of which it is part (1 Thess 2: 1–16) was added to the epistle in the later stages of redactional accretion in the period between A.D. 135 and 140, whereas other parts of the stratum were introduced earlier. If the earlier parts are associated with 1 Clement, then the beginnings of the Pastoral stratum are to be dated at approximately the same time as this work, and perhaps somewhat earlier.[101]

If the parallels C. Eggenberger claims exist between 1 Clement and various writers at the time of Trajan and Hadrian prove convincing,[102] it can be agreed that a date near the beginning of Hadrian's reign in A.D. 118 is feasible in both instances.

This dating is more likely than the latter part of Trajan's reign, when people were liable to be arrested and executed for the name of Christian unless they recanted by worshipping the emperor's image, even though imperial policy discouraged seeking them out, and cautioned against anonymous accusations.[103] It is difficult to reconcile this with the confident assertion of Rom 13: 1–7 that the ruling authorities have only to be obeyed in order to win their praise and avoid punishment.

On the other hand the rescript of Hadrian, cited by Justin in his First Apology to Antoninus Pius (cf. Ap I 69), provides more positive legal protection in that it requires charges against Christians to be brought before a court of justice and punishment meted out in accordance with offences, and those guilty of bringing libellous charges are to be punished. This falls short of actual recognition of the new faith, and there is nothing to indicate the repeal of Trajan's edict forbidding societies, mentioned in Pliny's letter to the emperor. Thus considerable uncertainty concerning the position of Christians vis-à-vis the Roman state probably continued, though there is no direct evidence of Roman-supported persecution of Christians during Hadrian's reign.[104] The fact that the first recorded instances of Christian apologies directed to a Roman emperor are those of Quadratus and Aristides to Hadrian (Eusebius, *H. E.* IV 3) suggests a more favourable climate than formerly for the public profession of Christianity.

If this is indeed the time when the Pastoral stratum and the subjection material began to emerge in Christian writings, much within it receives illumination. The situation of Christians described above is precisely one in which one may expect strong expressions of loyalty to the imperial authority, coupled with exhortations to obedience and good behaviour so that popular charges may be proved false. The continued danger of accusations by informers as well as mob outcries against Christians[105] could well account for the exhortations to behave in such a way as to gain the good will of fellow citizens, superiors, and neighbours, and to avoid giving offence by contradicting accepted social patterns. This kind of ethic is understandable at a time when the Christian movement began to surface cautiously from obscurity and secrecy in expectation of possible official recognition.

On the other hand, the same expectations could conceivably have been roused after the death of Domitian under the more tolerant regime of Nerva (96–98) and at the beginning of Trajan's reign, before his edict banning unrecognized associations. Such a dating would accord with the generally accepted view that 1 Clement was written in A.D. 96 or shortly thereafter,[106] the Pastoral epistles in the opening years of the second century,[107] and Ignatius' letters and Polycarp's epistle later in Trajan's reign.[108]

The generally accepted chronology, however, leaves unexplained the strong reaction against the Jews and Judaism reflected in certain parts of the Pastoral stratum and in Ignatius' epistles,[109] and does not account for the visitation of wrath on the Jews of Judaea referred to in 1 Thess 2: 14–16. It is evident from the correspondence between Pliny and Trajan that Christians had by this time become distinguishable from Jews in Roman eyes. Even so, some identification with Judaism would have been to the advantage of Christians since it could have supported claims to the kind of recognition they enjoyed, even after the Jewish revolts of 115–17.

Such association with the Jewish heritage and cult, combined with protestations of loyalty and repudiation of sedition as occur in 1 Clement would, perhaps, have been particularly advantageous in the opening years of Hadrian's reign if Baron is correct in thinking that the new emperor tried to pacify his Jewish subjects by expressing intentions to rebuild Jerusalem and even the temple.[110]

In the conflict that followed it is understandable that Christians had no alternative but to continue their pro-Roman stance and side with the Romans, unless they were to suffer the same uncompromising repression as was inflicted on Judaism after the rebellion.[111] Nothing could better explain the change in relations between Christians and Jews in the writings under consideration than to assume that these events are indeed the historical context of those writings. The rejection of the Jewish God and scriptures by Cerdo and Marcion[112] then falls into place as a more extreme reaction against Judaism than the parallel one manifested in the Pastoral epistles, as well as in the Ignatian letters and the writings of Justin.

On this basis it can be posited that Marcion used the version of Paul's letters as he found it in early catholic circles[113] immediately after the Jewish war, and that his corpus did not contain the Pastoral epistles because they had not yet appeared, or had not yet reached him. If he had known them he could easily have incorporated them with only minor excisions.[114] Why, then, should he have invited criticism unnecessarily by rejecting them?

Similarly, the Pastoral epistles are directed against heresy of a Jewish type rather than against Marcionism, except perhaps in the reference to 'antitheses of knowledge falsely so-called' in 1 Tim 6: 20, though this phrase could have in mind dualistic heresy in general, rather than Marcion's Antitheses in particular. Either way Marcionism has apparently not yet become a major issue; thus a date beyond A.D. 145 for 1 Timothy, the latest of the Pastoral epistles, is unlikely.

For reasons already given, the Pastoral layer in 1 Peter is to be ascribed to the same time as the Pastoral epistles or somewhat later.[115] On the basis of the earlier dating for 1 Clement and the other writings under consideration, it would seem to have been written in the latter half of Trajan's reign, in response to the sporadic persecution experienced at that time.[116] On the basis of the later dating it may be assigned to the beginning of the reign of Antoninus Pius, who apparently did nothing to prevent the execution of people for the name of Christian,[117] including Telesphoros, bishop of Rome.[118]

Rom 1: 19 – 2: 1 may be assigned to approximately the same time as the Pastorals and the later material in 1 Peter, for reasons already given.[119] It is best understood as a refutation of the kinds of accusations commonly made against Christians, for instance in the oration of Cornelius Fronto, probably during his consulship in A.D. 143.[120]

If the generally accepted dating of 1 Clement, the Pastoral epistles, and the letters of Ignatius and Polycarp is followed, the Pastoral stratum may be assumed to belong to the period between 95 and 117, which is to say, the reigns of Nerva and Trajan. If the later dating suggested above is preferred, it would seem to have emerged in the period between 118 and 150, that is to say, the reign of Hadrian and the early years of Antoninus Pius' reign, or, expressed differently, the time before and after the second Jewish war. The latter has appeared to offer the most adequate explanation for the various factors involved, but is put forward tentatively and provisionally, pending fuller exploration of the impact of the events of 132-5 upon Christian tradition.

In many respects, however, a very similar situation in life can be deduced whichever dating is preferred. Internally the church was beset by divisions caused by the activities of charismatic leaders and groups who were often gnostic and enthusiastic in character. Externally the church was actually illegal and subject to calumny and suspicion of subversion. Arrest, interrogations, and extreme punishment were a continual possibility, though systematic persecution was not official policy, so that action against Christians was sporadic. Whether or not charges were brought against them depended largely on the good will or hostility of immediate neighbours, acquaintances, and superiors. Survival therefore depended on maintaining friendly relations with all, living according to approved customs, giving satisfaction to masters, providing as little cause as possible for criticism, and avoiding the impression that Christian influence was disturbing to or undermining the peace and security of the household and the state.

Moreover, it would have been in the interests of Christian apologetic to maintain traditional authority at a time when patriarchal authority had become much weakened and family ties had loosened.[121] The father had lost the power of life and death over his children, laid down in the Twelve Tables and the Royal Laws, as also the right to sell a child into slavery.[122] The older legally recognized forms of marriage (*confarreatio, coemptio,* and *usus*[123]) had given way to recognition of marriage *sine manu*, which left the wife free from the husband's legal control (*manus viri*).[124] In addition, restrictions on the master's power over his slaves culminated in Antoninus Pius' prohibition against the killing of a slave by the sole order of the master.[125] These legal changes evidently went hand in hand with greater laxity in all three areas of patriarchal authority, in practice as well as attitude.[126] Monogamous marriage in particular was a failing institution owing partly to the concubinage that accompanied slavery,[127] and partly to the ease with which divorce could be obtained under marriage *sine manu*.

In such circumstances it is possible that the church stood to gain by upholding an ideal of authority and virtue that accorded with the traditional past rather than the present. The promise of the new faith to renew the decaying institutions of marriage and the household and to restore the power of the *pater familias* could indeed have exercised a strong appeal in many quarters.

It would also have accorded to some degree with imperial policy for, though the Flavian and Antonine emperors brought welcome relief from the terror and tyranny of Domitian's reign, and attempted to humanize patriarchal authority, there are signs that they also tried to overcome the laxity of the times. It was during the reign of Hadrian that the cult of discipline was introduced into the army, and under the Antonines in general discipline and duty became watchwords.[128] Thus, though Hadrian restricted the master's right of life and death over his slaves, there was also increased rigour in their treatment during his reign.[129] Indeed, imperial rule was essentially as autocratic as ever, though the excesses of Domitian had ceased, and the empire as a whole was a military dictatorship which it was not possible to defy with impunity.[130]

In these circumstances the subjectionist teaching of the New Testament would have commended itself as a means of meeting both the internal and the external problems of the church. It not only provided the basis for the development of the episcopal ministry and the concept of apostolic tradition in the struggle against heresy, but also served as an assurance of loyalty to the institutions of existing society and a source of support for their continuance. Within this setting, then, it is assumed the Pastoral version of the Pauline corpus and 1 Peter emerged.

The Pastoral stratum in the history of the text

The question has still to be answered, however, how such a far-reaching revision and expansion of the Pauline writings and 1 Peter could have won acceptance so effectively that no pre-Pastoral version survived or left its mark on manuscript transmission.

There is external evidence that the Pastoral epistles were probably not always part of the collection,[131] but such indications of an earlier version of the ten letters are much less decisive. The textual variation placing 1 Cor 14: 34f after vs. 40 is not such as to have arisen from the absence of the fragment in some manuscripts, but rather from an attempt to bring about a smoother reading.[132] Otherwise, apart from minor glosses,[133] evidence is confined to the possible absence of Rom 1: 19 - 2: 1 in Marcion's text and the lack of any explicit mention of Rom 13: 1-7, 14: 1 - 15: 6, and Col 3: 18 - 4: 1 in Tertullian's analysis of Marcion's version.[134]

The fact that the closing benediction in Romans (16: 25-7) appears after 14: 23, 15: 33, and 16: 33 in different manuscripts[135] suggests that the epistle ended at varying points in different versions. Since, however, the Pastoral material thought to begin at 14: 1 extends to 15: 6, none of these variations provides evidence for the original absence of that passage.

Direct evidence for the existence of an earlier shorter version of a text is not, however, a *sine qua non* for a theory of redactional expansion; else the Proto-Luke, Q, and Johannine source hypotheses would have to be ruled out of court in the study of the gospels, and theories of the combination of different letters in Pauline scholarship would likewise have to be discounted. Since, however, Paul was a major storm centre in early Christian history, and one of the controversies surrounding him after his death involved a different version of the epistolary text, some explanation of its relative stability in the manuscript tradition is needed.

For the Pastoral epistles and 1 Peter the question is one relating to the acceptance or otherwise of entire letters as canonical because of an eventual consensus that they are both apostolic and orthodox. It can be assumed that 1 Peter was constructed from a small and obscure deutero-Pauline-type letter which provided verisimilitude with earlier Christian writings. The real problem relates to the Pauline ten-letter corpus. How could extensive additions and editorial rearrangement have been introduced into the writings of a prominent apostle and found acceptance without undue influence from the earlier version? Under what circumstances and at what stage in the development of the corpus is it feasible that this could have happened?

At first sight the simplest explanation would seem to be that the Pastoral editor was the original collector who brought the corpus into being, or else that he revised and reissued the corpus after it had fallen into obscurity and disuse. The latter has the advantage of not having to contend with the influence of the local circulation of individual letters before the formation of the collection. It can also accommodate the finding of C. L. Mitton that Ephesians has knowledge of all the other letters in the ten-letter corpus and is therefore subsequent to the rest, and the finding of the present study that Ephesians contains Pastoral material which has been added to an earlier version. It leaves room more easily too for the possibility of further deutero-Pauline and pre-Pastoral material in the corpus, including the earlier version of 2 Thessalonians, some portions of 1 Corinthians, and all or most of pre-Pastoral Colossians. A remaining question would be, then, how the writings of an apostle thought sufficiently important to have pseudonymous material ascribed to him could have been forgotten and virtually discarded.

Even more serious for the two possibilities mentioned above is the question of motive. Why should a later, Pastoral redactor have taken the trouble either to assemble or to revive what was, to a considerable degree, in tension and even outright conflict with his point of view? From the following listing it is evident that such material is to be found in all the ten letters to some degree:

1 Sharp (day vs. night, light vs. darkness) dichotomy between the church and the world: Rom 12, 13 (earlier stratum); 1 Cor 6, 10: 1–22, 2 Cor 6: 14 – 7: 1; Eph 4: 17–19, 5: 7f, 6: 10–20; 1 Thess 5: 3–5.
2 Rejection of the Gentile (Roman) state and law courts: Rom 8: 38; 1 Cor 2: 8, 6: 1–4, 15: 24, Eph 6: 12.

3 Elevation of celibacy above marriage: 1 Cor 7: 8, 25–40.
4 Women on equal terms with men: Rom 16: 1–16; 1 Cor 7: 1–4, 32–4, 14: 26, 31; Gal 3: 28.
5 Slaves on equal terms with the free: 1 Cor 7: 21–3, 12: 13; Gal 3: 28; Col 3: 11, 4: 9 with Phm 15–17.
6 Persecution of Paul and his followers without any explanation of Jewish instigation: Rom 8: 18, 35f; 1 Cor 4: 11–13; 2 Cor 1: 5–10, 6: 3–10, 7: 5, 12: 10; Eph 4: 1, 6: 20; Phil 1: 7, 12–14; Col 1: 24, 4: 10; 1 Thess 3: 3f, 7; 2 Thess 1: 5–7.
7 Rejection of hellenistic philosophic wisdom: 1 Cor 1: 18–21, 2: 1, 6, 13, 3: 18–20; Col 2: 8.
8 Judaic-Christian orientation:[136] Rom 2: 10, 3: 1–4; 4: 1, 9: 1–5, 11: 1–32; 1 Cor 5: 6–8, 10: 1–22; 2 Cor 6: 14 – 7: 1; Gal 3: 29; Eph 2: 11–13.
9 Divergent community meal, and rigour regarding food sacrificed to idols: 1 Cor 10: 1–22.
10 Paul's authority in question: 1 Cor 4: 1–5, 9: 1–3; 2 Cor 11: 5 – 12: 13.
11 Conflict among earlier Christian leaders: 1 Cor 1–3, 9; 2 Cor 11: 5 – 12: 13; Gal 1, 2.

Some parts of the pre-Pastoral corpus, such as Rom 2: 12–24, 1 Cor 7: 10–16, 9: 7–14, 13, Phil 2: 1–11, and Col 2: 16–23, affirm the Pastoral point of view in some way, but there is far more which does not. An original Pastoral redactor would surely have excluded much that finds a place in the corpus and added more of his own, and so too if he were seeking to resuscitate a forgotten corpus. It can be surmised that under such circumstances the ratio of Pastoral to pre-Pastoral material would be closer to the two-to-one of 1 Peter than the approximately seven-to-one of the ten-letter corpus.

The inescapable conclusion is that the ten-letter collection was in circulation at the time of the Pastoral revision. That means that it must have been taken over from an opposition group and revised in order to counteract its influence.

That such an opposition existed has transpired repeatedly in the analysis of the Pastoral and related writings. What has emerged is that Pastoral circles were attempting to deal with Jewish-oriented ascetics, in the Aegean region and Asia Minor, at first internally, and later as a rival faction distinct from the Pastoral circles. It follows that they looked, in part at least, to Paul's epistles for the bases of their teachings. In this case the Pastoral version would immediately have become a point of demarcation between the Jewish-oriented Paulinists and the adherents of ecclesiastical orthodoxy.

The Pastoral material implies as much in the objections it anticipates regarding the ostensible Pauline directive for women to be silent in church gatherings. The threat of rejection and exclusion of those not accepting the passage is clear in the warning: 'If anyone thinks he is a prophet or spiritual he should acknowledge that what I am writing to you is a command of the Lord. If anyone does not recognise this he is not recognised' (1 Cor 14: 37f). It is unmistakable too in 2 Thess 2: 14 regarding the activities of unauthorized charismatics: 'If anyone refuses to obey what we say in this letter, note that man, and have nothing to do with him . . .', though at this stage of the conflict an attempt is being made to win over the opposition (3: 14*c*, 15).

It follows that the sharper the division between orthodoxy and an opposition in a particular region, the more distinct the differentiation between them in their practices, tenets, and scriptures. As already indicated, the history of the Pastoral stratum seems to coincide with a history of growing cleavage between the Pastoral circles and their opponents. Increasingly, it can be expected, dissociation and avoidance of the heretical outgroup would have involved avoidance of their version of the Pauline writings.

Thus, though episcopacy was probably not yet firmly established in the Aegean region, it would have been possible to maintain a standard text within orthodox circles. Acceptance of this ecclesiastical authority would have involved adherence to the scriptures and versions of scripture it authorized, and rejection or deviation therefrom would have spelt expulsion. No doubt the Jewish-oriented group had a closely knit sectarian character which involved a sharp distinction between itself as of the light and the day, and all others and all else as in darkness. 2 Cor 6: 14 – 7: 1, with its call for strict separation between believers and unbelievers, would have been precisely the kind of text to reinforce such tendencies. Self-induced isolation, together with that issuing from exclusion and avoidance by the orthodox, could have contributed to the isolation of the earlier version of the Pauline writings from the Pastoral version.

Then too, the Jewish orientation of the Pastoral opposition would certainly have accentuated the odium attached to them. That anti-Jewish feelings were widespread in the Roman world is well documented.[137] This factor has particular relevance if the later dating for the Pastoral material is accepted. Disturbances involving Jews in the second decade of the second century, and above all the second Jewish war of 133–5, would have inflamed already existing antagonism. That Jewish–Christian relations worsened during this period and thereafter is no accident.[138] The Martyrdom of Polycarp has it that Jews joined the Gentile populace in bringing about the death of Polycarp, Bishop of Smyrna (12: 2, 13: 1, 18: 1). Whether factual or not, the account is indicative of considerable enmity between Christians and Jews in the area of Smyrna, as is attested also in Rev. 2: 8f.

In such circumstances, how would Jewish-oriented Paulinism have fared? Though weakened and isolated, various brands of Jewish-oriented Christianity survived the aftermath of the war ending in 135, and persisted into the fourth century.[139] There seems to be no trace, however, of any distinctly Jewish Paulinism in the later second century. Beyond the Pastoral and related writings there is no recorded attack on any such heresy. The conclusion to be drawn is that most of the Pastoral opponents capitulated to orthodoxy, or abandoned Paul and were absorbed into some kind of Judaic Christianity, or turned to orthodox Judaism. The faithful remainder were probably too few in number to warrant attention, and eventually disappeared completely, along with their version of Paul's letters.

How this could have happened is no mystery. If the epistle to the Ephesians is any indication of their stance, it can be assumed that their post-Pauline forebears had tried to unite Jews and Gentiles in the sub-apostolic Pauline churches on the basis of the Pauline concept of the believing Gentiles as engrafted into the already existing reality of Israel (Eph 2: 11–22, cf. Rom 11: 1–32). That would have meant, in effect, that the church was regarded as in a close relation to Judaism, being from the Jewish point of view in the heterodox category. In the second-century context, Jewish-related identity would have been unacceptable to Gentile Christians. The Pastoral view of the church as a unity in a positive relationship with Roman-hellenistic society and distinct from Judaism would have found far greater support among them.

The legalists and rigorists evidently gained the upper hand among the Pastoral opponents, especially after their separation from the orthodox, as the polemic of the Pastoral epistles seems to indicate (cf. 1 Tim 1: 6–11, 4: 1–4). The tensions and contradictions within this kind of Paulinism would, if anything, have been even more severe than in the Pastoral variety. It can be expected that they reached the breaking-point in the period during and after the second Jewish war. That Marcion placed Galatians at the beginning of his *Apostolikon*, no doubt to demonstrate Pauline repudiation of Judaism, illustrates the problematic nature of Paul for Jewish Christians at that time.

That Marcion's career began within early catholic orthodoxy is consonant with his use of the Pastoral text of the ten letters as the basis for his abbreviated version. His appropriation of Luke perhaps indicates a connection between Luke–Acts and the Pastoralist ten letters. More than this, his attempt to purge the Pauline letters of their Jewishness represents a more thorough-going reaction against Jewish-oriented Paulinism than that of early catholic orthodoxy. It may indeed have arisen to some extent from some direct association with the former in Asia Minor which continued to influence him even after his reaction against it. According to Irenaeus Marcion derived his basic tenets from Cerdo in Rome, whom he succeeded as leader of a school, and Cerdo's ideas originated with Simon Magus. This, however, represents a polemic placing opponents in a heretical succession in contrast to the true succession from the apostles.[140]

Marcion's dualism is not unlike that of heterodox Jewish sects such as the Minim, and the thought of the Qumran community was not far removed from it. It could be argued that all Marcion did initially was to change names, so that the evil power of darkness was identified with the Jewish Creator God and the Demiurge, and the head of the power of light with the Father of Jesus Christ. The dualism of the Pastoral opponents seems indeed to be tending toward a rejection of the created order which could quite easily have moved toward a rejection of God as Creator.[141] Like the Pastoral opposition, Marcion advocated celibacy, and together with them he looked to Paul as the apostle par excellence, even, according to Irenaeus, the only apostle.[142]

Given such contact, Marcion would no doubt have known of any divergent text of Paul's letters in use among the Jewish-oriented Paulinists. While the orthodox would have argued that their version retained certain passages that the heretics had excised, someone with a knowledge of both could also have come to the conclusion that before their withdrawal or expulsion the Jewish Paulinists had also perverted the orthodox text with Jewish importations. In other words, the hypothesis of Pastoral expansion of an earlier version of Paul's writings finds some corroboration in the existence of the shorter Marcionite version, even though its variations from the Pastoral text were of a very different nature.[143]

Whether this is so or not, Marcion was very probably responsible for extending the knowledge and use of the Pauline collection beyond Asia Minor and the Aegean region. To combat his version on the same scale, the Pastoral text evidently came into play, as a standard of correctness from which he had diverged. This factor could have been a major one in affirming the Pastoral version of the text and bringing about the eventual acceptance of the Pauline writings in orthodoxy.

In view of the finding that the Pauline letters were in circulation before the Pastoral editing, avoidance of them is likely to have been deliberate. It seems probable that the writer of the Acts did know these letters, but shunned them to avoid any impression of association. On this assumption it can be argued that in a number of ways the Acts pointedly and obviously counteracts the Paul of the earlier ten letters.[144] Viewed as part of the rehabilitation of Paul, it is obvious that the Acts must have been written before the revised corpus had become established, and perhaps even before the Pastoral material had been introduced.

1 Clement is the earliest document of early catholicism to recognize and endorse the Pauline letters, though it does so to a limited degree. There is explicit reference to 1 Corinthians as 'the letter of the blessed apostle Paul' which 'he first wrote to you at the beginning of the gospel' (47:1f),[145] and argument based on some of the contents of this epistle. Otherwise there are only slight allusions to the ten letters, specifically to Romans and Ephesians. Nevertheless these allusions do exist, so that the conclusion that 1 Clement knows only 1 Corinthians, and that the rest of the corpus had not yet been gathered together with it is questionable.[146] Rather, 1 Clement probably demonstrates hesitant and guarded use of writings regarded in orthodox circles with suspicion and hostility.[147] Similarly, the fact that 1 Clement shows no signs of literary dependence on the subjectionist teaching, though giving expression to the same ideas in very similar terms, does not mean that the Pastoral revision of the ten letters could not yet have taken place. Issuing as it evidently does from the same circles, and standing in a close relation to the Pastoral material, the writer would probably have known of it, and so would have chosen to build his case on that which had an assured place in the version of the heretical opponents.

Polycarp's letter, by comparison, is a patchwork of allusions, to the Pauline writings, the Pastorals, and 1 Peter, as well as the four gospels, the Acts, Hebrews, James, and 1 John. Though Pauline thought has had little impact on either Ignatius or Polycarp, the latter accords him recognition and endorsement, with the caveat: 'Neither am I, nor is anyone like me, able to follow the wisdom of the blessed and glorious Paul' (Pol Phil 3: 2). A similar warning accompanies the endorsement in 2 Peter of what 'our beloved brother Paul' wrote 'in all his letters', to the effect that 'there are some things in them hard to understand, which the ignorant and unstable twist to their own destruction . . .' (2 Pet 3: 15f). In other words, the elements in Paul which orthodoxy found indigestible or subject to heretical use are ascribed to the apostle's obscurity.

Polycarp's letter suggests too that the Pauline texts were being preserved within orthodoxy, not in isolation, but within a larger collection, alongside the reputed writings of other apostles. At this stage of inclusion it is possible that the later Pastoral contributions to the ten letters were added, together with finishing touches in the form of glosses.

Paul continued, however, to be suspect in orthodoxy, for once wrested from the Jewish-oriented ascetics, he quickly became a favourite apostle of hellenizing gnostics, such as the Valentinians. They were not concerned to limit the text of the ten letters, as was Marcion, but resorted rather to esoteric interpretations.[148] Ambivalence and avoidance continued among the orthodox, but the use to which Irenaeus in particular put him in the refutation of heresy established his credentials, so that his place in the canon was assured.

So it was that the teaching on authority and subjection became part of the Pauline corpus and 1 Peter, and found a place in the Christian scriptures. Intended as part of a reshaping and domesticating of both apostles to serve the purposes of a church bent on survival, it no doubt played an important part in the preservation of the writings of Paul and his immediate successors.

5 CONCLUSIONS AND REFLECTIONS

The finding of this study is that the balance of probability favours the hypothesis that the teaching on authority and subjection to it in the Pauline corpus and 1 Peter is part of an extensive literary stratum extending across these writings, except in the Pastoral epistles, which appear to belong to the stratum in their entirety. Since the major part of it is found in these epistles, it is referred to as the Pastoral stratum.

Though the subjectionist teaching in the ten-letter corpus occurs in units which could stand on their own independently, it is usually attached to additional Pastoral material which has facilitated its introduction into disparate earlier material. This applies also to its presence in 1 Peter, except that most of this epistle is of a Pastoral character. In both sets of material there is adaptation to the earlier stratum or strata, and a very similar mingling of earlier and later strands. The later redactor does not seem, however, to have engaged in rewriting of what he found. Thus it proved possible to differentiate between the Pastoral and earlier material on grounds of literary dependence, and of ideological and stylistic tendencies, with important confirmation from the reconstruction of disrupted rhetorical or hymnic patterning. The greater the amount of material of the later stratum identified in these ways, the clearer its character became, and the easier its identification by reference to its internal qualities, with contextual considerations continuing, however, to play an essential confirming role. It should, perhaps, be reiterated that the numerical data presented are not intended to provide statistical proof that more than one hand has been at work in the text, but simply to bring to attention discernible differences which could well be relevant to the issue.

In the ten letters the analysis of 1 Cor 11: 2–16 proved crucial for the nature and extent of the later stratum, for if this passage can be retained as genuinely Pauline, that which coheres with it in its context must be also. The determination that it is not Pauline but is intrinsically related to the Pastoral material had extensive repercussions. At this point it became clear that the investigation could not be confined to a few subjectionist passages in the ten letters, but that much else is involved.

Since the analysis did not begin with or depend on the Pastoral epistles, the conclusion that the later stratum in the ten letters and 1 Peter stands in a close relation to them serves as an independent line of evidence corroborating the existence of the stratum outside the Pastorals. Here the agenda and programme of the stratum are revealed most explicitly. Yet at virtually every point the concerns of the Pastoral epistles find a parallel in the material identified as later in other epistles. Some differences emerged in the three sets of Pastoral material. Time lapse and changed circumstances proved capable of explaining the difference in the attitude to the Jewish-oriented opposition in the later material in the ten letters as compared with the Pastoral epistles. Time lapse seemed also to explain the accentuation of certain stylistic characteristics in the Pastorals as compared with the Pastoral material in the ten letters. The unusual paucity of *hapax legomena* in the latter (except for Rom 1:19 – 2:1) could indeed be due to a more careful effort to emulate Pauline and primitive Christian vocabulary in the earlier stages of the stratum. Some differences were also discerned in the patterning of the subjection material in 1 Peter as compared with the Ephesians–Colossians complex. Here the explanation proved to be, not differing tendencies, but adaptation to varying contexts.

The study did not set out to establish whether a single writer, or a school or circle of tradition is responsible for the stratum. The argument proceeded in terms of a circle, but the impression gained in the analysis was of following the method, and more than this, the twists and turns in the mental processes of a single individual over a period of time, but this remains an untested possibility. If, however, two, three, or more writers and redactors are involved, they must have been so closely associated with each other that they operated together as if possessed of a single mind. That the entire literary phenomenon issued from a single influential individual may be the more economical hypothesis. At the same time it could not have occurred in a vacuum. The stratum throughout assumes a supporting group, and requires assenting officials prepared to use the weapons placed in their hands. The revised and expanded corpus, together with the Acts, would have made possible a reinterpreted Paul to be used against the Pastoral opposition.

The extra-canonical writings associated with the stratum: 1 Clement, the Ignatian corpus, and Polycarp's letter, would have served a similar purpose. Here too the question of authorship arises perplexingly. 1 Clement and Polycarp's letter both have striking affinities with the Pastoral material, both in 1 Peter and in the Pauline collection; yet the former is written as from Rome, and the latter as from Asia Minor. Were the view of von Campenhausen to be adopted, that Polycarp is the writer of the Pastoral epistles, that would point to him as the single eminent personage at the centre of the Pastoral phenomenon. Yet in this capacity Polycarp raises more problems than he solves. He is an enigma in his relations with the Roman church being, apparently, recognized there as representative of the east, and yet at one point on the brink of a radical breach with Rome, together with the whole church of Asia Minor. Moreover, Polycarp was, according to Irenaeus, of the Johannine school. Was he the initiator and propagator of Pastoral ecclesiology in the region, or was he the vehicle (except regarding the date of Easter) of something that came from the outside? The problem remains.

The problem remains also regarding the precise origin of the teaching on authority and subjection in the New Testament epistles. The search for its context has led so far afield that the question arises whether the passages in which it occurs are after all only peripheral and incidental to a far larger literary and ecclesiastical development. On the contrary, they provide an indispensable basis for it, in that the concept of authority and subjection to it that governs Pastoral church order is obviously modelled on the household pattern. Transferred to the ecclesiastical sphere, the authority of the patriarch over wife, children, and slaves is ascribed to the presbyter or bishop over the flock, and the obedience which custom and formerly also law had required of the household members to the patriarch was required of church members in relation to the bishop. An important corollary is the exclusion of women from the prominent role they played in the Christian movement from the outset, and their silencing, so that their active leadership became confined to groups deemed to be heretical.

The subjectionist teaching is also crucial in the Pastoral affirmation of prevailing social structures, including the subordinate place of women, the vast institution of slavery, and the imperial authority of Rome. The longer dissertation version of this study shows, moreover, how the thought of the Pastoral material and related Christian literature accords with the rhetoric of Roman imperial policy in the first half of the second century. The possibility that the stratum is to be dated more probably in the period before, during, and after the second Jewish war of 133–5 gives special relevance to the teaching on subjection to the state. Clearly, any suggestion of connections with insubordination, rebellion, or insurrection, whether by women, slaves, or local populations such as the Jews, would have been abhorrent to the Pastoral circles, and embarrassing for the amity they sought to achieve with society at large and with governing authorities.

Connections with the Jews, it seems, came to be considered a distinct liability. In common with early catholicism in general, the Pastoral stratum affirms the Jewish God and scriptures, and a Jewish Messiah, but repudiates the Jewish people. Marcion went further and repudiated all these excepting the Jewish Messiah Jesus. Jews then became the scapegoat for the death of Jesus, and also for all persecution of Christians, which was blamed on their instigation.

Such factors would have been important in relations with the Jewish-oriented Paulinist opposition. If in addition their gatherings were of a charismatic, ecstatic nature, this would have accentuated their alienation from the Pastoral circles. A sharp division between the two groups is assumed to have been a major influence in differentiating the Pastoral text of the Pauline writings from any other version or versions. The Marcionite controversy, extending long after the middle of the second century, could have been responsible for further stabilization.

Thus far the conclusions of the study go. The mark of a good hypothesis is that it proves fruitful for further research. In this respect the concept of a Pastoral stratum potentially qualifies. The further questions to be answered are such that they cannot be undertaken by any one scholar. There is enough here to occupy many scholars for a considerable time to come if the theory is taken to have even general validity.

Most obviously, further, more thorough and comprehensive examination of the extent of the stratum in all epistles of the ten-letter corpus is needed, and this should perhaps be extended to the epistle to the Hebrews as well, which seems to contain some Pastoral-type paraenesis. The question also needs to be answered what relation this stratum of redaction bears to the glosses identified by Zuntz, and to the theories of J. C. O'Neill concerning glosses and interpolations in Galatians. Possible Pastoral rearrangement of earlier material is also a matter for exploration with reference to theories of letter combination.

It is not to be expected, however, that the complete peeling away of the layer of Pastoral redaction will bring us face to face with the original and genuine Paul. As already mentioned, it is very likely that an intermediary layer exists, corresponding with the eschatological–gnostic stage of catechesis postulated by A. Loisy. Ephesians, most of Colossians, and 2 Thessalonians may be strains within it, one or more of which are possibly present in a redactional capacity in other letters. To identify such material would probably be a more difficult task than that of locating the Pastoral stratum, because it stands closer to Paul in language and outlook.

In the meantime, the implication for the study of Paul is that we know him only as others have seen fit to present him, in the Acts and in the

Pauline and post-Pauline epistles. This applies in the ten letters, even apart from redactional additions, by virtue of selection and arrangement. On the other hand, despite considerable accretion and editing, there is no doubt that much genuinely Pauline writing has been preserved within the ten letters. If the same principles applied to the determination of genuine *verba Christi* and historicity of the gospel material were to be applied to the material concerning Paul, the results could be illuminating.

The endeavour to identify the historical Paul could, however, prove as frustrating as the search for the historical Jesus has been. The suspicion that one seeks to carve out a Paul in one's own theological and political image, as did Marcion, may be hard to dispel. A Paul who did not silence women and subject them to men, who did not oppose the manumission of slaves and subject them perpetually to their masters, who did not subject everyone unconditionally to the state and all other instituted authority is obviously preferable to one who did. If, however, there is sound reason to think that the Paul we in fact prefer is the true one, to reject the finding on the ground of suspected ulterior motivation would also be a distortion of critical judgement.

The identification of post-Pauline material does not mean that it is stripped away and discarded. Rather it is simply placed in its true context that it may be better understood both for what it says and why. Its presence in the canon means that it preserves for the church that which warrants attention in its own past. Both Paul and the way Paul was represented after his death are aspects of our past that are essential for our self-understanding. To recognize what has happened to the tradition in the past does not bind us to it unalterably, but on the contrary frees us with freedom similar to that claimed by our forebears to shape and change the present and future.

APPENDIX A The earlier form of 1 Peter

A reconstruction

1 Pet 1: 1–12 as in canonical text.

1: 13 Διὸ ἀναζωσάμενοι τὰς ὀσφύας τῆς διανοίας ὑμῶν, νήφοντες, τελείως ἐλπίσατε ἐπὶ τὴν φερομένην ὑμῖν χάριν ἐν ἀποκαλύψει Ἰησοῦ Χριστοῦ. 20 προεγνωσμένου μὲν πρὸ καταβολῆς κόσμου, φανερωθέντος δὲ ἐπ᾽ ἐσχάτου τῶν χρόνων δι᾽ ὑμᾶς 21 τοὺς δι᾽ αὐτοῦ πιστοὺς εἰς θεὸν τὸν ἐγείραντα αὐτὸν ἐκ νεκρῶν καὶ δόξαν αὐτῷ δόντα, ... 2: 4 πρὸς ὃν προσερχόμενοι, λίθον ζῶντα, ὑπὸ ἀνθρώπων μὲν ἀποδεδοκιμασμένον παρὰ δὲ θεῷ ἐκλεκτὸν ἔντιμον, 5 καὶ αὐτοὶ ὡς λίθοι ζῶντες οἰκοδομεῖσθε οἶκος πνευματικὸς εἰς ἱεράτευμα ἅγιον, ἀνενέγκαι πνευματικὰς θυσίας εὐπροσδέκτους θεῷ διὰ Ἰησοῦ Χριστοῦ. 6 διότι περιέχει ἐν γραφῇ,

> Ἰδοὺ τίθημι ἐν Σιὼν λίθον
> ἐκλεκτὸν ἀκρογωνιαῖον ἔντιμον,
> καὶ ὁ πιστεύων ἐπ᾽ αὐτῷ
> οὐ μὴ καταισχυνθῇ.
> (7 ὑμῖν οὖν ἡ τιμὴ τοῖς πιστεύουσιν· ἀπιστοῦσιν δὲ)*
> λίθος ὃν ἀπεδοκίμασαν οἱ οἰκοδομοῦντες
> οὗτος ἐγενήθη εἰς κεφαλὴν γωνίας
> 8 καὶ* λίθος προσκόμματος καὶ πέτρα σκανδάλου·
> 9 Ὑμεῖς δὲ γένος ἐκλεκτον,
> Βασίλειον ἱεράτευμα,
> ἔθνος ἅγιον
> λαὸς εἰς περιτοίησιν
> ὅπως τὰς ἀρετας ἐξαγγείλητε
> τοῦ ἐκ σκότους ὑμᾶς καλέσαντος
> εἰς τὸ θαυμαστὸν αὐτοῦ φῶς·

*These portions seem to be additions to adapt the series of hymnic stanzas to an epistolary context.

10 οἵ ποτε οὐ λαὸς
νῦν δὲ λαὸς Θεοῦ,
οἱ οὐκ ἠλεημένοι
νῦν δὲ ἐλεηθέντες . . .

21ab εἰς τοῦτο γὰρ ἐκλήθητε,
ὅτι καὶ Χριστὸς ἔπαθεν . . .

18c ἵνα ἡμᾶς προσαγάγῃ τῷ Θεῷ·

18ab ἀπέθανεν περὶ ἁμαρτιῶν
δίκαιος ὑπὲρ ἀδίκων

18de θανατωθεὶς μὲν σαρκὶ
ζωοποιηθεὶς δὲ πνεύματι, . . .

22bc πορευθεὶς εἰς οὐρανόν
ὑποταγέντων αὐτῷ ἀγγέλων
καὶ ἐξουσιῶν καὶ δυνάμεων.

4:1 Χριστοῦ οὖν παθόντος σαρκὶ καὶ ὑμεῖς τὴν αὐτὴν ἔννοιαν ὁπλίσασθε . . .
3 ἀρκετὸς ὁ παρεληλυθὼς χρόνος τὸ βούλημα τῶν ἐθνῶν κατειργάσθαι,
πεπορευμένους ἐν ἀσελγείαις, ἐπιθυμίαις, . . . καὶ ἀθεμίτοις εἰδωλολατρίαις . . .
10 ἕκαστος καθὼς ἔλαβεν χάρισμα, εἰς ἑαυτοὺς αὐτὸ διακονοῦντες ὡς
καλοὶ οἰκονόμοι ποικίλης χάριτος θεοῦ.
11 εἴ τις λαλεῖ, ὡς λόγια θεοῦ· εἴ τις διακονεῖ, ὡς ἐξ ἰσχύος ἧς χορηγεῖ ὁ
θεός . . .
17 ὅτι ὁ καιρὸς τοῦ ἄρξασθαι τὸ κρίμα ἀπὸ τοῦ οἴκου τοῦ θεοῦ· εἰ δὲ πρῶτον
ἀφ' ἡμῶν, τί τὸ τέλος τῶν ἀπειθούντων τῷ τοῦ θεοῦ εὐαγγελίῳ;
18 καὶ εἰ ὁ δίκαιος μόλις σώζεται,
ὁ ἀσεβὴς καὶ ἁμαρτωλὸς ποῦ φανεῖται; . . .
5:5c Ὁ θεὸς ὑπερηφάνοις ἀντιτάσσεται,
ταπεινοῖς δὲ δίδωσιν χάριν.
6 Ταπεινώθητε οὖν ὑπὸ τὴν κραταιὰν χεῖρα τοῦ θεοῦ,
ἵνα ὑμᾶς ὑψώσῃ ἐν καιρῷ, 7 πᾶσαν τὴν μέριμναν ὑμῶν
ἐπιρίψαντες ἐπ' αὐτόν, ὅτι αὐτῷ μέλει περὶ ὑμῶν.
7 Πάντων δὲ τὸ τέλος ἤγγικεν.
8 Νήψατε, γρηγορήσατε. ὁ ἀντίδικος ὑμῶν διάβολος ὡς
λέων ὠρυόμενος περιπατεῖ ζητῶν [τινα] καταπιεῖν

1 Pet 5: 9–12 as in canonical text.

APPENDIX B Rom 1:19 – 2:1 and the later or Pastoral stratum

Further to the summary of P. N. Harrison's reasons for thinking Rom 1:19 – 2:1 is a Pastoral insertion,[1] it is possible first to strengthen his contextual argument by pointing to the fact that besides the repetition of ὦ ἄνθρωπε ὁ κρίνων in Rom 2:1 and 2:3, οἱ τὰ τοιαῦτα πράσσοντες ... αὐτὰ ποιοῦσιν in Rom 1:32 is almost identical to ὁ κρίνων τοὺς τὰ τοιαῦτα πράσσοντας καὶ ποιῶν αὐτά in Rom 2:3. The latter appears to come as an expanded version of τοὺς τὰ τοιαῦτα πράσσοντες in Rom 2:2, with which it forms a synthetic parallel. The words in Rom 1:32 by contrast bear no such structural relationship to Rom 2:2f, and in view of other evidence pointing in the same direction, can be regarded as part of the seam connecting later to earlier material.

Then too, to turn to the beginning of the passage, Rom 1:19ff, concerning the revelation of God through the creation, follows awkwardly after Rom 1:18, which speaks of the revelation of God's wrath from heaven. If, however, Rom 2:2ff is joined to Rom 1:18, a smooth sequence results. The theme of the judgement of God in Rom 2:2 follows naturally after that of the wrath of God in Rom 1:18, and the thought of God's judgement 'according to truth' in Rom 2:2 forms an effective contrast to 'the ungodliness and unrighteousness of men who possess the truth in unrighteousness' (Rom 1:18).

Next, the passage contains connecting links with the later stratum which become evident on examining some of its terminology and key concepts.

Relating the material to the Pastorals as well as the later stratum is the word πάθος in Rom 1:26. It occurs elsewhere in the New Testament only in the brief catalogue of vices in Col 3:5 and in the later material in 1 Thess 4:5, where it appears in a context concerning Christians who err in the area of sexual relationships and become guilty of immorality (vs. 3). To fall in this way into the 'passion of lust' is to be like the heathen who do not know God (vs. 5). In Rom 1:19–21 there is also a connection with not knowing God, and for this reason being given over to immoral passions and other evils (Rom 1:24, 26ff).

There are significant connections also with 1 Cor 11:2–16, in that both passages use the relatively unusual New Testament words εἰκών, φύσις, κτίζειν, ἀτιμία and do so in very similar ways. Εἰκών occurs twenty-three times in the New Testament: once in each synoptic gospel to refer to Caesar's image on a coin (Matt 22:20, Mark 12:16, Luke 20:24), ten times in Revelation in the sense of an idol,[2] once in Hebrews to denote the shadow or copy of the real (10:1), and seven times in the ten-letter collection apart from the occurrences in Rom 1:23 and 1 Cor 11:7.

All the uses in the ten-letter corpus refer to the image of God as applied to man. In 2 Cor 4:4 and Col 1:15 the Christ is described as the 'image of God'. In Rom 8:29, 1 Cor 15:49, 2 Cor 3:18, and Col 3:10 it has a future reference in that it has to do with the transformation of believers into the image and glory of God, and therefore also the new creation in Jesus Christ. So too in 1 Cor 15:45 the $εἰκών$ is 'the image of the heavenly man', the 'second man' from heaven (vs. 47), whose image is yet to be acquired (vs. 49). This image of the new man stands over against the lesser image of the 'man of dust', who is equivalent to 'the first man from the earth' (vss. 47, 49), a contrast that appears to underlie all seven uses mentioned above. In 1 Cor 11:7, however, it is quite clear that the 'image and glory of God' has reference to the original creation without qualification. M. D. Hooker has argued that the use of $εἰκών$ in Rom 1:23, in the puzzling phrase, $ἐν ὁμοιώματι εἰκόνος φθαρτοῦ ἀνθρώπου$, is not to be distinguished from other uses of the word in Paul, because of its connections with the account of the creation of man in Gen 1:26 LXX, where the word also occurs in close proximity to $ὁμοίωσιν$, and with the story of the fall of Gen 3.[3] Hooker, however, can point only to 1 Cor 11:7 for another instance in the Pauline corpus of a direct connection between $εἰκών$ and Gen 1:26f.[4] Here, then, is a most significant point of contact between Rom 1:19 – 2:1 and the later stratum.

The contrast between $φθαρτός$ and $ἄφθαρτος$ (corruptible and incorruptible) in Rom 1:23 is reminiscent of 1 Cor 15:42. Whereas, however, 1 Cor 15 draws a distinction between the body ($σῶμα$) before and after the resurrection, Rom 1:19 – 2:1 is concerned with the difference between God as the supreme Creator, on the one hand, and on the other, humanity as belonging to the category of created beings along with birds, animals, and reptiles. In Rom 1:23 $ὁμοιώματι εἰκόνος$ obviously refers to idol images, the worship of which is thought to disturb the original ordering of the world. Thus worship and honour that properly belongs to God is transferred to lesser beings (vs. 25). As a result of this disruption of priorities, the proper distinctions between male and female are also confused, and male and female homosexuality results (vss. 26f). Similarly according to 1 Cor 11:2–16, the failure on the part of women to wear a head-covering violates the pre-eminence of man over woman derived from his creation in God's image (1 Cor 11:7f).

Both passages, indeed, base their argument on the order of creation, which is a concept that underlies much of the later stratum and the Pastorals.[5] The verb $κτίζειν$ is used in Rom 1:25 to refer to the worship of the creation ($κτίσει$) instead of the Creator ($τὸν κτίσαντα$), and in 1 Cor 11:9 to refer to Gen 2:21f, according to which woman is created ($ἐκτίσθη$) for man. Elsewhere in the New Testament it occurs eleven times: once in each of the synoptic gospels, twice in Revelation, and eight times in other parts of the Pauline corpus. Of these occurrences, four are in Ephesians (2:10, 15, 3:9, 4:24) and three in Colossians (two in 1:16, and one in 3:10). In both of these writings the word refers to the new creation, except in Eph 3: 9 and Col 1: 16, where there is a christological interpretation of creation. The remaining occurrence in the corpus is in 1 Tim 4: 3, where the use resembles those in Rom 1: 25 and 1 Cor 11: 9 in that it refers to creation as the norm for moral judgement. In all three contexts evil consists in rejecting or opposing the world as God has created and ordered it.

The word φύσις does not occur in the Pastorals, but appears in Rom 1: 26 and 1 Cor 11: 14 with connotations that are very similar. According to Rom 1: 26 the outcome of idolatry is the abandoning of natural sexual relations (τὴν φυσικὴν χρῆσιν) for the kind that is contrary to nature (παρὰ φύσιν). According to 1 Cor 11: 14 for woman's head to be covered is what nature herself (ἡ φύσις αὐτή) teaches. Obviously, then, in both contexts, to err is to behave in such a way as to oppose or change nature, and right conduct is behaviour that accords with nature.

Elsewhere in the Pauline corpus the word is used nine times, but the connotations are morally neutral, since the word is used to denote matters of fact with no assumption that 'nature' is either intrinsically good or bad. According to Rom 2: 14 when Gentiles do 'by nature' what the law requires, this occurs, not through following nature, but because what the law requires is written on their hearts, and therefore has become natural to them. This does not mean, however, that what is done 'by nature' is automatically good and right. In Rom 11: 24, the term refers simply to the physical fact of being uncircumcized. So too in Rom 11: 21, and twice in Rom 11: 24, the phrase κατὰ φύσιν is used to denote the facts of biological origin of Jews and Gentiles respectively, under the figure of the wild olive tree from which branches are grafted onto a cultivated tree. The incorporation of Gentiles into the stock of Abraham, which Paul obviously thinks desirable, therefore represents something contrary to nature (παρὰ φύσιν, Rom 11: 24). In Gal 2: 15 the word also refers simply to the fact of ethnic origin, and in Gal 4: 8 to beings who in fact or 'by nature' (φύσει) are not gods. The same probably applies also to the phrase 'by nature (φύσει) children of wrath' in Eph 2: 3.

Only two of the thirteen New Testament occurrences appear outside the Pauline corpus, one in Jas 3: 7, where the word refers to kind or species of animals, and 2 Pet 1: 4, where it refers to the divine nature. It seems, then, that Rom 1: 19 – 2: 1 and 1 Cor 11: 2–16 are alone in the New Testament in representing nature, clearly identifiable with the created order, as the norm for right behaviour.

Finally, these two passages share the word ἀτιμία (Rom 1: 26, 1 Cor 11: 14), which is a relatively rare word occurring only seven times in all in the New Testament, and then only in the Pauline collection. Of the other five uses, one is in the Pastorals (2 Tim 2: 20), and the other four in Romans and 1 and 2 Corinthians. Once again, there is a distinct difference in the connotations in the two passages in question and the Pastorals as compared with the rest of the corpus.

Outside the later stratum and the Pastorals the word is used to refer simply to lack of prominence and external importance, without necessarily implying any blame. According to Rom 9: 21 God ordains one vessel (σκεῦος) for honour and prominence (εἰς τιμήν), and another for ordinary, undistinguished existence (ἀτιμία). According to 1 Cor 15:43 the physical body is sown in ἀτιμία, a weak, perishable, inglorious state, but raised in 'glory' (δόξῃ) and 'power'. According to 2 Cor 6:8 the apostle experiences both δόξα and ἀτιμία, which find parallels in the terms δυσφημία and εὐφημία, ill repute and good repute. That is to say, δόξα and ἀτιμία have to do with the opinions and treatment meted out by others. The same applies to the dishonour the apostle suffers according to 2 Cor 11:21, which seems to refer to treatment actually bearing an inverse relationship to the apostle's deserts.

In 2 Tim 2:20, Rom 1:26, and 1 Cor 11:14, however, the term refers to dishonour in the sense of 'blameworthy disgrace' which is the result of culpable error. So in 2 Tim 2:20f the ἀτιμία of some vessels as opposed to the τιμή of others bears a direct relation to the 'youthful passions' mentioned in vs. 22, and the controversy and quarrelling condemned in vs. 23.[6] The disgraceful passions (πάθη ἀτιμίας) castigated in Rom 1:26 result from failing to give God the honour (ἐδόξασαν) as pre-eminent over all things (vs. 21). Accordingly human beings 'dishonour' (ἀτιμάζεσθαι) their bodies among themselves, with women turning to women instead of men, and men to men (vss. 27f). As in 1 Cor 11:14, dishonour is connected with the disturbance of the relation deemed proper between the sexes. The same implications are present in 1 Cor 11:2–16, though here ἀτιμία and δόξα (dishonour and glory) issue from hair length distinguishing the two sexes (vss. 14f). For a man to wear his hair long would presumably cause confusion as to his identity as a man, and thus result in loss of honour.

This use of the concept accords closely with what is to be found in the later stratum and the Pastorals as a whole. Here honour is due to all in that they are to receive recognition according to their assigned place in the hierarchical ordering of all things. Taking all the relevant passages in conjunction with one another, it can be said that according to this material rendering honour (τιμή) to whom honour is due (Rom 13:7) and honouring all (cf. πάντας τιμήσατε, 1 Pet 2:17) means amongst other things that subjects give homage to rulers (Rom 13:1–7, 1 Pet 2:17, 1 Tim 2:1f), that children honour and obey parents (Eph 6:2), that husbands honour wives as weaker than themselves (1 Pet 3:7), that slaves honour their masters (1 Tim 6:1), and that all honour elders (1 Tim 5:17) and widows who are genuine widows (1 Tim 5:3). It follows that honour involves appropriate behaviour and attitudes depending on one's own status and role, as well as the status and role of those to be honoured. To behave in such a way as to divest oneself of one's proper status must, then, lead to loss of honour, as in the instances discussed in Rom 1:19 – 2:1 and 1 Cor 11:2–16.

If it is assumed that the same outlook underlies Rom 1:19 – 2:1 as is present in the later stratum and the Pastorals, the presence of the phrase γονεῦσιν ἀπειθεῖς (disobedient to parents) in the catalogue of vices in this passage (Rom 1:30) is by no means accidental. Indeed, all the evils listed in Rom 1:29–31 can be interpreted as rebellion against the proper ordering of the world and society. That this is what is intended receives confirmation, moreover, from the fact that the list is introduced by the phrase ποιεῖν τὰ μὴ καθήκοντα (to do what is not fitting or proper). Καθήκειν is used nowhere else in the New Testament save in Acts 22: 22, where it occurs in the cry of the multitude in Jerusalem that Paul is not fit to live. Elsewhere in early Christian writings it is used only in 1 Clement, where it has quite explicit connections with a hierarchical ordering of human relationships. It occurs first in the catalogue of duties which the Corinthians are commended for obeying in 1 Clem 1: 3, in the phrase 'rendering proper honour (τιμήν) to the elders among you', which follows immediately after the words 'submitting to your rulers', and is followed by a statement to the effect that they trained the young to think restrained and seemly thoughts, and instructed the women to maintain a blameless conscience, rendering affection fittingly (καθηκόντως) to their husbands, remaining in the rule of obedience and managing their households properly.

The word καθήκειν appears also in 1 Clem 3: 4, where duty to Christ (τὸ καθηκόν τῷ Χριστῷ) stands in contrast to the strife, sedition, disorder, and rebellion against authority by the worthless (οἱ ἄτιμοι) against the worthy (τοὺς ἐντίμους), the foolish against the wise, and the young against the old (1 Clem 3: 3), all of which is equated with the wickedness and evil envy (ζῆλον) which originally brought death into the world by setting Cain against Abel (1 Clem 3: 4). The reference to the events involved in the Fall according to the early chapters of Genesis (cf. Gen 4) is yet another link with Rom 1: 19 - 2: 1.

Lastly, καθήκειν occurs in 1 Clem 41: 3, where duty (τὸ καθήκον) according to God's will is set over against disobedience to orderly ministrations within the church according to one's assigned place or rank (1 Clem 41: 1). Once again, the context displays a hierarchical view of duty and relationships, in that there is comparison with the positions of high priest, priests, Levites, and laity (cf. 1 Clem 40: 5, 41: 2).

That this contact with 1 Clement is by no means fortuitous appears from the similarity in wording as between the vice list of Rom 1: 29–32 and that of 1 Clem 35: 5f. Harrison pointed out that it has usually been assumed that 1 Clement is dependent on Paul in this passage, but in view of the data indicating that Rom 1: 19 - 2: 1 is probably later than the apostle, it is possible that the reverse is the case.[7] Alternatively both, in common with 2 Tim 3: 2–5, are dependent on an earlier source, or issue from a similar or identical source. However this may be, there is evidently a close connection among all three sets of material that goes beyond this particular passage.

The test for antithetic parallelism, used to assist identification of passages adhering to the later stratum, yields a positive result here too. There are six instances in 34.5 lines, which is to say, one to every 5.8 lines, a rate which is close to the range of two to five for the later stratum,[8] and falls well within the range of four to eight for the Pastorals.[9] This evidence does not, however, provide an assured means of dissociating the passage from the epistle as a whole, for antithetic parallels abound in Romans,[10] unlike any other letter in the collection apart from the Pastorals.

Such parallels in the rest of Romans coincide, however, with its dialectic style of argument. As in 1 Cor 7,[11] many of the parallels in the second and third chapters involve rhetorical questions, often posed positively and combined with some form of negative reply, whereas Rom

1: 19 – 2: 1 lacks this characteristic entirely. It can be said, moreover, that since the result is in conformity with what has been found throughout the later stratum, it tends to confirm other evidence favouring association with the stratum. The same may be said of the relation of Rom 1: 19 – 2: 1 to the Pastoral epistles, where the same stylistic trait is in evidence.[12]

APPENDIX C Antithetic parallels in the Pastoral stratum and in adjacent material

In the tables given below all passages assigned to the Pastoral stratum, and the data pertaining to them, are underscored, except for the Pastoral epistles and sum totals. References and figures in parentheses pertain to passages not analysed in this shorter, revised version of the study, but included in the Pastoral stratum in the longer version.[1]

Romans

In Romans the test for antithetic parallelism serves less well to distinguish the Pastoral stratum from its surroundings than elsewhere, for it is used relatively frequently in this epistle, though, as observed elsewhere, it is generally of a different character.[2] What is significant is that the material in Romans assigned to the Pastoral stratum for other reasons does not diverge from it in its use of antithetic parallels. The results are as follows:

Passages in Romans	No. of antithetic parallels	No. of lines	No. of lines to each occurrence
1:1–18	0	34.3	–
1:19–2:1	6	34.5	5.8
2:2–29	13	48	3.7
Chap. 3	8	38.4	4.8
Chap. 4	8	42	5.3
Chap. 5	5	49	9.8
Chap. 6	13	42.5	3.3
Chap. 7	16	50	3.1
Chap. 8	12	72	6.0
Chap. 9	7	41	5.9
Chap. 10	2	31	15.5
Chap. 11	9	51	5.7
12:1f	1	6	6
12:3–8*bd* 11*bc*, 12*ab*	1	13.5	13.5
12:8*c*, 9–11*a* 12*b*–21	7	18.5	2.6
13:1–7	5	16	3.2
13:8–10	3	6.4	2.1
13:11–14	1	8	8
14:1–15:6	13	49	3.7

Passages in Romans	No. of antithetic parallels	No. of lines	No. of lines to each occurrence
15:7–33	0	47	–
Chap. 16	2	50.2	25.3
Totals			
Earlier Material	97	623.7	6.4
Pastoral Stratum	34	124.4	3.7

1 Corinthians

Antithetic parallels occur sporadically in 1 Corinthians as a whole, but with regularity in the material judged to belong to the Pastoral stratum, as shown below:

Passages in 1 Corinthians	No. of antithetic parallels	No. of lines	No. of lines to each occurrence
Chap. 1	6	53.5	8.9
Chap. 2	5	28.6	5.9
Chap. 3	3	35.6	11.9
4:1–11, 13*bc*	4	24.6	6.2
(4:12, 13*a*, 14–21)	(4)	(15.6)	(3.9)
(5:1–5, 9–13)	(5)	(19)	(3.8)
5:6–8, 6:1–20	4	41.6	10.4
7:1–16, 18f, 21–23, 25	24	70	2.9
7:17, 20, 24	0	5	–
Chap. 8	6	25	4.1
Chap. 9	7	51	25.5
10:1–13	1	23	23.0
10:14–22, 11:30–32	2	17.6	8.8
10:23–11:1	4	17	4.25
11:2–16	6	25	4.2
11:17–22	3	11	3.7
11:23–25	0	9	–
11:27–29, 33f	2	8	4.0
Chap. 12	2	51	25.5
Chap. 13	3	51	17.0
14:1–31, 39f	4	59	14.8
14:32–38	2	10.5	5.3
Chap. 15	5	97	19.4
16:1–14, 17, 18*a*, 19–24	0	33.5	–
(16:15f, 18*b*)	(0)	(4)	(–)
Totals			
Earlier Material	70	637.5	9.1
Pastoral Stratum	32	149.1	4.6

2 Corinthians

There is no significant use of antithetic parallels in the first nine chapters of 2 Corinthians. The results for the last four chapters are as follows:

Passages in 2 Corinthians	No. of antithetic parallels	No. of lines	No. of lines to each occurrence
10: 1–5, 7, 12–18	2	26.4	13.3
(10: 6, 8–11)	(2)	(9)	(4.5)
Chap. 11	3	59.4	19.8
Chap. 12, 13: 11–14	8	54	6.8
(13: 1–10)	(5)	(19)	(3.8)
Totals for Chaps. 10–13			
Earlier Material	13	139.8	10.7
(Pastoral Stratum)	(7)	(28)	(4.0)

Ephesians

In Ephesians antithetic parallels are relatively rare except in 5: 1–14, 18*b*–20, which follows the darkness–light contrast, and in the Pastoral stratum, as shown below:

Passages in Ephesians	No. of antithetic parallels	No. of lines	No. of lines to each occurrence
Chap. 1	2	46	23.0
Chap. 2	4	42	10.5
Chap. 3	0	37	–
4: 1–27, 30–32*ab*	4	40.5	10.1
5: 2*b*–14*a*, 18*b*–20	4	23.5	5.9
4: 28f, 32*c*, 5: 1, 2*a*, 5: 15–18*a*	4	11	2.8
5: 21 – 6: 9	7	34	4.8
6: 10–24	1	31	31.0
Totals			
Earlier Material	15	220	14.7
Pastoral Stratum	11	45	4.1

Colossians

In Colossians much the same obtains as in Ephesians:

Passages in Colossians	No. of antithetic parallels	No. of lines	No. of lines to each occurrence
Chap. 1	2	63.5	31.8
Chap. 2	3	47.5	15.8
3: 1–17	4	32.5	8.1
3: 18 – 4: 1, 5	4	16.1	4.0
4: 2–4, 6–18	0	36.5	–
Totals			
Earlier Material	9	180	20.0
Pastoral Stratum	4	16.1	4.0

1 Thessalonians

In 1 Thessalonians the results follow the same pattern except for 5: 1–11, where the darkness–light dichotomy is expressed in antithetic parallelism:

Passages in 1 Thessalonians	No. of antithetic parallels	No. of lines	No. of lines to each occurrence
1:1, 5a, 6b–10	2	20	10.0
1:5b, 6a, 7, 2:1–16	8	38.5	4.8
2:7–3:13	1	36.5	36.5
4:1–12	6	23	3.8
4:13–18	0	14	–
5:1–11	3	18.5	6.2
5:12–15, 21b, 22	2	9.5	4.8
5:16–21a, 23–28	0	10.5	–
Totals			
Earlier Material	6	99.5	16.6
Pastoral Stratum	16	71.0	4.4

2 Thessalonians

The contrast in the use of antithetic parallels is even more obvious in 2 Thessalonians:

Material in 2 Thessalonians	No. of antithetic parallels	No. of lines	No. of lines to each occurrence
Earlier Material	1	74	74
2:15, 3:4, 6–15	6	22.5	3.8

Remainder of the Ten-letter corpus

The occurrence of antithetic parallels in the other epistles of the ten-letter corpus is relatively low:

	No. of antithetic parallels	No. of lines	No. of lines to each occurrence
Galatians	12	280	23.3
Philippians	9	175	19.4
Philemon	3	37	12.3

The Pastorals

Antithetic parallels occur with regularity in the Pastoral epistles, as shown below:

	No. of antithetic parallels	No. of lines	No. of lines to each occurrence
1 Timothy			
Chap. 1	5	39	7.8
Chap. 2	5	24	4.8
Chap. 3 (excluding vs. 17)	5	24	4.8
Chap. 4	5	28.3	5.7
Chap. 5	6	41.6	6.9
Chap. 6	10	45	4.5
Total	36	201.9	5.6

	No. of antithetic parallels	No. of lines	No. of lines to each occurrence
2 Timothy			
Chap. 1	6	29.6	4.9
Chap. 2	8	44.3	5.5
Chap. 3	5	30	6.0
Chap. 4	5	33.3	6.7
Total	23	137.2	5.9
Titus			
Chap. 1	5	27.5	5.5
Chap. 2	5	26	5.2
Chap. 3	5	29	5.8
Total	15	82.5	5.5

1 Peter

In 1 Peter there is also a marked difference between earlier and later strata in their use of antithetic parallels, as shown below:

Passages in 1 Peter	No. of antithetic parallels	No. of lines	No. of lines to each occurrence
1:1–12	2	26.5	13.3
1:13, 20, 21ab, 2:4–7, 9f, 21ab, 3:18, 22c	4	24.6	6.2
1:14–19, 21c–23, 2:1–3, 8b	4	18.5	4.6
2:11–20, 21c, 22–25	7	29.5	4.2
3:1–9	4	19.5	4.9
3:13–17, 19–22a	5	16.3	3.3
4:1a, 3, 7a, 10, 11a, 17f, 5:6–14	1	28.3	28.3
4:1b, 2, 3c, 4–6, 7b, 8f, 11b–16, 19	7	29.5	4.2
5:1–5b	3	9.3	3.1
Totals			
Earlier Material	7	79.4	11.3
Pastoral Stratum	30	122.6	4.1

Sum totals for Pastoral material

	No. of antithetic parallels	No. of lines	No. of lines to each occurrence
Ten-Letter Corpus	105	415.6	4.0
Pastoral Epistles	74	421.6	5.7
1 Peter	30	122.6	4.1
Totals	209	959.8	4.6

It is to be observed that the fragments which P. N. Harrison claimed to have identified as originally Pauline[1] contain only four antithetic parallels, yielding the following scores:

Passages in the Pastorals	No. of antithetic parallels		No. of lines		No. of lines to each occurrence
Tit 3:12–15	1		7.5		7.5
2 Tim 4:9–15	0		10		–
2 Tim 1:16–18	1		5		
2 Tim 3:10–11	0		4.8		
2 Tim 4:1, 2a	0		4		
2 Tim 4:5b–8	1	3	7	32	10.7
2 Tim 4:16–19	1		8.4		
2 Tim 4:21b–22a	0		2.8		

Despite this difference from the Pastorals as a whole and the Pastoral stratum, Harrison's theory is on balance unacceptable, for other characteristics tend to associate these passages with, rather than to dissociate them from, the Pastoral material.

There is first the frequent use of compound words formed from the combination of adjectives or nouns with nouns or verbs, which are distributed fairly evenly throughout the three epistles.[2] The occurrence of such words in Harrison's third fragment ($\mu\alpha\kappa\rho o\vartheta\upsilon\mu\acute{\iota}\alpha$ in 2 Tim 3:10, $\pi\lambda\eta\rho o\varphi\acute{o}\rho\eta\sigma o\nu$ in 2 Tim 4:5, and $\pi\lambda\eta\rho o\varphi o\rho\eta\vartheta\tilde{\eta}$ in 2 Tim 4:17) tends to associate it with the rest of the Pastoral material.

Moreover, the thought in 2 Tim 3:10f accords with the imitation theme which characterizes 2 Timothy as a whole. In addition the idea of Timothy's fulfilment of his ministry in 2 Tim 4:1f and 4:5 forms what seems to be an obviously intended contrast to the condemnation of heretical teaching in 4:3f, such as the Pastoral writer himself is likely to have devised.

Also linking 2 Tim 4:5b–8 with the Pastorals is the occurrence of the word $\dot{\epsilon}\pi\iota\varphi\acute{\alpha}\nu\epsilon\iota\alpha$ for the *parousia* concept in vs. 8, a term which is peculiar to these epistles in the New Testament[3] except for 2 Thess 2:8, where it is used together with $\pi\alpha\rho o\upsilon\sigma\acute{\iota}\alpha$, which does not appear in the Pastorals.

Reminiscent of the later stratum and the Pastorals is the use of $\ddot{\epsilon}\rho\gamma\alpha$ with $\kappa\alpha\kappa\acute{\alpha}$ in 2 Tim 4:14, which has the opposite force of the expression καλὰ ἔργα. This expression is particularly prominent in 1 Timothy and Titus,[4] and occurs in 1 Pet 2:12 as well. So too in Tit 3:14 one finds the expression καλῶν ἔργων with προΐστασθαι and χρείας. The latter two appear in the later stratum in Rom 12 (cf. 12:8c, 13), the first being implied in προνοούμενοι καλὰ (Rom 12:17). Significantly, προΐστημι occurs elsewhere in the New Testament only in the Pastorals (cf. 1 Tim 3:4, 5, 5:17, Tit 3:8). In Tit 3:8, moreover, the word is also used in combination with καλὰ ἔργα as in Tit 3:14. In addition the use of πάντα with τὰ ἔθνη in 2 Tim 4:17 concerning Paul's proclamation of the word to the Gentiles at his first defence accords with the universalist tendency of the Pastorals in common with the later stratum.[5]

It seems, then, that each of Harrison's fragments has significant connections with the trito-Pauline material which tend to outweigh its Pauline characteristics. Moreover, in a body of literature which is a virtual mosaic of literary borrowing from the earlier letters of the Pauline corpus, the occurrence of words and phrases which also appear in original Pauline material is scarcely surprising. It is understandable that a later imitator would attempt to simulate the personal details and greetings that appear toward the end of Pauline letters. In so doing it would be natural to take a particular passage, such as 1 Cor 16, as a model. Though realistic, the Pastoral passages in question are by no means beyond the devising of a moderately lively imagination.

The less frequent use of antithetic parallels as compared with the rest of the Pastoral epistles is understandable in material that is not paraenetic or discursive, but that consists of short, concrete statements, requests, and greetings such as occur in similar material in Pauline letters.[6] Their straightforward content would also have made for the use of simple, well-known words. Thus the fact that in these sections there are relatively few words that are peculiar to the Pastorals in the New Testament[7] is not unexpected either. Moreover, the words which Harrison cited as shared by these passages with the ten-letter corpus but occurring nowhere else in the Pastorals are, for the most part, frequently used in the rest of the New Testament, and so do not serve as convincing evidence of Pauline affinity. Of those that are less common, all are used also in Luke–Acts and/or other writings representing later New Testament tradition.[8]

There seem, then, to be insufficient grounds for concluding that Harrison identified a primitive substratum in the Pastoral epistles, and sufficient evidence to associate his fragments with the Pastoral epistles, and so with the Pastoral stratum as a whole.

APPENDIX E Vocabulary analysis

Compound words

A marked characteristic of the later or Pastoral stratum in the Pauline corpus and 1 Peter is the use of compound words other than those formed only by the addition of prefixes, which is to say, words formed from nouns and/or adjectives or adverbs, and/or verbs. The use is more frequent in the Pastoral epistles and the Pastoral material in 1 Peter than in the equivalent material in the ten-letter corpus. In the latter the trait is not sufficiently prominent to serve as a distinguishing mark, and does not exceed the same phenomenon in Ephesians, though it differs from the relatively sparse occurrence of such words in primitive Pauline material. The use of such compounds in the Pastoral stratum in the ten-letter corpus accords, however, with the generalization that it was a tendency present in earlier stages which was accentuated in later stages of the stratum.

The occurrences in the various parts of the Pastoral stratum[1] are as follows:

Ten-letter corpus

Romans

1:21	εὐχαριστεῖν	12:14	εὐλογεῖν (twice)
1:23	τετράπους	14:5	πληροφορεῖν
1:25	εὐλογητός	14:6	εὐχαριστεῖν (twice)
1:29	κακοήθεια	14:18	εὐάρεστος
1:30	θεοστυγής	14:19	οἰκοδομή
1:32	συνευδοκεῖν	15:2	οἰκοδομή
12:10	φιλαδελφία	15:6	ὁμοθυμαδόν
12:13	φιλοξενία		

Number of occurrences: 17   Number of lines: 124.4
Number of lines to each occurrence: 7.3

1 Corinthians

(4:12	εὐλογεῖν)	8:10	οἰκοδομεῖν, εἰδωλόθυτος
(4:13	δυσφημεῖν)	10:23	οἰκοδομεῖν
(4:15	παιδαγωγός, εὐαγγέλιον)	10:28	ἱερόθυτος
(5:11	εἰδωλολάτρης)	10:30	εὐχαριστεῖν
8:1	εἰδωλόθυτος	11:15	φιλόνεικος
8:4	εἰδωλόθυτος	11:16	φιλόνεικος
8:7	εἰδωλόθυτος	11:24	εὐχαριστεῖν

Ṅo. of occurrences: 16 Number of lines: 149.1
Number of lines to each occurrence: 9.3

2 Corinthians
 (10:8 οἰκοδομή)   (13:10 οἰκοδομή)
Number of occurrences: 2 Number of lines: 28
Number of lines to each occurrence: 14

Ephesians
    4:29 οἰκοδομή   6:9 προσωπολημψία
    6:5 ὀφθαλμοδουλία, ἀνθρωπάρεσκος
Number of occurrences: 4 Number of lines: 45
Number of lines to each occurrence: 11.3

Colossians
    3:20 εὐαρεστός   3:24 κληρονομία
    3:22 ὀφθαλμοδουλία, ἀνθρωπάρεσκος 3:25 προσωπολημψία
Number of occurrences: 5 Number of lines: 16.1
Number of lines to each occurrence: 3.2

1 Thessalonians
    1:5*b* πληροφορία   2:13 εὐχαριστεῖν
    2:2 εὐαγγέλιον   4:9 φιλαδελφία, θεοδίδακτος
    2:4 εὐαγγέλιον   4:11 φιλοτιμεῖσθαι
    2:5 πλεονεξία   4:12 εὐσχημόνως
    2:8 εὐδοκεῖν, εὐαγγέλιον   5:14 ὀλιγόψυχος, μακροθυμεῖν
    2:9 εὐαγγέλιον
Number of occurrences: 14 Number of lines: 71
Number of lines to each occurrence: 5.1

2 Thessalonians
    3:13 κακοποιεῖν
Number of occurrences: 1 Number of lines: 22.5
Number of lines to each occurrence: 22.5

Pastoral epistles

1 Timothy
    1:3 ἑτεροδιδασκαλεῖν   3:2 φιλόξενος
    1:4 γενεαλογία, οἰκονομία   3:3 φιλάργυρος
    1:6 ματαιολογία, νομοδιδάσκαλος   3:6 νεόφυτος
    1:9 πατρολῴας, μητρολῴας,   3:8 αἰσχροκερδής
         ἀνδροφόνος   3:16 ὁμολογουμένως, εὐσεβεία
    1:10 ἀρσενοκοίτης, ἀνδραποδιστής   4:2 ψευδολόγος
    1:11 εὐαγγέλιον   4:3 εὐχαριστία
    1:16 μακροθυμία   4:4 εὐχαριστία
    2:1 εὐχαριστία   4:7 εὐσέβεια
    2:2 εὐσέβεια   4:8 εὐσέβεια
    2:10 θεοσέβεια   5:4 εὐσεβεῖν
    2:15 τεκνογονία   5:10 τεκνοτροφεῖν

1 Timothy (continued)

5:14	τεκνογονεῖν, οἰκοδεσποτεῖν	6:11	εὐσέβεια, πραϋπαθία
5:23	ὑδροποτεῖν	6:12	ὁμολόγησις, ὁμολογία
6:2	εὐεργεσία	6:13	ζῳογονεῖν, ὁμολογία
6:3	εὐσέβεια, ἐτεροδιδασκαλεῖν	6:17	ὑψηλοφρονεῖν
6:5	εὐσέβεια	6:18	ἀγαθοεργεῖν, εὐμετάδοτος
6:6	εὐσέβεια, αὐτάρκεια	6:20	κενοφωνία, ψευδώνυμος
6:10	φιλαργυρία		

Number of occurrences: 50   Number of lines: 201.9
Number of lines to each occurrence: 4

2 Timothy

1:6	ἀναζωπυρεῖν, εὐαγγέλιον	3:3	ἀφιλάγαθος
1:8	συγκακοπαθεῖν	3:4	φιλήδονος, φιλόθεος
1:10	εὐαγγέλιον	3:5	εὐσεβεία
2:3	συγκακοπαθεῖν	3:10	μακροθυμία
2:4	στρατολογεῖν	3:12	εὐσεβῶς
2:8	εὐαγγέλιον	3:16	θεόπνευστος
2:9	κακοπαθεῖν, κακοῦργος	4:2	μακροθυμία, εὐκαίρως
2:15	ὀρθοτομεῖν	4:5	κακοπάθεια, εὐαγγελιστής,
2:16	κενοφωνία		πληροφορεῖν
2:21	εὔχρηστος	4:11	εὔχρηστος
3:2	φιλάργυρος, φίλαυτος	4:17	πληροφορεῖν

Number of occurrences: 28   Number of lines: 137.2
Number of lines to each occurrence: 4.9

Titus

1:1	εὐσέβεια	2:9	εὐάρεστος
1:7	οἰκονόμος, αἰσχροκερδής	3:1	πειθαρχεῖν
1:8	φιλόξενος, φιλάγαθος	3:4	φιλανθρωπία
1:10	ἀνυπότακτος, ματαιολόγος	3:7	κληρονόμος
1:16	ὁμολογεῖν	3:9	γενεαλογία
2:3	ἱεροπρεπής, καλοδιδάσκαλος	3:11	αὐτοκατάκριτος
2:4	φίλανδρος, φιλότεκνος, οἰκουργός		

Number of occurrences: 19   Number of lines: 82.5
Number of lines to each occurrence: 4.3

1 Peter

1:17	ἀπροσωπολήμπτως	3:9	εὐλογεῖν, εὐλογία
1:18	πατροπαραδότος	3:17	ἀγαθοποιεῖν, κακοποιεῖν
1:22	φιλαδελφία	3:20	μακροθυμία
2:2	ἀρτιγέννητος	4:3	οἰνοφλυγία
2:12	κακοποιεῖν	4:6	εὐαγγελίζειν
2:14	κακοποιεῖν, ἀγαθοποιεῖν	4:9	φιλόξενος, οἰκονόμος
2:15	ἀγαθοποιεῖν	4:15	κακοποιός, ἀλλοτριεπίσκοπος
2:20	κολαφίζειν, ἀγαθοποιεῖν	4:19	ἀγαθοποιΐα
3:6	ἀγαθοποιεῖν	5:2	αἰσχροκερδῶς
3:8	ὁμόφρων, φιλάδελφος,	5:4	ἀρχίποιμην
	εὔσπλαγχνος, ταπεινόφρων	5:5	ταπεινοφροσύνη,
			ἐγκομβοῦσθαι

Number of occurrences: 31   Number of lines: 122.6
Number of lines to each occurrence: 3.9

Earlier material in 1 Peter

1:3	εὐλογητός	3:18	ζωοποιεῖν
1:7	πολύτιμος	4:3	εἰδωλολατρία
1:12	εὐαγγελίζεσθαι	4:9	οἰκονόμος
2:5	οἰκοδομεῖν, εὐπηόσδεκτος		

Number of occurrences: 8   Number of lines: 79.4
Number of lines to each occurrence: 9.9

Comparison between the Pastoral stratum and earlier material in the Pauline corpus

	No. of occurrences	No. of lines	No. of lines to each occurrence
Ten-letter corpus	59	415.6	7.0
Pastoral epistles	97	421.6	4.3
1 Peter	31	122.6	3.9

These results may be compared with the following summarized data for earlier material in the Pauline corpus:

	No. of occurrences	No. of lines	No. of lines to each occurrence
Rom 1–4	23[2]	162.5	7.1
1 Cor 1–3	10	147.7	14.8
Earlier material in Ephesians	36	220	6.1

Words peculiar to given material in the New Testament including New Testament hapax legomena

The occurrence in 1 Peter of words peculiar to each stratum and occurring nowhere else in the New Testament, to be referred to as distinctive words, is as follows:

The later or Pastoral stratum

1 Pet 1: 14–19, 21c–23, 2: 1–3, 8b

1:17	ἀπροσωπολήμπτως	
1:18	πατροπάραδοτος	5 words in 18.5 lines,
1:23	σπορά	or 9 per page
2:2	ἄδολος, ἀρτιγέννητος	

1 Pet 2: 11–20, 21c, 22–25

2:12	ἐποπτεύειν	
2:12, 14	κακοποιός (cf. 1 Pet 4: 15)	
2:16	ἐπικάλυμμα	
2:19	ἀδίκως	10 words in 29.5 lines,
2:20	κλέος	or 11.2 per page
2:21	ὑπολιμπάνειν, ὑπογραμμός	
2:23	ἀντιλοιδορεῖν	
2:24	ἀπογίνεσθαι, μώλωψ	

1 Pet 3: 1–9
3:3	ἐμπλοκή, ἔνδυσις, περίθεσις, τριχῶν	
3:6	πτόησις	12 words in 19.5 lines,
3:7	ἀπονεμεῖν, συνοικεῖν, γυναικεῖος	or 13.4 per page
3:8	ὁμόφρων, συμπαθής, ταπεινόφρων, φιλάδελφος	

1 Pet 3: 13–17, 19–22a
3:21	ἐπερώτημα, ῥύπος	2 words in 16.3 lines, or 4 per page

1 Pet 4: 1b, 2, 3c, 4–6, 7b, 8f, 11b–16, 19
4:2	βιοῦν, ἐπίλοιπος	
4:3	οἰνοφλυγία, πότος	
4:4	ἀνάχυσις	10 words in 29.5 lines,
4:8	ἐκτενής	or 11.2 per page
4:15	κακοποιός, ἀλλοτριεπίσκοπος	
4:19	ἀγαθοποιΐα, κτίστης	

1 Pet 5: 1–5b
5:1	συμπρεσβύτερος	
5:2	ἀναγκαστῶς, προθύμως, αἰσχροκερδῶς	7 words in 9.3 lines, or 24.8 per page
5:4	ἀμαράντινος, ἀρχιποίμων	
5:5b	ἐγκομβοῦσθαι	

Totals: 43 words in 122.6 lines, or 11.6 per page

Earlier material
1 Pet 1: 1–12
1:4	ἀμάραντος	
1:8	ἀνεκλάλητος	4 words in 26.5 lines,
1:10	ἐξεραυνᾶν	or 4.9 per page
1:11	προμαρτύρεσθαι	

1 Pet 1: 13, 20, 21ab, 2: 4–7, 9f, 21ab, 3: 18, 22c
1:13	ἀναζώννυναι	
2:5, 9	ἐξαγγέλλειν	3 words in 24.6 lines, or 4.4 per page
2:9	ἱεράτευμα	

1 Pet 4: 1a, 3, 7a, 10, 11a, 17f, 5: 6–14
4:1	ὁπλίζεσθαι	
5:6	κραταιός	
5:10	σθενοῦν	5 words in 28.3 lines,
5:12	ἐπιμαρτυρεῖν	or 5.8 per page
5:13	συνεκλεκτός	

Totals: 12 words in 79.4 lines, or 5 per page

The occurrence of words peculiar to the Pastoral stratum of the ten-letter corpus and found nowhere else in the New Testament is as follows:
Rom 1: 19–21
1:20	θειότης, καθορᾶν
1:20, 2:1	ἀναπολόγητος

Rom 1:19–21 (continued)

1:21	ματαιοῦσθαι	
1:25	σεβάζεσθαι	
1:25	μεταλλάσσειν	
1:27	ἐκκαίεσθαι, ὄρεξις	16 words in 35 lines,
1:29	ψιθυριστής, κακοηθεία	or 15.1 per page
1:30	κατάλαλος, ἐφευρετής, θεοστυγής	
1:31	ἀνελεήμων	
1:21,31	ἀσύνετος	
1:26, 27	χρῆσις	

Rom 12:8c, 9–11a, 12b–21, 13:1–10

12:10	προηγεῖσθαι, φιλόστοργος	3 words in 36.1 lines,
13:4	ἔκδικος (cf. 1 Thess 4:6)	or 2.7 per page

Rom 14:1 – 15:6

14:1	κρέας (cf. 1 Cor 8:13)	1 word in 49 lines,
		or 0.7 per page

(1 Cor 4:12, 13a, 14–21, 5:1–5, 9–13)

4:13	δυσφημεῖν	2 words in 34.6 lines,
5:9, 11	συναναμείγνυναι (cf. 2 Thess 3:14)	or 1.9 per page

1 Cor 7:17, 20, 24
No words peculiar to this material in the New Testament

1 Cor 8

8:10	εἰδωλεῖον	2 words in 25 lines,
8:13	κρέας (cf. Rom 14:1)	or 2.6 per page

1 Cor 10:23 – 11:29, 33f, 14:32–8

10:25	μακέλλον	
10:27	ἀναξίως	
10:28	ἱερόθυτον	
11:5, 13	ἀκατακάλυπτος	8 words in 80.5 lines,
11:6, 7	κατακαλύπτειν	or 3.3 per page
11:14, 15	κομᾶν	
11:15	κόμη	
11:16	φιλόνεικος	

(1 Cor 16:15f, 18b)
No words peculiar to this material in the New Testament

(2 Cor 10:6, 8–11, 13:1–10)

10:9	ἐκφοβεῖν	1 word in 28 lines,
		or 1.2 per page

Eph 4:28f, 32c, 5:1, 2a, 15–18a, 5:21 – 6:9

5:15	ἄσοφος	
5:27	ῥυτίς	
5:29, 6:4	ἐκτρέφειν	6 words in 45 lines,
5:29	θάλπειν (cf. 1 Thess 2:7)	or 3.7 per page
6:6	ὀφθαλμοδουλία (cf. Col 3:22)	
	ἀνθρωπάρεσκος (cf. Col 3:22)	

Col 3:18 – 4:1, 5
 3:22   ὀφθαλμοδουλία (cf. Eph 6:6)
        ἀνθρωπάρεσκος (cf. Eph 6:6)   4 words in 16.1 lines,
 3:21   ἀθυμεῖν   or 8.2 per page
 3:24   ἀνταπόδοσις

1 Thess 1:5*b*, 6*a*, 7, 2:1-16
 2:2   προπάσχειν
 2:5   κολακεία
 2:7   τροφός (cf. Eph 5:29)   7 words in 38.5 lines,
 2:8   ὁμείρεσθαι   or 6 per page
 2:10   ὁσίως
 2:14   συμφυλέτης

1 Thess 4:1-12
 4:6   ὑπερβαίνειν
 4:9   θεοδίδακτος   3 words in 23 lines,
 4:6   ἔκδικος (cf. Rom 13:4)   or 4.3 per page

1 Thess 5:12-15, 21*b*, 22
 5:14   ἄτακτος, ὀλιγόψυχος   2 words in 9.5 lines,
                                             or 6.6 per page

2 Thess 2:15, 3:4, 6-15
 3:6   ἀτάκτως
 3:7   ἀτακτεῖν
 3:13   καλοποιεῖν   5 words in 22.5 lines,
 3:14   συναναμείγνυναι (cf. 1 Cor 5:9, 11) or 7.2 per page
        σημειοῦσθαι

Totals for passages in the ten-letter corpus, excluding Rom 1:19 – 2:1
which is atypical, are as follows: 38 words in 381.1 lines, or 3.3 per page.
These figures exclude repetitions.

The rate of 3.3 words peculiar to the ten-letter Pastoral stratum in the
New Testament is relatively low as compared with the rest of the corpus.
According to the calculations of P. N. Harrison, the figures for the epistles
of the ten-letter corpus are as follows:

Romans	4	Philippians	6.2
1 Corinthians	4.1	Colossians	5.5
2 Corinthians	5.6	1 Thessalonians	3.6
Galatians	3.9	2 Thessalonians	3.3
Ephesians	4.6	Philemon excluded	

If the passages assigned in this study to the Pastoral stratum were to be
excluded, the figures for some of these epistles would be significantly
higher. This applies particularly to 1 and 2 Thessalonians.

The implication is that the vocabulary of the Pastoral material in the
ten-letter corpus is more typical of the New Testament as a whole than
that of the rest of the corpus, which could be a sign of verbal camouflage.

ABBREVIATIONS

ATR	*Anglican Theological Review*
BAG	W. Bauer, *A Greek-English Lexicon of the New Testament and Other Early Christian Literature*, tr. and rev. W. F. Arndt, F. W. Gingrich, 4th edn, London 1952.
CBQ	*Catholic Biblical Quarterly*
ConNT	*Coniectanea neotestamentica*
ET	*Expository Times*
FRLANT	*Forschungen zur Religion und Literatur des Alten und Neuen Testaments*
HTR	*Harvard Theological Review*
JAAR	*Journal of the American Academy of Religion*
JBL	*Journal of Biblical Literature*
JQR	*Jewish Quarterly Review*
JRS	*Journal of Roman Studies*
JTS	*Journal of Theological Studies*
LCL	Loeb Classical Library
LSJ	H. G. Liddell and R. Scott, *A Greek-English Lexicon*, rev. H. S. Jones, 9th edn, Oxford 1940.
NTS	*New Testament Studies*
NovT	*Novum Testamentum*
RGG	*Religion in Geschichte und Gegenwart*
SNTP	*Studien zum Neuen Testament und zum Patristik*
ST	*Studia theologica*
TDNT	G. Kittel (ed.), *Theological Dictionary of the New Testament*, tr. and ed. G. W. Bromiley, Grand Rapids, Mich. 1967.
TLZ	*Theologische Literaturzeitung*
ZNW	*Zeitschrift für die neutestamentliche Wissenschaft*
ZTK	*Zeitschrift für Theologie und Kirche*

NOTES

1. Introduction

1 See T. S. Kuhn, *The Social Structure of Scientific Revolutions* (Chicago 1962).

2 W. Munro, 'Authority and Subjection in Early Christian "Paideia" with Particular Reference to the Pauline Corpus and 1 Peter' (Columbia University and Union Theological Seminary Ed. D., 1974; University Microfilms, Ann Arbor, Michigan).

3 K. Weidinger, *Die Haustafeln ein Stuck urchristliche Paränese* (Leipzig 1928), 1–2.

4 K. von Weizsäcker, *The Apostolic Age of the Christian Church* (tr. from 2nd edn, J. Millar, New York 1895), 391f.

5 *Ibid.*, 391.

6 M. Dibelius, *An die Kolosser Epheser an Philemon* (3rd edn, Tübingen 1953), 48–50.

7 Weidinger, 6–12.

8 *Ibid.*, 3–5.

9 A. Seeberg, *Der Katechismus der Urchristenheit* (Leipzig 1903), *Die beiden Wege und das Aposteldekret* (Leipzig 1906), and *Die Didache des Judentums und der Urchristenheit* (Leipzig 1908).

10 G. Klein, *Der alteste Christliche Katechismus und die judische Propaganda-Literatur* (Berlin 1909).

11 P. Carrington, *The Primitive Christian Catechism* (London 1940).

12 *Ibid.*, 6–21, 67–77.

13 E. G. Selwyn, *The First Epistle of St. Peter* (2nd edn, London 1961), 363–466.

14 W. D. Davies, *Paul and Rabbinic Judaism* (London 1958), 122–36.

15 Selwyn, 17–24, 268–81, 363–466.

16 O. D. Foster, *The Literary Relations of 'The first epistle of Peter'* (New Haven 1913).

17 A. E. Barnett, *Paul Becomes a Literary Influence* (Chicago 1941), 52–69.

18 C. L. Mitton, *The Epistle to the Ephesians* (Oxford 1951), 280–315.

19 Carrington, 23–9, 31f, 35, 38–43.

20 Selwyn, 370f, 376–8, 383, 390f, 394f, 403, 408–11, 416, 418, 427, 430, 432f, 442–9.

21 *Ibid.*, 386, 389.

22 *Ibid.*, 438f.
23 *Ibid.*, 437f.
24 *Ibid.*, 467–88.
25 D. Daube, *The New Testament and Rabbinic Judaism* (London 1956), chs. 4, 5.
26 *Ibid.*, 126, 129.
27 *Ibid.*, 130.
28 Selwyn, 9–17.
29 Acts 15:22, 27, 32.
30 Selwyn, 369, 372, 382.
31 *Ibid.*, 454–8.
32 *Ibid.*, 441, 450.
33 F. W. Beare, *The First Epistle of Peter* (Oxford 1945), ix.
34 F. W. Beare, *The First Epistle of Peter* (2nd edn, Oxford 1958), 186–204.
35 *Ibid.*, 188–90.
36 *Ibid.*, 189, citing W. L. Knox, 'The First Epistle of St. Peter', *Theology*, 49 (1946), 342–4.
37 C. L. Mitton, *The Epistle to the Ephesians.*
38 'The Relation of 1 Peter and Ephesians', *JTS*, 1 (1950), 67–73.
39 M. S. Enslin, 'The First Epistle of St. Peter', *JQR*, N.S. 37 (1946–7), 295–9.
40 Beare (1958), 196.
41 P. Feine & J. Behm, *Introduction to the New Testament* (rev. W. G. Kümmel, tr. from 14th edn, A. J. Mattill, Nashville 1966).
42 R. H. Fuller, *A Critical Introduction to the New Testament* (London 1966), 158.
43 See, e.g., R. P. Morgan, 'The Composition of 1 Peter in Recent Study', *Vox Evangelica* (London 1962), 3–42, and J. H. Elliott, 'The Rehabilitation of an Exegetical Stepchild: 1 Peter in Recent Research', *JBL*, 95 (1976), 243–54.
44 R. Perdelwitz, 'Die Mysterienreligion und das Problem des 1. Petrus-briefes', *Religionsgeschichtliche Versuche und Vorarbeiten*, 9:3 (1911).
45 W. Bornemann, 'Der erste Petrusbrief – eine Taufrede des Silvanus?', *ZNW*, 39 (1919), 143–65.
46 B. H. Streeter, *The Primitive Church* (New York 1929), 136–9.
47 H. Windisch, 'Der erste Petrusbrief', *Die katholischen Briefe* (Tübingen 1930), 49–82.
48 R. Bultmann, 'Bekenntnis- und Liedfragmente im ersten Petrusbrief', *ConNT*, 11 (1947), 1–14.
49 H. Preisker, 'Anhang zum ersten Petrusbrief', *Die katholischen Briefe* (rev. of H. Windisch, Tübingen 1951), 152–62.
50 E. Lohse, 'Paränese und Kerygma im 1 Petrusbrief', *ZNW*, 45 (1954), 68–89.
51 F. L. Cross, *1 Peter: A Paschal Liturgy* (London 1954).
52 T. C. G. Thornton, '1 Peter, A Paschal Liturgy?', *JTS*, 12 (1961), 14–26.
53 E. Best, '1 Peter and the Gospel Tradition', *NTS*, 16 (1970), 95–113. The article replies in the first instance to R. H. Gundry, '"Verba Christi" in 1 Peter: their implications concerning the authorship of 1 Peter and the authenticity of the Gospel tradition', *NTS*, 12 (1966–7), 336–50, and

C. Spicq, 'La 1 Petri et le témoignage évangélique de saint Pierre', *ST*, 20 (1966), 37–61. Gundry's argument has antecedents, however, in Selwyn's category, *verba Christi*, as also in other writers whom Best lists.
54 Mitton, *Epistle*, 112, takes as one of his tests of literary dependence a tendency for parallels to be concentrated in certain impressive passages.
55 Fuller, 57, 65.
56 *Ibid.*, 133.
57 Feine, Behm, Kümmel, 261.
58 *Ibid.*
59 *Ibid.*
60 *Ibid.*
61 H. J. Holtzmann, *Die Pastoralbriefe* (Leipzig 1880).
62 B. Weiss, 'The Present Status of the Inquiry concerning the Genuineness of the Pauline Epistles', *American Journal of Theology*, 1 (1897), 328–403, 392.
63 *Ibid.*, 393f.
64 P. N. Harrison, *The Problem of the Pastorals* (London 1921).
65 For consideration of these passages, see appendix D.
66 Cf. F. R. M. Hitchcock, 'Tests for the Pastorals', *JTS*, 30 (1929), 272–9; W. Michaelis, 'Pastoralbriefe und Wortstatistik', *ZNW*, 27 (1929), 69–76; B. M. Metzger, 'A Reconsideration of Certain Arguments against the Pauline Authorship of the Pastoral Epistles', *ET*, 70 (1958–9), 91–4; D. Guthrie, *The Pastoral Epistles* (London 1957), 46–8, where there is objection to statistical methods *per se* in establishing authorship; and K. Grayston & G. Herdan, 'The Authorship of the Pastorals in the Light of Statistical Linguistics', *NTS*, 6 (1959–60), 1–15, where the weaknesses of Harrison's methods are countered by alternative methods confirming his conclusions.
67 A. Q. Morton & J. McLeman, *Christianity in the Computer Age* (New York 1964), and *Paul, the Man and the Myth* (London 1966).
68 J. Jeremias, 'Zur Datierung der Pastoralbriefe', *ZNW*, 12 (1961), 101–9.
69 Cf. Guthrie, *Pastoral Epistles*; J. N. D. Kelly, *A Commentary on the Pastoral Epistles* (London 1963); E. F. Harrison, *Introduction to the New Testament* (Grand Rapids 1964); and, postulating an amanuensis, J. Jeremias, 'Die Briefe an Timotheus und Titus', *Das Neue Testament Deutsch*, vol. 9 (7th edn, Göttingen 1954), 1–67.
70 Cf., e.g., Harrison, *Problem*; A. H. McNeile, *An Introduction to the Study of the New Testament* (rev. C. S. C. Williams, 2nd edn, Oxford 1953).
71 Cf. amongst others E. J. Goodspeed, *An Introduction to the New Testament* (Chicago 1937); B. S. Easton, *The Pastoral Epistles* (New York 1947); Fuller; Feine, Behm, Kümmel.
72 Guthrie, 14.
73 Note, however, A. C. Sundberg, 'Canon Muratorii: A Fourth Century List', *HTR*, 66 (1973), 1–41.
74 Fuller, 133.
75 Brown, *The Pastoral Epistles*, xxiv, with reference to 1 Clem 5, Rom 15:24, and the reference in the Muratorian canon to a visit to Spain.
76 For discussion of the question see Easton, 21; Feine, Behm, Kümmel, 268–71; Kelly, 13–16.
77 Feine, Behm, Kümmel, 267f.
78 Easton, 10–13; Kelly, 16–21; Fuller, 134; Feine, Behm, Kümmel, 269f.

79 Harrison, *Problem*, 20–5; Grayston & Herdan, 8–13. Fuller, 135, points out that of the 306 words in the Pastorals not found in Paul some are key terms taking the place of Pauline key terms.
80 Harrison, *ibid.*, 30–8; Feine, Behm, Kümmel, 263.
81 Harrison, *ibid.*, 44.
82 Feine, Behm, Kümmel, 263.
83 Fuller, 135.
84 Harrison, *Problem*, appendix IV, following 184.
85 Feine, Behm, Kümmel, 252.
86 E. Percy, *Die Probleme der Kolosser- und Epheserbriefe* (Lund 1946), 2.
87 H. J. Holtzmann, *Kritik der Epheser- und Kolosserbriefe* (Leipzig 1872).
88 Mitton, *Epistle*, 26.
89 J. Moffatt, *An Introduction to the Literature of the New Testament* (New York 1922), 375–81.
90 E. J. Goodspeed, *The Meaning of Ephesians* (Chicago 1933), and *Introduction*, 222–39.
91 Goodspeed, *Introduction*, 222, n. 1.
92 J. Knox, *Philemon among the Letters of Paul* (Nashville 1935), 76–90, and *Marcion and the New Testament* (Chicago 1942), 58–69, found support for the possibility from the order of the letters in Marcion's corpus according to Tertullian and Epiphanius, which he thought reflects the displacement of Ephesians by Galatians as the first letter, and in this he has the concurrence of C. L. Mitton, *The Formation of the Pauline Corpus of Letters* (London 1955), 61–74. Both, like Goodspeed, assumed a connection between the collecting of the letters and the writing of Ephesians.
93 Mitton, *Epistle*, 49.
94 *Ibid.*, part III.
95 *Ibid.*, 4–40.
96 Soon after the publication of Mitton's study, J. N. Sanders and D. E. Nineham presented the case for and against Pauline authorship respectively, in *Studies in Ephesians* (ed. F. L. Cross, London 1956), 9–35, indicating that the matter had become controversial among English scholars.
97 Percy, 215–48.
98 G. Schille, 'Der Autor des Epheserbriefes', *TLZ*, 82 (1957), 326–34.
99 N. A. Dahl, 'Adresse und Proömium des Epheserbrief', *TLZ*, 7 (1951), 241–64.
100 J. C. Kirby, *Ephesians: Baptism and Pentecost* (Montreal 1968).
101 J. P. Sampley, *'And the Two shall become One Flesh'* (London 1971), vii, 1, 3.
102 E. Käsemann, 'Epheserbrief', *RGG*, 3 (1958), 517–20.
103 W. Marxsen, *Introduction to the New Testament* (tr. G. Buswell, Philadelphia 1968), 195f.
104 See below, 33f.
105 W. Munro, 'Col III.18–IV.1 and Eph V.21–VI.9: Evidences of a Late Literary Stratum?', *NTS*, 18 (1971–2), 448–51.
106 Sampley, '. . . One Flesh'.
107 Fuller, 62; Feine, Behm, Kümmel, 240f.
108 Feine, Behm, Kümmel, 240–3; Fuller, 60–2.
109 Another explanation accounting for some difficulties is that Colossians

uses hymnic sources, e.g., in 1:15–20; cf. Fuller, 62; E. Käsemann, 'A Primitive Christian Baptismal Liturgy', *Essays on New Testament Themes* (tr. W. J. Montague, Naperville, Ill. 1964) , 149–68. Yet another explanation is that of an amanuensis, favoured by Fuller, 62.

110   E. P. Sanders, 'Literary Dependence in Colossians', *JBL*, 85 (1966), 28–45.

111   Mitton, *Epistle*, 107–10.

112   Holtzmann, *Kritik*.

113   Dibelius, *Kolosser Epheser*, 49; Weidinger, *Haustafeln*, 51.

114   K. E. Kirk, *The Vision of God* (2nd edn, New York 1932), 126f.

115   E. Lohse, *Colossians and Philemon* (tr. W. & R. J. Karris, Philadelphia, 1971), 154.

116   J. E. Crouch, *The Origin and Intention of the Colossian Haustafel* (Göttingen 1972), 10f, 144, 149–51, and *passim*; D. G. Bradley, 'The Origins of the Hortatory Materials in the Letters of Paul' (Ph.D. thesis, Yale University, 1947), 181. For support for Crouch's stance, cf. W. Schrage, 'Zur Ethik der neutestamentlichen Haustafeln', *NTS*, 21 (1971), 1–22.

117   See J. A. Beet, *A Commentary on St. Paul's Epistles to the Corinthians* (London 1882), 256; C. J. Ellicot, *St. Paul's First Epistle to the Corinthians* (London 1882), 282. The latter thought that Paul had in mind the office of teaching in public, a rule which was 'carefully maintained'.

118   W. B. Harris, *The First Epistle of St. Paul to the Corinthians, Introduction and Commentary*(Madras 1958), 185f; H. Wendland, *Die Briefe an die Korinther* (Göttingen 1968), 131f.

119   J. Héring, *The First Epistle of Saint Paul to the Corinthians* (tr. from 2nd edn A. W. Heathcote & P. J. Allcock, London 1962), 154f. He does not think, however, that the passage intends to silence all women, but only those merely present at worship with no right to bring a message. Wendland, 132, expressed the view that what is at stake is church order in the sense of what has general approval in the church.

120   G. Zuntz, *The Text of the Epistles* (London 1946), 16.

121   M. E. Thrall, *The Ordination of Women to the Priesthood* (London 1958), 76.

122   T. B. Allworthy, *Women in the Apostolic Church* (Cambridge 1917), 95–7.

123   C. K. Barrett, *A Commentary on the First Epistle to the Corinthians* (London 1968), 330–3.

124   J. Weiss, *Der erste Korintherbrief* (Göttingen 1910); A. Loisy, *Remarques sur le Littérature épistolaire du Nouveau Testament* (Paris 1935), 73; Easton, 127f; E. Schweizer, *Church Order in the New Testament* (London 1961), 203, n. 783; J. Ruef, *Paul's First Letter to Corinth* (Harmondsworth 1971); H. Conzelmann, *Der erste Brief an die Korinther* (Göttingen 1969); W. Munro, 'Patriarchy and Charismatic Community in "Paul"', *Women and Religion: 1972 Proceedings* (Montana, AAR, 1973), 141–59, 141; R. Scroggs, 'Paul and the Eschatological Woman', *JAAR*, 40 (1972), 291–2; R. Jewett, 'The Redaction of 1 Corinthians and the Trajectory of the Pauline School', *JAAR*, 44 (1978), sup. 389–444, 420–3.

125   C. Clemen, *Die Einheitlichkeit der paulinische Briefen* (Göttingen 1894), 49.

126   Barrett, 330f.

127 Wendland, 131; Loisy; Munro, 'Patriarchy'; Jewett, 'The Redaction . . . School'.

128 O. Cullmann, *Christ and Time* (tr. F. V. Filson, Philadelphia 1949), 191–210, and *The State in the New Testament* (2nd edn, London 1963), 70–88.

129 Cullmann, *State*, 70–88.

130 C. Morrison, *The Powers That Be* (London 1960), 42f.

131 Cf. Col 1:16, 2:10, 15, Eph 1:20f, 3:10, 6:11f, 1 Cor 15:24, 1 Pet 3:22.

132 Cf. Luke 12:11, Tit 3:1, Rom 13:1.

133 Morrison, 43, 45.

134 *Ibid.*, 114–27.

135 E. Käsemann, Principles of the Interpretation of Romans 13', *New Testament Questions of Today* (tr. W. J. Montague, Philadelphia 1969), 196–211, 204.

136 A. Strobel, 'Zum Verständnis von Röm 13', *ZNW*, 47 (1956), 67–93.

137 Käsemann, 'Principles', 206f.

138 W. Schmithals, *Paul and the Gnostics* (tr. J. E. Steely, Nashville 1972), 219–38, could cite only Rom 16:17–20 for direct reference to gnostic opponents in Romans. Even if the passage gives a similar polemical character to the whole epistle, there is no evidence that those attacked in Rom 16 were necessarily eschatologically minded opponents of the Roman state, nor did he argue along these lines.

139 To give a sampling of views, T. Zahn, *Der Brief des Paulus an die Römer* (3rd edn, Leipzig 1925), 555, found no syntactical connection, but considered the general rule of obedience to civil power follows from the instructions regarding relations to enemies in Rom 12:17–21, on the assumption that state authorities were hostile to Christians and therefore their enemies. F. A. Philippi, *Commentary on St. Paul's Epistle to the Romans*, vol. 2 (tr. from 3rd edn J. S. Banks, Edinburgh 1879), 299, rejected efforts by earlier critics to bridge the hiatus by assuming that the apostle is exhorting Christians to submit humbly to pagan authorities in the same way as to the hostile acts of individuals as in Rom 12:14–21, or by seeing the state as an instrument of the divine wrath and vengeance mentioned in 12:19. He thought the injunctions were more generally related together in a discussion of behaviour toward those outside the Christian community. C. K. Barrett, *A Commentary on the Epistle to the Romans* (London 1957), 244, described the passage as self-contained and as at first sight introduced 'somewhat abruptly'. He found a connection, however, in the exhortations to humility and to live in peace in the preceding chapter. C. E. B. Cranfield, *A Commentary on Romans 12–13* (Edinburgh 1965), 62, favoured the explanation that since the state serves the good of humanity, to support it is part of one's debt to one's neighbour.

140 H. A. W. Meyer, *Critical and Exegetical Handbook to the Epistle to the Romans*, vol. 2 (tr. from 5th edn J. C. Moore, Edinburgh 1881), 275, and F. Godet, *Commentary on St. Paul's Epistle to the Romans*, vol. 2 (tr. A. Cusin, Edinburgh 1892), 303, concurred in finding the various connections suggested by scholars unsatisfactory. H. W. Schmidt, *Der Brief des Paulus an die Römer* (Berlin 1963), 218, saw Rom 13:1–7 as breaking

the obviously close connection between Rom 12:21 and 13:8, but thought the subject of love leads impellingly to that of relations with the state.

141 O. Michel, *Der Brief an die Römer* (2nd edn, Göttingen 1955), 38f.
142 Cranfield, 62.
143 Käsemann, 'Principles', 198f.
144 D. G. Bradley, 'The Topos as a Form in the Pauline Paraenesis', *JBL*, 72 (1953), 238–46.
145 H. Windisch, 'Imperium und Evangelium im Neuen Testament', *Kieler Universitätsreden*, 14 (1913), 27f; M. Dibelius, *Botschaft und Geschichte*, vol. 2 (Tübingen 1956), 182; A. Pallis, *To the Romans, A Commentary* (Liverpool 1920), 141; Loisy, 30f.
146 E. Barnikol, 'Der nichtpaulinische Ursprung der absoluten Obrigkeitsbejahung von Römer 13:1–7', *SNTP*, 77 (1961), 65–133.
147 J. Kallas, *The Satanward View* (Philadelphia 1966), and *Jesus and the Power of Satan* (Philadelphia 1968).
148 Kallas, 'Romans xiii. 1–7: An Interpolation', *NTS*, 11 (1965), 365–74.
149 H. Gamble, 'The Redaction of the Pauline Letters and the Formation of the Pauline Corpus', *JBL*, 94 (1975), 403–18, 403.
150 See above, n. 92. For discussion of a possible original seven-letter corpus, to which Colossians, Ephesians, and Philemon were added later, see W. Schmithals, 'On the Composition and Collection of the Major Epistles of Paul', *Paul and the Gnostics*, 239–74. For consideration of the place of the Pastoral stratum in the history of the corpus, see below, 140–7.
151 P. N. Harrison, *Paulines and Pastorals*, 79–85; W. O. Walker, '1 Corinthians and Paul's Views regarding Women', *JBL*, 94 (1975), 94–110 (cf. the rejection of the hypothesis by J. Murphy-O'Connor, 'The Non-Pauline Character of 1 Corinthians 11: 2–16?', *JBL*, 95 (1976), 615–21); W. Munro, 'Patriarchy', 141–5.
152 J. Weiss, *Der erste Korintherbrief*; G. Zuntz, *Text of the Epistles*.
153 E. Käsemann, 'Ministry and Community in the New Testament', *Essays on New Testament Themes* (tr. W. J. Montague, Naperville, Ill. 1964), 63–94, and 'Paul and Early Catholicism', in *New Testament Questions of Today* (tr. W. J. Montague, Philadelphia 1969), 236–51.
154 Käsemann, 'Ministry', 66, 71, 75f, 78, 81–6, and *Jesus Means Freedom* (tr. from 3rd rev. edn F. Clarke, Philadelphia 1970), 59–65.
155 W. Schmithals, *Die Gnosis in Korinth* (Göttingen 1965), and *Paul and the Gnostics*.
156 R. H. Fuller, 'Early Catholicism in the New Testament', unpublished manuscript.
157 H. von Campenhausen, *Polycarp von Smyrna und die Pastoralbriefe* (Heidelberg 1951), 49–51.
158 R. T. Fortna, *The Gospel of Signs* (London 1970), 15–21.
159 *Ibid.*, 16f.
160 *Ibid.*, 17–19.
161 *Ibid.*, 19.
162 *Ibid.*, 19–21.
163 J. Barr, *The Semantics of Biblical Language* (London 1961), 263–71.
164 R. Jewett, *Paul's Anthropological Terms* (Leiden 1971), 4–10.
165 Fortna, 19.

166 *Ibid.*, 19f.
167 Here Fortna followed E. Hirsch, 'Stilkritik und Literaranalyse im vierten Evangelium', *ZNW*, 43 (1950-1), 129-43; Fortna, 21.
168 Cf., e.g., Rom 10: 18-21, 11: 33-6; 1 Pet 2: 4-10.
169 Mitton, *Epistle*, part III.
170 Mitton, 'The Relation of 1 Peter and Ephesians', *JTS*, 1 (1950), 67-73.

2. The identification of a later stratum in the Pauline corpus and 1 Peter

1 This section largely reproduces the short study by W. Munro, 'Col III. 18- IV. 1 and Eph V. 21-VI. 9: Evidences of a Late Literary Stratum?', *NTS*, 18 (1971-2), 448-51.
2 Dibelius, *An die Kolosser Epheser an Philemon*, 46-50, and Weidinger, *Die Haustafeln Ein Stück urchristlicher Paränese*, 50-73, postulated a gradual christianization of a code or codes which they consider were current in hellenism and hellenistic Judaism, with Col 3: 18-4: 1 representing its most primitive form in Christian circles, and Eph 5: 21-6: 9 a more christianized version. Those rejecting the code theory, however, have taken a similar view. For instance Beare, *The First Epistle of Peter* (1958), 195, cited a letter from E. J. Goodspeed to the effect that he and his colleagues at Chicago were unable to find any supposed *Haustafel* such as is claimed existed in ancient times, and that it appeared to them more likely that a germ in Colossians had been expanded in Ephesians, and then in 1 Peter. Sampley, *'And the Two Shall Become One Flesh'*, 24, accepted the code theory but cautioned against assuming too easily that Col 3: 18-4: 1 is the more primitive version.
3 See above, 13.
4 Mitton, *The Epistle to the Ephesians*, 280-315.
5 *Ibid.*, 192, 194; Mitton, 'The Relation between 1 Peter and Ephesians'.
6 Cf. R. H. Fuller, *The Foundations of New Testament Christology* (London 1965), 237f, n. 28, for references to hymnic reconstructions of Col 1: 15-20 indicating that the phrase does not accord with the poetic parallelism which seems to be present.
7 Twelve parallels of three or more words, excluding articles, have been found between different parts of the rest of Ephesians. Of these only one (Eph 4: 29, 3: 2, 6: 19; Col 3: 8) clearly resembles what was observed in 5: 21-6: 9 in that there is apparent dependence by one set of words on another which has closer links with material outside Ephesians in the ten-letter corpus. Eph 4: 28f will, however, be associated with Eph 5: 21- 6: 9 in due course; see below, 35. For details concerning the other parallels, see Munro, 439.
8 Mitton, *Epistle*, 304f.
9 See, e.g., Kirk, *The Vision of God*, 127.
10 See K. Aland, *et al.* (eds.), *The Greek New Testament* (New York 1966), 676, n. 7.
11 *Ibid.*, 701, n. 6.
12 Arguing that the form reflects semitic usage, D. Daube, 'Participle and Imperative in 1 Peter', rejected the view of J. H. Moulton, *A Grammar of New Testament Greek*, vol. 1 (3rd edn, Edinburgh 1908), 180ff, 232ff, that the use of the participle as an imperative predicate was acceptable in

the common Greek of the first century. H. G. Meecham, 'The Use of the Participle for the Imperative in the New Testament', *ET*, 58 (1947), 207f, ruled out most of the instances both these scholars cited from the New Testament on the grounds that they are textually uncertain, grammatically connected with a preceding or following verb, or due to case apposition or anacoluthon. F. Blass and A. Debrunner, *A Greek Grammar of the New Testament* (9–10th edn by R. W. Funk, Chicago 1961), 245f, treated the matter as an instance of anacoluthon, with a growing tendency to use the participle as an imperative independent from the preceding verb.

13   Cf. Eph 1:9f, 18f, 21, 23–2:6, 19, 3:6, 10, 17, 4:4–6, 9f, 14, 16, 18, 5:3f, 9, 6:13, 18.

14   The text used to calculate the frequency in the occurrence of linguistic traits is that of B. F. Westcott and F. J. A. Hort, *The New Testament in the Original Greek* (London 1914), selected for the usually unvarying length of its pages. Eph 5:21–6:9 is reckoned as 32 lines (excluding the quotations from LXX in Eph 5:31 and 6:2f), and the rest of Ephesians as 242 lines, excluding the quotation in 4:8. In the former, paired words occur in 5:27, 29; 6:4f, and in the latter, in 1:3, 4, 8, 17–2:1, 3, 6, 19, 20–3:10, 12, 17; 4:2, 14, 16, 17, 32; 5:19; 6:18.

15   See Eph 1:5, 6, 7, 9, 10, 11, 12, 13, 14, 17, 18, 19; 2:2, 3, 7, 12, 14, 15; 3:2, 7, 9, 16; 4:4, 7, 13, 17, 18, 22; 5:6, 8, 9, 11; 6:10, 12, 14, 15, 16, 17, 19. All these instances may be categorized as adjectival genitives, of the kind N. Turner characterized as the genitive of quality and the *genitivus materiae* and *epexegeticus* or appositive genitive in *A Grammar of New Testament Greek*, vol. 3 (Edinburgh 1963), 212–15. In Eph 5:21–6:9 all genitives that are in any sense adjectival are clearly partitive or objective, cf. 5:23, 26, 30; 6:6, 9; and Turner, 208–12.

16   H. Schlier, *Christus und die Kirche im Epheserbrief* (Tübingen 1930), 38.

17   In Eph 2:3 the mind and the flesh (σαρκὸς ... διανοιῶν) are regarded as evil because they are under the sway of demonic powers (cf. 2:2). These, not αἷμα καὶ σάρκα, are seen as the true enemies (6:12). In 2:11 σάρξ refers to the morally neutral fact of ethnic origin, and in 2:14 to the physical being of Christ.

18   There may well be an allusion also to the lustration of the bride in the marriage rites which were widely current in ancient times. According to N. D. Fustel de Coulanges, *The Ancient City* (tr., New York 1956), 45f, the marriage ceremony of earlier Greek and Roman times represented an initiation of the bride into the domestic religion of her husband after being freed from that of her father. The rites within the husband's home included both a ceremonial washing and a shared meal. Sampley, '*And the Two shall become One Flesh*', 41–5, found similar significance in Eph 5:26, because of his association of the Christ–church theme with the YHWH–Israel, YHWH–Jerusalem sacred marriage motif in Jewish tradition. His citation of a Sumerian sacred marriage text (44) reinforces the impression of allusions to the marriage lustration in Ezekiel (43).

19   Cf. Mitton, *Epistle*, 91.

20   H. A. A. Kennedy, *St. Paul and the Mystery Religions* (New York 1913), 127; G. Bornkamm, 'μυστήριον', TDNT, vol. 4 (1967), 802–28, 822. R. E. Brown, *The Semitic Background of the Term 'Mystery' in the New*

Testament (Philadelphia 1968), 65f, considers the word refers in Eph 5:32 to scripture with a deeper meaning; though pursuing semitic origins, he could point only to second-century writers, especially Justin, for similar use. J. Coppens, '"Mystery" in Paul's Theology', *Paul and Qumran*, ed. J. Murphy-O'Connor (Chicago 1968), 132–58, 146f, attempted to align the use with that in the rest of Ephesians, which he related to similar concepts in the Qumran writings, but his exegesis is somewhat forced. Sampley, *'And the Two shall become One Flesh'*, 95f, has tried to connect the use of the term in Eph 5:32 with the idea of unity in the rest of the epistle, but the unity commended in the subjection material is of quite a different kind, as already indicated.

21 K. G. Kuhn, 'Der Epheserbrief im Lichte der Qumrantexte', *NTS*, 7 (1960–1), 334–46, 346. Sampley, 72f, pointed to a possible connection between the idea of holiness for the church, and the purity and physical perfection required for membership in the Qumran community and for participation in the eschatological battle. The argument hinges on the use of ἀμώμος in Eph 5:27, which recalls the use of μῶμος in the LXX to translate the Hebrew מום in passages concerning the perfection required of sacrificial animals and priests. Sampley argued that the same applied to brides. This is feasible in regard to his Old Testament references, and Hebrew sacrificial notions probably do underlie Eph 5:27, even if only via the LXX and earlier New Testament writings, since Eph 5:27 appears to be dependent on Col 1:22, 28, and 2 Cor 11:2 (see above, 30). Any direct connection with the Qumran use of the same ideas is a tenuous assumption, however, since the writings of the sect do not employ the sacred marriage symbolism.

22 This is a common assumption for which those adhering to the theory of literary dependence and those adhering to the catechetical theory account in different ways; cf. Beare, *The First Epistle of Peter*, 9; Mitton, 'The Relation', over against Selwyn, *The First Epistle of St. Peter*, 365–419.

23 Among the similarities in style are the prolongation of the thanksgiving period through the use of repeated relative clauses, frequent prepositional phrases and present participles, the use of the genitive, the repetition of roughly synonymous words, and the liturgical quality of the rhythm. P. Schubert, *Form and Function of the Pauline Thanksgiving* (Berlin 1939), 8f, pointed out that the form of the thanksgiving in 2 Cor 1:3–11 is similar to, and he suggested imitated by, Eph 1:3–14 and 1 Pet 1:3–12. He found only traces of the form in the Pastorals (cf. 1 Tim 1:12–17, 2 Tim 1:3–5), and only feeble echoes of it in the Christian literature of the second century, while it does not occur at all in the catholic epistles. J. Coutts, 'Ephesians 1:3–14 and 1 Peter 1:3–12', *NTS*, 3 (1956–7), 115–27, argued that forms of baptismal, liturgical prayer, similar in structure but not exactly the same in context, lie behind these two passages. In regard to Ephesians he attempted to reconstruct the original form, which he arranged in three six-line strophes (123f).

24 Apart from the opening formula in 1 Pet 1:3 and Eph 1:3, it appears from the parallels in Mitton, *Epistle*, 280–315, that the correspondence in wording does not extend beyond scattered similarity in vocabulary and certain characteristic phrases.

25   See below,

26   See below,

27   See 1 Pet 1:17 as compared with 1 Pet 2:17f, 3:2, Eph 5:33, 6:5, Col 3:22.

28   Evidence confirming this conclusion is to be found in the parallel to which Foster pointed in *The Literary Relations of 'The first epistle of Peter'*, 424, between 1 Pet 1:20 and Rom 16:25, for the parallel is more extensive and clearer if it is assumed that 1 Pet 1:20 originally followed directly after vs. 13, as shown below:

> 1 Pet 1:13 Διὸ ἀναζωσάμενοι τὰς ὀσφύας τῆς διανοίας ὑμῶν, νήφοντες, τελείως ἐλπίσατε ἐπὶ τὴν φερομένην ὑμῖν χάριν ἐν ἀποκαλύψει Ἰησοῦ Χριστοῦ... 20 προεγνωσμένου μὲν πρὸ καταβολῆς κόσμου, φανερωθέντος δὲ ἐπ' ἐσχάτου τῶν χρόνων δι' ὑμᾶς 21 τοὺς δι' αὐτοῦ πιστοὺς εἰς θεὸν τὸν ἐγείραντα αὐτὸν ἐκ νεκρῶν καὶ δόξαν αὐτῷ δόντα

> Rom 16:25 Τῷ δὲ δυναμένῳ ὑμᾶς στηρίξαι κατὰ τὸ εὐαγγέλιόν μου καὶ τὸ κήρυγμα Ἰησοῦ Χριστοῦ, κατὰ ἀποκάλυψιν μυστηρίου χρόνοις αἰωνίοις σεσιγημένου 26 φανερωθέντος δὲ νῦν διά τε γραφῶν προφητικῶν κατ' ἐπιταγὴν τοῦ αἰωνίου θεοῦ εἰς ὑπακοὴν πίστεως εἰς πάντα τὰ ἔθνη γνωρισθέντος, 27 μόνῳ σοφῷ θεῷ διὰ Ἰησοῦ Χριστοῦ [ᾧ] ἡ δόξα εἰς τοὺς αἰῶνας ἀμήν.

    In addition R. Bultmann, 'Bekenntnis- und Liedfragmente im ersten Petrusbrief', *ConNT*, 10, in examining the hypothesis put forward by Windisch, that 1 Pet 1:18–20 is a hymnic fragment, concluded that while 1:20 has a poetic and liturgical quality, what immediately precedes it has a purely prosaic character. This impression accords with the present argument that there is a change of style at 1:20.

29   Preisker, 'Anhang zum ersten Petrusbrief', 157f.

30   In the LXX προσέρχεσθαι occurs in the opening to some of the psalms, though more often of the worshipper's call upon God to respond than of the approach to God; cf., e.g., Pss 21(22):1, 54(55):2, 79(80):1. In 77(78):1 the verb occurs in the divine call: 'Come, my people to my law.' The preposition πρός is used fairly frequently in regard to the approach to God (cf. Pss 24(25):1, 27(28):1, etc), sometimes with προσευχῇ, e.g., 54(55):1, 60(61):1. Thus the phrase in 1 Pet 2:4a does not necessarily have any direct connection with προσέλθατε πρὸς αὐτόν in Ps 33(34):5, though 1 Pet 2:3 seems to be a citation from this psalm (cf. vs. 8), and the psalm is cited also in 1 Pet 3:10–12. If, however, 1 Pet 2:4a does issue from Ps 33(34), it is very likely that it does belong to the later stratum. In that case, λίθον ζῶντα in 1 Pet 2:4b probably followed directly after ἐγείραντα αὐτὸν ἐκ νεκρῶν in 1 Pet 1:21.

31   See, among others, Selwyn, 268–81, concerning the theory that a hymnic source underlies 1 Pet 2:4–10, as also Windisch, 'Der erste Petrusbrief'.

32   Perdelwitz, 'Die Mysterienreligionen und das Problem des 1. Petrusbriefes', 69f, and Beare, 95, have tried to reconcile the two by reference to the Phrygian cult of the stone image in which milk was given to initiates, but this is not what one would expect of material so closely aligned with the thought of the Qumran sect as 1 Pet 2:4–10. See below, 39.

33 B. Lindars, *New Testament Apologetic* (Philadelphia 1961), 170, 179f, related the New Testament use of Ps 118:22, concerning the rejected stone which becomes the head cornerstone, with the resurrection, very particularly in his exegesis of 1 Pet 2:4–10. Selwyn, 286, put forward the view that 2:5–9 belongs to the circle of ideas pertaining to the resurrection, because of the connection drawn in John 2:19 between the destruction of the temple and its raising up (ἐγερῶ αὐτόν) in three days, which he took to refer to the superseding of the temple of stone by that of his body.

34 Supporting this view is the fact that both hellenistic and Jewish authors used ἐγείρω in the sense of raising up, erecting, or restoring buildings. See BAG, 213. R. J. McKelvey, 'Christ the Cornerstone', *NTS*, 8 (1961–2), 352–9, maintained that ἀκρογωνιαῖος is used in 1 Pet 2:6 and Eph 2:20 in the sense of a cornerstone placed on the foundation at the foot of a building, following the use of the equivalent Hebrew expression אבן פנה in Isa 28:16. Countering the view of J. Jeremias that in all three contexts the reference is to the stone at the top of the arch, he conceded that the Hebrew could have this meaning, but that the Rabbis understood it otherwise (355f). He also correctly pointed out that a stone causing stumbling could scarcely be conceived as being at the top of a building (357). Selwyn, 163, interpreted the word as meaning both 'cornerstone' and 'foundation stone'. Lindars, 180, accepted 'cornerstone' but rejected 'foundation'. J. H. Elliott, *The Elect and the Holy* (Leiden 1966), 24, concurred. For those supporting Jeremias' view cf. Schlier, *Der Brief an die Epheser*, 142, n. 3.

35 B. Gärtner, *The Temple and the Community in Qumran and the New Testament* (London 1965), discussing the idea of the new temple (16–46), suggested that the concept may have arisen from the use of the expression 'House of God' for the people of Israel as well as the temple. In the Qumran writings it clearly replaces the official temple from which the sectaries were separated (21f). Elliott, 157f, identified οἶκος in 1 Pet 2:5 with 'temple' though it was not a technical term for it, because the concept was held by the Qumran sect. Similarly the related idea of 'spiritual sacrifices' by a 'holy priesthood' (1 Pet 2:5) or 'royal body of priests' (2:9) has parallels in Qumran literature, as indicated by Gärtner (30–46).

36 Cf. 1 Pet 3:13 (ὁ κακώσων ... τοῦ ἀγαθοῦ), 3:16 (μετὰ ... φόβου, συνείδησιν ἔχοντες ἀγαθήν), 3:17 (ἀγαθοποιοῦντας ... κακοποιοῦντας), 2:12 (κακοποιῶν), 2:14 (κακοποιῶν ... ἀγαθοποιῶν), 2:17 (τὸν Θεὸν φοβεῖσθε), 2:18 (ἐν παντὶ φόβῳ τοῖς δεσπόταις ... τοῖς ἀγαθοῖς ... τοῖς σκολιοῖς), 2:20 (ἀγαθοποιοῦντες), 3:2 (ἐν φόβῳ), 3:6 (ἀγαθοποιοῦσαι καὶ μὴ φοβούμεναι), Eph 4:28 (ἐργαζόμενος ... τὸ ἀγαθόν), 5:33 (φοβῆται τὸν ἄνδρα), 6:5 (μετὰ φόβου), 6:8f (ποιήσῃ ἀγαθόν ... τὰ αὐτὰ ποιεῖτε), Rom 13:3 (οὐκ εἰσὶν φόβος τῷ ἀγαθῷ ἔργῳ ἀλλὰ τῷ κακῷ ... μὴ φοβεῖσθαι τὴν ἐξουσίαν; τὸ ἀγαθὸν ποίει), 13:4 (τὸ ἀγαθόν ἐὰν δὲ τὸ κακὸν ποιῇς φοβοῦ ... κακὸν πράσσοντι).

37 Cf. Eph 5:15–18a, 21–6:9, where the ten uses are proportionately far greater than in the rest of the epistle; Col 3:18–4:1, of which the same may be said in regard to its nine uses in relation to the rest of Colossians; 1 Pet 3:6, 15.

38 Contrasts between ἀγαθός and κακός and their compounds occur five

times in the material under consideration as compared with seven times in
the rest of the New Testament. The combined use of ἀγαθός and ποιεῖν
occurs six times in this material, four instances in 1 Peter in compounds,
and nine times in the rest of the New Testament, involving compounds
four times. Κακός and ποιεῖν are used twice in combination, once as a
compound in this material, and nine times in the rest of the New Testament, three times as a compound. Κακοποιός occurs three times, only in
1 Peter, and ἀγαθοποιία in 1 Pet 4:19 is a *hapax legomenon*. The proportionately more concentrated use of these expressions in the catalogues
of duties is thus very evident; see above, n. 36. Their occurrence in combination with φόβος and φοβεῖσθαι is confined to the passages under consideration in the New Testament.

39 E. K. Lee, 'Words Denoting "Pattern" in the New Testament', *NTS*, 8
(1961–2), 166–73, listed the word, with four others including τύπος,
used in the New Testament and having the sense of pattern or example.
He cited Clement of Alexandria (Strom V:675) to point to the sense of a
copy-head for children to trace as basic to the meaning of the word (173).
40 Bultmann, 'Bekenntnis- und Liedfragmente im ersten Petrusbrief'.
41 See above, 34.
42 See above, n. 39. BAG associate ἀντίτυπος with the Platonic notion of
types. G. W. Blenkin, *The First Epistle General of Peter* (London 1914),
79, pointed out that the word is used in the Apostolic Constitutions and
other church fathers for the bread and wine of the eucharist, and by the
Valentinians for the earthly church as a copy of the heavenly.
43 Cf. 1 Pet 2:19, 3:16, Rom 13:5; see below, 10.
44 Bultmann's reconstructed hymn (cf. above, n. 40) consists of an assumed
introductory affirmation, 1 Pet 1:20*ab*, 3:18*a*, with ὅς inserted in place
of Χριστός and ὅτι καί omitted, 3:18*cde*, 3:19 without πορευθείς, and
3:22*bc* with ἐκάθισεν ἐν δεξιᾷ inserted after οὐρανον. In this way he
brought the structure into alignment with the pattern found in Phil 2:
6–11, 1 Tim 3:16, Pol Phil 2:1, and Ign Trall 9:1f. In view of this reconstruction Fuller accepted the plausibility of Windisch's theory of hymnic
sources; cf. Windisch, 218, 238f.
45 Selwyn, *The First Epistle of St. Peter*, 197f, 415, 317, rejected πνεύματι
as the antecedent to ἐν ᾧ, and suggested instead that the antecedent is the
preceding context. Cross, 31f, found a creed in the passage, eliminating
vss. 19–22 as an *ad hoc* addition for the baptismal ceremony.
46 Bultmann, 14, excluded these words as editorial, and Fuller, 238, n. 38,
decided it was a gloss, since it disturbs the poetic structure and conforms
with the immediate context, which, however, the present analysis largely
retains.
47 Cf. Eph 4:31, 5:3–5 in the main body of the epistle, and 5:18 in the later
stratum.
48 See, e.g., Mark 7:21f, Luke 21:34, Rom 1:29f, Gal 5:19f, Col 3:8, 1 Tim
6:4, Tit 3:3. For a more complete listing and discussion of origins, see
N. J. McEleney, 'The Vice Lists of the Pastoral Epistles', *CBQ*, 36 (1974),
203–19, the conclusion being that they issue from manifold influences.
49 See above,

50 Windisch, 'Der erste Petrusbrief', 73, took παθών to refer to death, as also in Ign Smyr 2, Barn 7:11. Beare, *The First Epistle of Peter*, 153, found an equivalent saying in Rom 6:7, but here there is no suggestion of death as freeing one from the evil of flesh. Selwyn, *The First Epistle of St. Peter*, 209, judged the thought to be that bodily suffering purifies the soul, as in certain Jewish intertestamental writings, the Rabbis, and Melito. Cross, *1 Peter: A Paschal Liturgy*, 20, found 1 Pet 4:1*b* 'a hard saying' that had defeated the exegetes, but his reference to 'the Pasch' at this point adds nothing to the solution of the problem.

51 E. Schweizer, 'πνεῦμα', TDNT, vol. 6 (1968), 332–451, 447f, found that the word refers to disembodied spirits in 1 Pet 3:19, 4:2, and 4:6, whereas in 1:2 it is a general endowment and in 1:11f is given to certain individuals (prophets and apostles). In 4:14, he pointed out, it applies only to martyrs. B. Reicke, *The Disobedient Spirits and Christian Baptism* (Copenhagen 1946), 52–9, concluded that, as in 1 Enoch (cf. 22:3, 6, 7, 9, 12f, 9:3, 10), the word in 1 Pet 3:19 could be referring both to angels and the souls of the human dead, though it is not usual to find the word used in this sense in Greek. The explanation that the preaching refers to that heard by Christians who have subsequently died is a forced one. If this were the intended meaning it is difficult to understand why the writer did not qualify νεκροῖς in some way to narrow the application, instead of emphasizing the extraordinary nature of such preaching by the addition of καί before this word. Cf. Kelly, *A Commentary on the Pastoral Epistles*, 174f.

52 There is an obvious resemblance too to the words ἤγγικεν ἡ βασιλεία in Matt. 3:2, 4:17, 10:7, Mark 1:15, Luke 10:9, 11, but these passages do not share the other motifs accompanying 1 Pet 4:7*a*. Cf. also ἡ παρουσία τοῦ κυρίου ἤγγικεν in Jas 5:8.

53 Selwyn, 375–82, found a roughly similar sequence of thought in 1 Pet 1, 4, 5:8 as compared with 1 Thess 5:1–9, as well as significant parallels in Rom 13:11–14 and the latter parts of Ephesians and Colossians.

54 Cf. Eph 6:8f, Col 3:24, 4:1, 1 Pet 2:20, 5:2–4.

55 Cf. Eph 5:21, 1 Pet 3:1, 2, 5, 6, 7, 8, 9, 16, 17. Concerning the same phenomenon in Rom 12:9–21, cf. below, 60–1.

56 See appendix E.

57 Selwyn, 220, pointed out that a doxology does not necessarily indicate an intention to bring a letter to a close, for of the sixteen in the New Testament only three conclude an epistle, Rom 16:27, Jude 25, and 2 Pet 3:18. Streeter, *The Primitive Church*, correctly observed, however, that the doxology and 'amen' have the effect of detaching the rest of the letter from the earlier parts. Going further than this, C. F. D. Moule, 'The Nature and Purpose of 1 Peter', *NTS*, 3 (1956–7), 1–11, postulated two letters in 1 Peter, sharing 1:1–2:10 in common but with one continuing from 2:11 to 4:11, and the other from 4:12 to 5:11, and both concluding with 5:12–14.

58 Cf. Beare, 162. Moule ('Nature and Purpose') argued, on the basis of this difference, that of the two letters he found in 1 Peter, the first was addressed to those threatened with persecution and the second to those actually suffering it. W. Nauck, 'Freude im Leiden', *ZNW*, 46 (1955),

68–80, by contrast, maintained that no distinction exists between hypothetical and actual suffering in 1 Peter. He therefore rejected the view that 4:12–5:14 was appended later.

59   See appendix E.

60   See above, 40.

61   Cf. ἀγαλλιᾶσθε ... πειρασμοῖς ... πυρὸς ... δόξαν ... ἐν ἀποκαλύψει ... χαρᾷ ... Χριστὸν παθήματα ... δόξας (1 Pet 1:6–8, 11), μακάριοι ... χαίρετε καὶ ἀγαλλιᾶσθε (Matt 5:11f), and πυρώσει ... πειρασμόν ... Χριστοῦ παθήμασιν χαίρετε ... ἐν τῇ ἀποκαλύψει τῆς δόξης ... χαίρετε ἀγαλλιώμενοι ... μακάριοι (1 Pet 4:12f, 14).

62   Regarding contact with the gospels as probably due to literary dependence, see above, 9.

63   Cf. 1 Pet 1:6f, 5:9; see below, 51.

64   See below, 51, 64.

65   The connection between suffering, humility, and elevation features also in Pauline tradition (cf. Phil 2:1–11).

66   Apart from the lack of any mention of a Petrine letter before Cyprian, there is no evidence for A. von Harnack's theory that the epistolary salutation and close were added after the middle of the second century; see Beare, 24.

67   Babylon denotes Rome in Sib Or 5:139, 143, 159ff, 2 Bar 11:1, 67:7, 4 Ezra 3:1f, 28, 31, as also in the Talmud; cf. H. L. Strack and P. Billerbeck, *Kommentar zum Neuen Testament aus Talmud und Midrash*, vol. 3 (3rd edn, München 1961), 816. Eusebius HE II 15 referred to the reputedly metaphorical use of the term to denote Rome, and Kelly, 218, pointed out that two cursives have 'Rome' instead of 'Babylon'. For the arguments for Rome, Babylon on the Euphrates, and Babylon in Egypt, see Blenkin, xxx–xxxiii. Scholarly consensus, however, favours Rome, though not necessarily as the place of writing; see, e.g., Beare, *The First Epistle of Peter*, 31.

68   Cf. Rev 13:2 for a description of the beast kingdom, the instrument of the satanic dragon, as having a mouth like a lion's. For an association between the beast and 'Babylon', see Rev 14:8–11.

69   Concerning Babylon as a city of evil, doomed to fall, see Rev 14:8, 16:19, 17:5, 18:2, 10, 21. Streeter, 121–4, 131, found the use of 'Babylon' for Rome quite extraordinary in a letter urging obedience to the emperor and provincial governors, and used this as an argument for rejecting the view of Petrine authorship which associates the epistle with Rome. He therefore understood 'Babylon' in a literal sense.

70   See Appendix A, 'The Earlier Form of 1 Peter'.

71   BAG, 39.

72   LSJ, 70, cited Polybius to indicate that ἀλλοτριοπραγεῖν means meddling in other people's affairs and exciting disturbances.

73   For use of these words in other teaching concerning authority and subjection, cf. Tit 2:5, 1 Tim 2:9, 3:4f, 5:4, 8.

74   BAG, 299.

75   A. Bischoff, 'Ἀλλοτρι(ο)επίσκοπος', *ZNW*, 7 (1906), 271–4, finding the usual explanation for the word inadequate, concluded that the crime involved must be politically subversive activity which fell under the *lex*

maiestatis and could be taken as treason. C. J. Cadoux, *The Early Church and the World* (Edinburgh 1925), 100, n. 2, cited W. M. Ramsay, *The Church in the Roman Empire before A.D. 170* (New York 1893), 293, 348, to the effect that it may involve tampering with family relations and causing disobedience among slaves. Beare, 167, rendered the term 'revolutionary activity', as did also J. Knox, 'Pliny and 1 Peter', *JBL*, 72 (1953), 187.

76 Cf. W. Nauck, 'Freude im Leiden', *ZNW*, 46 (1955), 68–80. For similar expectations cf. among others Dan 12:1, Ass Mos 8, 1 Enoch 47:4, 90:16, Mark 13:12 and parallels, 1 Thess 3:3f, Rev 6:11.

77 See above, 44.

78 Cf. Elliott, *The Elect and the Holy*, 174–9, 186–8; Gärtner, *The Temple and the Community in Qumran and the New Testament*, 44–6, 84, with reference more particularly to 1 Pet 1:1–12 and 2:4–10.

79 Cf. 1 Pet 2:12, 14, 19, 20, 3:4, 9, 4:14, 5:4–6.

80 W. C. van Unnik, 'The Teaching of Good Works in 1 Peter', *NTS*, 1 (1954–5), 92–110.

81 Cf. Selwyn, 124, to the effect that in Jewish thought that which is predestined is laid up in heaven. He also saw a connection with the treasure in the heavens referred to in Luke 12:32–4. Beare, 58, pointed to Col 1:5, concerning the hope 'laid up ... in heaven' as the precedent for 1 Pet 1:4.

82 Van Unnik, 96f.

83 Reicke, *The Disobedient Spirits and Christian Baptism*, 212f.

84 Selwyn, 173, mentioned recognition of meritorious service in the honours lists referred to by Plutarch Mor 368 B. Cf. W. C. van Unnik, 'A Classical Parallel to 1 Peter ii.14 and 20', *NTS*, 2 (1955–6), 198–202, where Josephus is cited to the effect that the practice was not Jewish. Van Unnik referred too to Diodorus Siculus' view of the historian's task as being to render praise (ἔπαινος) to the good for their good deeds (καλῶν ἔργων), and to blame the evil. So similar is the terminology that van Unnik argued that 1 Pet 2:14 should be interpreted accordingly.

85 See Eph 5:21f, vss. 23–9 on Christ and the church as his body, and vs. 31 (Gen 2:24); Eph 6:1, vss. 2f (Exod 20:12); Eph 6:5, vss. 6–8 on servanthood to Christ and divine reward; Eph 6:9a, vs. 9b on divine judgement; 1 Pet 2:13–20, vss. 21–5 on the passion of Christ, vs. 22 (Isa 2:22); 1 Pet 3:1–4, vss. 5f on Sarah and others; 1 Pet 5:1–5, with reference to Christ and the apostle Peter, vs. 5b (Prov 3:34).

86 See above, 34.

87 BAG, 111f.

88 For a tabulation of occurrences see appendix C.

89 See appendix E.

90 See appendix E.

91 See above, 17–8.

92 The theory that two strata are present in Rom 12 is implicit in the analysis of C. H. Talbert, 'Tradition and Redaction in Romans XII.9–21', *NTS*, 16 (1969–70), 83–93.

93 Kallas, 'Romans XIII.1–7: An Interpolation', 366.

94 Evidence that Rom 13:1–7 has in mind Luke 20:20–6 or a version of it is to be found in the use in each of certain key terms (cf. ἐξουσία in Luke

20:20 and Rom 13:12; ἀρχή in Luke 20:20 and Rom 13:3; φόρος in Luke
20:22 and Rom 13:6, 7, whereas Mark 12:14 and Matt 22:17 use κῆνσος;
and ἀποδίδωμι in Luke 20:25 and Rom 13:7). There is similarity also in
the sentence structure and rhythm of Luke 20:25 (ἀπόδοτε τὰ Καίσαρος
Καίσαρι καὶ τὰ τοῦ Θεοῦ τῷ Θεῷ) and Rom 13:7 (ἀπόδοτε πᾶσιν τὰς
ὀφειλάς, τῷ τὸν φόρον, τὸν φόρον, τῷ τὸ τέλος τὸ τέλος, τῷ τὸν φόβον τὸν
φόβον, τῷ τὴν τιμὴν τὴν τιμήν). In addition, A. Strobel, 'Zum Verstandnis
von Rom 13', *ZNW*, 47 (1956), 67–93, pointed to the correspondence
between the two passages in their use of terminology which seems to
reflect Latin political and military language.
95 Cf. Matt 19:16–22, Mark 10:17–22, Luke 18:18–23. The wording in Rom
13:9 is closest to the Matthean version, cf. Matt 19:18f.
96 Cf. Ἀγαπήσεις ... ὅλος ὁ νόμος κρέμαται καὶ οἱ προφῆται in Matt 22:38f
as compared with Ἀγαπήσεις ... πλήρωμα οὖν νόμου ἡ ἀγάπη in Rom
13:9f.
97 It is noteworthy that outside the New Testament the closest approxi-
mation to the subjectionist passages in the Pauline corpus occurs in Philo's
treatise on the decalogue; cf. De Decal 165–7.
98 Of the four *topoi* Bradley found loosely connected together in Rom 13,
only vss. 11–14, he pointed out, has no link word connecting it with what
precedes it, 'The Topos as a Form in Pauline Paraenesis'; see above, 18.
99 BAG, 393f, include this kind of phrase in their comments on the
'explicative' use of καί.
100 This explanation is favoured by Michel, *Der Brief an die Römer*, 291, who
suggested that ποιεῖτε is to be understood. Cf. also F. Blass and A.
Debrunner, *A Greek Grammar of the New Testament* (tr. & rev. from 10th
edn R. W. Funk, Chicago 1961), 480 (5).
101 With specific reference to Rom 12, see C. H. Talbert, 83, ns. 1 and 2,
where there is a survey of the discussion.
102 See above, 32–3.
103 Cf. Did 1–6 concerning the ways of life and death, and Barn 18–20 concerning the ways of light and darkness.
104 Talbert, 85.
105 Concerning compound words of this kind in the later stratum see
appendix E.
106 Cf. Talbert, 89, and Michel, 273. Both point out that the Hebrew word
רדף may mean both pursue, as in Rom 12:13, and persecute as in 12:14.
This helps Talbert to sustain his theory that a semitic source underlies
Rom 12:10–14 *inter alia*, but in the context of Rom 12 the use of the
word in both senses could be due to the fact that the Greek word had
acquired a connection with persecution through such use in the LXX and
in other writings of hellenistic Judaism. It has the sense of 'persecute' in
the early patristic writings (cf., e.g., Ign Mag 8:2, Ign Trall 9:1, 1 Clem
4:9, Barn 20:2). See BAG, 200.
107 Michel, 273, saw a definite relation with a synoptic *Jesuswort*, but
regarded the correspondence as in the nature of a targum-like paraphrase
rather than a strictly accurate rendering. For this reason, as also the
presence of what he characterized as 'Greek' imperatives in 12:14, Talbert
decided that this verse is part of the hellenistic redaction that he argued

overlies Rom 12:9–21; Talbert, 87f.

108   In supporting D. Daube's thesis that the present participles in Rom 12:9ff
        and other similar contexts reflect an underlying semitic code, cf. *The New
        Testament and Rabbinic Judaism*, 90–7, and 'Participle and Imperative in
        1 Peter', Talbert argued that since the usage applies only to secondary rules
        and customary behaviour, it would be unsuitable for dominical teaching;
        ibid., 87. Whether or not the Hebrew usage underlies the passage, the dis-
        tinction could apply to loosely attached participles in a hortatory sentence
        as compared with the stronger effect of the imperative form.

109   Talbert, *ibid.*, 93, n. 4, observed that Rom 12:15 is not integral to the
        'finished structure' of Rom 12:9–21, and therefore concluded that it must
        have been joined to 12:14 before the latter was attached to 12:13,
        particularly since it enlarges on 12:14.

110   See above, 58.

111   The verb προκόπτειν can have the sense of the progressing or increasing of a
        trend either good or bad, and in Josephus is used of time going from bad
        to worse; see BAG, 714f.

112   R. Bultmann, *Der Stil der paulinischen Predigt und die kynisch-stoische
        Diatribe*, *FRLANT*, 13 (1910), 1–109, 75f, arranged Rom 12 in a very
        similar way.

113   It is suggested here that κατὰ τὴν ἀναλογίαν τῆς πίστεως in 12:6b has
        been substituted for ἐν τῇ προφητείᾳ, which accords with the structure of
        the other phrases in 12:6b, 7. The former is the kind of amendment one
        could expect in a stage of formalization of the content of faith which did
        not apply in the primitive period. It may then be translated 'in accordance
        with the pattern of faith', or 'in agreement with the faith'. W. A. Sanday
        and A. C. Headlam, *The Epistle to the Romans* (New York 1895), 356f,
        pointed out that most of the Latin fathers interpreted τῆς πίστεως in the
        sense of a standard of truth that would rule out private and fanatical
        aberrations, but they thought that this conflicts with the sense of the word
        in 12:3. Similarly, Michel, 267, mentioned that the Latin church translated
        ἀναλογία with the words *mensura, regula, ratio*, and *gratia*, which suggest
        that the Greek term refers to the norm of faith or the apostolic credal
        symbol, but he rejected this sense in the context of Rom 12.

114   It is evident that one of the phrases in Rom 12:8 breaks the pattern of
        paired phrases in the reconstructed passage. The third is the most likely,
        since it detracts from the correspondence between 12:8b and 12:8c. The
        participle προϊστάμενος could have the meaning of 'caring for' or 'giving
        aid', but in the context of the later stratum it is very possible that it carries
        the more obvious sense of 'holding a position of preeminence' with poss-
        ible reference to the bearing of authority in the household or church; cf.,
        e.g., 1 Tim 3:4f, 12, 5:17. See BAG, 713f.

115   See appendix C.

116   Rom 14:1–15:6 is, however, an exception, but it will transpire in due
        course that it probably belongs with the later stratum; see below, 78–9.

117   For references to scholars who have pointed to the similarity in the
        sequence of ideas in Rom 12 and 1 Cor 12, see Talbert, 'Tradition and
        Redaction in Romans XII.9–21', 85, n. 7.

118   Cf. the repetition of οὐ with each imperative from the decalogue in Rom

13: 9 as compared with the series of negatives with finite verbs in 1 Cor
13: 4f, as well as the correspondence between ἀγάπη . . . κακὸν οὐκ
ἐργάζεται in Rom 13: 10 and ἀγάπη . . . οὐ λογίζεται τὸ κακον in 1 Cor
13: 4–6.

119   Cf. εἰς ἀλλήλους in Rom 12: 9a and 1 Thess 5: 16; πονηρόν . . . τῷ ἀγαθῷ
in Rom 12: 9b and πονηροῦ in 1 Thess 5: 22 with τὸ ἀγαθόν in 1 Thess
5: 15; τῷ πνεύματι in Rom 12: 11b and τὸ πνεῦμα in 1 Thess 5: 19;
χαίροντες in Rom 12: 12 and χαίρετε in 1 Thess 5: 17; προσευχῇ in Rom
12: 12b and προσεύχεσθε in 1 Thess 5: 16; χαίρειν μετὰ χαιρόντων in
Rom 12: 15 and χαίρετε in 1 Thess 5: 15; εἰρηνεύοντες in Rom 12: 18 and
εἰρηνεύετε in 1 Thess 5: 14. It will transpire that some material in 1 Thess
5: 12–22 probably emanates from the later stratum; cf. μηδενὶ κακὸν ἀντὶ
κακοῦ ἀποδιδόντες in Rom 12: 17, μὴ . . . ἀλλὰ . . . ἐν τῷ ἀγαθῷ τὸ κακον
in Rom 12: 21, and μή τις κακὸν ἀντὶ κακοῦ τινι ἀποδῷ, ἀλλὰ . . . τὸ
ἀγαθόν in 1 Thess 5: 15.

120   Cf. n. 119 above. According to Talbert, 86f, in 1 Thess 5: 21 Paul has re-
written in acceptable Greek the code from which both passages are derived,
whereas Rom 12: 9–21 more directly reflects the original semitic version
with its assumed participial imperatives. The suggestion fails, however, to
explain how it is that in the parallel to Rom 12: 17 in 1 Pet 3: 9 one of the
present participles is εὐλογοῦντες, which corresponds with εὐλογεῖτε in
Rom 12: 14, an ordinary imperative. This fact undermines his reconstructed code, since he excluded Rom 12: 14 on the ground that it echoes
synoptic material which he characterized as hellenistic rather than semitic.
Thus Talbert's attempt to explain why the imperative participle occurs in
material which he judged to contain hellenistic elements and link words
breaks down. The suggestion by C. E. B. Cranfield, *A Commentary on
Romans 12–13* (Edinburgh 1965), 40, n. 3, that the participial imperative
reflects familiarity with rabbinic usage, avoids the difficulties in the views
of Daube (see above, ns. 10, 106) and of Talbert. It is, however, not
strictly necessary in the context of the theory of two strata in Rom 12
presented here, for the participles in the material judged to be earlier are
syntactically attached to a complete sentence (cf. 12: 7f, 11bc, 12ab),
while the imperative participles in the material judged to be later can be
ascribed to an exaggerated attempt to imitate the style of the original
(cf. 12: 9bc, 10b, 12c, 13a, b, 16a, b, 18, 19a).

121   Cf. 1 Cor 7: 29–31, where detachment from all present ties and activities
is counselled, for 'the time is short' (vs. 29), and the present form of the
world is passing away (vs. 31); 1 Cor 2: 6, according to which the ruling
powers of this age are being abolished; and 1 Cor 15: 24, concerning 'the
end', when every rule, authority, and power will be done away with.

122   Thus according to 1 Cor 6: 1–7 heathen courts are to be avoided and their
judges are referred to as 'the unrighteous' (vs. 1), and instead the saints are
to try their own cases. Further than this, however, Paul is concerned with
the appearing of the new creation, for the old is dying of itself; cf. Rom 8:
18–21, 2 Cor 5: 17.

123   D. W. Riddle, 'Early Christian Hospitality: A Factor in the Gospel Transmission', *JBL*, 42 (1938), 141–54, 143f.

124   Rom 12: 14f, 17–21; cf. Matt 5: 38–48, Luke 6: 27–36.

125 A reciprocal injunction to church authorities corresponding with that in
1 Pet 5:1-4 may be present in the phrase ὁ προϊστάμενος ἐν σπουδῇ in
Rom 12:8, which was excluded from the earlier material; see above, 62,
and n. 114.

126 According to BAG, 712f, the phrase was understood in this way in Old
Latin versions, including the Vulgate, and in the Syriac and Armenian.
Cranfield, *A Commentary on Romans 12-13*, 41, cited Oecumenius,
Theophylact, and Chrysostom in favour of this rendering, but opted for
the rendering 'in honour preferring one another', on the ground that the
genitive rather than the accusative is to be expected for a direct object with
προηγούμενοι. This conclusion depends on the use of the accusative with
ἡγεῖσθαι in Phil 2:3. If, however, Rom 12:10b is dissociated from Paul,
Pauline usage is not necessarily definitive for it. Furthermore, it is possible
that Rom 12:10b is dependent on Phil 2:3, where the accusative ἀλλήλους
is used with ἡγούμενοι, as in Rom 12:10b.

127 H. Kleinknecht, 'Nomos in the Greek and Hellenistic World', TDNT, vol. 4
(1967), 1022-91, pointed out that the hellenism of the Graeco-Roman
period took over the Greek philosophical concept of the king as the source
of law and as expressing the universal law of supreme reason or moral law
binding on all people. If the circles of the later stratum held such a view,
the unconditional acceptance of state authority as valid for Christian conscience (Rom 13:5) is understandable. Concerning a similar treatment of
the law and the decalogue in 1 Timothy, see below, 110.

128 With the exception of the section on 1 Cor 7, what follows was originally
presented as a paper to the Society of Biblical Literature, Paul Section,
Atlanta, Ga., Oct. 1971, though some revision has been made in the light
of the article by Walker, '1 Corinthians 11:2-16 and Paul's Views Regarding Women', in which he argues that this passage is an interpolation, and
the reply by J. Murphy-O'Connor, 'The Non-Pauline Character of 1 Corinthians 11:2-16?' *JBL*, 95 (1976), 615-21.

129 See above, 15-6.

130 See above, 53-4.

131 Cf. Rom 1:3, 1 Cor 1:10, 2 Cor 1:8, Gal 1:11, Phil 1:12, 1 Thess 1:4, etc.

132 See, e.g., Barrett, *The First Epistle to the Corinthians*, 332, to the effect
that if the passage comes from Paul, he took steps to silence women, not
on principle, but because in Corinth they were disturbing good order. By
contrast J. Moffatt, *The First Epistle of Paul to the Corinthians* (New York
1938), 231-4, viewing 1 Cor 14:33b-35 as 'a pendant' to the rest of the
chapter, regarded it as an objection to a 'local innovation' diverging from
the practice of other churches. Jewett, *Paul's Anthropological Terms*, 39,
followed Schmithals, *Die Gnosis in Korinth*, 230-2, in ascribing the prohibition to Paul's opposition to gnostic libertinism among the Corinthians,
but from the other parts of the chapter it could be said that Paul himself is
guilty of similar 'libertinistic' tendencies. More recently Jewett has decided
it is a Pastoral interpolation; see above, ch. 1, n. 123.

133 The word νόμος is usually taken to refer to the Jewish scriptures, and in
particular to Gen 3:16; cf., e.g., Barrett, *The First Epistle to the Corinthians*, 330, but neither here nor elsewhere in the Old Testament is there
a specific command silencing women.

134 Cf. σιγάτω ἐν ἐκκλησίᾳ... λαλείτω in 1 Cor 14:28 and ἐν ταῖς ἐκκλησίαις σιγάτωσαν... λαλεῖν in 14:34. The similarity in wording could be due to deliberate imitation by an interpolator, if the present hypothesis is correct.

135 The word however is used in two other contexts in the ten-letter corpus; cf. 2 Cor 6:5, where it is listed among Paul's hardships and sufferings (2 Cor 6:4–10), and 2 Cor 12:20, where it concludes a list of vices. In 1 Clement, which will be associated with the later stratum (see below, 120–4), it clearly has the sense of rebellion as well as disorder (cf. 1 Clem 3:2, 14:2, 43:6), which is of special relevance for the subjectionist teaching of 1 Cor 14:33b–35.

136 E. Schweizer, 'πνεῦμα', TDNT, vol. 6 (1968), 332–455, 435, n. 689, found no reference to demons in 1 Cor 14:32, but conceded that animistic ideas may be 'in the background'.

137 Aland *et al.*, *The Greek New Testament*, 611, n. 3. The plural could be a grammatical improvement to accord with the plural relative pronoun ἅ and the various exhortations in 1 Cor 14. Thus it is more likely that the singular was changed to the plural in the process of transmission than the other way round.

138 *Ibid.*, 611, n. 2; 612, n. 6; see above, 15.

139 Walker, '1 Corinthians 11:2–16 and Paul's Views Regarding Women'. A. C. Thiselton, 'Realized Eschatology at Corinth', *NTS*, 24 (1978), 510–26, arguing for the unity of 1 Corinthians, rejects Walker's view on the grounds that Paul is counteracting a realized eschatology of resurrection and 'theology of enthusiasm' that leads women to imagine that they are raised above the order of nature and restraints of convention (521). He does not apply the same argument to support the genuineness of 1 Cor 14:32ff, where it would be just as applicable. In neither instance, however, is there any hint that the instructions are intended to curb ideas flowing from the idea of present resurrection.

140 Cf. αἰσχρόν in 1 Cor 11:6, 14:35, and πρέπον in 11:13.

141 For evidence that the veil is intended see below, n. 154. F. A. Wright, *Feminism in Greek Literature* (New York 1923), 61, pointed out that in ancient Athens a woman could not leave her husband's house without wearing a veil, and only a slave woman could walk abroad with her face exposed. In Greek culture the disgrace of exposure seems to have been a prominent factor. Wright, *ibid.*, cited Euripides as having Andromache bewail her exposed state on becoming a captive, which meant there was nothing about her head but 'hideous slavery', and as having Hecuba crouch to the ground to hide herself from the eyes of men. The custom was evidently also related to the idea of protection from malignant spiritual powers; see J. G. Frazer, *The Golden Bough, Part II, Taboo and the Perils of the Soul* (3rd edn, New York 1966), 120–6. For the idea of demons as harbouring erotic desires toward human women, see H. Lietzmann, *An die Korinther I.II* (rev. W. G. Kümmel, 4th edn, Tübingen 1949), 55, with reference to both Jewish and pagan writings. For a listing of literature dealing with the question of the veil in relation to spirits, demons, or angels see J. A. Fitzmyer, 'A Feature of Qumran Angelology and the Angels of Qumran', *Paul and Qumran* (ed. J. Murphy-O'Connor, Chicago

1968), 31–47, 36, n. 18; or '1 Cor. xi, 10', *NTS*, 4 (1957), 48–58.

142 See Strack and Billerbeck, *Kommentar zum Neuen Testament aus Talmud und Midrash*, vol. 3, 432–40, for references to the effect that according to Jewish custom the veil was the sign of the married woman, for a bride went bare-headed until married, and was veiled to indicate her subjection to her husband. Similar significance seems to have prevailed more widely. Wright, 161, mentioned the incident in Aristophanes' *Lysistrata* in which the heroine informs the magistrate that henceforth women will direct the affairs of state while men keep silent. The magistrate protests, on the grounds that she is wearing a veil, whereupon she places her veil on his head and bids him keep silent forthwith. Here the feminine headdress clearly connotes subjection and silence in the presence of men. The story of Joseph and Aseneth, which Scroggs cites in 'Paul and the Eschatological Woman: Revisited', *JAAR*, 42 (1974), 532–7, 536, confirms that the veil normally distinguished between the married and unmarried woman. 1 Cor 11:2-16 certainly attempts to maintain the distinctions between women and men, but Scroggs' suggestion that the passage attacks those in Christian circles who had similar ideas that female asceticism gives a woman male identity finds no support in the text.

143 This suggestion goes some way in answering the objection of Murphy-O'Connor that Walker is unable to give 'a satisfactory reason why the interpolation was made at precisely this point in the letter', 'The Non-Pauline Character of 1 Corinthians 11:2-16?', 616. For further reasons for selecting this location, see below, 80–1.

144 Mitton, *Epistle*, 306f.
145 See above, 29.
146 Cf. αὐτός ἐστιν ἡ κεφαλή in Col 1:18, αὐτὸν ... ἐστιν ἡ κεφαλή, Χριστός in Eph 4:15, and ἡ κεφαλὴ ὁ Χριστός ἐστιν in 1 Cor 11:3.
147 Cf. τὴν κεφαλήν, ἐξ οὗ πᾶν τὸ σῶμα διὰ τῶν ἁφῶν ... καὶ συνβιβαζόμενον in Col 2:19, ἐξ οὗ πᾶν τὸ σῶμα ... συνβιβαζόμενον διὰ ... ἁφῆς in Eph 4:15, and παντὸς ... ἡ κεφαλή in 1 Cor 11:3.
148 See above, 33–4.
149 See above, 34.
150 See above, 34.
151 R. Scroggs, 'Paul and the Eschatological Woman', 298f, with reference, amongst others, to S. Bedale, 'The Meaning of κεφαλή in the Pauline Epistles', *JTS*, 5 (1954), 211–15.
152 BAG, 431, recognize the word as denoting superior rank, and include the uses in 1 Cor 11:3, Ephesians, and Colossians in this category.
153 BAG, 180; N. Turner, *A Grammar of New Testament Greek*, vol. 3 (Edinburgh 1963), 267–8.
154 That the wearing of the veil is to be understood at this point receives confirmation from the variant reading κάλυμμα by various early authorities, the Latin rendering *velamen* by Irenaeus, and *velamen et potestatem* by Origen; see Aland *et al.*, 601, n. 1, and Fitzmyer, 37. Fitzmyer (34–8) sets out the varying views of commentators on the word. First the term has been taken to refer to the veil as a symbol of woman's subjection by man, which Fitzmyer objects gives an inadmissible passive meaning to the word. There is no reason, however, why man should not be understood as the

active agent in exercising authority here, particularly since masculine pre-eminence receives strong emphasis in the passage as a whole, though the wording is unusual. For further explanation, see next note and below, 79. Secondly the term has been taken to indicate the veil as a symbol of the power and authority of woman in the primitive Christian cult, a view elaborated by M. D. Hooker, 'Authority on Her Head: an Examination of 1 Cor XI.10', *NTS*, 10 (1963–4), 410–16, on the grounds that the word is parallel to δόξα over against αἰσχρός, but this is tortuous, considering, as Fitzmyer points out (35) that the passage concerns woman's subordination to man. See also the observation of E. H. Pagels, 'Paul and Women: A Response to Recent Discussion', *JAAR*, 42 (1974), 538–49, that the reading 'seems to strain the context beyond credibility' (543). The same applies to the article by A. Jaubert, 'La voile des femmes (1 Cor xi.2–16)', *NTS*, 18 (1971–2), 419–30. On the basis of the reference to the veil in 2 Cor 3, she argues that 1 Cor 11 requires that since woman is man's glory she must veil herself in the presence of God's glory, and that ἐξουσία in 1 Cor 11:10 indicates the special right, capacity, permission, or freedom she gains in the Christian cult. Thirdly, the word has been connected with the magical power of the veil to ward off evil spirits (see above, n. 141). Fitzmyer objects that the suggestion lacks evidence. Fourthly, he himself follows G. Kittel in thinking the word is intended to refer to a veil or head ornament, but is a mistranslation or a matter of popular etymology derived from the fact that the root of the Aramaic word for veil means to have power or dominion. Whether or not an aramaism is present here, his argument does point to a connection between a head-covering and the idea of authority in antiquity. As applied to woman in this passage, the question at issue is whose authority, man's over woman, or woman's over herself, is intended. In the context of 1 Cor 11, the former seems to apply.

155 See W. Foerster, 'ἔξεστιν', TDNT, vol. 2 (1964), 560–75. Relevant to the expression ἐξουσίαν ἔχειν in 1 Cor 11:10 are the words μὴ ἔχων κατ' αὐτῆς ἐξουσίαν cited by Foerster from the Oxyrhynchus Papyri, VII, 1120:17f as referring to someone who has taken a female slave illegally. He mentions too that the word can signify individual liberty, but that does not seem to be relevant to the present context.

156 For scholars supporting this view, see J. C. Hurd, *The Origin of 1 Corinthians* (London 1965), 184, n. 4.

157 Concerning this view see Fitzmyer, 'A Feature of Qumran Angelology and the Angels of 1 Cor 11:10', 40–1.

158 *Ibid.* As Hurd observes, *Origin of 1 Cor*, his parallels are 'rather distant'.

159 Murphy-O'Connor, 'The Non-Pauline Character of 1 Corinthians 11:2–16?' does not reply adequately to Walker at this point, especially regarding the uncharacteristic use of κεφαλή here as also in Eph 5:21ff; but arguments concerning content and vocabulary require stronger confirmation than that which Walker furnishes.

160 Murphy-O'Connor, 616, correctly points to the 'unambiguous . . . unity' of ch. 11, and to the comprehensible transition from the end of ch. 10.

161 All partition theories postulate a break at this point; cf. Hurd, 43–7; Jewett, 'The Redaction of 1 Corinthians and the Trajectory of the Pauline School', 435–8.

162   Though the mood in 1 Cor 10: 21 is indicative, the statement has imperative
      force and could be rendered less literally: 'Do not try to drink the cup of
      the Lord and the cup of demons', etc.

163   See R. Bultmann, *Der Stil der paulinischen Predigt und die kynisch-stoische
      Diatribe, FRLANT*, 13 (1910), 1-109.

164   Hurd, 45, lists J. Weiss, A. Loisy, P.-L. Couchoud, M. Goguel, and W.
      Schmithals to this effect. See also Jewett's revised version of Schmithals'
      proposals, 'The Redaction . . .', 396-438.

165   BAG, 115.

166   *Ibid.*, 109.

167   *Ibid.*, 383-4.

168   Concerning the view that 2 Cor 6: 12-7: 1 preceded 1 Cor 10: 1-22 in an
      earlier letter see Hurd, 44-5. For a survey of views see G. D. Fee, 'II Corin-
      thians vi. 14-vii. 1 and Food Offered to Idols', *NTS*, 23 (1977), 140-61,
      140f, and *passim* for his defence of the original Pauline character of the
      passage, against J. A. Fitzmyer, 'Qumran and the Interpolated Fragment
      in 2 Cor 6: 14-7: 1', *CBQ*, 23 (1961), 271-80, among others, because of its
      links with 1 Corinthians, particularly 1 Cor 6: 12-20. See also the survey
      by M. E. Thrall, 'The Problem of II Cor. vi. 14-vii. 1 in Some Recent Dis-
      cussion', *NTS*, 24 (1977), 132-48, 132-44.

169   Jewett, 395. Fee, *ibid.*, defends the original location of the passage in
      2 Cor 6, 7 via the connections with 1 Corinthians, while Thrall, *ibid.*,
      passim, attempts to bring it into relation with the preceding parts of
      2 Corinthians, proposing at the same time that it is 'the real continuation
      of vi 2, after a digression in vi 3-13'. Both explanations, however, seem
      strained since there is no other explicit reference to idolatry in 2 Corin-
      thians. Thrall's points of contact with earlier chapters of 2 Corinthians
      concern common NT concepts found in many parts of the NT, and do
      little to establish thought continuity. Her suggestion of an allusion to
      Deut 11: 16 in 2 Cor 6: 11 is ingenious, but would surely have been too
      obscure for ordinary perception.

170   Hurd, 45, indicates that Loisy, Couchoud, Goguel, de Zwaan, Schmithals,
      and Dinkler assume that 10: 23-11: 1 or 10: 24-11: 1 was originally
      separate from the earlier part of chapter ten and was originally part of the
      same letter as chapters seven and eight, which they judged contains a
      later, more lenient approach to the subject of sacrifices to idols. Only
      Goguel, however, expressed the view that 10: 23(24)-11: 1 belonged to
      the same letter as 11: 2-34. It is to be observed too that none of these
      critics divides 1 Cor 8 from 1 Cor 7, but it is evident that the concept of
      marriage in 1 Cor 7 differs markedly from that in the later stratum. Hence
      it probably issues from a different source.

171   For a more detailed discussion of the problems presented by 1 Cor 8-11: 1,
      see Hurd, 115-49. His own argument for the integrity of this part of the
      epistle consists partly in an attempted reconstruction of the situation, so
      that the difference between 10: 1-22 and 1 Cor 8 and 10: 23-11: 1 is
      explained largely as reflecting that between Paul and the Corinthians. He
      concludes, however, by concurring with H. J. Cadbury, 'The Macellum of
      Corinth', *JBL*, 53 (1934), 134-6, that Paul seems to be of two minds on
      the issue of food sacrificed to idols. He also maintains that 1 Cor 10: 23-

11:1 is a summary of 1 Cor 8 and 9, on the basis of a series of parallels (128–31). They certainly apply to 1 Cor 8, but 1 Cor 9 has a very different thrust from 1 Cor 8 and 10:23–11:1, for it is a vigorous defence of Paul's apostleship, ranging over a variety of topics. Its position at this point is problematic, and it may be displaced, to bolster the case for greater freedom in the matter of food taboos. However this may be, its genuine Pauline character is scarcely to be questioned, for it is unlikely that a later follower would have chosen to stress the uncertainty of Paul's standing among the Corinthians and over against other apostles (9:5f). By contrast the apostle's position is quite assured, according to 10:23ff (cf. 11:1f, 16f, 34), despite blasphemous criticism (10:30). It seems then that 10:23–11:1 is an attempt by the interpolator to bind together 1 Cor 8 and 9 versus 10:1–22 rather than a genuine summary.

172 Motifs characteristic of the later stratum which appear in Rom 14:1–15:6 include the pleasing of others as a guiding ethical principle (15:2), the importance of agreement and harmony (14:1, 15:5f), Christ as a model for imitation (15:2–4).

173 Included among the parallels are some containing rhetorical questions, construed as a form of statement.

174 For the occurrence of antithetic parallels in Romans, see appendix C.

175 See above, n. 154.

176 It is to be observed that each of the two strata in 1 Cor 10 and 11 contains a different version of the community meal; cf. 10:14–22 and 11:23–6. While in each there is reference to the bread and the cup, in 10:14–22 there is nothing to suggest anything other than a meal following the Jewish custom of pronouncing a blessing at the filling of the cup and the breaking of the bread; see J. Weiss, *The History of Primitive Christianity*, vol. 1 (New York 1937), 62–6, with supporting citations from the Mishnah tractate Berakoth, and from the eucharistic prayers in Did 9. The significance attached to the meal in 10:14–22 follows without difficulty from the Jewish notion that those who join in table fellowship are made one; cf. J. Jeremias, *The Eucharistic Words of Jesus* (New York 1955), 153f. According to 11:17–29, by contrast, the 'Lord's supper' (vs. 20) is to be sharply distinguished from ordinary eating and drinking (vs. 21), such as could, and in the view of the later stratum should, take place at home (vss. 22, 24). Then too, 10:14–22, like Did 9, and unlike 11:23–6, first mentions the cup and then the bread. Clearly 11:17–29, 33f is much concerned with correct procedure, and its prescriptive character receives emphasis from its juridical and decretal-like style, to which Käsemann drew attention in 'The Pauline Doctrine of the Lord's Supper', *Essays on New Testament Themes*, 108–35, 119. Hence it is likely that 11:23–6 represents the order which was to be followed in practice. Käsemann argued that the traditional sequence was altered in 10:14–22 to shift the emphasis (110). Jewett, *Paul's Anthropological Terms*, 254–65, following Schmithals, *Die Gnosis in Korinth*, accounted for the differences between the two versions by postulating that the idea of the body of Christ is used in 10:14ff to oppose the participation of libertinistic gnostics in heathen cultic meals, and in 11:17ff to check gnostic libertinistic disregard for traditional ecclesiastical order and the somatic Jesus, in both instances in

the name of pseudo-enlightenment which held that what one did in the body was irrelevant. The finding that 11:17–29, 33f is to be associated with 11:2–16 as belonging to the later stratum raises the possibility that each version of the Lord's supper in 1 Cor 10 and 11 issues from a different source and represents a different tradition. The later stratum, it seems, has incorporated 11:23–6 from earlier tradition related to that used by Luke. Jeremias, 102–31, maintained that 1 Cor 11:23–6 incorporates liturgical formulae, and that the common use in 1 Cor 11:24*b*, 25 and Luke 22:19*b*–20 explains their similarities in these two contexts, particularly since the language is both un-Lukan (102) and un-Pauline (131). This is not to deny, however, that each stratum in 1 Cor 10 and 11 probably contends with gnosticism in some form, though at different times.

177 Barrett, *A Commentary on the First Epistle to the Corinthians*, 120, translated μᾶλλον χρῆσαι 'rather put up with your present status', on the grounds that the more obvious meaning does not make sense of the context, but his rendering seems somewhat arbitrary, particularly since what is to be used (χρῆσαι), according to vs. 21*b*, is not the state of slavery, but more probably the possibility of freedom; cf. H. Lietzmann, *An die Korinther I.II* (4th edn, rev. W. G. Kümmel, Tübingen 1949), 32.

178 Cf. ἐν πάσαις ταῖς ἐκκλησίαις τῶν ἁγίων ὑποτασσέσθωσαν in 1 Cor 14: 33f. Similarly 1 Cor 4:17 and 11:16 appeal to that which finds acceptance in all the churches to validate the teaching and instructions imputed to the apostle Paul. Jewett, 426, follows J. Weiss in accepting 7:17*b* as a Pastoral interpolation.

179 Concerning the concept of calling in each stratum in 1 Peter, see above, 50–1.

180 Cf., e.g., τῆς χάριτος . . . ἧς ἐχαρίτωσεν (Eph 1:6), κατὰ τὴν ἐνέργειαν ἐνήργησεν (1:19f), and ὀνόματος ὀνομαζόμενου (1:21). Other instances occur in 2:4, 3:7, and 6:19f.

181 Eph 4:1, 4 with 4:1–14, 6:10–20.

182 For a history of earlier criticism, see J. E. Frame, *A Critical and Exegetical Commentary on the Epistles of St. Paul to the Thessalonians* (New York 1912), 39–43. Among those rejecting 2 Thessalonians were F. C. Baur, H. J. Holtzmann, and W. Wrede (40). For a more recent account of critical theory, see E. Best, *A Commentary on the First and Second Epistles to the Thessalonians* (London 1972), 35–9. Scholars currently rejecting the integrity of the epistle include H. Braun, 'Zur nachpaulinischen Herkunft des zweiten Thessalonicherbriefes', *ZNW*, 44 (1952–3), 152–6, W. Marxsen, *Introduction to the New Testament*, 37–44, and J. A. Bailey, 'Who Wrote II Thessalonians?' *NTS*, 25 (1979), 131–45.

183 W. Schmithals, 'Die Thessalonicherbriefe als Briefkompositionen', *Zeit und Geschichte* (ed. E. Dinkler, Tübingen 1964), 295–315, put forward the theory that the two Thessalonian epistles are constructed from four original letters, the first of which consisted of 2 Thess 1:12 and 3:6–16, and the second of 2 Thess 2:13f, 2:1–12, 2:15–3:5, and 3:17f. Thus he judged that there is a break at 3:5, and that 3:6ff originally followed 1:12. There is no reason, however, to associate 1:1–12 with the later stratum, and no obvious continuity as between 1:1–12 and 3:6ff. According to

Best, 338, 3:6–15 is traditional paraenesis akin to the *Haustafeln*, and may indeed have been replaced by the teaching to servants in Eph 6:5–9, etc.

184 Cf. οὐκ ... ἀλλ' in 2 Thess 3:8 and 3:9, μηδὲν ... ἀλλὰ with present participles and ἵνα in 3:11f, and μὴ ... ἵνα ... καὶ μὴ ὡς ... ἀλλὰ ... ὡς in 3:14f.

185 Cf. also 1 Thess 4:11f, which also occurs in material it will be concluded belongs to the later stratum; see below, 86–8.

186 Cf. also 1 Thess 1:7, which is to be assigned to the later stratum; see below, 92–3.

187 See above,

188 Cf., e.g., Frame, 298, 305; and Best, 331–45. Both scholars also include the sense of busybody or meddler.

189 LSJ, 1373. BAG, 652, mention that the word is used in Acts 19:13 of itinerant exorcists. In 1 Tim 5:13 it refers to the activities of heretics; see below, 102.

190 LSJ, 267.

191 Cf. 1 Cor 11:2, 23, and below, 98.

192 Best, 334, with reference to 230, indicated that some scholars have favoured the sense of the disorderly or unruly, notably C. Spicq, 'Les Thessaloniens "inquiets" étaient-ils des paresseux?' *ST*, 10 (1956), 1–13, who concluded that those admonished oppose the order of society and nature or God, in rejecting Paul's example of self-supporting work. According to W. Schmithals, *Die Gnosis in Korinth*, 90–157, they are gnostic libertinists of the same kind as Paul opposes in the Corinthian correspondence. W. Marxsen, *Introduction to the New Testament*, 38–40, found fanatical gnostic eschatologists.

193 Cf. κατὰ τὴν παράδοσιν ἣν παρελάβοσαν ... δεῖ μιμεῖσθαι ἡμᾶς ... ἵνα ἑαυτοὺς τύπον δῶμεν ὑμῖν εἰς τὸ μιμεῖσθαι ἡμᾶς in Thess 3:6, 9, μου μέμνησθε καὶ καθὼς παρέδωκα ὑμῖν τὰς παραδόσεις κατέχετε in 1 Cor 11:2, and ἐγὼ γὰρ παρέλαβον ἀπὸ τοῦ κυρίου, ὃ καὶ παρέδωκα ὑμῖν ... ἀνάμνησιν in 1 Cor 11:23–5.

194 See above, 69.

195 The same motif appears in 1 Cor 4:12, 14ff, which is among passages assigned to the later stratum in the longer version of this study; see below, n. 234.

196 Best, 49, pointed out that 2 Thess 2:16–3:5 follows the usual sequence for a Pauline epistolary conclusion, though he did not find the position of 3:6–15 unnatural.

197 J. L. White, 'Introductory Formulae in the Body of the Pauline Letter', *JBL*, 90 (1971), 91–7, 97, found that the opening thanksgiving is followed by a formula introducing the body of the epistle, and that this formula is followed by a section which introduces the subject of the body and establishes mutuality.

198 Cf., e.g., Frame, *The Epistles of St. Paul to the Thessalonians*, 300; L. Morris, *The First and Second Epistles to the Thessalonians* (Grand Rapids, Mich. 1959), 251; R. C. Kelcy, *The Letters of Paul to the Thessalonians* (Austin, Tex. 1968), 174; and Best, 334f, who suggested that scorn for manual work and ideas of Christian freedom may also have contributed to the idleness of the 'loafers'.

199 The preposition πρός with the accusative is taken to have the sense of relationship to or among; see BAG, 717f.
200 Cf. ἐν σοφίᾳ περιπατεῖτε πρὸς τοὺς ἔξω in Col 4: 5, 1 Pet 2:12f, 3:15f, Rom 12:17f, 13: 3, 1 Cor 10: 32f; see above, 52–3, 65, 75, and below, 103–4.
201 See above, 50.
202 See above, 83–4.
203 C. Maurer, 'σκεῦος', TDNT, vol. 7 (1971), 358–67, pointed out that while there are Jewish precedents for the sense of a sexual partner, Greek body-soul dualism accords with the sense of body (365). Best, 161f, followed Maurer in preferring the translation 'wife' in the context of Paul's thought. Body-soul dualism is, however, present in the later stratum; see above, 34, 44.
204 Though the word can mean possess, the more usual sense is to procure or acquire, sometimes with particular reference to marriage; cf. BAG, 456, and Best, 161.
205 Cf. Frame, 150.
206 In this respect the passage resembles 1 Cor 7 (cf. vss. 2, 5, 9). It differs, however, in its encouragement of marriage, whereas 1 Cor 7 discourages it and advises the unmarried to marry only in cases of physical necessity (1 Cor 7: 8f, 26–8, 32–7, 39), at the same time commending those who remain celibate (1 Cor 7: 38).
207 Cf. Tim 4:1–3 and below, 106–8.
208 Elsewhere in the New Testament only Mark 4:11 uses ἔξω to refer to those outside the community of faith.
209 See above, 35f.
210 Aland *et al.*, *The Greek New Testament*, 709, n. 2.
211 The reference to drunkenness in 1 Thess 5:7 does, however, recall similar references in the material assigned to the later stratum; cf. Eph 5:18 and 1 Cor 11:31. Here, however, it is probably intended to contrast with and strengthen the exhortation to watchfulness and readiness for the *parousia*, rather than to condemn drunkenness in Christian assemblies, as in Eph 5:8 and 1 Cor 11:31.
212 Cf. above, 63.
213 See above, 59.
214 Cf. μή τις κακὸν ἀντὶ κακοῦ τινι ἀποδῷ in 1 Thess 5:15 and μηδενὶ κακὸν ἀντὶ κακοῦ ἀποδιδόντες in Rom 12:17a.
215 Cf. χαίρετε . . . προσεύχεσθε . . . πνεῦμα in 1 Thess 5:16–19, and πνεύματι . . . χαίροντες . . . προσευχή in Rom 12:11f. The last-mentioned occurs in a phrase assigned to the later stratum. Its occurrence in Rom 12:12 could be due to knowledge of 1 Thessalonians.
216 Cf. Phil 4: 4–6, Col 3:17, 4:2, as also Eph 5:20 with 6:18.
217 Cf. Rom 12:6, 11b, 1 Cor 12:1–4, 14: 39.
218 See above, 83.
219 See above, 88.
220 P. Schubert, *Form and Function in the Pauline Thanksgiving* (Berlin 1939), 7, had difficulty in determining where the opening thanksgiving ends in 1 Thessalonians, and concluded that the three thanksgivings at 1:2, 2:13, and 3:9 are part of a long thanksgiving section which continues till 3:13. As pointed out, however, by J. T. Sanders, 'The Transition from the Body

Opening Epistolary Thanksgiving to Body in the Letters of the Pauline Corpus', *JBL*, 81 (1962), 348-62, 355, an eschatological climax does in fact occur at 1:10. White, 'Introductory Formulae in the Body of the Pauline Letter', 97, concurs.

221 *Ibid.*

222 In Rom 1:13 and 2 Cor 1:8 the wish to disclose is expressed negatively (οὐ θέλω ... ἀγνοεῖν).

223 Sanders, 'The Transition from the Body Opening Epistolary Thanksgiving to Body in the Letters of the Pauline Corpus', 356, observed that the form is less precise here than elsewhere, but suggested that Ἀυτοὶ οἴδατε replaces the more usual ἀγνοεῖν.

224 White, 93f.

225 *Ibid.*, 94f.

226 Schubert, 7.

227 With reference to 1 Thess 4:1-12 and 5:12-15, see above, 86-9.

228 D. M. Williams, 'The imitation of Christ in Paul with special reference to Paul as teacher' (unpublished Ph.D. dissertation, Columbia University, 1967), 39, 47, 49, 51f, 101f, 107.

229 Concerning the same phenomenon in 1 Peter and Rom 12 and 13, see above, 40-1, 61f.

230 For a discussion of these two possibilities as well as 'to the end' and 'forever', see Best, 119-21. He favoured 'finally', interpreting the perfect form ἔφθασεν in a proleptic sense (120).

231 See below, 134-7.

232 See above, 52-3, 65f, 75.

233 To some extent these findings receive corroboration from K.-G. Eckart, 'Der zweite echte Brief des Apostels Paulus an die Thessalonicher', *ZTK*, 58 (1961), 30-44, who claimed to identify a series of non-Pauline catechetical paraenetic passages incorporated into the canonical epistle in the process of combining two genuine Pauline epistles. He found that this material (1 Thess 2:13-16, 4:1-8, 10*b*-12, and 5:12-22) falls into a series of parallels which distinguishes it from the rest of 1 Thessalonians. The extent to which these sections coincide with the passages included in the later stratum is striking. For further comment and references cf. Best, 29f. The view that 2:13-16 is an interpolation is argued by B. A. Pearson, '1 Thessalonians 2:13-16: A Deutero-Pauline Interpolation', *HTR*, 64 (1971), 79-94, in contrast to the view that the passage uses traditional material akin to Matt 23:29-38; cf. amongst others R. Schippers, 'The pre-synoptic tradition in 1 Thessalonians ii 13-16', *NovT*, 8 (1966), 223-34.

234 The following passages are included in the later stratum in the earlier, longer version of this study (see above, ch. 1, n. 2), though the contextual evidence is not as strong as elsewhere, so that the argument depends to a greater degree on ideological and stylistic considerations: 1 Cor 4:12, 13*b*, 5:5, 9-13, 16:15f, 18*b*, 2 Cor 10:6, 8-11, 13:1-10. Other passages suspected of belonging to the later stratum are Rom 16:17-20*a*, 1 Cor 1:2*b*, 15:1-11, and Phil 3:17. The kind of rearrangement that emerged as a possibility in the analysis of 1 Cor 10, 11 may also be present elsewhere, especially in the Corinthian correspondence; cf. Jewett, 'The Redaction ...', 411-20.

3. The later stratum and the Pastoral epistles

1 See above, 28-31.
2 Dibelius, *An die Kolosser Epheser an Philemon*, 48f, and *Die Pastoralbriefe* (4th edn, Tübingen 1966), 5f.
3 Weidinger, *Die Haustafeln ein Stück urchristliche Paränese*, 2.
4 Carrington, *The Primitive Catechism*, 42f.
5 Selwyn, *The First Epistle of St. Peter*, 427, 430, 432f.
6 E. Barnikol has suggested that the requirement in 1 Tim 2:2f that prayer be offered for those in authority, including kings, is an interpolation; cf. 'Der nichtpaulinische Ursprung', 79. 1 Tim 2:2f accords, however, with the universalist emphasis of 1 Tim 2:1-7, calling for prayer for 'all people' (vs. 1) and the teaching that salvation is for all (vss. 4, 6). Similarly in the later stratum in Rom 12, 13, the emphasis on conciliation with all (12:17f) precedes the teaching on obedience to the authorities in Rom 13:1-7, and in 1 Pet 2:13-17 it is combined with the injunction to 'honour all' (vs. 17a).
7 For attempts to identify interpolations in the Pastorals, see Moffatt, *An Introduction to the Literature of the New Testament*, 402-6.
8 Cf. Rom 12:21 and 13:1ff, 13:7 and 8ff, 1 Cor 11:1 and 2ff, 11:16 and 17ff, 11:22 and 23ff, 1 Pet 2:25 and 3:1ff, 4:19 and 5:1ff.
9 1 Tim 3:16 is probably drawn from an earlier source since it has the appearance of a typical christological formula; cf. R. H. Fuller, *The Foundations of New Testament Christology*, 216-18, with reference to the structural analysis of E. Schweizer. In addition, P. N. Harrison isolated biographical material as genuine Pauline fragments; see *The Problem of the Pastoral Epistles*, 93-135, and *Paulines and Pastorals* (London 1964), 106-28.
10 Cf. Tit 3:12-15, 1 Cor 4:17, 19, 2 Cor 10:9-11, 13:1, 10, 1 Thess 2:2, 9, 2 Thess 3:8.
11 Dibelius recognized the close connection between the *Haustafel* material and church order in the Pastorals by tracing the outlines of a church order in 1 Timothy and Titus following much the same form as the *Haustafeln*. He noted too that there is a merging of rules concerning the household and the church, as also in Polycarp's letter to the Philippians; see *Die Pastoralbriefe*, 5f.
12 Cf. H. von Campenhausen, *Ecclesiastical Authority and Spiritual Power* (tr. J. A. Baker, London 1969), who considered that the instructions in the Pastorals follow the pattern of the 'so-called *Haustafeln*' (107), and that the institution of elders represents the taking over of a Jewish patriarchal form (76, 116). Concerning the idea in the Pastorals of the church as a household, see E. Schweizer, *Church Order in the New Testament*, 78f; and T. M. Lindsay, *The Church and Ministry in the Early Centuries* (London 1902), 145.
13 The same theme appears in 1 Cor 4:14-21, 5:1-5, 9-13, which may also be part of the later stratum; see above, ch. 2, n. 234. If these passages are in fact Pauline, they must be accounted Pauline anticipations of what was to become prominent in later legitimation of ecclesiastical authority.
14 Cf. above, 91.
15 Cf. Lindsay, 145-7; von Campenhausen, 113.

16 For the view that the πρεσβύτεροι represent a development from Judaism, see Schweizer, 71; G. Bornkamm, 'πρέσβυς', TDNT, vol. 5 (1967), 651–83, 667; von Campenhausen, 77. Von Campenhausen went so far as to associate elders with Jewish Christian circles, and bishops and deacons with gentile Christian congregations (77f).

17 See above, 50.

18 To what extent an office corresponding with that of the later bishop has emerged, however, is uncertain and unsettled. For a summary of views, see Feine, Behm, Kümmel, *Introduction to the New Testament*, 268f. According to von Campenhausen, 107f, the simple explanation is that there is now one bishop at the head of the presbyterate, since the letters are addressed to individuals who act as apostolic representatives. Perhaps then it should be said that Titus points in the direction of a head presbyter though it is not yet a distinct office.

19 Regarding the dual sense of the word in Judaism and Christianity, see Dibelius, *Die Pastoralbriefe*, 60f, and Bornkamm, 654.

20 1 Cor 4: 18–21, 5: 3–5, 9–13, 2 Cor 10: 8–11, 13: 1–4, 10 are also relevant if included in the later stratum; see above, ch. 2, n. 234.

21 Cf. above, 70.

22 W. Lock, *A Critical and Exegetical Commentary on the Pastoral Epistles* (New York 1924), 56, suggested that the rules implied that the order was not yet fully established. The fact, however, that 1 Timothy seeks to correct past and present abuses contradicts this view. In addition the vow against remarriage conflicts with the Pastoral view in favour of marriage (1 Tim 5: 14), and so cannot have originated in Pastoral circles. The regulations in the Pastorals were apparently not universally applied, however, for Lock cited evidence indicating that an order of widows performing official functions in the church did exist at a somewhat later stage (56); cf. Barrett, *The Pastoral Epistles*, 73f. The latter, however, found no direct connection with the order referred to in 1 Tim 5: 3–16.

23 See above, 70.

24 A. T. Hanson, *Studies in the Pastoral Epistles* (London 1968), 71–3, 76f, points out that the implication is that woman is more gullible than man, and that the transgression is evidently regarded as sexual, since the words used for 'deceive' (ἀπατᾶν, ἐξαπατᾶν) and for 'fell into transgression' (ἐν παράβασει γέγονεν) can be related to seduction and illegitimate birth respectively.

25 See above, 70, 73f.

26 Cf. Tertullian's protest against the boldness of heretical women, who teach, argue, perform exorcisms, undertake cares, and baptise (On the Prescription of Heresies 41); the criticism of Montanist prophetesses in Eusebius, *HE*, V 16–18; Mary and Salome among Jesus' disciples in the Coptic Gospel of Thomas; Mary Magdalene as the most loved disciple who imparts special revelations in the gnostic Gospel of Mary.

27 Easton, *The Pastoral Epistles*, 127, followed Dibelius in comparing the requirements with those for a consecrated woman, according to the mystery inscription of Andania, to the effect that she must not wear cosmetic adornment nor a headband nor braided shoes or hair; see W. Dittenberger (ed.), *Sylloge Inscriptionum Graecarum*, vol. 2 (3rd edn,

Lipsia 1917), 736. Easton did not, however, draw any direct connection with 1 Timothy, for he considered it common for men to prefer women to dress inexpensively.

28 For the relation of 1 Tim 2:1f to the prayer for rulers in 1 Clem 59:3–61:3, see below, 122.

29 Commenting on the regard for the reactions of non-Christians as a motivation in early Christian paraenesis, W. C. van Unnik, 'Die Rucksicht auf die Reaktion der Nicht-Christen als Motiv in der altchristliche Paränese', *Judentum Urchristentum Kirche:Festschrift für Joachim Jeremias* (ed. W. Eltester, Berlin 1960), 221–34, has pointed to most of these passages in the Pastoral epistles, and also to various parts of the ten-letter corpus and 1 Peter (229f). Almost every instance he cites, apart from the patristic writers and the Pastorals, appears in material associated with the later stratum; cf. 1 Thess 4:11f, 1 Cor 14:33, Col 4:5, 1 Cor 10:32f, Rom 14:13–15:3 (227–9), 1 Pet 2:15, 3:16, 3:1, 2:12 (230). The only exception is 1 Cor 9:19ff, concerning Paul's efforts to win both Jews and Greeks to the gospel.

30 1 Pet 2:12–14, 20f, 5:1–4; cf. above, 51.

31 Rom 13:4, Eph 6:5–7, Col 3:23f, 1 Thess 4:11f. The expression καλὰ ἔργα does not occur, but the connotations are present in terminology concerning doing good; cf. above, 40.

32 Regarding the use of the word in this way in hellenistic writings, the Jewish wisdom literature, Philo, and Josephus, see BAG, 794; where the same sense is accepted also for Heb 10:2, 1 Pet 2:19, and 1 Cor 8:7. Jewett provides a useful historical survey of views on the New Testament use in *Paul's Anthropological Terms*, 402–20, where there is mention of H. J. Holtzmann's association of the word with νοῦς (402f), and the conclusion of W. Gutbrod, C. Spicq, R. Bultmann, and G. Bornkamm that the term has the meaning of knowledge in regard to oneself and one's actions (408–10). This comes close to the Latin *conscientia* as used by Seneca; see J. N. Sevenster, *Paul and Seneca* (Leiden 1961), 85.

33 So too in 1 Clement the word is used in 1:3 in the phrase ἐν ἀμώμῳ καὶ σεμνῇ καὶ ἀγνῇ συνειδήσει in the course of an account of the instructions given to women to render fitting affection to their husbands, to remain in the rule of obedience, and to keep house with propriety. Similarly in 41:1 to maintain a good conscience or consciousness (ἐν ἀγαθῇ συνειδήσει ὑπάρχων) is equivalent to pleasing God in one's own rank and not going beyond the appointed limits of one's own office. In 34:7 the word occurs concerning the gathering together of Christians ἐν ὁμονοίᾳ...τῇ συνειδήσει (in harmony as to conscience). Significantly, this follows from an exhortation to be subject to the will of God (34:5) who is to be honoured as the Creator who has ordered all things (ch. 33). Cf. also Pol Phil 5:3, where an exhortation to virgins to walk ἐν ἀμώμῳ καὶ ἀγνῇ συνειδήσει comes directly after a call for subjection to elders and deacons, and Ign Trall 7:2, where schismatics are described as impure as to conscience. For other instances in early Christian literature where συνείδησις is qualified as good or bad, see 2 Clem 6:4, Did 4:14, Herm Man 3:4, Dial Tryph 93:2. Concerning the Pastoral distinctions between different kinds of συνείδησις, Dibelius, *Die Pastoralbriefe*, 16, found a parallel in the Latin *mala* and

bona conscientia as used by Seneca; cf. Sevenster, 87, regarding the relation of an unperverted mind, as opposed to *mala conscientia*, to the tranquillity of the state in Seneca. Josephus also referred to συνείδησις as good and pure, or bad, but it is not clear whether he meant conscience or consciousness; see C. Maurer, 'σύνοιδα', TDNT, vol. 7 (1971), 898–919, 911.

34 Rom 13:5, 1 Cor 8:7, 10, 12, 10:25, 27, 28, 29 (twice). The word is used only five times elsewhere in the ten-letter corpus (Rom 2:15, 9:1, 2 Cor 1:12, 4:2, 5:11). Σύνοιδα in 1 Cor 4:4 may be added as a virtually synonymous word.

35 See above, 75.

36 See below, 134f.

37 See above, 78.

38 See above, 78f.

39 See above, 78f.

40 Jewett, *Paul's Anthropological Terms*, 421–30, expresses the view that the use of συνείδησις in these passages is taken over from Paul's gnostic opponents, who regarded the weak as bound to the material realm and tried to enlighten them through a libertinistic disregard of their scruples. In such contexts the word appears to Jewett to be identical with mind and pneumatic being, whereas in others in the Corinthian correspondence it seems to him to refer to an autonomous faculty. He explains the difference by assuming that the two senses are in letters addressed to different groups in Corinth who use the word differently. The later stratum may well have hellenistic gnostics within its purview as well as Jewish ascetic gnostics (cf. the use of the gnosis concept in 1 Cor 8:1–6), but it is clear that the latter rather than the former are in obvious conflict with the point of view of the later stratum and the Pastorals on the subject of food sacrificed to idols.

41 See above, 79.

42 The occurrence of καθαρά or the verb καθαρίζειν with κοινός in the account in Acts 10 and 11 (cf. 10:14, 28, 11:8) of Peter's vision sanctioning the setting aside of Jewish food taboos is significant. There it is evident that to reject certain food as unclean is to oppose God who has made them clean (Acts 10:15). Concerning the affinities of the Acts with the later stratum and the Pastorals, cf. below, 116–8.

43 Jewett, *Paul's Anthropological Terms*, 439–41, found a similarity as between this phrase and its use in 1 Cor 10:25, in that both involve the avoidance of acts which if performed would cause pangs of conscience. Here he followed the distinctions in meaning drawn by C. A. Pierce, *Conscience in the New Testament* (London 1955), 71, 75–83.

44 Selwyn, *The First Epistle of St. Peter*, 177, pointed out that some manuscripts read συνείδησιν ἀγαθήν, and two have ἀγαθήν after Θεοῦ. The explanation probably is, however, that copyists have been influenced by the use of the adjective with συνείδησις in 1 Pet 3:16 and 21, and not that the phrase originally contained ἀγαθήν.

45 Selwyn, 205, prefers this rendering and considers the meaning is close to the word *sacramentum* (military oath) which was applied to baptism and the eucharist. Concerning the use of μυστήριον in the same sense in Eph 5:32, see above, 34.

46 See above, 41.

47 That Paul strives to maintain a blameless conscience toward God and man (ἀπόσκοπον συνείδησιν ἔχει πρὸς τὸν Θεὸν καὶ τοὺς ἀνθρώπους, Acts 24: 16), suggests the same affirmative consciousness held to be pure and good in the Pastorals, and in this case it can be concluded that the 'good conscience' toward God mentioned in Acts 23: 1 has similar significance. Regarding the close relation between the Pastorals and the Acts, see below, 116-8.

48 M. E. Thrall, 'The Pauline Use of ΣΥΝΕΙΔΗΣΙΣ', *NTS*, 14 (1967-8), 118-25, 124f, pointed out that according to Rom 2: 15 the word serves the same judging function for Gentiles as the law for Jews (vs. 12). Cf. also Rom 9: 1, according to which the word bears witness to the truth of the apostle's contention; 2 Cor 1: 12, where he claims the testimony of conscience that he has conducted himself well in the world; and 2 Cor 4: 2 and 5: 11, where he commends himself to the 'conscience' or judgement of others.

49 Detailed consideration of the material involved is outside the scope of the present study, but it is tentatively postulated that Heb 13: 1-9, 16-19 belongs to the later stratum; see φιλαδελφία (Heb 13: 1) shared only with the later stratum (Rom 12: 10, 1 Thess 4: 9, 1 Pet 1: 22, and 2 Pet 1: 7) in the New Testament; φιλοξενία (Heb 13: 2) shared only with the later stratum (Rom 12: 13); the ideas of remembering and imitating in close proximity (Heb 13: 3, 7), as in the later stratum (cf. 1 Cor 11: 1f, 1 Thess 1: 6, 2: 9, 14, 2 Thess 3: 7-9); the citation of a psalm to combat the fear of man (Heb 13: 6, Ps. 118: 6) as in the later stratum (1 Pet 3: 10-15, Ps 34: 12-16); instructions to respect and obey church authorities (Heb 13: 7, 17) as in the later stratum (cf. 1 Pet 5: 5); the frequent use of antithetic parallels (six uses in 22.6 lines, one per 3.8 lines) distinguishing the passages from Heb 12 and the rest of Heb 13; and finally the fact that the context is considerably more coherent if read without these passages.

50 This suggests that the gnostic dualism in question may be a development from earlier eschatological dualism. According to J. Massingberd Ford, 'A Note on Proto-Montanism in the Pastoral Epistles', *NTS*, 17 (1970-1), 338-46, the heresy opposed in the Pastorals may be of a Montanist kind.

51 For a comparison between Rom 13: 1-7 and the eschatological dualism of the earlier surrounding material, cf. above, 57f, 64f, 66.

52 Cf. 1 Pet 2: 20f, 3: 17, 4: 14-16.

53 1 Cor 11: 19, 2 Cor 10: 18, 13: 7. Something of the same significance would seem to be attached to the word ἀγνοεῖται in 1 Cor 14: 38, concerning those who do not recognize the ruling that women should keep silent in assemblies (11: 34f).

54 1 Cor 5: 11, 13, 11: 17-19, 2 Thess 3: 14f.

55 Cf. 1 Tim 1: 3-7, 4: 1-5, 7, 2 Tim 2: 16-18, 3: 6-9, 4: 3f, Tit 1: 10-16, 3: 9.

56 1 Tim 4: 2, 6: 3-5, 2 Tim 2: 16, 19, 25f, 3: 8, Tit 1: 10-12, 16.

57 See above, 78.

58 See above, 89-93.

59 See above, 93.

60 As Easton indicates in *The Pastoral Epistles*, 110f, the first three commandments are reflected in the reference to the 'lawless and rebellious,

irreligious and sinful, unholy and profane' in 1 Tim 1:9*ab*; the fifth in the reference to patricide and matricide in 1 Tim 1:9*c*; the sixth, to 'murderers' in 1 Tim 1:9*c*; the seventh, to fornicators and homosexuals in 1 Tim 1:10*a*; the eighth, to kidnappers in 1 Tim 1:10; and the ninth, to liars and perjurors in 1 Tim 1:10. The fourth commandment concerning the sabbath, and the tenth, are omitted. Dibelius, *Die Pastoralbriefe*, 20, also remarks on the connection of the passage with the decalogue.

61   See, e.g., 1 Tim 2:9f, 3:3–7, 5:1f, 13, 2 Tim 1:7–9, 2:24f, Tit 1:7–9, 2:10, 3:4–6.
62   See appendix C.
63   *Ibid.*
64   *Ibid.*
65   See Harrison, *Problem*, 93–135; and *Paulines and Pastorals*, 106–28.
66   See appendix D.
67   Harrison, *Problem*, 20f. Harrison mistakenly termed all words peculiar to the Pastorals but found nowhere else in the New Testament *hapax legomena*, as pointed out by Grayston and Herdan, 'The Authorship of the Pastorals in the Light of Statistical Linguistics', 4. Harrison's mode of calculation has, however, been followed in the present investigation to make possible comparison with his results.
68   Harrison's results are given as 11.8, 10.3, and 11.25 respectively; cf. *ibid.*, 21. The discrepancy may be due to a difference in calculating the length of each Pastoral epistle, for the present results are based on the vocabulary listings for each Pastoral epistle (without repetitions) which Harrison provided in an appendix (137f).
69   *Ibid.* Cf. appendix E.
70   See above,
71   Harrison, *Paulines and Pastorals*, 79–85.
72   Cf. T. Zahn, *Geschichte des Neutestamentlichen Kanons*, vol. 2 (Erlangen 1892), 516; A. von Harnack, *Marcion* (2nd edn, Leipzig 1924), 48, 103.
73   Harrison, *Paulines and Pastorals*, 81.
74   *Ibid.*
75   P. Carrington, 'The Problem of the Pastoral Epistles. Dr. Harrison's Theory Reviewed', *ATR*, 21 (1939), 32–9.
76   *Ibid.*, 35–9.
77   See appendix B.
78   See Tertullian, *Ad Marc* V 7 for references to 1 Cor 5:1ff, 10:23–7; *Ad Marc* V 8 to 1 Cor 11:2ff, *Ad Marc* V 12 to 2 Cor 13:1, 10, *Ad Marc* V 14 to Rom 12:9–21, 13:8–10, *Ad Marc* V 15 to 1 Thess 2:15, 4:3–5, *Ad Marc* V 16 to 2 Thess 3:10, *Ad Marc* V 18 to Eph 5:18, 22–32, 6:1f, 4. This means that Tertullian furnishes evidence for the existence in Marcion's corpus of all the passages associated with the later stratum in the ten letters, excepting Rom 13:1–7, 14:1–15:6, Eph 4:28f, and Col 3:18–4:1, 5. There is no mention of Colossians, probably because of its resemblance to Ephesians, which is to say, Marcion's Epistle to the Laodiceans. As for the other passages, there is no compelling evidence that Marcion omitted them. Tertullian's commentary on Marcion's text suggests that Rom 13:1–7 may have been wanting, but the evidence is not conclusive, for he did not mention any omission, though he evidently knew the

passage; see Aland *et al.*, *The Greek New Testament*, 565, n. 1.

79 Harrison, *Problem*, 36f.

80 The uses in the later stratum are as follows: πλήν, two times out of five; διότι, four times out of ten; ἔξω, four times out of five; οὔτε, seven times out of twenty-two; ἀντί, three times out of five; ἄρα, three times out of eleven; ὥστε, five times out of thirteen; τε, seven times out of twenty-five; and ἔκαστος, eight times out of sixteen.

81 Harrison, *Problem*, 31f.

82 Of the eight uses of ἐξουθενεῖν in the corpus three are in the later stratum; of the thirteen uses of ἀσθενής, five; of the seven uses of νουθετεῖν, four; of the nine uses of φοβεῖσθαι, three; of the eighteen uses of πράσσειν, five; of the thirteen uses of ψυχή, four; of the eighteen uses of ἐργάζεσθαι, eight; of the twenty-five uses of εὐχαριστεῖν, five; and of the thirty-two uses of περιπατεῖν, eight.

83 Harrison, *Problem*, 34, Diagram iv.

4. The literary and historical context of the Pastoral stratum

1 Matt 22:15–22, Mark 12:13–17, Luke 20:20–6.

2 Matt 22:21, Mark 12:14, Luke 20:25.

3 R. Eisler, *The Messiah Jesus and John the Baptist* (tr. A. H. Krappe, New York 1931), 331–5, maintained that Jesus lacked a denarius because, like the Essenes, he eschewed the whole monetary system of the Roman empire, as the evil mammon (Matt 6:24, Luke 6:13). This interpretation differs radically from that usually favoured, that the pericope to some degree supports the state in the duties it requires. See, e.g., V. Taylor, *The Gospel according to St. Mark* (2nd edn, New York 1966), 480. I. S. Kennard, 'Syrian Coin Hoards and the Tribute Question', *ATR*, 27 (1945), 248–52, suggested on the basis of a study of coin hoards that the Jewish masses did not use the Roman denarius, and that those who did had ceased to be Jews. The interpretation is perhaps too extreme. More probably use of Roman currency denoted some degree of collaboration with Rome. Significantly most denarii of the time in the area were found in the houses of priests (*ibid.*, 250). G. Bornkamm, *Jesus of Nazareth* (tr. I. and F. McLuskey, J. M. Robinson, New York 1960), 120–4, understood the pericope as recognizing the authority of Caesar, but with the intent of stressing the claims of God. In this way, at least, he avoided the questionable exegesis which constructs a doctrine of two realms from the tribute saying.

4 Cf. Luke 9:59f and Matt 8:21ff, concerning the would-be disciple who desired first to bury his father; Luke 12:51–3 and Matt 10:34–6 concerning division between father and son, mother and daughter/daughter-in-law and mother-in-law; Luke 14:26, which speaks even of hating father, mother, wife, and children, brothers and sisters, where the parallel passage in Matt 10:37–8 asserts that anyone who loves them more than the Christ is not worthy of him; and Luke 8:19–21 (Matt 12:46–50, Mark 3:31–5), where the kinship of those who hear the word of God takes precedence over natural kinship when the mother and brothers of Christ seek to see him.

5 See Acts 4:19 and 5:29 in the contexts of Acts 4:1–31 and 5:12–42. The

two passages are commonly compared with the similar saying in Plato, *Apology*, 29D; F. J. Foakes Jackson and K. Lake (eds.), *The Beginnings of Christianity*, vol. 4 (London 1933), 45. Assuming the writer or redactor knew Plato, the sayings could be intended as a brief apology for the apostolic defiance of authority.

6 Acts 13: 45, 50, 14: 2, 14-19, 17: 5, 18: 12f, Acts 21: 27f, 22: 22f, 23: 1-10, 12-15, 24: 1-9, 25: 2f.

7 Acts 16: 19-24, 35-9, 18: 12-17, 24: 22-7, 25: 1-27, 26: 1, 30-2.

8 Acts 21: 31-6, 22: 22-30, 23: 10-35, 27: 1-3, 28: 16. See H. J. Cadbury, *The Book of Acts in History* (New York 1955), 65-82, concerning the role of Roman citizenship and the Roman army in assisting Paul. On the Roman military background of Luke-Acts, see T. R. S. Broughton, 'Note XXXIII. The Roman Army', Jackson and Lake (eds.), *The Beginnings of Christianity*, vol. 4, 427-45.

9 For summaries of views on the use of sources in Acts, see C. S. C. Williams, *A Commentary on the Acts of the Apostles* (London 1957), 7-13, and E. Haenchen, *The Acts of the Apostles* (ET Philadelphia 1971), 81-90.

10 See above, 112f, and appendix B.

11 Cf. P. Vielhauer, 'On the Paulinism of Acts', *Studies in Luke-Acts* (ed. E. Keck and J. L. Martyn, Nashville 1966), 33-50, on the differences between the two passages.

12 E. Norden, *Agnostos Theos* (Leipzig 1913), 3-83, maintained that the speech follows a common form of religious propaganda literature in Jewish and pagan writers, and that it is an imitation of a speech by Apollonius of Tyana in the second century. On the Stoic background see M. Dibelius, *Studies in the Acts of the Apostles* (London 1956), 26-77, and H. Conzelmann, 'The Address of Paul on the Areopagus', *Studies in Luke-Acts* (ed. E. Keck and J. L. Martyn, Nashville 1966), 217-30.

13 See below, 138.

14 Cf. below, n. 19.

15 Acts 15: 2, 4, 6, 23, 16: 4.

16 Acts 15: 6, 12-30, 21: 17-26.

17 See above, 98.

18 1 Cor 4: 12, Eph 4: 28, 1 Thess 2: 9, 4: 11, 2 Thess 3: 8; cf. above, 84, 86.

19 See amongst others C. K. Barrett, *Luke the Historian in Recent Study* (London 1961), 63, concerning similarity in opposition to gnosticism, in the treatment of Paul, and in apologetic purpose; J. C. O'Neill, *The Theology of Acts* (2nd edn, London 1970), 8f, where there is mention also of the common emphasis on a good relation to rulers, and the completion of Paul's mission with his defence in Rome (Acts 28: 28, 2 Tim 4: 16-18); C. F. D. Moule, *The Birth of the New Testament* (New York 1962), 220f; and C. H. Talbert, *Luke and the Gnostics* (Nashville 1966), 46f, 67, concerning striking agreements, despite some differences, in the opposition to gnosticism.

20 O'Neill, 9.

21 Cf. πραΰς: 1 Pet 3: 4 and 3 times in Matthew; ἀφιλάργυρος: 1 Tim 3: 3, Heb 13: 5; λειτουργός: Rom 13: 6, Phil 2: 25; Heb 1: 7, 8: 2; τιμᾶν: Eph 6: 2, 1 Tim 5: 3, 1 Pet 2: 17, and elsewhere in the New Testament 15 times.

22 Cf. Rom 13:11-14, 1 Thess 5:3-10, 2 Thess 1:5-2:12, as also the synoptic apocalypse in Matt 24, Mark 13, and Luke 21. The reference to false prophets and lawlessness in the last days (Did 16:3f) finds parallels in 1 Tim 4:1-5 and 2 Tim 3:1-5, but the latter lack other accompaniments of the *parousia* expectation, and are aimed at Jewish heretics.

23 The earlier dating (*c*. A.D. 100) is preferred to the later at the end of the second century and the beginning of the third, following E. J. Goodspeed, 'The Didache, Barnabas and the Doctrina', *ATR*, 27 (1945), 228-47, as opposed to F. E. Vokes, *The Riddle of the Didache* (New York 1938). Cf. Dibelius, *A Fresh Approach to the New Testament and Early Christian Literature*, 236; B. Altaner, *Patrology* (tr. from 5th edn H. C. Graef, New York 1960), 51; and R. M. Grant, *The Apostolic Fathers*, vol. 1 (New York 1964), 75.

24 While both works may be dependent on a common source, as surmised by Goodspeed, *ibid.*, Barnabas could be directly dependent on the Didache, for there is some slight sign of possible contact with the rest of the latter; cf. Barn 4:9, Did 16:2.

25 Cf. 1 Cor 10:14-22, Rom 14:1-15:6; above, 78, 106.

26 Barn 13, Acts 28:23-8; cf. above, 117.

27 Cf. Rom 12:9-21, 13:8-10, 1 Tim 1:5, 2 Tim 2:22, 1 Pet 3:8f, 5:5.

28 The use of the same word in 1 Pet 2:21 is noteworthy considering that it is a New Testament *hapax legomenon*; cf. also 1 Clem 5:7; 16:17, Pol Phil 8:2.

29 See above, 73, 105-8.

30 See above, 40.

31 See above, 83, 88.

32 W. Schmithals, *The Office of Apostle in the Early Church* (tr. J. E. Steely, Nashville 1969), 244, found approximately the same doctrine of apostolic succession in the Pastorals and 1 Clement, but with greater emphasis in the latter.

33 See appendix B.

34 See above, 99.

35 Another interpretation, however, is that both 1 Clement and the Pastorals belong to a stage prior to mon-episcopacy; cf., e.g., Schmithals, *The Office*, 244f.

36 Cf. K. W. Clark, 'Worship in the Jerusalem Temple after A.D. 70', *NTS*, 6 (1959-60), 269-80, for evidence and argument to the effect that the temple cult was operative after A.D. 70 until the destruction of Jerusalem in A.D. 135.

37 See above, 116f.

38 Cf. 1 Cor 10:30, 1 Tim 4:4.

39 1 Tim 1:3-29, Tit 3:10f. At the same time 2 Tim 2:25f holds out the possibility that correction will persuade heretics to repent; cf. also 2 Thess 3:14f.

40 The long recension is thought to contain interpolations and additional letters from the fourth century and the middle ages, and the shorter Syriac recension to be an abridged version; see J. B. Lightfoot, *The Apostolic Fathers*, part II, 1 (New York 1889), 70-126, 587-98; K. Lake, *The Apostolic Fathers*, vol. 1 (LCL), 166-71; C. C. Richardson (ed.), *Early Christian Fathers* (New York 1970), 81-3.

41 See above, 97–9, 120.
42 Cf. von Campenhausen, *Ecclesiastical Authority*, 102, and 101–6 on the concept of the bishop's office in Ignatius.
43 Prov 3:34 is cited also in Jas 4:6, where the context concerns submission to God, 1 Pet 5:5, where it reinforces exhortation to submit to elders, and 1 Clem 30:2, where it occurs among general moral exhortations. That there is a connection between the citation from Prov 3:34 in these three instances as well as in Ign Eph 5:3, appears from the use in each of Θεός where the LXX has κύριος; cf. Lightfoot, 45.
44 Cf. Eph 5:33, 6:5, Col 3:22, 1 Pet 2:18. There is also mention of fear as unnecessary if authority is obeyed and one does good, as in Rom 13:3f, 1 Pet 3:6, 13f.
45 Either way there is accord with the thought of the Pastoral stratum. Τύπον, however, has the support of Ign Trall 3, as well as similar language concerning ecclesiastical authority in Apost Constit 2:26, Barn 19, Clem Hom 3:62. Cf. Lightfoot, 119.
46 Cf. von Campenhausen, 97–9, on the more advanced stage of the ministry in Ignatius as compared with 1 Clement. He found it closer to the Pastorals in this respect, but pointed out that the position of the bishop receives far more emphasis in Ignatius (107).
47 Cf. *ibid.*, 99.
48 Cf. 1 Pet 1:22, 3:8, and above, 120–2. For other exhortations to unity, peace, and harmony, cf. Ign Eph 2:2, 3:2, 4:1, 5:1, 13:1f, 20:3, Ign Mag 6:2, Ign Philad Inscription, 3:2, 4, 8:1, Ign Pol 1:2.
49 See above, 78–80.
50 Cf. above, 106–7.
51 Cf. above, 109f.
52 1 Clem 5:2–7, 6:2, 45:4–7.
53 See above, 122.
54 Cf. 1 Tim 2:1f, 1 Clem 61.
55 Cf. above, 103f.
56 Pol Phil 2:1–3, 4:1, 6:3, 7:1–10:3.
57 For similar teaching in the Pastoral epistles, cf. 1 Tim 3:1–13, 5:4–22, Tit 1:7–9, 2:3–10.
58 H. von Campenhausen, *Polycarp*, commented that Polycarp did not take up the cudgels in Ignatius' battle for the mon-episcopacy, but that he simply included the bishop among the presbyters. He also suggested that Polycarp did not want to stress his own episcopal dignity (34f), but that the absence of any clear distinction between the bishop and the elders aligns the epistle more closely with the Pastorals in its understanding of the ministry (36).
59 Cf. above, 124f.
60 P. N. Harrison remarks on the 'schoolmasterly tone' of Ignatius' letter to Polycarp; cf. *Polycarp's Two Epistles to the Philippians* (London 1936), 65.
61 Virtually the same words appear in 1 Pet 2:22, 24 as in Pol Phil 8:1f, though the order is changed, and ὑπογραμμός occurs in Pol Phil 8:2 and 1 Pet 2:21; cf. J. B. Lightfoot, *The Apostolic Fathers*, part II, 3 (New York 1889), 336.
62 Cf. above, 127.

63 Cf. above, 52, 104.
64 These are ματαιολογία (Pol Phil 2:1, 1 Tim 1:6), ἐγκρατής (Pol Phil 5:2, Tit 1:8), the adjective διάβολος (Pol Phil 5:2, 1 Tim 3:11, 2 Tim 3:3, Tit 2:3), and δίλογος (Pol Phil 5:2, 1 Tim 3:8); von Campenhausen, *Polycarp*, 25f and 26, n. 99.
65 *Ibid.*, 26 and n. 103, which mentions other somewhat similar constructions in Polycarp's letter.
66 *Ibid.*, 26f and n. 104.
67 *Ibid.*, 27 and ns. 105, 106, 108.
68 Occurrences of such compound words in Polycarp's epistle are as follows: παντοκράτωρ (superscription), ἀγιοπρεπής (1:1), καρποφορεῖν (1:2), ματαιολογία (2:1), ψευδομαρτυρία (2:2), οἰκοδομεῖν (3:2), φιλαργυρία (4:1), ψευδομαρτυρία, φιλαργυρία, μωμοσκοπεῖσθαι (4:3), ἀφιλάργυρος (5:2), χαλιναγωγεῖν, ἀρσενοκοίτης (5:3), φιλάργυρια (6:1), ψευδάδελφος (6:3), ψευδοδιδασκαλία, παντεπόπτης (7:2), total 17, excluding repetitions, 13.
69 Occurrences of antithetic parallels are as follows: Pol Phil 1:3 (1), 2:2 (1), 3:1 (1), 4:3 (2), 5:2 (2), 5:3 (3), 6:1 (2), 6:3 (1), 7:1 (1), 7:2 (1), 8:1 (1), 9:1 (1), 9:2 (2), 10:2 (1), 11:2 (1), 11:4 (1), 12:1 (1), total 23.
70 Von Campenhausen, *Polycarp*, 27, 51.
71 Cf. appendix E.
72 See above, 110, 116f.
73 See above, 123.
74 See above, 116.
75 This may be construed from the greeting to Prisca and Aquila, 2 Tim 4:19; cf. Acts 18:18f, 24–6.
76 For Paul's presence in Antioch see Acts 11:25f, 13:1–3, 14:25f, 15:35. For Peter's connections with this church see Gal 2:11, and also Apost Const 7:46, according to which Peter ordained Euodias a bishop, and Paul ordained Ignatius, both in Antioch. A tradition that Peter was actually the first bishop of Antioch is evident from Eusebius, *HE* III 22. Lightfoot, part II, 1, 29, has discussed this and other evidence.
77 Ign Eph 21:2, Ign Mag 14, Ign Trall 13:1, Ign Rom 9:1.
78 Ign Philad 10:1f, Ign Pol 7:1–3.
79 W. Bauer, *Orthodoxy and Heresy in Earliest Christianity* (tr. Philadelphia Seminar on Christian Origins, Philadelphia 1971), 67–70, argued that the episcopal ministry was insecure in Asia Minor. So too B. H. Streeter, *The Primitive Church* (New York 1929), 169f, contended that the system Ignatius championed was of recent origin in Antioch, and was strongly opposed. H. E. W. Turner, *The Pattern of Christian Truth* (London 1954), 60f, conceded that Ignatius was fighting a battle not yet won, but he contested the tenuous nature of orthodoxy as envisaged by Bauer.
80 See above, 122f. Ignatius, moreover, refers to the Roman church as the instructor of others (Ign Rom 3:1). Streeter, 165–6, considered Ign Rom 3:1 a reference to 1 Clement, the existence of which is the reason for an absence of admonitions to the Roman church. He thought Ignatius interpreted it as advocating mon-episcopacy.
81 Turner, *The Pattern of Christian Truth*, 74, challenged the extent rather than the fact of Roman influence in the growth of orthodoxy as maintained

by W. Bauer, arguing that Asian orthodoxy was collateral with that of Rome rather than derived from that of Rome. He cited amongst others Polycarp's difference from the bishop of Rome on the date of Easter (Eusebius, *HE* V 24, 14–17) in support of his view.

82   F. M. Hitchcock, 'Latinity of the Pastorals', *ET*, 39 (1928), 347–52, 350, found 160 Latin words and phrases.

83   Lightfoot, *The Apostolic Fathers*, II, 1, 629–60.

84   For a summary of Harrison's proposal cf. *Polycarp's Two Epistles to the Philippians*, 15–19, and for a history of critical explanation, 27–72. Pol Phil 13, 14 is identified as a note originally attached to Ignatius' letter in the same year as Ignatius' martyrdom, and Pol Phil 1–12 as a separate letter written toward the end of Hadrian's reign, the two being combined after Polycarp's death. This, if correct, means that the final version of the letter came into being after A.D. 155.

85   See above, 27–37.

86   See the reckoning of A. von Harnack, *Marcion*, 24, 27, based on the statement by Tertullian that the Marcionites reckoned 115 years between Christ and Marcion (*Ad Marc* 1:19). Knox, *Marcion and the New Testament*, 5, 11, n. 19, followed the same dating.

87   See above,

88   Cf. Eusebius, *HE* IV 6; J. Goldin, 'The Period of the Talmud', *The Jews: Their History, Culture, and Religion* (ed. L. Finkelstein, New York 1960), 115–215, 154f; S. W. Baron, *A Social and Religious History of the Jews*, vol. 2, pt. 2 (2nd edn, New York 1952), 97. Hadrian's ban against circumcision did not necessarily follow the second Jewish war, but may indeed have preceded it as a would-be enlightened act to eliminate a custom considered barbarous. This prohibition, along with Hadrian's well-meaning intentions to transform Jerusalem into a typical hellenistic city, may well have been the occasion for the outbreak of the war (276).

89   According to Goldin, 'The Period of the Talmud', 155, 209, n. 27, the new emperor revoked most of Hadrian's measures in response to appeals by the Jewish embassy and influential Gentiles, but retained those against Jewish entry into Jerusalem and the receiving of proselytes.

90   C. Eggenberger, *Die Quellen der politischer Ethik des 1. Klemens Briefes* (Zürich 1951), 187; cf. 1 Clem 40, 41. See above, 123.

91   1 Cor 10:23–11:31, 33f; cf. above,

92   See above, 106.

93   See above, 123f.

94   See above, 88–93.

95   See above, ch. 3, n. 78.

96   Cf. Rom 2:17–3:4, 11:1–29, 2 Cor 11:21f. In addition H. D. Betz, '2 Cor 6:14–7:1: An Anti-Pauline Fragment?' *JBL*, 92 (1973), 88–108, indicates the intensely Jewish character of this passage.

97   In a survey of evidence by A. Fuks, 'The Jewish Revolt in A.D. 115–117', *JRS*, 51 (1961), 98–104, there is mention of hostilities in Cyrenaica, Egypt, Cyprus, and Mesopotamia. According to Eusebius, *HE* IV 2, Trajan had Mesopotamia cleared of Jews, many of whom were killed, and Lucius Quietus, who was responsible for this action, was rewarded with the governorship of Judaea. This appointment was probably intended as a

warning to the Judaean Jews rather than an outcome of disturbances among them. The only evidence that the disturbances extended to Judaea occurs in Megillat Ta'anit, but S. W. Baron rejected the entry, since it is missing in the best manuscripts; see *A Social and Religious History*, vol. 2, pt. 2, 390, n. 9.

98   Baron, *ibid.*, cited the thirteenth-century Syriac Chronology of Bar-Hebraeus to this effect, with some doubts as to its reliability.

99   Circumcision is characterized as a mark distinguishing Jews from all other nations in order that they might suffer from afflictions they deserve for slaying Jesus and the prophets, persecuting Christians, and failing to repent but instead spreading calumnies throughout the world against Christians (Dial Tryph 16, 17, 19). For these sins the Jews are regarded as having forfeited their inheritance with the patriarchs and prophets, which has been transferred to the Gentiles who believe (Dial Tryph 26). Moreover, their scriptures are now said to belong not to the Jews but to the Christians (Dial Tryph 29).

100   Here the Jews are said not to understand their scriptures, and to have been persecutors of the Christians, particularly during the recent Jewish war, when Bar Kochba is alleged to have ordered them to be tortured if they did not deny Christ (Justin Ap I 31, cf. I 36). Jews are characterized also as rejecting Christ whereas the Gentiles turned from idol-worship and accepted him (I 49). They are also said to have suffered the judgement of Christ in the recent devastation of their land, which is compared to the destruction of Sodom and Gomorrah (I 53).

101   It appears that 1 Clement represents a slightly later stage in the controversy with Jewish or Jewish-oriented gnostics; cf. above, 124.

102   Eggenberger, *Die Quellen*, cites evidence to the effect that 1 Clement is acquainted with the writings of Flavius Josephus dating from 93 until after 97 (113-17); Dio of Prusa from 100 till after 105, with a much heightened reputation after his death in the reigns of Trajan and Hadrian (74-106); Pliny the Younger, from 111 to 113 (121-27); Tacitus' Annals dated 116 or 117 (127-31); Plutarch during the time of Trajan (131-34). For a summary of the evidence and conclusions, cf. 182.

103   See Plinii Caecilii Secundi Epistulae X 97.

104   Indirect evidence that the situation was by no means ideal under Hadrian exists in the fact that Justin in his First Apology cited only Hadrian's rescript, and made no mention of actual practice, which one might expect if all persecution had ceased.

105   Hadrian's rescript is testimony to the frequent occurrence of both informing and mob outcries against Christians; cf. Justin Ap I 69.

106   Cf. W. K. L. Clarke, *The First Epistle of Clement to the Corinthians* (New York 1937), 11-13; Lake, *The Apostolic Fathers*, vol. 1, 3-5. The evidence for this dating is, however, extremely slender. There is nothing substantial to relate the calamities referred to in 1 Clem 1:1 with Domitian's reign, the connection some make with the household of Titus Flavius Clemens, a cousin of Domitian executed in A.D. 95, is highly speculative, and the evicted presbyters in Corinth were not necessarily the apostolic appointees mentioned in 1 Clem 44:3.

107   See, amongst others, Feine, Behm, Kümmel, *Introduction to the New*

Testament, 271f; Easton, *The Pastoral Epistles*, 20–2.

108 See, amongst others, Grant, *The Apostolic Fathers*, vol. 1, 47f, 64–71; Richardson, *Early Christian Fathers*, 124f.

109 See above, 110, 126.

110 See above, n. 88.

111 Such a position would have received reinforcement from reports of the persecution of Christians by Bar Kochba (Justin Ap I 31). That Hadrian enjoyed positive Christian support is evident from Eusebius' claim that Christians were among those who settled in Jerusalem in place of the expelled Jews (*HE* IV 7).

112 Cf. Eusebius, *HE* IV 11, citing Irenaeus to the effect that Marcion's teaching followed that of Cerdo, whom he succeeded as leader of a school.

113 This conclusion differs from the view of Knox, *Marcion and the New Testament*, 72f, that Marcion's version of Paul was independent of the catholic text.

114 Marcion could have omitted the requirement that bishops and deacons be married and be heads of households (1 Tim 3: 2*b*, 4f, 12, Tit 1: 6), the criticism of those who oppose marriage (1 Tim 4: 3f), the requirement that younger widows marry (1 Tim 5: 14), and the antagonistic reference to antitheses (1 Tim 6: 20).

115 See above, 111–4.

116 It is noteworthy that this material is decidedly less confident than Rom 13: 1–7 that authorities will mete out reward and punishment according to just deserts, and while arguing that those who do good enjoy divine protection and need have no fear, admits the possibility and actuality of righteous suffering (1 Pet 2: 18f, 3: 10–16, 4: 12–16, 19).

117 Cf. Justin's complaint to Antoninus Pius, that he decreed death for those who have done no wrong, as if they were enemies, ignoring the decree of his father Hadrian (Ap I 68).

118 Eusebius reported Telesphoros' death as taking place in the first year of the reign of Antoninus, citing Irenaeus to the effect that he died a martyr's death (*HE* IV 10).

119 See above, 111–4.

120 See R. M. Grant, *The Sword and the Cross* (New York 1955), 75f. Fronto accused Christians of fornication and incest, hinting at orgiastic nocturnal rites, the inclusion of an infant's body in their common meals, and worship of an animal's head and the genitals of their leader.

121 For a survey of the situation see J. Carcopino, *Daily Life in Ancient Rome* (tr. E. D. Lorimer, New Haven 1940), 76–100.

122 *Ibid.*, 77f.

123 The first was a religious ceremony which transferred a woman from the authority and family religious worship of her father to that of her husband; the second simulated a sale of a woman by her plebeian father to her husband; and the third brought a woman under the *manus* of a man through a year's uninterrupted cohabitation; *ibid.*, 80. See also W. C. Morey, *Outlines of Roman Law* (New York 1894), 244f.

124 Morey, 245, 247f; Carcopino, 84.

125 Carcopino, 57f. Regarding humanitarian change affecting slaves, see W. Westermann, *The Slave System of Greek and Roman Antiquity*

(Philadelphia 1955), 113–15.

126   Carcopino, 55–65 regarding slaves, 78–80 regarding the relaxation of Roman severity in the control of children, and 84f, 88, 90–3 regarding the increased independence of women.

127   *Ibid.*, 95–103.

128   M. I. Rostovtzeff, *The Social and Economic History of the Roman Empire* (2nd edn, Oxford 1957).

129   Westermann, 115, 116, n. 119.

130   C. G. Starr, *Civilization and the Caesars* (Ithaca, New York 1954), 158, maintained that by the time of Trajan the Roman system of surveillance, organized largely through the army, had reached its zenith.

131   See above, 11.

132   Crouch, *The Origin and Intent of the Colossian Haustafel*, 133, n. 61, correctly points out that the unit extends beyond 14: 34f, which occurs after vs. 40 in some western mss. See above, 69.

133   See the analysis of G. Zuntz, *The Text of the Epistles*, concerning variant readings.

134   See above, 113, and ch. 3, n. 7.

135   See Feine, Behm, Kümmel, 222–6. The passage has a striking affinity with 1 Pet 1: 13, 20, assigned consecutively to the earlier form of 1 Peter, which goes far beyond mere verbal correspondence; cf. ch. 2, n. 28. If it owes its presence to Marcion, as Zuntz thinks (cf. 227f) following Harnack, he most certainly derived it from a pre-Pastoral source, probably in post-Ephesian circles of a Jewish–Christian character, which Marcion may have known; see below, 144f. Cf. L. Mowry, 'The Early Circulation of Paul's Letter', *JBL*, 63 (1944), 73–86, 78f.; but according to Origen he omitted it.

136   That such passages would have found favour with the Pastoral opposition is evident from its Jewish character or leanings; see above, 110, 126.

137   See J. R. Daniel, 'Anti-Semitism in the Hellenistic-Roman Period', *JBL*, 98 (1979), 45–65.

138   See above, ns. 99, 100; and R. Wilde, *The Treatment of the Jews in the Greek Christian Writers of the First Three Centuries* (Washington, D.C. 1949), 78–147.

139   See G. Strecker, 'On the Problem of Jewish Christianity', in appendix 1 of W. Bauer, *Orthodoxy and Heresy in Earliest Christianity*, 241–85; and A. F. J. Klijn, 'The Study of Jewish Christianity', *NTS*, 20 (1973–4), 419–31. Klijn, 422f, citing F. J. A. Hort, *Judaistic Christianity* (Cambridge and London 1894), 200, and R. Seeberg, *Lehrbuch der Dogmengeschichte* (Leipzig 1922, reprint Darmstadt 1965), 255, points to the 'isolation and antagonism' in which they came to live from the Gentile Christian church in Jerusalem after 135. The same could very well have occurred in other regions also.

140   Irenaeus Against Heresies I 27 1f with III 3.

141   See above, 105f.

142   Irenaeus Against Heresies III 13, 14.

143   J. C. O'Neill, *The Recovery of Paul's Letter to the Galatians* (London 1972), 11, in arguing for the existence of many glosses and some extended interpolations in Galatians, suggests that Marcion's treatment of the text may have issued from a desire to determine what Paul actually wrote,

having 'heard that Paul's original letters were overlaid by commentary, without possessing accurate information about what was original and what was secondary', in other words, in awareness of a shorter version which had undergone expansion.

144 It is noteworthy that the Acts contradicts the pre-Pastoral Pauline letters at a number of the points listed above: 2, in its pro-Roman stance and representation of the Roman system of law and its courts as protecting Paul; 6, in accounting for opposition from local populations as instigated by Jews; 7, in representing Paul as a philosophic teacher in the Stoic mode; 8, in representing the Jews as rejecting the Christian preaching by and large, while Gentiles respond gladly; 10, in presenting a picture of unfailing amity between Paul and all Christian churches, with disagreements relegated to later times (20:29f); 11, in depicting Paul's relations with Peter and James as cordial, and controversy as minimal between them.

145 W. Schmithals, 'The Collection of the Major Epistles of Paul', *Paul and the Gnostics*, 239–74, 257f, n. 43, argues that 1 Clem 47:1f gives testimony to a letter collection at the head of which stood 1 Corinthians. The possibility that ἐπιστολή has such a collective meaning here is not to be dismissed.

146 The discussion of Abraham in 1 Clem 10 seems to show knowledge of Rom 4, and there are possible allusions to Rom 9:3 and 6:1 in 1 Clem 32 and 33:1. The similarity between 1 Clem 35:5 and Rom 1:29–32 seems to be of a different character (see appendix B). There is also a fairly clear allusion to Eph 4:4–6 in 1 Clem 46:5.

147 Concerning the hesitation, mistrust, and outright hostility toward Paul both from the Jewish-Christian and the early catholic side in the second century, see G. Strecker, 'Paulus in Nachpaulinische Zeit', *Kairos* N. F., 12 (1970), 208–16, and C. K. Barrett, 'Pauline Controversies in the Post-Pauline Period', *NTS*, 20 (1973–4), 229–45. E. H. Pagels, *The Gnostic Paul* (Philadelphia 1975), having amply documented the gnostic use of Paul, finds this a more than adequate explanation for orthodox avoidance and hostility (161).

148 Pagels, *passim*.

Appendix B. Rom 1:19–2:1 and the later or Pastoral stratum

1 See above, 112f.
2 Rev 13:14, 15 (three occurrences), 14:9, 11, 15:2, 16:2, 19:20, 20:4.
3 M. D. Hooker, 'Adam in Romans 1', *NTS*, 6 (1959–60), 297–306; cf. 298, 300–2.
4 *Ibid.*, 304.
5 See above, 73, 105–8, 121.
6 2 Tim 2:20f appears to draw on Rom 9:21, or a common or similar source, but has evidently adapted it to Pastoral paraenetic purposes.
7 Harrison, *Paulines and Pastorals*, 84f.
8 Appendix C.
9 Appendix C.
10 Appendix C.
11 Appendix C.
12 Cf. appendix C.

Appendix C. Antithetic parallels in the Pastoral stratum and adjacent material

1 See ch. 1, n. 2.
2 See above, 63.

Appendix D. Harrison's theory of Pauline fragments in the Pastorals

1 See above, 97.
2 See appendix E.
3 Cf. 1 Tim 6: 14, 2 Tim 1: 10, 4: 1, 8, Tit 2: 13.
4 Cf. 1 Tim 3: 1, 5, 10, 25, 6: 18, Tit 2: 7, 14, 3: 8, 14.
5 Cf. the references to 'all people' in Rom 12: 17f, 1 Cor 10: 33, 1 Thess 5: 15, 1 Pet 2: 17, 4: 8, 1 Tim 2: 4, 4: 10, Tit 2: 11.
6 Cf. Rom 16: 1-23, 1 Cor 16: 1-24, 2 Cor 11: 30-3, Phil 4: 14-23, Col 4: 7-18.
7 Harrison, *The Problem of the Pastoral Epistles*, 96, indicated that there are four such words on the last page of 2 Timothy as compared with an average of 17.4 per page in the Pastorals as a whole.
8 Harrison, *ibid.*, 974. Of the eleven words cited for Tit 3: 12-15, five are rare or relatively rare (i.e., occur less than a dozen times) in the New Testament, and of these, four occur in Luke–Acts ($\pi\alpha\rho\alpha\chi\epsilon\iota\mu\acute{\alpha}\xi\epsilon\iota\nu$, $\sigma\pi\text{ou}\delta\alpha\acute{\iota}\omega\varsigma$, $\pi\rho\text{o}\pi\acute{\epsilon}\mu\pi\epsilon\iota\nu$, $\dot{\alpha}\nu\alpha\gamma\kappa\alpha\acute{\iota}\text{o}\varsigma$), one also in 1 and 3 John ($\pi\rho\text{o}\pi\acute{\epsilon}\mu\pi\epsilon\iota\nu$), and one in 2 Peter ($\ddot{\alpha}\kappa\alpha\rho\pi\text{o}\varsigma$). Of the fourteen words cited for 2 Tim 4: 6-22, only one ($\dot{\epsilon}\gamma\kappa\alpha\tau\alpha\lambda\epsilon\acute{\iota}\pi\epsilon\iota\nu$) can be termed rare, and it occurs twice in the Acts. Of the fifteen cited for the residue of Harrison's fragments, seven are relatively rare, and of these five occur in Luke–Acts ($\ddot{\alpha}\lambda\text{u}\sigma\iota\varsigma$, $\sigma\pi\text{ou}\delta\alpha\acute{\iota}\omega\varsigma$, $\delta\iota\omega\gamma\mu\acute{\text{o}}\varsigma$, $\epsilon\grave{\text{u}}\alpha\gamma\gamma\epsilon\lambda\iota\sigma\tau\acute{\eta}\varsigma$), and one in the later material in 1 Peter ($\grave{\text{u}}\pi\text{o}\phi\acute{\epsilon}\rho\epsilon\iota\nu$, 2: 19).

Appendix E. Vocabulary analysis

1 Passages in parenthesis are assigned to the Pastoral stratum in the longer version of this study.
2 This figure is considerably conflated by the repetition of the word $\dot{\alpha}\kappa\rho\text{o}\beta\text{u}\sigma\tau\acute{\iota}\alpha$, used ten times.

INDEX OF NAMES

Turner, N. 184 n. 15

Unnik, W. C. van 52, 191 nn. 80, 82,
84, 207 n. 29

Vielhauer, P. 212 n. 11
Vokes, F. E. 213 n. 23

Walker, W. O. 20, 69, 74, 182 n. 151,
195 n. 128, 196 n. 139, 198 n. 159
Weidinger, K. 3, 4, 8, 14, 16, 95, 176
nn. 3, 7, 8, 183 n. 2
Weiss, B. 10, 13, 20, 178 nn. 62, 63
Weiss, J. 180 n. 124, 182 n. 152, 199
n. 164, 200 n. 176, 201 n. 178
Weizsacker, K. von 3, 4, 176 nn. 4, 5
Wendland, H. 16, 180 nn. 118, 119,
181 n. 127

Westcott, B. F. 184 n. 14
Westermann, W. 218 n. 125, 219 n. 129
White, J. L. 89, 90, 202 n. 197, 204
nn. 224, 225
Wilde, R. 219 n. 138
Williams, C. S. C. 178 n, 70, 212 n. 9
Williams, D. M. 204 n. 228
Windisch, H. 8, 18, 177 n. 47, 182 n.
145, 186 nn. 28, 31, 188 n. 44,
189 n. 50
Wrede, W. 201 n. 182
Wright, F. A. 196 n. 141, 197 n. 142

Zahn, T. 181 n. 139
Zuntz, G. 15, 20, 151, 180 n. 120, 182
n. 152, 219 n. 13
Zwaan J. de 199 n. 170